e English | 21

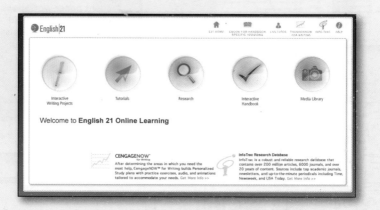

English 21

E21 HOME   EBOOK FOR HANDBOOK   LIVE TUTOR   THOMSONNOW   HARD TRAC   HELP
SPECIFIC VERSIONS   FOR WRITING

Interactive   Tutorials   Research   Interactive   Media Library
Writing Projects   Handbook

Welcome to English 21 Online Learning

CENGAGENOW
For Writing
After determining the areas in which you need the
most help, CengageNOW™ for Writing builds Personalized
Study plans with practice exercises, audio, and animations
tailored to accommodate your needs. Get More Info >>

InfoTrac Research Database
InfoTrac is a robust and reliable research database that
contains over 200 million articles, 6000 journals, and over
20 years of content. Sources include top academic journals,
newsletters, and up-to-the-minute periodicals including Time,
Newsweek, and USA Today. Get More Info >>

www.cengage.com/english21

Supporting students through every step of the writing process

More than just the largest compilation of online resources
ever organized for composition courses, English21 supports
students through every step of the writing process, from
assignment to final draft. This complete
support system weaves robust, self-paced
instruction with interactive assignments
to engage students as they become better
prepared and more effective writers.

**OPEN HERE TO LEARN MORE ABOUT
HOW English21 CAN WORK FOR YOU!**

www.cengage.com/english21

Writing Analytically

Writing Analytically

FIFTH EDITION

David Rosenwasser

Muhlenberg College

Jill Stephen

Muhlenberg College

WADSWORTH
CENGAGE Learning

Australia • Brazil • Japan • Korea • Mexico • Singapore • Spain • United Kingdom • United States

WADSWORTH
CENGAGE Learning

Writing Analytically,
Fifth Edition
David Rosenwasser
Jill Stephen

Publisher: Lyn Uhl

Development Editor: Mary Beth
    Walden

Assistant Editor: Lindsey
    Veautour

Technology Project Manager:
    Stephanie Gregoire

Marketing Manager: Mandee
    Eckersley

Marketing Assistant: Kathleen
    Remsberg

Marketing Communications
    Manager: Stacey Purviance

Senior Content Project Manager:
    Michael Lepera

Senior Art Director: Cate Barr

Print Buyer: Mary Beth
    Hennebury

Text Permissions Editor: Mardell
    Glinski Schultz

Photo Permissions Editor: Sheri
    Blaney

Production Service: Graphic
    World Publishing Services

Text Designer: John Ritland

Compositor: Graphic World Inc.

Cover Designer: Maxine Ressler

Cover Image: © Thinkstock/RF/
    Ron Chapple/Jupiter Images

For product information and
technology assistance, contact us at **Cengage Learning
Customer & Sales Support, 1-800-354-9706**
For permission to use material from this text or product,
submit all requests online at **cengage.com/permissions**
Further permissions questions can be emailed to
permissionrequest@cengage.com

Library of Congress Control Number: 2007939138

ISBN-13: 978-1-413-03310-6

ISBN-10: 1-413-03310-5

Wadsworth
25 Thomson Place
Boston, MA 02210
USA

Cengage Learning is a leading provider of customized learning solutions with office locations around the globe, including Singapore, the United Kingdom, Australia, Mexico, Brazil, and Japan. Locate your local office at: **international.cengage.com/region**

Cengage Learning products are represented in Canada by Nelson Education, Ltd.

For your course and learning solutions, visit
academic.cengage.com

Purchase any of our products at your local college store or at our preferred online store **www.ichapters.com**

Printed in Canada
4 5 6 7 11 10 09

BRIEF CONTENTS

CONTENTS

PREFACE

Writing Analytically focuses on ways of using writing to discover and develop ideas. That is, the book treats writing as a tool of thought—a means of undertaking sustained acts of inquiry and reflection.

For some people, learning to write is associated less with thinking than with arranging words, sentences, and ideas in clear and appropriate form. The achievement of good writing does, of course, require attention to form, but writing is also a mental activity. Through writing we figure out what things mean (which is our definition of analysis). The act of writing allows us to discover and, importantly, to interrogate what we think and believe.

All the editions of *Writing Analytically* have evolved from what we learned while establishing and directing a cross-curricular writing program at a four-year liberal arts college (a program we began in 1989 and continue to direct). The clearest consensus we've found among faculty is on the kind of writing that they say they want from their students: not issue-based argument, not personal reflection (the "reaction" paper), not passive summary, but analysis, with its patient and methodical inquiry into the meaning of information. Yet most books of writing instruction devote only a chapter, if that, to analysis.

The main discovery we made when we first wrote this book was that none of the reading we'd done about thesis statements seemed to match either our own practice as writers and teachers or the practice of published writers. Textbooks about writing tend to present thesis statements as the finished products of an act of thinking—as inert statements that writers should march through their papers from beginning to end. In practice, the relationship between thesis and evidence is far more fluid and dynamic.

In most good writing, the thesis grows and changes in response to evidence, even in final drafts. In other words, the relationship between thesis and evidence is reciprocal: the thesis acts as a lens for focusing what we see in the evidence, but the evidence, in turn, creates pressure to refocus the lens. The root issue here is the writer's attitude toward evidence. The ability of writers to discover ideas and improve on them in revision depends largely on their ability to use evidence as a means of testing and developing ideas rather than just supporting them.

By the time we came to writing the third edition, we had begun to focus on observation skills. We recognized that students' lack of these skills is as much a problem as thought-strangling formats like five-paragraph form or a too-rigid notion of thesis. We began to understand that observation doesn't come naturally; it needs to be taught. The book advocates locating observation as a separate phase of thinking before the writer becomes committed to a thesis. Much weak writing is prematurely and too narrowly thesis driven precisely because people try to formulate the thesis before they have done much (or any) analyzing.

The solution to this problem sounds easy to accomplish, but it isn't. As writers and thinkers, we all need to slow down—to dwell longer in the open-ended, exploratory, information-gathering stage. This requires specific tasks that will reduce the anxiety for answers, impede the reflex move to judgments, and encourage a more hands-on engagement with materials. *Writing Analytically* supplies these tasks for each phase of the writing and idea-generating process: making observations, inferring implications, and making the leap to possible conclusions.

WHAT'S NEW IN THIS EDITION

This edition of *Writing Analytically* marks the fourth time we've had the chance to revisit the book's initial thinking on writing. The difficult but also exciting thing about repeatedly revising the same book is that the writer must keep learning how to see the logic of the book as a whole, even as new thinking rises from earlier thinking and threatens to displace it. We believe that we have now succeeded at what we couldn't quite manage to do in the fourth edition—to integrate the early versions of the book, oriented largely toward thesis and evidence, with the later editions of the book, oriented toward observation and interpretation.

Here in brief (and in boldface) are the suggestions and criticisms to which this extensively rewritten and reorganized version of the book responds:

- **Put back the definition-of-analysis chapter containing the five analytical moves, which disappeared in the third edition.** This edition starts with a revised version of the older chapter, now called Analysis: What It Is and What It Does.

- **Make things easier to find! Make core ideas stand out more clearly.** And so . . . :

    1. We have organized the book into four units to make the book's arguments and advice clearer and more clearly incremental. These units are:

        I. The Analytical Frame of Mind: Introduction to Analytical Methods

        II. Writing the Analytical Essay

        III. Writing the Researched Paper

        IV. Grammar and Style

    2. We have created separate chapters on matters that were not adequately pulled together and foregrounded in previous editions.

        - The book's observational strategies, such as 10 on 1 and The Method, now appear prominently in a single chapter called A Toolkit of Analytical Methods (Chapter 3).

        - A revised chapter called Interpretation: What It Is, What It Isn't, and How to Do It (Chapter 4) reunites materials on interpretation that were split up in the fourth edition.

        - The book's advice on analyzing and producing arguments now appears in a single chapter called Analyzing Arguments (Chapter 5).

- A new chapter called Topics and Modes of Analysis (Chapter 6) adds explicit discussion of rhetorical analysis, acknowledging it as an ongoing topic of the book, and restores attention to ways of making the traditional rhetorical modes, such as comparison and contrast, more analytical.

- The book's advice on organizing papers is now pulled together in a largely new chapter on organization called Structuring the Paper: Forms and Formats (Chapter 10), which also includes a new section on paragraphing. Readers will now know where to look for alternatives to five-paragraph form. The chapter invites readers to think of organization in terms of movement of mind at both the paper and paragraph levels.

- **Get rid of the overstuffed first chapter and restore the unexpurgated version of counterproductive habits of mind as a separate chapter.** Done. We recognize that in the fourth edition we attempted to do what all writers, not just our students, too often do—pack everything into the opening. The parts of this opening chapter have now been broken up and redistributed more logically. We have also reorganized and rewritten our chapter on counterproductive habits of mind, which now appears as Chapter 2. We continue to believe, as the chapter argues, that it is hard to develop new thinking skills without first becoming aware of what's wrong with our customary modes of response.

- **Put the book's advice on reading with the chapters on researched writing.** A pared-down chapter called Reading Analytically (Chapter 13) now opens the book's unit on research-based writing. In this chapter, we make it clear that all of the book's strategies can be applied to reading, but we now foreground some that are particular to writing about reading—such as using a reading as a lens—in this revised reading chapter.

- **Make the book shorter and less repetitive.** We have tried to prune every sentence—in fact, every clause, phrase, and word—wherein we had succumbed to the temptation to say something twice when once would do. We think we have made the book more readable in both clarity and tone and lighter to carry.

We continue to believe that the book's schematic way of describing the analytical thought process will make students more confident thinkers, better able to contend with complexity and to move beyond the simplistic agree/disagree response and passive assembling of downloaded information. We have faith in the book's various formulae and verbal prompts for their ability to spur more thoughtful writing and also for the role they can play in making the classroom a more genuinely engaging and collaborative space. When students and teachers can share the means of idea production, class discussion and writing become better connected, and students can more easily learn that good ideas don't just happen—they're made.

HOW TO USE THIS BOOK

Writing Analytically is designed to be used in first-year writing courses or seminars, as well as in more advanced writing-intensive courses in a variety of subject areas.

Though the book's chapters form a logical sequence, each can also stand alone and be used in different sequences.

We assume that most professors will want to supply their own subject matter for students to write about. The book does, however, contain writing exercises throughout that can be applied to a wide range of materials—print and visual, text-based (reading), and experiential (writing from direct observation). In the text itself we suggest using newspapers, magazines, films, primary texts (both fiction and nonfiction), academic articles, textbooks, television, historical documents, places, advertising, photographs, political campaigns, and so on.

There is, by the way, an edition of this book that contains readings—*Writing Analytically with Readings.* It includes writing assignments that call on students to apply the skills in the original book to writing about the readings and to using the readings as lenses for analyzing other material.

The book's writing exercises take two forms: end-of-chapter assignments that could produce papers and informal writing exercises called "Try This" that are embedded inside the chapters near the particular skills they employ. Many of the Try This exercises could generate papers, but usually they are more limited in scope, asking readers to experiment with various kinds of data-gathering and analysis.

The book acknowledges that various academic disciplines differ in their expectations of student writing. Interspersed throughout the text are boxes labeled Voices from across the Curriculum. These were written for the book by professors in various disciplines who offer their disciplinary perspective on such matters as reasoning back to premises and determining what counts as evidence. Overall, however, the text concentrates on the many values and expectations that the disciplines share about writing.

THEORETICAL ORIENTATIONS

We have had the good fortune to interest others enough in our work to stimulate attack, much of it, we think, the result of misunderstanding. In an effort to clarify our own premises and origins, we offer the following disclosure of our influences and orientations.

The book is aligned with the thinking of Carl Rogers and others on the goal of making argument less combative, less inflected by a vocabulary of military strategizing that discourages negotiation among competing points of view and the evolution of new ideas from the pressure of one idea against another.

The book is also heavily influenced by the early proponents of the process movement in writing pedagogy. Books such as Peter Elbow's *Writing Without Teachers* and Ken Macrorie's *Telling Writing* were standard fare in graduate programs when we began to teach. We came of age, so to speak, accepting that writing instruction should focus on writers' process and not just on ways of shaping finished products. As is now generally recognized, the inherent romanticism and expressivist bias of the process approach to writing limited its usefulness for people who were interested in teaching students how to write for academic audiences. Despite the social scientific approach that researchers such as Janet Emig, James Britton, and Linda Flower (to name a few) brought to the understanding of students' writing process, the process approach to writing instruction suffered a decline in status as trends in college writing programs took up other causes. (See, for example, the arguments of Patricia Bizzell, David Bartholomae, Charles Bazerman, and others, who reoriented compositionists toward discourse analysis and ethnographic research on the writing practices of other disciplines.)

We continue to believe that attention to process and attention to the stylistic and epistemological norms of writing in the disciplines can and should be brought into accord. We think, further, that a relatively straightforward and teachable set of strategies can go a long way toward achieving this goal. The process approach is not necessarily expressivist, at least not exclusively so. Analytical strategies with the power to enrich students' writing process can be taught, and they shed light on the otherwise mysterious-seeming nature of individuals' creativity as thinkers.

The book has drawn some interesting critiques, based on people's assumptions about our connection to particular theoretical orientations. One such critique comes from people who think the book invites students to think in a "New Critical" vacuum— that it is uncritically aligned with an unreformed, unself-conscious and old-fashioned New Critical mind-set. The midcentury interpretive movement known as the New Criticism has come to be misunderstood as rigidly materialist, deriving meaning only from the physical details that one can see on the page, on the screen, on the sidewalk, and so on. This is not the place to take up a comprehensive assessment of the ideas and impact of the New Criticism, but, as the best of the New Critics clearly knew, things always mean (as our book explicitly argues) in context. *Interpretive contexts,* which we discuss extensively in Chapter 4 and elsewhere, are determined by the thing being observed; but, in turn, they also determine what the observer sees. Ideas are always the products of assumptions about how best to situate observations in a frame of reference. Only when these interpretive frames, these ways of seeing and their ideological underpinnings, are made clear do the details begin to meaningfully and plausibly "speak."

We are aware that the language of binary oppositions, patterns of repetition, and organizing contrasts suggests not just the methods of the New Critics but those of their immediate successors, structuralists. Without embarking here on an extended foray into the evolution of theory in the latter half of the twentieth century, we will just say that the value assumptions of both the New Criticism (with its faith in irony, tension, and ambiguity) and structuralism (with its search for universal structures of mind and culture) do not automatically accompany their methods. Any approach to thinking and writing that values complexity will subscribe to some extent to the necessity of recognizing tension and irony and paradox and ambiguity. As for finding universal structures of mind and culture, we haven't so grand a goal, but we do think that there is value in trying to state simply and clearly in nontechnical language some of the characteristic moves of mind that make some people better thinkers than others and better able to arrive at ideas.

Here are some other ways in which *Writing Analytically* might lend itself to misunderstandings. Its employment of verbal prompts like So what? and its recommendation of step-by-step procedures, such as the procedure for making a thesis evolve, should not be confused with prescriptive slot-filler formulae for writing. Our book does not prescribe a fill-in-the-blank grid for analyzing data, but it does try to describe systematically what good thinkers do—as acts of mind—when they are confronted with data.

Our focus on words has also attracted critique. The theoretical orientation that has come to be called performance theory has emphasized the idea that words alone don't adequately account for the meanings we make of them. Words exist—their interpretations exist—in how and why they are spoken in particular circumstances, genres, and traditions. Our view is that this essential emphasis on the significance of context does not diminish the importance of attending to words. The situation is rather like the one we addressed earlier in reference to the New Criticism. Words mean in particular contexts. It is reductive to assume that attention to language means that only words matter or that words matter in some context-less vacuum. The methods we define in *Writing Analytically* can be applied to nonverbal and verbal data.

Interestingly, we were aware of, but had not actually studied, the work of John Dewey as we evolved our thinking for this book. Looking more closely at his writing now, we are struck by the number of key terms and assumptions our thinking shares with his. In his book *How We Think,* Dewey speaks, for example, of "systematic reflection" as a goal. He was interested, as are we, in what goes on in the production of actual thinking, rather than "setting forth the results of thinking" after the fact, in the manner of formal logic. On this subject Dewey writes, "When you are only seeking the truth and of necessity seeking somewhat blindly, you are in a radically different position from the one you are in when you are already in possession of the truth" (revised edition 1933, 74–75).

Dewey thought, as do we, that habits of mind can be trained, but first people have to be made more conscious of them. This is what *Writing Analytically* tries to accomplish. It begins with some of the same premises that Dewey and others have offered:

- The importance of being able to dwell in and tolerate uncertainty
- The importance of curiosity and knowing how to cultivate it
- The importance of being conscious of language
- The importance of observation

Dewey also said that people cannot make themselves have ideas. This we believe is not true. People can make themselves have ideas, and it is possible to describe the processes through which individuals enable themselves to make interpretive leaps. It is also possible (and necessary) for people to learn how to differentiate ideas from other things that are often mistaken for ideas, such as clichés and opinions—products of the deadening effect of habit (about which we have much to say in the book's opening unit). Although the interpretive leaps from observation to idea can probably never be fully explained, we are not thus required to relegate the meaning-making process to the category of imponderable mystery.

ABOUT THE AUTHORS

David Rosenwasser and Jill Stephen are Professors of English at Muhlenberg College in Allentown, Pennsylvania, where they have co-directed a Writing Across the Curriculum (WAC) program since 1987. They began teaching writing to college students in the 1970s—David at the University of Virginia and then at the College of William and Mary, and Jill at New York University and then at Hunter College (CUNY). *Writing Analytically* has grown out of their undergraduate teaching and the seminars on writing and writing instruction that they have offered to faculty at Muhlenberg and at other colleges and universities across the country.

ACKNOWLEDGMENTS

Our greatest debt in this edition of the book is to Kenny Marotta, who helped us rethink the book. Like all great teachers, he let us see more clearly the shape and implications of our own thinking. Those of you unaware of his gifts as a fiction writer are missing a rare pleasure. Major thanks also go to developmental editor extraordinaire Mary Beth Walden for her tireless efforts on our behalf—her understanding of how we work; her ability to help us hide from distractions; her sound advice, patience, and good cheer. We are also very grateful to departing acquisitions editor Aron Keesbury for his frank talk and occasional flights of poetry.

We have over the years been fortunate to work with a range of talented and dedicated editors: Dickson Musslewhite, who saw us through the third and fourth editions; Julie McBurney and John Meyers, who nurtured the book in its early days; and Michell Phifer and Karen R. Smith, who looked over our shoulders with acuity and wit. And we remain grateful to Karl Yambert, our original developmental editor, whose insight and patience first brought this book into being.

Christine Farris at Indiana University has been a great friend of the book since its early days; we heard her voice often in our heads as we revised this edition. She and her colleagues John Schilb and Ted Leahey gave us what every writer needs— a discerning audience. Similar thanks are due to Wendy Hesford and Eddie Singleton of Ohio State University, as well as their graduate students, whom we have had the pleasure of working with over the past few years. The book has enabled us to make many new friends just starting their college teaching careers in rhetoric and composition—Matthew Johnson and Matt Hollrah, to name two. Our friend Dean Ward at Calvin College has been a source of inspiration and good conversation on writing for many years. So have two old friends, Richard Louth and Lin Spence, who offer the benefit of their long experience with the National Writing Project. And we always learn something about writing whenever we run into Mary Ann Cain and George Kalamaras, inspiring teachers and writers both. We have also benefited from stimulating conversations about writing with Chidsey Dickson.

Among our colleagues at Muhlenberg College, we are especially grateful to reference librarian Kelly Cannon for his section on library and Internet research in Chapter 16. For writing the Voices from across the Curriculum boxes that appear throughout the book, thanks to Karen Dearborn, Laura Edelman, Jack Gambino, James Marshall, Rich Niesenbaum, Fred Norling, Mark Sciutto, Alan Tjeltveit, and Bruce Wightman. For their good counsel and their teaching materials, thanks to Anna Adams, Jim Bloom, Chris Borick, Ted Conner, Joseph Elliot, Barri Gold, Mary Lawlor, Jim Peck, Jeremy Teissere, and Alec Marsh, with whom we argue endlessly about writing. Carol Proctor in the English Department looks out for us. We also thank Muhlenberg

College, especially its provost, Marjorie Hass, for continuing to support our participation at national conferences.

We are indebted to our students at Muhlenberg College, who have shared their writing and their thinking about writing with us. Chief among these (of late) are Sarah Kersh, Robbie Saenz di Viteri, Laura Sutherland, Andrew Brown, Meghan Sweeney, Jen Epting, Jessica Skrocki, and Jake McNamara. Thanks also go to the following students who have allowed us to use their writing in our book (most recently): Jen Axe, Wendy Eichler, Theresa Leinker, and Kim Schmidt.

Finally, thanks to our spouses (Deborah and Mark) and our children (Lizzie, Lesley, and Sarah) for their love and support during the many hours that we sit immobile at our computers.

━   ━   ━

We would also like to thank the many colleagues who reviewed the book; we are grateful for their insight:

Diann Ainsworth, *Weatherford College*
Jeanette Adkins, *Tarrant County College*
Joan Anderson, *California State University–San Marcos*
Candace Barrington, *Central Connecticut State University*
Maria Bates, *Pierce College*
Karin Becker, *Fort Lewis College*
Laura Behling, *Gustavus Adolphus College*
Stephanie Bennett, *Monmouth University*
Tom Bowie, *Regis University*
Roland Eric Boys, *Oxnard College*
David Brantley, *College of Southern Maryland*
Jessica Brown, *City College of San Francisco*
Christine Bryant Cohen, *University of Illinois–Urbana-Champaign*
Alexandria Casey, *Graceland University*
Anthony Cavaluzzi, *Adirondack Community College*
Johnson Cheu, *Michigan State University*
Jeff Cofer, *Bellevue Community College*
Helen Connell, *Barry University*
Cara Crandall, *Emerson College*
Rose Day, *Central New Mexico Community College*
Susan de Ghize, *University of Denver*
Virginia Dumont-Poston, *Lander University*
David Eggebrecht, *Concordia University*
Karen Feldman, *University of California*
Dan Ferguson, *Amarillo College*
Gina Franco, *Knox College*
Sue Frankson, *College of DuPage*
Anne Friedman, *Borough of Manhattan Community College*
Tessa Garcia, *University of Texas–Pan American*

Susan Garrett, *Goucher College*
Edward Geisweidt, *University of Alabama*
Nate Gordon, *Kishwaukee College*
Glenn Hutchinson, *University of North Carolina–Charlotte*
Habiba Ibrahim, *University of Washington*
Charlene Keeler, *California State University–Fullerton*
Douglas King, *Gannon University*
Constance Koepfinger, *Duquesne University*
Anne Langendorfer, *The Ohio State University*
Kim Long, *Shippensburg University*
Laine Lubar, *Broome Community College*
Phoenix Lundstrom, *Kapi`olani Community College*
Cynthia Martin, *James Madison University*
Andrea Mason, *Pacific Lutheran University*
Darin Merrill, *Brigham Young University–Idaho*
Sarah Newlands, *Portland State University*
Emmanuel Ngwang, *Mississippi Valley State University*
Leslie Norris, *Rappahannock Community College*
Ludwig Otto, *Tarrant County College*
Adrienne Peek, *Modesto Junior College*
Adrienne Redding, *Andrews University*
Julie Rivera, *California State University–Long Beach*
John Robinson, *Diablo Valley College*
Pam Rooney, *Western Michigan University*
Linda Rosekrans, *The State University of New York–Cortland*
Becky Rudd, *Citrus College*
Arthur Saltzman, *Missouri Southern State University*
Vicki Schwab, *Manatee Community College*
John Sullivan, *Muhlenberg College*
Eleanor Swanson, *Regis University*
Kimberly Thompson, *Wittenberg University*
Kathleen Walton, *Southwestern Oregon Community College*
James Ray Watkins, *The Art Institute of Pittsburgh, Online; Colorado Technical University, Online; and The Center for Talented Youth, Johns Hopkins University*
Lisa Weihman, *West Virginia University*
Robert Williams, *Radford University*
Nancy Wright, *Syracuse University*
Robbin Zeff, *George Washington University*

UNIT I

The Analytical Frame of Mind: Introduction to Analytical Methods

CHAPTER 1

Analysis: What It Is and What It Does

FIRST PRINCIPLES

Writing takes place now in more forms than ever before. Words flash by on our computer and cell phone screens and speak to us from iPods. PowerPoint bulleted lists are replacing the classroom blackboard, and downloadable entries from Wikipedia and Google offer instant reading on almost any subject. Despite the often-heard claim that we now inhabit a visual age—that the age of print is passing—we are, in fact, surrounded by a virtual sea of electronically accessible print. What does all this mean for writers and writing?

If what is meant by writing is the form in which written text appears on page or screen, then presumably the study of writing would focus on the new forms of organization that characterize writing on the web. But what if we define writing as the act of *recording our thoughts in search of understanding?* In that case, the writing practices and mental habits that help us to think more clearly would be, as they have long been, at the center of what it means to learn to write.

This book is primarily about ways of using writing to discover and develop ideas. Its governing premise is that learning to write well means learning to use writing to think well. This does not mean that the book ignores such matters as sentence style, paragraphing, and organization, but that it treats these matters in the context of writing as a way of generating and shaping thinking.

Although it is true that authors of web pages and PowerPoint demonstrations display their finished products in forms unlike the traditional essay, people rarely arrive at their ideas in the form of PowerPoint lists and hypertext. Whatever form the thinking will finally take, first comes the stage of writing to understand—writing as a sustained act of reflection. Implicit throughout this book is an argument for the value of reflection in an age that seems increasingly to confuse sustained acts of thinking with information downloading and formatting.

ANALYSIS DEFINED

We have seized upon analysis as the book's focus because it is the skill most commonly called for in college courses and beyond. The faculty with whom we work encourage analytical writing because it offers alternatives both to oversimplified thinking of

3

the like/dislike, agree/disagree variety and to the cut-and-paste compilation of sheer information. It is the kind of writing that helps people not only to retain and assimilate information, but to use information in the service of their own thinking about the world.

More than just a set of skills, analysis is a frame of mind, an attitude toward experience. It is a form of detective work that typically pursues something puzzling, something you are seeking to understand rather than something you are already sure you have the answers to. Analysis finds questions where there seemed not to be any, and it makes connections that might not have been evident at first.

Analyzing, however, is often the subject of attack. It is sometimes thought of as destructive—breaking things down into their component parts, or, to paraphrase a famous poet, murdering to dissect. Other detractors attack it as the rarefied province of intellectuals and scholars, beyond the reach of normal people. In fact, we all analyze all of the time, and we do so not simply to break things down but to *construct* our understandings of the world we inhabit.

If, for example, you find yourself being followed by a large dog, your first response, other than breaking into a cold sweat, will be to analyze the situation. What does being followed by a large dog mean for me, here, now? Does it mean the dog is vicious and about to attack? Does it mean the dog is curious and wants to play? Similarly, if you are losing a game of tennis, or you've just left a job interview, or you are looking at a painting of a woman with three noses, you will begin to analyze. How can I play differently to increase my chances of winning? Am I likely to get the job, and why (or why not)? Why did the artist give the woman three noses?

If we break things down as we analyze, we do so to search for meaningful patterns, or to uncover what we had not seen at first glance—or just to understand more closely how and why the separate parts work as they do.

As this book tries to show, analyzing is surprisingly formulaic. It consists of a fairly limited set of basic moves. People who think well have these moves at their disposal, whether they are aware of using them or not. Having good ideas is less a matter of luck than of practice, of learning how to make best use of the writing process. Sudden flashes of inspiration do, of course, occur; but those who write regularly know that inspirational moments can, in fact, be courted. The rest of this book offers you ways of courting and then realizing the full potential of your ideas.

Next we offer five basic "moves"—reliable ways of proceeding—for courting ideas analytically.

THE FIVE ANALYTICAL MOVES

Each of the five moves is developed in more detail in subsequent chapters; this is an overview. As we have suggested, most people already analyze all the time, but they often don't realize that this is what they're doing. A first step toward becoming a better analytical thinker and writer is to become more aware of your own thinking processes, building on skills that you already possess, and eliminating habits that get in the way. Each of the following moves serves the primary purpose of analysis: to figure out what something means, why it is as it is and does what it does.

Move 1: Suspend Judgment

Suspending judgment is a necessary precursor to thinking analytically because our tendency to judge everything shuts down our ability to see and to think. It takes considerable effort to break the habit of responding to everything with likes and dislikes, with agreeing and disagreeing. Just listen in on a few conversations to be reminded of how pervasive this phenomenon really is. Even when you try to suppress them, judgments tend to come.

Judgments usually say more about the person doing the judging than they do about the subject being judged. The determination that something is boring is especially revealing in this regard. Yet people typically roll their eyes and call things boring as if this assertion clearly said something about the thing they are reacting to but not about the mind of the beholder.

Consciously leading with the word *interesting* (as in, "What I find most interesting about this is. . . ") tends to deflect the judgment response into a more exploratory state of mind, one that is motivated by curiosity and thus better able to steer clear of approval and disapproval. As a general rule, you should seek to understand the subject you are analyzing before deciding how you feel about it. (See the Judgment Reflex in Chapter 2, Counterproductive Habits of Mind, for more.)

Move 2: Define Significant Parts and How They're Related

Whether you are analyzing an awkward social situation, an economic problem, a painting, a substance in a chemistry lab, or your chances of succeeding in a job interview, the process of analysis is the same:

- Divide the subject into its defining parts, its main elements or ingredients.
- Consider how these parts are related, both to each other and to the subject as a whole.

In the case of analyzing the large dog encountered earlier, you might notice that he's dragging a leash, has a ball in his mouth, and is wearing a bright red scarf. Having broken your larger subject into these defining parts, you would try to see the connections among them and determine what they mean, what they allow you to decide about the nature of the dog: apparently somebody's lost pet, playful, probably not hostile, unlikely to bite me.

Analysis of the painting of the woman with three noses, a subject more like the kind you might be asked to write about in a college course, would proceed in the same way. Your result—ideas about the nature of the painting—would be determined, as with the dog, not only by your noticing its various parts, but also by your familiarity with the subject. If you knew little about art history, scrutiny of the painting's parts would not tell you, for instance, that it is an example of the movement known as Cubism. Even without this context, however, you would still be able to draw some analytical conclusions—ideas about the meaning and nature of the subject. You might conclude, for example, that the artist is interested in perspective or in the way we see, as opposed to realistic depictions of the world.

One common denominator of all effective analytical writing is that it pays close attention to detail. We analyze because our global responses, to a play, for example, or to a speech or a social problem, are too general. If you comment on an entire football game, you'll find yourself saying things like "great game," which is a generic response, something you could say about almost anything. This "one-size-fits-all" kind of comment doesn't tell us very much except that you probably liked the game. To say more, you would necessarily become more analytical—shifting your attention to the significance of some important aspect of the game, such as "they won because the offensive line was giving the quarterback all day to find his receivers" or "they lost because they couldn't defend against the safety blitz."

This move from generalization to analysis, from the larger subject to its key components, is characteristic of good thinking. To understand a subject, we need to get past our first, generic, evaluative response to discover what the subject is "made of," the particulars that contribute most strongly to the character of the whole.

If all that analysis did, however, was to take subjects apart, leaving them broken and scattered, the activity would not be worth very much. The student who presents a draft of a paper to his or her professor with the words, "Go ahead, rip it apart," reveals a disabling misconception about analysis—that, like dissecting a frog in a biology lab, analysis takes the life out of its subjects. Clearly, analysis means more than breaking a subject into its parts. When you analyze a subject you ask not just "What is it made of?" but also "How do these parts help me to understand the meaning of the subject as a whole?"

Move 3: Make the Implicit Explicit

One definition of what analytical writing does is that it makes explicit (overtly stated) what is implicit (suggested but not overtly stated), converting suggestions into direct statements. Some people fear that, like the emperor's new clothes, implications aren't really there, but are instead the phantasms of an overactive imagination. "Reading between the lines" is the common and telling phrase that expresses this anxiety. We will have more to say in Chapter 4 against the charge that analysis makes something out of nothing—the spaces between the lines—rather than out of what is there in black and white. Another version of this anxiety is implied by the term *hidden meanings.*

Implications are not hidden, but neither are they completely spelled out so that they can be simply extracted. The word *implication* comes from the Latin *implicare,* which means "to fold in." The word *explicit* is in opposition to the idea of implication. It means "folded out." This etymology of the two words, *implicit* and *explicit,* suggests that meanings aren't actually hidden, but neither are they opened to full view. An act of mind is required to take what is folded in and fold it out for all to see.

The process of drawing out implications is also known as making inferences. *Inference* and *implication* are related but not synonymous terms, and the difference is essential to know. The term *implication* describes something suggested by the material itself; implications reside in the matter you are studying. The term *inference* describes your thinking process. In short, you infer what the subject implies.

Now, let's move on to an example that suggests not only how the process of making the implicit explicit works, but also how often we do it in our everyday lives. Imagine that you are driving down the highway and find yourself analyzing a billboard advertisement for a brand of beer. Such an analysis might begin with your noticing what the billboard photo contains, its various parts—six young, athletic, and scantily clad men and women drinking beer while pushing kayaks into a fast-running river. At this point, you have produced not an analysis but a summary—a description of what the photo contains. If, however, you go on to consider what the particulars of the photo imply, your summary would become analytical.

You might infer, for example, that the photo implies that beer is the beverage of fashionable, healthy, active people. Thus, the advertisement's meaning goes beyond its explicit contents. Your analysis would lead you to convert to direct statement meanings that are suggested but not overtly stated, such as the advertisement's goal of attacking common stereotypes about its product (that only lazy, overweight men drink beer). By making the implicit explicit (inferring what the ad implies) you can better understand the nature of your subject. (See Chapter 4 for more on implications versus hidden meanings.)

▬ **Try this 1.1:** *Making Inferences*

Locate any magazine ad that you find interesting. Ask yourself, "What is this a picture of?" Use our hypothetical beer ad as a model for rendering the implicit explicit. Don't settle for just one answer. Keep answering the question in different ways, letting your answers grow in length as they identify and begin to interpret the significance of telling details. If you find yourself getting stuck, add to the question: "and why did the advertiser choose this particular image or set of images?"

VOICES FROM ACROSS THE CURRICULUM

Science as a Process of Argument

I find it ironic that the discipline of science, which is so inherently analytical, is so difficult for students to think about analytically. Much of this comes from the prevailing view of society that science is somehow factual. Science students come to college to learn the facts. I think many find it comforting to think that everything they learn will be objective. None of the wishy-washy subjectivity that many perceive in other disciplines. There is no need to argue, synthesize, or even have a good idea. But this view is dead wrong.

Anyone who has ever done science knows that nothing could be further from the truth. Just like other academics, scientists spend endless hours patiently arguing over evidence that seems obscure or irrelevant to laypeople. There is rarely an absolute consensus. In reality, science is an endless process of argument, obtaining evidence, analyzing evidence, and reformulating arguments. To be sure, we all accept gravity as a "fact." To not do so would be intellectually bankrupt, because all reasonable people agree to the truth of gravity. But to Newton, gravity was an argument for which evidence needed to be produced, analyzed, and discussed. It's important to remember that a significant fraction of his intellectual contemporaries were not swayed by his argument. Equally important is that many good scientific ideas of today will eventually be significantly modified or shown to be wrong.

—Bruce Wightman, *Professor of Biology*

Move 4: Look for Patterns

We have been defining analysis as the understanding of parts in relation to each other and to a whole, as well as the understanding of the whole in terms of the relationships among its parts. But how do you know which parts to attend to? What makes some details in the material you are studying more worthy of your attention than others? Here are three principles for selecting significant parts of the whole:

1. *Look for a pattern of repetition or resemblance.* In virtually all subjects, repetition is a sign of emphasis. In a symphony, for example, certain patterns of notes repeat throughout, announcing themselves as major themes. In a legal document, such as a warranty, a reader quickly becomes aware of words that are part of a particular idea or pattern of thinking: for instance, disclaimers of accountability.

   The repetition may not be exact. In Shakespeare's play *King Lear,* for example, references to seeing and eyes call attention to themselves through repetition. Let's say you notice that these references often occur along with another strand of language having to do with the concept of proof. How might noticing this pattern lead to an idea? You might make a start by inferring from the pattern that the play is concerned with ways of knowing (proving) things—with seeing as opposed to other ways of knowing, such as faith or intuition.

2. *Look for binary oppositions.* Sometimes patterns of repetition that you begin to notice in a particular subject matter are significant because they are part of a contrast—a basic opposition—around which the subject matter is structured. A binary opposition is a pair of elements in which the two members of the pair are opposites; the word *binary* means "consisting of two." Some examples of binary oppositions that we encounter frequently are nature/civilization, city/country, public/private, organic/inorganic, voluntary/involuntary. One advantage of detecting repetition is that it will lead you to discover binaries, which are central to locating issues and concerns. (For more on working with binary oppositions, see Chapters 3 and 5.)

3. *Look for anomalies—things that seem unusual, seem not to fit.* An *anomaly* (*a = not, nom = name*) is literally something that cannot be named, what the dictionary defines as deviation from the normal order. Along with looking for pattern, it is also fruitful to attend to anomalous details—those that seem not to fit the pattern. Anomalies help us to revise our stereotypical assumptions. A TV commercial, for example, advertises a baseball team by featuring its star reading a novel by Dostoyevsky in the dugout during a game. In this case, the anomaly, a baseball player who reads serious literature, is being used to subvert (question, unsettle) the stereotypical assumption that sports and intellectualism don't belong together.

   Just as people tend to leap to evaluative judgments, they also tend to avoid information that challenges (by not conforming to) opinions they already hold. Screening out anything that would ruffle the pattern they've begun to see, they ignore the evidence that might lead them to a better theory. (For more on this process of using anomalous evidence to evolve an essay's main idea, see Chapter 9, Making a Thesis Evolve.) Anomalies are important because noticing them often leads to new and better ideas. Most advances in scientific thought, for example, have arisen when a scientist observes some phenomenon that does not fit with a prevailing theory.

Move 5: Keep Reformulating Questions and Explanations

Analysis, like all forms of writing, requires a lot of experimenting. Because the purpose of analytical writing is to figure something out, you shouldn't expect to know at the start of your writing process exactly where you are going, how all of your subject's parts fit together, and to what end. The key is to be patient and to know that there are procedures—in this case, questions—you can rely on to take you from uncertainty to understanding.

The following three groups of questions (organized according to the analytical moves they're derived from) are typical of what goes on in an analytical writer's head as he or she attempts to understand a subject. These questions work with almost anything that you want to think about. As you will see, the questions are geared toward helping you locate and try on explanations for the meaning of various patterns of details.

Which details seem significant? Why?

What does the detail mean?

What else might it mean?

(Moves: Define Significant Parts; Make the Implicit Explicit)

How do the details fit together? What do they have in common?

What does this pattern of details mean?

What else might this same pattern of details mean? How else could it be explained?

(Move: Look for Patterns)

What details don't seem to fit? How might they be connected with other details to form a different pattern?

What does this new pattern mean? How might it cause me to read the meaning of individual details differently?

(Moves: Look for Anomalies and Keep Asking Questions)

The process of posing and answering such questions—the analytical process—is one of trial and error. Learning to write well is largely a matter of learning how to frame questions. One of the main things you acquire in the study of an academic discipline is knowledge of the kinds of questions that the discipline typically asks. For example, an economics professor and a sociology professor might observe the same phenomenon, such as a sharp decline in health benefits for the elderly, and analyze its causes and significance in different ways. The economist might consider how such benefits are financed and how changes in government policy and the country's population patterns might explain the declining supply of funds for the elderly. The sociologist might ask about attitudes toward the elderly and about the social structures that the elderly rely on for support.

ANALYSIS AT WORK: A SAMPLE PAPER

Examine the following excerpt from a draft of a paper about Ovid's *Metamorphoses*, a collection of short mythological tales dating from ancient Rome. We have included annotations in blue to suggest how a writer's ideas evolve as he or she looks for pattern, contrast, and anomaly, constantly remaining open to reformulation.

The draft actually begins with two loosely connected observations: that males dominate females, and that many characters in the stories lose the ability to speak and thus become submissive and dominated. In the excerpt, the writer begins to connect these two observations and speculate about what this connection means.

There are many other examples in Ovid's *Metamorphoses* that show the dominance of man over woman through speech control. In the Daphne and Apollo story, Daphne becomes a tree to escape Apollo, but her ability to speak is destroyed. Likewise, in the Syrinx and Pan story, Syrinx becomes a marsh reed, also a life form that cannot talk, although Pan can make it talk by playing it. *[The writer establishes a pattern of similar detail.]* Pygmalion and Galatea is a story in which the male creates his rendition of the perfect female. The female does not speak once; she is completely silent. Also, Galatea is referred to as "she" and never given a real name. This lack of a name renders her identity more silent. *[Here the writer begins to link the contrasts of speech/silence with the absence/presence of identity.]*

Ocyrhoe is a female character who could tell the future but who was transformed into a mare so that she could not speak. One may explain this transformation by saying it was an attempt by the gods to keep the future unknown. *[Notice how the writer's thinking expands as she sustains her investigation of the overall pattern of men silencing women: here she tests her theory by adding another variable—prophecy.]* However, there is a male character, Tiresias, who is also a seer of the future and is allowed to speak of his foreknowledge, thereby becoming a famous figure. (Interestingly, Tiresias during his lifetime has experienced being both a male and a female.) *[Notice how the Ocyrhoe example has spawned a contrast based on gender in the Tiresias example. The pairing of the two examples demonstrates that the ability to tell the future is not the sole cause of silencing because male characters who can do it are not silenced—though the writer pauses to note that Tiresias is not entirely male.]* Finally, in the story of Mercury and Herse, Herse's sister, Aglauros, tries to prevent Mercury from marrying Herse. Mercury turns her into a statue; the male directly silences the female's speech.

The woman silences the man in only two stories studied. *[Here the writer searches out an anomaly— women silencing men—that grows in the rest of the paragraph into an organizing contrast.]* In the first, "The Death of Orpheus," the women make use of "clamorous shouting, Phrygian flutes with curving horns, tambourines, the beating of breasts, and Bacchic howlings" (246) to drown out the male's songs, dominating his speech in terms of volume. In this way, the quality of power within speech is demonstrated: "for the first time, his words had no effect, and he failed to move them [the women] in any way by his voice" (247).

Next the women kill him, thereby rendering him silent. However, the male soon regains his temporarily destroyed power of expression: "the lyre uttered a plaintive melody and the lifeless tongue made a piteous murmur" (247). Even after death Orpheus is able to communicate. The women were not able to destroy his power completely, yet they were able to severely reduce his power of speech and expression. *[The writer learns, among other things, that men are harder to silence; Orpheus's lyre continues to sing after his death.]*

The second story in which a woman silences a man is the story of Actaeon, in which the male sees Diana naked, and she transforms him into a stag so that he cannot speak of it: "he tried to say 'Alas!' but no words came" (79). This loss of speech leads to Actaeon's inability to inform his own hunting team of his true identity; his loss of speech leads ultimately to his death. *[This example reinforces the pattern that the writer had begun to notice in the Orpheus example.]*

In some ways these four paragraphs of draft exemplify a writer in the process of discovering a workable idea. They begin with a list of similar examples, briefly noted. As the examples accumulate, the writer begins to make connections and formulate trial explanations. We have not included enough of this excerpt to get to the tentative thesis the draft is working toward, although that thesis is already beginning to emerge. What we want to emphasize here is the writer's willingness to accumulate data and to locate it in various patterns of similarity and contrast.

■ Try this 1.2: *Applying the Five Analytical Moves to a Speech*

Speeches provide rich examples for analysis, and they are easily accessible on the Internet. We especially recommend a site called American Rhetoric (You can Google it for the URL). Locate any speech and then locate its patterns of repetition and contrast. On the basis of your results, formulate a few conclusions about the speech's point of view and its way of presenting it. Try to get beyond the obvious and the general—what does applying the moves cause you to notice that you might not have noticed before?

DISTINGUISHING ANALYSIS FROM ARGUMENT, SUMMARY, AND EXPRESSIVE WRITING

How does analysis differ from other kinds of thinking and writing? A common way of answering this question is to think of communication as having three possible centers of emphasis—the writer, the subject, and the audience. Communication, of course, involves all three of these components, but some kinds of writing concentrate more on one than on the others. Autobiographical writing, for example, such as diaries or memoirs or stories about personal experience, centers on the writer and his or her desire for self-expression. Argument, in which the writer takes a stand on an issue, advocating or arguing against a policy or attitude, is reader-centered; its goal is to bring about a change in its readers' actions and beliefs. Analytical writing is more concerned with arriving at an understanding of a subject than it is with either self-expression or changing readers' views. (See Figure 1.1.)

These three categories of writing are not mutually exclusive. So, for example, expressive (writer-centered) writing is also analytical in its attempts to define and explain a writer's feelings, reactions, and experiences. And analysis is a form

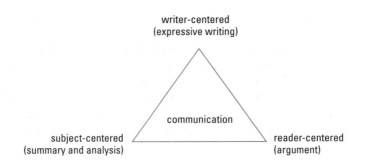

FIGURE 1.1
Diagram of Communication Triangle

of self-expression since it inevitably reflects the ways a writer's experiences have taught him or her to think about the world. But even though expressive writing and analysis necessarily overlap, they also differ significantly in both method and aim. In expressive writing, your primary subject is your self, with other subjects serving as a means of evoking greater self-understanding. In analytical writing, your reasoning may derive from your personal experience, but it is your reasoning and not you or your experiences that matter. Analysis asks not just "What do I think?" but "How good is my thinking? How well does it fit the subject I am trying to explain?"

In its emphasis on logic and the dispassionate scrutiny of ideas ("What do I think about what I think?"), analysis is a close cousin of argument. But analysis and argument are not the same. Analytical writers are frequently more concerned with persuading themselves, with discovering what they believe about a subject, than they are with persuading others. And, while the writer of an argument often goes into the writing process with some certainty about the position he or she wishes to support, the writer of an analysis is more likely to begin with the details of a subject he or she wishes to better understand.

Accordingly, argument and analysis often differ in the kind of thesis statements they formulate. The thesis of an argument is usually some kind of *should* statement: readers should or shouldn't vote for bans on smoking in public buildings, or they should or shouldn't believe that gays can function effectively in the military. The thesis of an analysis is usually a tentative answer to a what, how, or why question; it seeks to explain why people watch professional wrestling, or what a rising number of sexual harassment cases might mean, or how certain features of government health care policy are designed to allay the fears of the middle class. The writer of an analysis is less concerned with convincing readers to approve or disapprove of professional wrestling, or legal intervention into the sexual politics of the workplace, or government control of health care than with discovering how each of these complex subjects might be defined and explained. As should be obvious, though, the best arguments are built upon careful analysis: the better you understand a subject, the more likely you will be to find valid positions to argue about it.

Applying the Five Analytical Moves: The Example of *Whistler's Mother*

Summary differs from analysis because the aim of summary is to recount, in effect, to reproduce someone else's ideas. But summary and analysis are also clearly related and usually operate together. Summary is important to analysis because you can't analyze a subject without laying out its significant parts for your reader. Similarly, analysis is important to summary because summarizing is more than just copying someone else's words. To write an accurate summary you have to ask analytical questions, such as:

- Which of the ideas in the reading are most significant? Why?
- How do these ideas fit together? What do the key passages in the reading mean?

Like an analysis, an effective summary doesn't assume that the subject matter can speak for itself: the writer needs to play an active role. A good summary provides perspective on the subject as a whole by explaining, as an analysis does, the meaning and function of each of that subject's parts. Moreover, like an analysis, a good summary does not aim to approve or disapprove of its subject: the goal, in both kinds of writing, is to understand rather than to evaluate. (For more on summary, see Chapters 6 and 13.)

So summary, like analysis, is a tool of understanding and not just a mechanical task. But a summary stops short of analysis because summary typically makes much smaller interpretive leaps. A summary of the painting popularly known as *Whistler's Mother*, for example, would tell readers what the painting includes, which details are the most prominent, and even what the overall effect of the painting seems to be. A summary might say that the painting possesses a certain serenity and that it is somewhat spare, almost austere. This kind of language still falls into the category of *focused description*, which is what a summary is.

An analysis would include more of the writer's interpretive thinking. It might tell us, for instance, that the painter's choice to portray his subject in profile contributes to our sense of her separateness from us and of her nonconfrontational passivity. We look at her, but she does not look back at us. Her black dress and the fitted lace cap that obscures her hair are not only emblems of her self-effacement, shrouds disguising her identity like her expressionless face, but also the tools of her self-containment and thus of her power to remain aloof from prying eyes. What is the attraction of this painting (this being one of the questions that an analysis might ask)? What might draw a viewer to the sight of this austere, drably attired woman, sitting alone in the center of a mostly blank space? Perhaps it is the very starkness of the painting, and the mystery of self-sufficiency at its center, that attracts us. (See Figure 1.2.)

Observations of the sort just offered go beyond describing what the painting contains and enter into the writer's ideas about what its details imply, what the painting invites us to make of it and by what means. Notice in our analysis of the painting how intertwined the description (summary) is with the analysis. Laying out the data is key to any kind of analysis, not simply because it keeps the analysis accurate but also

REUNION DES MUSEES NATIONAUX, ART RESOURCE, NY. James Abbott McNeil Whistler.

FIGURE 1.2
Arrangement in Grey and Black: The Artist's Mother by James Abbott McNeill Whistler, 1871.

because, crucially, it is *in the act of carefully describing a subject that analytical writers often have their best ideas.*

You may not agree with the terms by which we have summarized the painting, and thus you may not agree with such conclusions as "the mystery of self-sufficiency." Nor is it necessary that you agree because there is no single, right answer to what the painting means. The absence of a single right answer does not, however, mean that all possible interpretations are equal and equally convincing to readers. The writer who can offer a careful description of a subject's key features is likely to arrive at conclusions about possible meanings that others would share.

Here are two general rules to be drawn from this discussion of analysis and summary:

1. Describe with care. The words you choose to summarize your data will contain the germs of your ideas about what the subject means.

2. In moving from summary to analysis, scrutinize the language you have chosen, asking, "Why did I choose this word?" and "What ideas are implicit in the language I have used?"

ANALYSIS AND PERSONAL ASSOCIATIONS

Although observations like those offered in the Interpretive Leaps column in Figure 1.3 go beyond simple description, they stay with the task of explaining the painting, rather than moving to private associations that the painting might prompt, such as effusions about old age, or rocking chairs, or the character and situation of the writer's own mother. Such associations could well be valuable unto themselves as a means of prompting a searching piece of expressive writing. They might also help a writer to interpret some feature of the painting that he or she was working to understand. But the writer would not be free to use pieces of his or her personal history as conclusions about what the painting communicates, unless these conclusions could also be reasonably inferred from the painting itself.

Analysis is a creative activity, a fairly open form of inquiry, but its imaginative scope is governed by logic. The hypothetical analysis we have offered is not the only reading of the painting that a viewer might make because the same pattern of details might lead to different conclusions. But a viewer would not be free to conclude anything he or she wished, such as that the woman is mourning the death of a son

Data	Method of Analysis	Interpretive Leaps
subject in profile, not looking at us	make implicit explicit (speculate about what the detail might suggest)	figure strikes us as separate, nonconfrontational, passive
folded hands, fitted lace cap, contained hair, expressionless face	locate pattern of same or similar detail; make what is implicit in pattern of details explicit	figure strikes us as self-contained, powerful in her separateness and self-enclosure— self-sufficient?
patterned curtain and picture versus still figure and blank wall; slightly frilled lace cuffs and ties on cap versus plain black dress	locate organizing contrast; make what is implicit in the contrast explicit	austerity and containment of the figure made more pronounced by slight contrast with busier, more lively, and more ornate elements and with little picture showing world outside
slightly slouched body position and presence of support for feet	anomalies; make what is implicit in the anomalies explicit	these details destabilize the serenity of the figure, adding some tension to the picture in the form of slightly uneasy posture and figure's need for support: she looks too long, drooped in on her own spine

FIGURE 1.3
Summary and Analysis of *Whistler's Mother* Diagram

or is patiently waiting to die. Such conclusions would be unfounded speculations be-cause the black dress is not sufficient to support them. Analysis often operates in areas in which there is no one right answer, but like summary and argument, it requires the writer to reason from evidence.

A few rules are worth highlighting here:

1. The range of associations for explaining a given detail or word must be governed by context.

2. It's fine to use your personal reactions as a way into exploring what a subject means, but take care not to make an interpretive leap stretch farther than the actual details will support.

3. Because the tendency to transfer meanings from your own life onto a subject can lead you to ignore the details of the subject itself, you need always to be ask-ing yourself: "What other explanations might plausibly account for this same pattern of detail?"

As we began this chapter by saying, analysis is a form of detective work. It can surprise us with ideas that our experiences produce once we take the time to listen to ourselves thinking. But analysis is also a discipline; it has rules that govern how we proceed and that enable others to judge the validity of our ideas. A good analytical thinker needs to be the attentive Dr. Watson to his or her own Sherlock Holmes. That is what the remainder of this book teaches you to do.

ASSIGNMENT: Analyze a Portrait or Other Visual Image

Locate any portrait, preferably a good reproduction from an art book or magazine, one that shows detail clearly. Then do a version of what we've done with *Whistler's Mother* in the preceding columns.

Your goal is to produce an analysis of the portrait with the steps we included in analyzing *Whistler's Mother*. First, summarize the portrait, describing accurately its significant details. Do not go beyond a recounting of what the portrait includes; avoid interpreting what these details suggest.

Then use the various methods offered in this chapter to analyze the data. What repetitions (patterns of same or similar detail) do you see? What organizing contrasts suggest themselves? In light of these patterns of similarity and difference, what anom-alies do you then begin to detect? Move from the data to interpretive conclusions.

This process will produce a set of interpretive leaps, which you may then try to assemble into a more coherent claim of some sort—about what the portrait "says."

CHAPTER 2

Counterproductive Habits of Mind

ANALYSIS, we have been suggesting, is a frame of mind, a set of habits for observing and making sense of the world. There is also, it is fair to say, an anti-analytical frame of mind with its own set of habits. These shut down perception and arrest potential ideas at the cliché stage. This chapter attempts to unearth these anti-analytical habits. Then the next chapter offers some systematic ways of improving your observational skills.

The meaning of observation is not self-evident. If you had five friends over and asked them to write down one observation about the room you were all sitting in, it's a sure bet that many of the responses would be generalized judgments—"it's comfortable"; "it's a pigsty." And why? Because the habits of mind that come readily to most of us tend to shut down the observation stage so that we literally notice and remember less. We go for the quick impression and dismiss the rest.

Having ideas is dependent on allowing ourselves to notice things in a subject that we wish to better understand rather than glossing things over with a quick and too easy understanding. The problem with convincing ourselves that we have the answers is that we are thus prevented from seeing the questions, which are usually much more interesting than the temporary stopping points we have elected as answers.

The nineteenth-century poet, Emily Dickinson, writes that "Perception of an object/Costs precise the object's loss." When we leap prematurely to our perceptions about a thing, we place a filter between ourselves and the object, shrinking the amount and kinds of information that can get through to our minds and our senses. The point of the Dickinson poem is a paradox—that the ideas we arrive at actually deprive us of material with which to have more ideas. So we have to be careful about leaping to conclusions, about the ease with which we move to generalization, because if we are not careful, such moves will lead to a form of mental blindness—loss of the object.

FEAR OF UNCERTAINTY

Most of us learn early in life to pretend that we understand things even when we don't. Rather than ask questions and risk looking foolish, we nod our heads. Soon, we even come to believe that we understand things when really we don't, or not nearly as well as we think we do. This understandable but problematic human trait means that to become better thinkers, most of us have to cultivate a more positive attitude toward not knowing. Prepare to be surprised at how difficult this can be.

Start by trying to accept that uncertainty—even its more extreme version, confusion—is a productive state of mind, a precondition to having ideas. The poet John Keats coined a memorable phrase for this willed tolerance of uncertainty. He called it *negative capability.*

> I had not had a dispute but a disquisition with Dilke, on various subjects; several things dovetailed in my mind, & at once it struck me, what quality went to form a Man of Achievement especially in Literature & which Shakespeare possessed so enormously—I mean *Negative Capability,* that is when man is capable of being in uncertainties, Mysteries, doubts, without any irritable reaching after fact & reason.
>
> —*Letter to George and Thomas Keats, December 1817*

The key phrases here are "capable of being in uncertainties" and "without any irritable reaching." Keats is not saying that facts and reason are unnecessary and therefore can be safely ignored. But he does praise the kind of person who can remain calm (rather than becoming irritable) in a state of uncertainty. He is endorsing a way of being that can stay open to possibilities longer than most of us are comfortable with. Negative capability is an essential habit of mind for productive analytical thinking.

PREJUDGING

Too often inexperienced writers are pressured by well-meaning teachers and textbooks to arrive at a thesis statement—a single sentence formulation of the governing claim that a paper will support—before they have observed enough and reflected enough to find one worth using. These writers end up clinging to the first idea that they think might serve as a thesis, with the result that they stop looking at anything in their evidence except what they want and expect to see. Writers who leap prematurely to thesis statements typically find themselves proving the obvious—some too-general and superficial idea—and worse, they miss opportunities for the better paper that is lurking in the more complicated evidence being screened out by the desire to make the thesis "work."

Unit II of this book, Writing the Analytical Essay, will have much to say about finding and using thesis statements. But this unit (especially Chapter 3, A Toolkit of Analytical Methods) first focuses attention on the kinds of thinking and writing you'll need to engage in before you can successfully make the move to thesis-driven writing. In this discovery phase, you will need to slow down the drive to conclusions to see more in your evidence.

Tell yourself that you don't understand, even if you think that you do. You'll know that you are surmounting the fear of uncertainty when the meaning of your evidence starts to seem less rather than more clear to you, and perhaps even strange. You will begin to see details that you hadn't seen before and a range of competing meanings where you had thought there was only one.

BLINDED BY HABIT

Some people, especially the very young, are good at noticing things. They see things that the rest of us don't see or have ceased to notice. But why is this? Is it just that people become duller as they get older? The poet William Wordsworth thought the problem was not age but habit. That is, as we organize our lives so that we can function more efficiently, we condition ourselves to see in more predictable ways and to tune out things that are not immediately relevant to our daily needs.

You can test this theory by considering what you did and did not notice this morning on the way to work or class or wherever you regularly go. Following a routine for moving through the day can be done with minimal engagement of either the brain or the senses. Our minds are often, as we say, "somewhere else." As we walk along, our eyes wander a few feet in front of our shoes or blankly in the direction of our destination. Moving along the roadway in cars, we periodically realize that miles have gone by while we were driving on automatic pilot, attending barely at all to the road or the car or the landscape. Arguably, even when we try to focus on something that we want to consider, the habit of not really attending to things stays with us.

The deadening effect of habit on seeing and thinking has long been a preoccupation of artists as well as philosophers and psychologists. Some people have even defined the aim of art as "defamiliarization." "The essential purpose of art," writes the novelist David Lodge, "is to overcome the deadening effects of habit by representing familiar things in unfamiliar ways." The man who coined the term *defamiliarization,* Victor Shklovsky, wrote, "Habitualization devours works, clothes, furniture, one's wife, and the fear of war. . . . And art exists that one may recover the sensation of life" (David Lodge, *The Art of Fiction.* New York: Penguin, 1992, p. 53).

Growing up we all become increasingly desensitized to the world around us; we tend to forget the specific things that get us to feel and think in particular ways. Instead we respond to our experience with a limited range of generalizations, and more often than not, these are shared generalizations—that is, clichés.

A lot of what passes for thinking is merely reacting: right/wrong, good/bad, loved it/hated it, couldn't relate to it, boring. Responses like these are habits, reflexes of the mind. And they are surprisingly tough habits to break. As an experiment, ask someone for a description of a place, a movie, a new CD, and see what you get. Too often it will be a diatribe. Offer a counterargument and be told, huffily, "I'm entitled to my opinion." Why is this so?

We live in a culture of inattention and cliché. It is a world in which we are perpetually assaulted with mind-numbing claims (Arby's offers "a baked potato so good you'll never want anyone else's"), flip opinions ("The Republicans/Democrats are idiots") and easy answers ("Be yourself"; "Provide job training for the unemployed, and we can do away with homelessness"). We're awash in such stuff.

That's one reason for the prominence of the buzz phrase "thinking outside the box"—which appears to mean getting beyond outworn ways of thinking about things. But more than that, the phrase assumes that most of the time most of us are trapped inside the box—inside a set of prefabricated answers (clichés) and like/dislike responses. This is not a new phenomenon, of course—250 years ago the philosopher David Hume, writing about perception, asserted that our lives are spent in "dogmatic slumbers," so ensnared in conventional notions of just about everything that we don't really see.

We turn now to three of the most stubbornly counterproductive habits of mind: the judgment reflex, generalizing, and overpersonalizing.

THE JUDGMENT REFLEX

It would be impossible to overstate the mind-numbing effect that the judgment reflex has on thinking. Why? Consider what we do when we judge something and what we ask others to do when we offer them our judgments. Ugly, realistic, pretty, wonderful, unfair, crazy: notice how the problem with such words is a version of the problem with all generalizations—lack of information. What have you actually told someone else if you say that something is ugly, or boring, or realistic?

In its most primitive form—most automatic and least thoughtful—judging is like an on/off switch. When the switch is thrown in one direction or the other—good/bad, right/wrong, positive/negative—the resulting judgment predetermines and overrides any subsequent thinking we might do. Rather than thinking about what X is or how X operates, we lock ourselves prematurely into proving that we were right to think that X should be banned or supported.

The psychologist Carl Rogers has written at length on the problem of the judgment reflex. He claims that our habitual tendency as humans—virtually a programmed response—is to evaluate everything and to do so very quickly. Walking out of a movie, for example, most people will immediately voice their approval or disapproval, usually in either/or terms: I liked it *or* didn't like it; it was right/wrong, good/bad, interesting/ boring. The other people in the conversation will then offer their own evaluation and their judgments of the others' judgments: "I think that it was a good movie and that you are wrong to think it was bad," and so on. Like the knee jerking in response to the physician's hammer, such reflex judgments are made without conscious thought (the source of the pejorative term "knee-jerk thinking"). They close off thinking with likes and dislikes and instant categories.

This is not to say that all judging should be avoided. Obviously our thinking on many occasions must be applied to decision-making: whether we should or shouldn't vote for a particular candidate, should or shouldn't eat French fries, should or shouldn't support a ban on cigarette advertising. Ultimately, in other words, analyti- cal thinking does need to arrive at a point of view—which is a form of judgment—but analytical conclusions are usually not phrased in terms of like/dislike or good/bad. They disclose what a person has come to understand about X rather than how he or she rules on the worth of X.

In some ways, the rest of this book consists of a set of methods for blocking the judgment reflex in favor of more thoughtful responses. For now, here are two moves to make in order to short circuit the judgment reflex and begin replacing it with a more thoughtful, patient, and curious habit of mind. First, try the cure that Carl Rogers recommended to negotiators in industry and government. Do not assert an agreement

THE PROBLEM

data (words, images, other detail) $\xrightarrow[\text{leaps to}]{}$ broad generalization

data $\xrightarrow[\text{leaps to}]{}$ evaluative claims (like/dislike; agree/disagree)

FIGURE 2.1
The Problems with Generalizing and Judging

or disagreement with another person's position until you can repeat that position in a way the other person would accept as fair and accurate. This is surprisingly hard to do because we are usually so busy calling up judgments of our own that we barely hear what the other person is saying.

Second, try eliminating the word "should" from your vocabulary for a while. Judgments take the form of *should* statements. We should pass the law. We should not consider putting such foolish restrictions into law. The analytical habit of mind is characterized by the words *why, how,* and *what.* Analysis asks: What is the aim of the new law? Why do laws of this sort tend to get passed in some parts of the country rather than others? How does this law compare with its predecessor?

You might also try eliminating evaluative adjectives—those that offer judgments with no data. "Green" is a descriptive, concrete adjective. It offers something we can experience. "Beautiful" is an evaluative adjective. It offers only judgment. (See Figure 2.1.)

■ **Try this 2.1:** *Distinguishing Evaluative from Nonevaluative Words*

The dividing line between judgmental and nonjudgmental words is often more difficult to discern in practice than you might assume. Categorize each of the terms in the following list as judgmental or nonjudgmental, and be prepared to explain your reasoning: monstrous, delicate, authoritative, strong, muscular, automatic, vibrant, tedious, pungent, unrealistic, flexible, tart, pleasing, clever, slow.

■ **Try this 2.2:** *Experiment with Adjectives and Adverbs*

Write a paragraph of description—on anything that comes to mind—without using any evaluative adjectives or adverbs. Alternatively, analyze and categorize the adjectives and adverbs in a piece of your own recent writing.

GENERALIZING

What it all boils down to is… What this adds up to is… The gist of her speech was…

Generalizing is not always a bad habit. Reducing complex events, theories, books, or speeches to a reasonably accurate summarizing statement requires practice and skill. We generalize from our experience because this is one way of arriving at ideas.

The problem with generalizing is that it removes the mind—usually much too quickly—from the data that produced the generalization in the first place.

People tend to remember their reactions and impressions. The dinner was dull. The house was beautiful. The music was exciting. But they forget the specific, concrete causes of these impressions (if they ever fully noticed them). As a result, people deprive themselves of material to think with—the data that might allow them to reconsider their initial impressions or share them with others.

Generalizations are just as much a problem for readers and listeners as they are for writers. Consider for a moment what you are actually asking others to do when you offer them a generalization such as "His stories are very depressing." Unless the recipient of this observation asks a question—such as "Why do you think so?"—he or she is being required to take your word for it: the stories are depressing because you say so.

What happens instead if you offer a few details that caused you to think as you do? Clearly, you are on riskier ground. Your listener might think that the details you cite are actually not depressing or that this is not the most interesting or useful way to think about the stories. He or she might offer a different generalization, a different reading of the data, but at least conversation has become possible.

Vagueness and generality are major blocks to learning because, as habits of mind, they allow you to dismiss virtually everything you've read and heard except the general idea you've arrived at. Often the generalizations that come to mind are so broad that they tell us nothing. To say, for example, that a poem is about love or death or rebirth, or that the economy of a particular emerging nation is inefficient, accomplishes very little, since the generalizations could fit almost any poem or economy. In other words, your generalizations are often sites where you stopped thinking prematurely, not the "answers" you've thought they were.

The simplest antidote to the problem of generalizing is to train yourself to be more self-conscious about where your generalizations come from. Remember to trace your general impressions back to the details that caused them. This tracing of attitudes back to their concrete causes is the most basic—and most necessary—move in the analytical habit of mind.

Here's another strategy for bringing your thinking down from high levels of generality. Think of the words you use as steps on an abstraction ladder. The more general and vague the word, the higher its level of abstraction. *Mammal,* for example, is higher on the abstraction ladder than *cow.*

You'll find that it takes some practice to learn to distinguish between abstract words and concrete ones. A concrete word appeals to the senses. Abstract words are not available to our senses of touch, sight, hearing, taste, and smell. *Submarine* is a concrete word. It conjures up a mental image, something we can physically experience. *Peace-keeping force* is an abstract phrase. It conjures up a concept, but in an abstract and general way. We know what people are talking about when they say there is a plan to send submarines to a troubled area. We can't be so sure what is up when people start talking about peace-keeping forces.

You might try using "Level 3 Generality" as a convenient tag phrase reminding you to steer clear of the higher reaches of abstract generalization, some so high up the ladder from the concrete stuff that produced them that there is barely enough air to sustain the thought. Why Level 3 instead of Level 2? There aren't just two categories, abstract and concrete; the categories are the ends of a continuum, a sliding scale. And too often when writers try to concretize their generalizations, the results are still too general: they change *animal* to *mammal,* but they need *cow* or, better, *black angus.*

■ Try this 2.3: *Locating Words on the Abstraction Ladder*
Find a word above (more abstract) and a word below (more concrete) for each of the following words: society, food, train, taxes, school, government, cooking oil, organism, story, magazine.

■ Try this 2.4: *Distinguishing Abstract from Concrete Words*
Make a list of the first ten words that come to mind and then arrange them from most concrete to most abstract. Then repeat the exercise by choosing key words from a page of something you have written recently.

OVERPERSONALIZING (NATURALIZING OUR ASSUMPTIONS)

In one sense all writing is personal: you are the one putting words on the page, and inevitably you see things from your point of view. Even if you were to summarize what someone else had written, aiming for maximum impersonality, *you* would be making the decisions about what to include and exclude. Most effective analytical prose has a strong personal element—the writer's stake in the subject matter. As readers, we want the sense that a writer is engaged with the material and cares about sharing it.

But in another sense, no writing is strictly personal. As contemporary cultural theorists are fond of pointing out, the "I" is not a wholly autonomous free agent who

VOICES FROM ACROSS THE CURRICULUM

Habits of Mind

Readers should not conclude that the "Counterproductive Habits of Mind" presented in this chapter are confined to writing. Psychologists who study the way we process information have established important links between the way we think and the way we feel. Some psychologists, such as Aaron Beck, have identified common "errors in thinking" that parallel the habits of mind discussed in this chapter. Beck and others have shown that falling prey to habits of mind is associated with a variety of negative outcomes. For instance, a tendency to engage in either/or thinking, overgeneralization, and personalization has been linked to higher levels of anger, anxiety, and depression. Failure to attend to these errors in thinking chokes off reflection and analysis. As a result, the person becomes more likely to "react" rather than think, which may prolong and exacerbate the negative emotions.

—Mark Sciutto, *Professor of Psychology*

writes from a unique point of view. Rather, the "I" is always shaped by forces out-side the self—social, cultural, educational, historical, etc. The extreme version of this position allots little space for what we like to think of as "individuality": the self is a site through which dominant cultural ways of understanding the world (ideologies) circulate. From this perspective we are like actors who don't know that we're actors, reciting various cultural scripts that we don't realize are scripts.

This is, of course, an overstated position. A person who believes that civil rights for all is an essential human right is not necessarily a victim of cultural brainwashing. The grounds of his or her belief, shaped by participation in a larger community of belief (ethnic, religious, family tradition, etc.) is, however, not merely personal.

But it's a mistake for a person to assume that because he or she experienced or believes *X*, everyone else does too. Rather than open-mindedly exploring what a sub-ject might mean, the overpersonalizer tends to use a limited range of culturally con-ditioned likes and dislikes to close the subject down. Overpersonalizing substitutes merely reacting for thinking.

It is surprisingly difficult to break the habit of treating our points of view as self-evidently true—not just for us but for everyone. What is "common sense" for one person, and so not even in need of explaining, can be quite uncommon and not so obviously sensible to someone else. More often than not, *common sense* is a phrase that really means "what seems obvious to me and therefore should be obvious to you." This is a habit of mind called "naturalizing your assumptions." The word *naturalize* in this context means you are representing—and seeing—your own assumptions as natural, as simply the way things are (and ought to be).

Overpersonalizers tend to make personal experiences and prejudices an unques-tioned standard of value. Your own disastrous experience with a health maintenance organization (HMO) may predispose you to dismiss a plan for nationalized health care, but your writing needs to examine in detail the holes in the plan, not simply evoke the three hours you lingered in some doctor's waiting room. Paying too much attention to how a subject makes you feel or fits your previous experience of life can seduce you away from analyzing how the subject itself operates.

This is not to say that there is no learning or thinking value in telling our ex-periences: narratives can be used analytically. Storytelling has the virtue of offering concrete experience—not just the conclusions the experience may have led to. Personal narratives can take us back to the source of our convictions. The problem comes when "relating" to someone's story becomes a habitual substitute for thinking through the ideas and attitudes that the story suggests.

The problem with the personal is perhaps most clear when viewed as half of a particularly vicious set of binary oppositions that might be schematized thus:

subjective vs. objective

personal expression vs. impersonal analysis

passionately engaged vs. detached, impassively neutral

genuinely felt vs. heartless

Like most vicious binaries, the personal/impersonal, heart/head binary overstates the case and obscures the considerable overlap of the two sides.

The antidote to the overpersonalizing habit of mind is, as with most habits you want to break, to become more self-conscious about it. Ask yourself, "Is this what I really believe?" Of course, some personal responses can provide valuable beginnings for constructive thinking, provided that, as with generalizing, you get in the habit of *tracing your own responses back to their causes.* If you find an aspect of your subject irritating or funny or disappointing, locate exact details that evoked your emotional response, and begin to analyze those details.

■ Try this 2.5: *Tracing Impressions Back to Causes*

One of Ernest Hemingway's principal rules for writing was to trace impressions back to causes. He once wrote to an apprentice writer, "Find what gave you the emotion; what the action was that gave you the excitement. Then write it down, making it clear so the reader will see it too and have the same feeling you had." You can try this exercise anywhere. Wait for an impression to hit, and then record the stimuli—the concrete details that produced your response—as accurately as you can.

■ Try this 2.6: *Looking for Naturalized Assumptions*

Start listening to the things people say in everyday conversation. Read some newspaper editorials with your morning coffee (a pretty disturbing way to start the day in most cases). Watch for examples of people naturalizing their assumptions. You will find examples of this everywhere. Also, try paraphrasing the common complaint "I couldn't relate to it." What does being able to "relate" to something consist of? What problems would follow from accepting this idea as a standard of value?

OPINIONS (VERSUS IDEAS)

Perhaps no single word causes more problems in the relation between students and teachers, and for people in general, than the word *opinion.* Consider for a moment the often-heard claim "I'm entitled to my opinion." This claim is worth exploring. What is an opinion? How is it (or isn't it) different from a belief or an idea? If I say that I am entitled to my opinion, what am I asking you to do or not do?

Many of the opinions people fight about are actually clichés, pieces of much-repeated conventional wisdom. For example, "People are entitled to say what they want. That's just my opinion." But, of course, this assertion isn't a private and personal revelation. It is an exaggerated and overstated version of one of the items in the U.S. Bill of Rights, guaranteeing freedom of speech. Much public thinking has gone on about this private conviction, and it has thus been carefully qualified. A person can't, for example, say publicly whatever he or she pleases about other people if what he or she says is false and damages the reputation of another person—at least not without threat of legal action.

Our opinions are learned. They are products of our culture and our upbringing—not personal possessions. It is okay to have opinions, but dangerous to give too many of them protected-species status, walling them off into a reserve, not to be touched by reasoning or evidence.

Some things, of course, we have to take on faith. Religious convictions, for example, are more than opinions, though they operate in a similar way: we believe where we can't always prove. But even our most sacred convictions are not really harmed by thinking. The world's religions are constantly engaged in interpreting and reinterpreting what religious texts mean, what various traditional practices mean, and how they may or may not be adapted to the attitudes and practices of the world as it is today.

WHAT IT MEANS TO HAVE AN IDEA

Thinking, as opposed to reporting or reacting, should lead you to ideas. But what does it mean to have an idea? This question lies at the heart of this book. It's one thing to acquire knowledge, but you also need to learn how to produce knowledge, to think for yourself. The problem is that people are daunted when asked to arrive at ideas. They dream up ingenious ways to avoid the task, or they get paralyzed with anxiety.

What is an idea? Must an idea be something that is entirely "original"? Must it revamp the way you understand yourself or your stance toward the world?

Such expectations are unreasonably grand. Clearly, a writer in the early stages of learning about a subject can't be expected to arrive at an idea so original that, like a Ph.D. thesis, it revises complex concepts in a discipline. Nor should you count as ideas

---

VOICES FROM ACROSS THE CURRICULUM

Ideas versus Opinions

Writers need to be aware of the distinction between an argument that seeks support from evidence and mere opinions and assertions. Many students taking political science courses often come with the assumption that in politics one opinion is as good as another. (Tocqueville thought this to be a peculiarly democratic disease.) From this perspective any position a political science professor may take on controversial issues is simply his or her opinion to be accepted or rejected by students according to their own beliefs/prejudices. The key task, therefore, is not so much substituting knowledge for opinions, but rather substituting well-constructed arguments for unexamined opinions.

What is an argument, and how might it be distinguished from opinions? Several things need to be stressed: (1) The thesis should be linked to evidence drawn from relevant sources: polling data, interviews, historical material, and so forth. (2) The thesis should make as explicit as possible its own ideological assumptions. (3) A thesis, in contrast to mere statement of opinion, is committed to making an argument, which means that it presupposes a willingness to engage with others. To the extent that writers operate on the assumption that everything is an opinion, they have no reason to construct arguments; they are locked into an opinion.

—Jack Gambino, *Professor of Political Science*

only those that lead to some kind of life-altering discovery. Ideas are usually much smaller in scope, much less grand, than people seem to expect them to be.

It is easiest to understand what ideas are by considering what ideas do and where they can be found. Here is a partial list:

- An idea answers a question; it explains something that needs to be explained or provides a way out of a difficulty that other people have had in understanding something.
- An idea usually starts with an observation that is puzzling, with something you want to figure out rather than something you think you already understand.
- An idea may be the discovery of a question where there seemed not to be one.
- An idea may make explicit and explore the meaning of something implicit—an unstated assumption upon which an argument rests or a logical consequence of a given position.
- An idea may connect elements of a subject and explain the significance of that connection.
- An idea often accounts for some *dissonance*—that is, something that seems to not fit together.
- An idea provides direction; it helps you see what to do next.

Most strong analytical ideas launch you in a process of resolving problems and bringing competing positions into some kind of alignment. They locate you where there is something to negotiate, where you are required not just to list answers but also to ask questions, make choices, and engage in reasoning about the significance of your evidence.

Some would argue that ideas are discipline-specific, that what counts as an idea in Psychology differs from what counts as an idea in History or Philosophy or Business. And surely the context does affect the way that ideas are shaped and expressed. This book operates on the premise, however, that ideas across the curriculum share common elements. All of the items in the list just given, for example, seem to us to be common to ideas and to idea-making in virtually any context. (See Figure 2.2.)

HAVING IDEAS

(doing something with the material)

versus

RELATING ← − → **REPORTING**

(personal experience   (information matters, but . . .)
matters, but . . .)

FIGURE 2.2
Having Ideas *Ideas occupy a middle ground between the extremes of sheer personal response and faceless reportage of information.*

RULES OF THUMB FOR HANDLING COMPLEXITY

This chapter has been about blocking habits of mind that allow you to evade a more complex way of approaching your writing. Almost all writers feel uncomfortable when encountering complexity. But discomfort need not lead to avoidance or to verbal paralysis. The following rules of thumb can help you to respond to the complexities of the subjects that you write about rather than oversimplifying or evading them.

1. *Reduce scope.* Whenever possible, reduce drastically the range of your inquiry. Resist the temptation to try to include too much information. Even when an assignment calls for broader coverage of a subject, you will usually do best by covering the ground up front and then analyzing one or two key points in greater depth.

   For example, if you were asked to write on Franklin Roosevelt's New Deal, you would obviously have to open with some general observations, such as what it was and why it arose. But if you tried to stay on this general level throughout, your paper would have little direction or focus. You could achieve a focus, though, by moving quickly from the general to some much smaller and more specific part of the subject, such as attacks on the New Deal. You would then be able to limit the enormous range of possible evidence to a few representative figures, such as Huey Long, Father Coughlin, and Alf Landon. Once you began to compare the terms and legitimacy of their opposition to the New Deal, you would be much more likely to manage a complex analysis of the subject than if you had remained at the level of broad generalization.

2. *Study the wording of topics for unstated questions.* Nearly all formulations of a topic contain a number of questions that emerge when you ponder the wording. Framing these questions overtly is often the first step to having an idea. Take a topic question such as "Is feminism good for Judaism?" It seems to invite you simply to argue yes or no, but it actually requires you to set up and answer a number of implied questions. For example, what does "good for Judaism" mean—that which allows the religion to evolve? That which conserves its tradition? The same kinds of questions might be asked of the term *feminism.* And what of the possibility that feminism has no significant effect whatsoever?

   As this example illustrates, even an apparently limited and straightforward question presses writers to make choices about how to engage it. So don't leap from the topic question to your plan of attack too quickly. One of the best tricks of the trade lies in smoking out the unstated assumptions implied by the wording of the topic, and addressing them. (See Chapter 5, Analyzing Arguments, for more on uncovering assumptions.)

3. *Suspect your first responses.* If you settle for these, the result is likely to be superficial and overly general. A better strategy is to examine your first responses for ways in which they might be inaccurate, and then develop the implications of these overstatements (or errors) into a new formulation. In many cases, writers go through this process of proposing and rejecting ideas ten times or more before they arrive at an angle or approach that will sustain an essay.

A first response is okay for a start, as long as you don't stop there. So, for example, most of us would agree, at first glance, that no one should be denied health care, or that a given film or novel that concludes with a marriage is a happy ending, or that the American government should not pass trade laws that might cause Americans to lose their jobs. On closer inspection, however, each of these responses begins to reveal its limitations. Given that there is a limited amount of money available, should everyone, regardless of age or physical condition, be accorded every medical treatment that might prolong life? And might not a novel or film that concludes in marriage signal that the society depicted offers too few options, or more cynically, that the author is feeding the audience an implausible fantasy to blanket over problems raised earlier in the work? And couldn't trade laws resulting in short-term loss of jobs ultimately produce more jobs and a healthier economy?

As these examples suggest, first responses—usually pieces of conventional wisdom—can blind you to rival explanations. Try not to decide on an answer to questions you're given—or those of your own making—too quickly.

4. *Begin with questions, not answers.* Whether you are focusing on an assigned topic or devising one of your own, you are usually better off to begin with something that you don't understand very well and want to understand better. Begin by asking what kinds of questions the material poses. So, for example, if you are convinced that Robinson Crusoe changes throughout Defoe's novel and you write a paper cataloging those changes, you essentially are composing a selective plot summary. If, by contrast, you wonder why Crusoe walls himself within a fortress after he discovers a footprint in the sand, you will be more likely to interpret the significance of events than just to report them.

5. *Write all of the time about what you are studying.* Doing so is probably the single best preparation for developing your own interest in a subject and for finding interesting approaches to it. Don't wait to start writing until you think you have an idea you can organize a paper around. By writing informally—as a matter of routine—about what you are studying, you can acquire the habits of mind necessary to having and developing ideas. Similarly, by reading as often and as attentively as you can, and writing spontaneously about what you read, you will accustom yourself to being a less passive consumer of ideas and information, and will have more ideas and information available to think actively with and about. (See Freewriting in Chapter 3, A Toolkit of Analytical Methods, for more.)

6. *Accept that interest is a product of writing—not a prerequisite.* The best way to get interested is to expect to become interested. Writing gives you the opportunity to cultivate your curiosity by thinking exploratively. Rather than approaching topics in a mechanical way, or putting them off to the last possible moment and doing the assignment grudgingly, try giving yourself and the topic the benefit of the doubt. If you can suspend judgment and start writing, you will often find yourself uncovering interests where you had not seen them before.

7. *Use the "backburner."* In restaurants, the backburner is the place that chefs leave their sauces and soup stocks to simmer while they are actively engaged in other, more immediately pressing and faster operations on the frontburners.

Think of your brain as having a backburner—a place where you can set and temporarily forget (though not entirely) some piece of thinking that you are working on. A good way to use the backburner is to read through and take some notes on something you are writing about—or perhaps a recent draft of something you are having trouble finishing—just before you go to sleep at night. Writers who do this often wake up to find whole outlines, whole strings of useful words already formed in their heads. Keep a notebook by your bed and record these early-morning thoughts. If you do this over a period of days (which assumes, of course, that you will need to start your writing projects well in advance of deadlines), you will be surprised at how much thinking you can do when you didn't know you were doing it. The backburner keeps working during the day as well—periodically insisting that the frontburner, your more conscious self, listen to what it has to say. Pretty soon, ideas start popping up all over the place.

In the context of this discussion, we'll end these rules of thumb with the following anecdote. The wife of the writer and cartoonist, James Thurber, reportedly was asked about her husband's behavior at dinner parties wherein he occasionally went blank and seemed to be staring off into space. "Oh, don't worry about that," she said. "He's all right. He's just writing."

ASSIGNMENT: Observation Practice

Among the habits of mind that this chapter recommends, one of the most useful (and potentially entertaining) is to trace impressions, reactions, sudden thoughts, moods, etc., back to their probable causes. Practice this skill for a week, recording at least one impression a day in some detail (that is, what you both thought and felt). Then determine at least three concrete causes of your response. That is, go after specific sensory details. For class purposes, pick one or two of your journal writings and revise them to a form that could be shared with other members of the class.

Interesting subjects for such writing might include your response to first-year student orientation, some other feature of the beginning of the school year, or your response to selected places on campus. What impact do certain places have on you? Why?

CHAPTER 3

A Toolkit of Analytical Methods

Once I begin the act of writing, it all falls away—the view from the window, the tools, the talismans, even the snoring cat—and I am unconscious of myself and my surroundings while I fuse language with idea, make a specific image visible or audible through the discovery of the right words . . . One's carping inner critics are silenced for a time, and, as a result, what is produced is a little bit different from anything I had planned. There is always a surprise, a revelation. During the act of writing I have told myself something that I didn't know I knew.

—Gail Godwin, "How I Write" (Boston: *The Writer,* October 1987)

IN A RECENT (AND FASCINATING) BESTSELLER ENTITLED *BLINK*, Malcolm Gladwell offers an exploration into intuitive knowing. Gladwell ultimately argues that there is a big difference between experts who make decisions in the blink of an eye and relative novices (people outside their area of expertise) who do so. He finds that although both novices and experts can make intuitive decisions based on rapid assessment of key details (a process he calls thin slicing), the accuracy and quality of these decisions is incomparably better in thinkers who have trained their habits of perception.

This chapter offers a set of procedures—tools—for training your habits of perception, especially those habits that allow you to see significant detail. The tools are presented as formulae that you can apply to anything you wish to better understand. We have deliberately given each of the tools a name and nameable steps so that they are easy to invoke consciously in place of the semi-conscious glide into such habits as overgeneralizing and the judgment reflex. (See Chapter 2, Counterproductive Habits of Mind, for more.)

Most of the items in the Toolkit share the trait of encouraging defamiliarization. In the last chapter we spoke of the necessity of defamiliarizing—of finding ways to see things that the veneer of familiarity would otherwise render invisible. This involves recognizing that the apparently self-evident meanings of things seem "natural" and "given" only because we have been conditioned to see them this way.

Most of us assume, for example, that the media is a site of public knowledge and awareness. But look what happens to that idea when defamiliarized by Jonathan Franzen in a recent essay ("Imperial Bedroom"):

Since really serious exposure in public today is assumed to be synonymous with being seen on television, it would seem to follow that televised space is the premier public space. Many things that people say to me on television, however, would never be tolerated in a genuine public space—in a jury box, for example, or even on a city sidewalk. TV is an enormous, ramified extension of the billion living rooms and bedrooms in which it's consumed. You rarely hear a person on the subway talking loudly about, say, incontinence, but on television it's been happening for years. TV is devoid of shame, and without shame there can be no distinction between public and private.

Franzen here enables us to see freshly by offering us details that challenge our conventional notions of public and private. Seeing in this way requires that we attend carefully to the concrete aspect of things.

We admit that in some cases it is the fear of the unfamiliar rather than the blindness bred of habit that keeps people from looking closely at things. Such is the situation of college students confronted with difficult and unfamiliar reading. And so, there is clearly some value in using habit to domesticate the unfamiliar in particular (and daunting) circumstances. Nevertheless, it's probably easier to overcome the fear of grappling with new material than it is to turn off the notion that meanings are obvious. (On strategies for tackling difficult reading, see the discussions of Paraphrase × 3 and Passage-Based Focused Freewriting later in this chapter. See also Chapter 13, Reading Analytically.)

Before introducing the Toolkit, we should say that what we are proposing is (in a sense) nothing new. There is a long history dating back to the ancient Greek and Roman rhetoricians of using formulae to discover and develop ideas. In classical rhetoric, the pursuit and presentation of ideas—of workable claims for arguments—was divided into five stages: *inventio, dispositio, elocutio, memoria,* and *pronuntiatio.* For present purposes we need to concentrate on only two—*inventio* (invention) and *dispositio* (disposition). Disposition includes the various means of effectively organizing a speech or piece of writing, given that rhetoric is concerned with the means of persuasion. Invention includes various ways of finding things to say, of discovering arguable claims to develop and dispose (arrange).

The early rhetoricians thought of invention in terms of what they called "topics," from the Greek word *topoi,* meaning place or region. The topics were "places" that an orator (speech-maker) could visit, mentally, to discover possible ways of developing a subject. The topics are what we might now think of as strategies—a word which, interestingly, has its roots in the Greek word for army, and, thus, with the idea of winning over an audience to your point of view and defeating enemies. Because the quality and plausibility of a writer's ideas constitute, arguably, the best means of persuading an audience, we here emphasize ways of discovering as much as possible about your evidence.

THE TOOLKIT

What follows are a set of fundamental analytical activities—tools that effective thinkers use constantly, whether they are aware of using them or not. Some people do indeed have ideas as sudden flashes of inspiration (in the blink of an eye), but there is method even in such seemingly intuitive leaps. And when the sudden flashes of inspiration don't come, method is even more essential.

One trick to becoming a better observer and thus a better thinker is to *slow down,* to stop trying to draw conclusions before you've spent time openly attending to the data, letting yourself notice more. Better ideas grow out of a richer acquaintance with whatever it is you are looking at. Observation and interpretation go hand in hand, but it helps greatly to allow yourself a distinct observation stage and to prolong this beyond what most people find comfortable. All of the activities in the Toolkit seek to create such a stage. The Toolkit will also help you to stave off anxiety about assimilating difficult material by giving you something concrete to do with it, rather than expecting yourself to leap instantly to understanding.

The activities in the Toolkit can be conducted either orally or in writing and should be practiced again and again, until they become habitual. The activities themselves do not produce ready-made papers, and may in fact produce an abundance of writing that never makes it through to the final draft. But the thinking these activities inspire ultimately produces much better final results.

There are, of course, more observational and idea-generating methods than we have offered here. In classical rhetoric, for example, the topics of invention include such things as the traditional rhetorical modes (comparison and contrast, classification, definition, etc.) and ways of inventorying an audience to discover things that need to be said. Our purpose in this chapter is narrower. We are concentrating on ways of looking at data—whether in print, visual, or the world—that will allow you to become more fully aware of the features that define your subject, that make it what it is. (Later chapters offer tools for other, mostly later-stage tasks such as making interpretive leaps, conversing with sources, and finding and evolving a thesis.)

PARAPHRASE × 3

The activity we call Paraphrase × 3 offers the quickest means of seeing how a little writing about something you're reading can lead to having ideas about it. Paraphrasing moves toward interpretation because it tends to uncover areas of uncertainty and find questions. It instantly defamiliarizes. It also keeps your focus small so that you can practice thinking in depth rather than going for an overly broad "big picture."

Paraphrasing is commonly misunderstood as summary (a way of shrinking material you've read) or perhaps as simply a way to avoid plagiarism by putting it in your own words. Too often when people wish to understand or retain information, they summarize—that is, they produce a general overview of what the words say. Paraphrasing stays much closer to the actual words than summarizing. The word *paraphrase* means to put one phrase next to *(para)* another phrase. When you paraphrase a passage, you cast and recast its key terms into near synonyms, translating it into a parallel statement. The goal of paraphrasing is to open up the possible meanings of the words; it's a mode of inquiry.

Why is paraphrasing useful? The answer has to do with words—what they are and what we do with them. When we read, it is easy to skip quickly over the words, assuming we know what they mean. Yet when people start talking about what they mean by particular words—the difference, for example, between *assertive* and *aggressive* or the meaning of ordinary words such as *polite, realistic,* or *gentlemanly*—they usually find less agreement than they expected. Most words mean more than one thing, and mean different things to different people.

What you say is inescapably a product of how you say it. Language doesn't merely reflect reality; what we see as reality is shaped by the words we use. This idea is known as the constitutive theory of language. It is opposed to the so-called "transparent" theory of language, wherein it is implied that we can see through words to some meaning that exists beyond and is independent of them. When you paraphrase language, whether your own or language you encounter in your reading, you are not just defining terms but opening out the wide range of implications those words inevitably possess.

We call this activity Paraphrase × 3 because usually one paraphrase is not enough. Take a sentence you want to understand better and recast it into other language three times. This will banish the problematic notion that the meaning of words is self-evident, and it will stimulate your thinking.

If you paraphrase a key passage from a reading several times, you will discover that it gets you working with the language. But you need to paraphrase *slavishly*. You can't let yourself just go for the gist; replace all of the key words. The new words you are forced to come up with represent first stabs at interpretation, at having (small) ideas about what you are reading by unearthing a range of possible meanings embedded in the passage.

In practice, Paraphrase × 3 has three steps:

1. Select a single sentence or phrase from whatever it is you are studying that you think is interesting, perhaps puzzling, and especially useful for understanding the material.

2. Do Paraphrase × 3. Find synonyms for all of the key terms—and do this three times.

3. Reflect. What have you come to recognize about the original passage on the basis of repeated restatement?

■ Try this 3.1: *Experimenting with Paraphrase × 3*

Recast the substantive language of the following statements using Paraphrase × 3:

- *I am entitled to my opinion.*
- *We hold these truths to be self-evident.*
- *That's just common sense.*

What do you come to understand about these remarks as a result of paraphrasing? Which words, for example, are most slippery (that is, difficult to define)?

It is interesting to note, by the way, that Thomas Jefferson originally wrote the words "sacred and undeniable" in his draft of the Declaration of Independence, instead of "self-evident." So what?

■ **Try this 3.2:** *Doing Paraphrase* × *3 with a Reading*

Recast the substantive language of a key sentence or short passage in something you are reading—say, a passage you find central or difficult in any of your assigned reading, the kind of passage most likely to attract yellow highlighter. Try not to make the language of your paraphrase more general than the original. This method is an excellent way to prepare for class discussion or to generate thinking about the reading that you might use in a paper. It is also, as we discuss in Unit III, a key method of analyzing the secondary sources that you draw on in your papers.

NOTICE AND FOCUS (RANKING)

The activity called Notice and Focus guides you to dwell longer with the data before feeling compelled to decide what the data mean. Repeatedly returning to the question, "What do you notice?" is one of the best ways to counteract the tendency to generalize too rapidly. "What do you notice?" redirects attention to the subject matter itself and delays the pressure to come up with answers.

So the first step is to repeatedly answer the question, "What do you notice?" being sure to cite actual details of the thing being observed rather than moving to more general observations about it. This phase of the exercise should produce an extended and unordered list of details—features of the thing being observed—that call attention to themselves for one reason or another.

The second step is the focusing part in which you *rank* (create an order of importance for) the various features of the subject that you have noticed. Answer the question "Which three details (specific features of the subject matter) are most interesting (or significant or revealing or strange)?" The purpose of relying on "interesting" or one of the other suggested words is that these will help to deactivate the like/dislike switch, which is so much a reflex in all of us, and replace it with a more analytical perspective.

The third step in this process is to say why the three things you selected struck you as the most interesting. Your attempts to answer this "why" question will trigger leaps from observation to interpretive conclusions.

Doing Notice and Focus is more difficult than it sounds. Remember to allow yourself to notice as much as you can about what you are looking at before you try to explain it. Dwell with the data (in that attitude of uncertainty we've recommended in Chapter 2). Record what you see. Resist moving to generalization or, worse, to judgment. The longer you allow yourself to dwell on the data, the more you will notice, and the richer your interpretation of the evidence will ultimately be.

Prompts: Interesting and Strange

What does it mean to find something "interesting"? Often we are interested by things that have captured our attention without our clearly knowing why. Interest and curiosity are near cousins.

The word *strange* is a useful prompt because it gives us permission to notice oddities. *Strange* invites us to defamiliarize things within our range of notice. *Strange,* in this context, is not a judgmental term but one denoting features of a subject or situation that aren't readily explainable. Where you locate something strange, you have something to interpret—to figure out what makes it strange and why.

Along similar lines, the words *revealing* and *significant* work by requiring you to make choices that can lead to interpretive leaps. If something strikes you as revealing or significant, even if you're not yet sure why, you will eventually have to produce some explanation.

▇ Try this 3.3: *Doing Notice and Focus with a Room*

Practice this activity with the room you're in. List a number of details about it, then rank the three most important ones. Use as a focusing question any of the four words suggested above—interesting, significant, revealing or strange. Or come up with your own focus for the ranking, such as the three aspects of the room that seem most to affect the way you feel and behave in the space.

▇ Try this 3.4: *Notice and Focus Fieldwork*

Try this exercise with a range of subjects: a photograph, a cartoon, an editorial, conversations overheard around campus, looking at people's shoes, political speeches, and so forth. Remember to include all three steps: notice, rank and say why.

10 ON 1

The exercise we call 10 on 1 is a cousin of Notice and Focus—it too depends on extended observation but with more focus and usually occurring at a later stage of analysis. Notice and Focus is useful because it frees you to look at the object with no constraints or prejudgments. Notice and Focus treats your subject matter as a broad canvas to move around in. 10 on 1 promotes a more intensive and elaborate exploration of a single representative piece of evidence. 10 on 1 is built on the idea that one sure way to notice more is to narrow your scope.

The term *10* on *1* is shorthand for the principle that it is better to make ten observations or points about a single representative issue or example (10 on 1) than to make the same basic point about ten related issues or examples (1 on 10). A paper that has evolved from detailed analysis of what the writer takes to be his or her single most telling example is far more likely to arrive at a good idea than a paper that settles prematurely for one idea and applies it mechanically to each piece of evidence it encounters (i.e., the same general idea attached to 10 similar examples).

The shift from making one observation about ten examples to making ten possible observations about your single best example is the aim of the exercise. Ten, in this case, is an arbitrary number. The ten are the observations you make about your representative example along with any ideas these observations start to give you. If you can keep the number 10 in mind, it will prod you to keep asking yourself questions rather than stopping the observation process too soon. What do I notice? What else do I notice? What might this imply? What else might it imply?

For extended discussion of doing 10 on 1 as an organizational principle for papers, see Chapter 8 (Using Evidence to Build a Paper) in Unit II, Writing the Analytical

Essay. We have included this brief discussion to better integrate 10 on 1 with our other observational strategies.

THE METHOD: WORKING WITH PATTERNS OF REPETITION AND CONTRAST

The Method is our shorthand for a systematic procedure for analyzing evidence by looking for patterns of repetition and contrast. It differs from other tools we have been offering in being more comprehensive. Whereas Notice and Focus and 10 on 1 cut through a wealth of data to focus on individual details, The Method goes for the whole picture, involving methodical application of a matrix or grid of observational moves upon a subject. Although these are separate moves, they also work together and build cumulatively to the discovery of an infrastructure, a blueprint of the whole.

Here is the procedure in its most pared-down form:

- What repeats?
- What goes with what?
- What is opposed to what?
- What doesn't fit?
- And for any of these, so what?

As you can see, these are the steps that we first presented as Move 4, Look for Patterns, in the Five Analytical Moves of Chapter 1. Now we are returning to this move in more elaborate form.

Before laying out these steps more precisely, we want first to mention that The Method can be applied to virtually anything you wish to analyze—an essay, a political campaign, a work of visual or verbal art, a dense passage from some secondary source that you feel to be important but can't quite figure out, and, last but not least, your own writing. It may be helpful to think of this method of analysis as a form of mental doodling, one that encourages the attitude of negative capability we spoke of in Chapter 2. Rather than worrying about what you are going to say, or about whether you understand, you instead get out a pencil and start tallying up what you see. Engaged in this process, you'll soon find yourself gaining entry to the logic of your subject matter.

The method of looking for patterns works through a series of steps. Hold yourself initially to doing the steps one at a time and in order. Later, you will be able to record your answers under each of the three steps simultaneously. Although the steps of The Method are discrete and modular, they are also consecutive. They proceed by a kind of narrative logic. Each step leads logically to the next, and then to various kinds of regrouping, which is actually rethinking. (Note: we have divided into two kinds of repetition, exact and similar, what was one step in the Five Analytical Moves.)

Step 1. *Locate exact repetitions*—identical or nearly identical words or details—and note the number of times each repeats.

For example, if the word *seems* repeats three times, write "seems × 3." Consider different forms of the same word—*seemed, seem*—as exact repetitions. Similarly, if you are working with images rather than words, the repeated appearance of high foreheads would constitute an exact repetition.

Concentrate on substantive (meaning-carrying) words. Only in rare cases do words like "and" or "the" merit attention as a significant repetition. If you are working with a longer text, such as an essay or book chapter or short story, limit yourself to recording the half-dozen or so words that call attention to themselves through repetition.

Step 2. *Locate repetitions of the same or similar kind of detail or word—which we call strands—and name the connecting logic.* (For example, *polite, courteous, mannerly* and *accuse, defense, justice, witness* are strands.)

Simply listing the various strands that you find in your evidence goes a long way toward helping you discover what is most interesting and important for you to address. But to use the discovery of strands as an analytical tool, you have to do more than list. You have to name the common denominators that make the words or details in your list identifiable as a strand. Naming and renaming your strands will trigger ideas; it is itself an analytical move. And again, when working with longer pieces, try to locate the half-dozen strands that seem to you most important.

Step 3. *Locate details or words that form or suggest binary oppositions, and select from these the most important ones, which function as organizing contrasts.* Sometimes patterns of repetition that you begin to notice in a particular subject matter are significant because they are part of a contrast—a basic opposition—around which the subject matter is structured. To find these oppositions, ask yourself, *What is opposed to what?*

When looking for binary oppositions, start with what's on the page. List words or details that are opposed to other words or details. Note that often these oppositions are not obvious; you need to become aware of what is repeatedly there and then ask yourself, is something opposed to this? And often the oppositions that you discover are not actual words in a text but implied meanings. For example, images of rocks and water might suggest the binary permanence/impermanence or unchanging/changing.

This process of constructing binary oppositions from the data usually leads you to discover what we call *organizing contrasts*. An organizing contrast is a central binary, one that reveals the central issues and concerns in the material you are studying and also provides—like the structural beam in a building—its unifying shape. Some examples that we encounter frequently are nature/civilization, city/country, public/ private, organic/ inorganic, and voluntary/involuntary.

Step 4. *Rank the data within your lists to isolate what you take to be the most important repetitions, strands, and binaries. Then write a paragraph—half a page or so—in which you explain your choice of one repetition or one strand or one binary as central to understanding whatever you have been observing.* Ranking your data in terms of its importance is a means of moving toward interpretive leaps. Your most important binaries might be a pair of opposed terms and/or ideas, but each might also be a strand that is opposed to another strand.

Step 5. *Search for anomalies—data that do not seem to fit any of the dominant patterns.* We have made this the last step because anomalies often become evident only after you have begun to discern a pattern, so it is best to locate repetitions, strands, and organizing contrasts—things that fit together in some way—before looking for things that seem not to fit. Once you see an anomaly, you will often find that it is part of a strand you had not detected (and perhaps one side of a previously unseen binary). In this respect, looking for anomalies encourages defamiliarizing—it's great for shaking yourself out of potentially limited ways of looking at your evidence and getting you to consider other possible interpretations.

Thinking Recursively with Strands and Binaries

Applying The Method has the effect of inducing you to get physical with the data—literally, for you will probably find yourself circling, underlining, and listing. Although you will thus descend from the heights of abstraction to the realm of concrete detail, the point of tallying repetitions and strands and binaries and then selecting the most important and interesting ones is to trigger ideas. The discipline required to notice patterns in the language produces more specific, more carefully grounded conclusions than you otherwise might produce.

You should expect ideas to suggest themselves to you as you move through the mechanical steps of The Method. The active thinking often takes place as you are grouping and regrouping. As you start listing, you will find that strands begin to suggest other strands that are in opposition to them. And you may find that words you first took to be parts of a single strand are actually parts of different strands and are, perhaps, in opposition. This process of noticing and then relocating words and details into different patterns is one aspect of using The Method that can push your analysis to interpretation.

To some extent using The Method is archaeological. It digs into the language or the material details of whatever you are analyzing in order to unearth its thinking. This is most evident in the discovery of organizing contrasts. Binary oppositions often indicate places where there is struggle among various points of view. And there is usually no single "right" answer about which of a number of binaries is the primary organizing contrast. One of the best ways to develop your analyses is to reformulate binaries, trying on different possible oppositions as the primary one. (For more on using binaries analytically, see Chapter 5, Analyzing Arguments.)

Thus far we have been talking about The Method as a grid for viewing other people's finished work. The Method also describes the processes by which writers, artists, scientists, and all manner of thinkers create those works in the first place. Much of the thinking that we do as we write and read happens through a process of association, which is, by its very nature, repetitive. In associative thinking, thoughts develop as words and details, which suggest other words and details that are like them. Thinking moves not just forward in a straight line, but sideways and in circles. We repeatedly make connections; we figure out what goes with what and what is opposed to what. In this sense, writing (making something out of words) and reading (arriving at an understanding of someone else's words) operate in much the same way.

Generating Ideas with The Method: An Example

See how the thinking in the following paragraph moves because the writer is noting strands and binaries. First he notes the differences in two kinds of fashion ads aimed at men. There are the high-fashion ads and the Dockers ads. In the first of these, the word *beautiful* repeats twice as part of a strand (including *gorgeous, interesting, supermodel, demure*). The writer then poses traits of the Dockers ads as an opposing strand. Instead of a beautiful face there is no face, instead of "gorgeous outfit," the author says "it's tough to concentrate on the clothes." These oppositions cause the writer to make his interpretive leap, that the Dockers ads "weren't primarily concerned with clothes at all" and that this was intentional.

> The most striking aspect of the spots is how different they are from typical fashion advertising. If you look at men's fashion magazines, for example, at the advertisements for the suits of Ralph Lauren or Valentino or Hugo Boss, they almost always consist of a beautiful man, with something interesting done to his hair, wearing a gorgeous outfit. At the most, the man may be gesturing discreetly, or smiling in the demure way that a man like that might smile after, say, telling the supermodel at the next table no thanks he has to catch an early-morning flight to Milan. But that's all. The beautiful face and the clothes tell the whole story. The Dockers ads, though, are almost exactly the opposite. There's no face. The camera is jumping around so much that it's tough to concentrate on the clothes. And instead of stark simplicity, the fashion image is overlaid with a constant, confusing patter. It's almost as if the Dockers ads weren't primarily concerned with clothes at all—and in fact that's exactly what Levi's intended. What the company had discovered, in its research, was that baby-boomer men felt that the chief thing missing from their lives was male friendship. Caught between the demands of the families that many of them had started in the eighties and career considerations that had grown more onerous, they felt they had lost touch with other men. The purpose of the ads—the chatter, the lounging around, the quick cuts—was simply to conjure up a place where men could put on one-hundred-percent-cotton khakis and reconnect with one another. In the original advertising brief, that imaginary place was dubbed Dockers World.
>
> *—Malcolm Gladwell, "Listening to Khakis"*

Doing The Method on a Poem: Our Analysis

Here is an example of how one might do The Method on a piece of text—in this case, a student poem. You might try it yourself first, using our version to check against your own.

Brooklyn Heights, 4:00 A.M.
Dana Ferrelli

sipping a warm forty oz.

Coors Light on a stoop in

Brooklyn Heights. I look

across the street, in the open window;

Blonde bobbing heads, the

smack of a jump rope, laughter

of my friends breaking

beer bottles. Putting out their

burning filters on the #5 of

a hopscotch court.

We reminisce of days when we were

Fat, pimple faced—

look how far we've come. But tomorrow

a little blonde girl will

pick up a Marlboro Light filter, just to play.

And I'll buy another forty, because

that's how I play now.

Reminiscing about how far I've come

1. *Words that repeat exactly:* forty × 2, blonde × 2, how far we've (I've) come × 2, light × 2, reminisce, reminiscing × 2, filter, filters × 2, Brooklyn Heights × 2

2. *Strands:* jump rope, laughter, play, hopscotch (connecting logic: childhood games representing the carefree worldview of childhood); Coors Light, Marlboro Light filters, beer bottles (connecting logic: drugs, adult "games," escapism?); smack, burning, breaking (violent actions and powerful emotion: burning)

3. *Binary oppositions:* how far we've come/how far I've come (a move from plural to singular, from a sense of group identity to isolation, from group values to a more individual consideration)

Blonde bobbing heads/little blonde girl

Burning/putting out

Coors Light, Marlboro Lights/jump rope, hopscotch

How far I've come (two meanings of *far*?, one positive, one not)

Heights/stoop

Present/past

4. *Ranked repetitions, strands and binaries plus paragraph explaining the choice of one of these as central to understanding.*

   Most important repetitions: forty, how far we've/I've come

   Most important strands: jump rope, laughter, play, hopscotch; Coors Light, Marlboro Light filters, beer bottles

   Most important binaries: jump rope, laugher, play, hopscotch versus Coors Light, Marlboro Light filters, beer bottles; burning/putting out

Paragraph(s):

This is a poem about growing up—or failing to grow up, both being subjects about which the poem expresses mixed emotions. The repetition of *forty* (forty-ounce beer) is interesting in this context. It signals a certain weariness—perhaps with a kind of pun on forty to suggest middle age and thus the speaker's concern about moving toward being older in a way that seems stale and flat. The beer, after all, is warm—which is not the best state for a beer to be in, once opened, if it is to retain its taste and character. Forty ounces of beer—"supersizing"—suggest excess.

This reading of forty as excess along with the possible allusion to middle age takes us to what is, in our reading of the poem, the most important (or at least most interesting) binary opposition: *burning* versus *putting out*. We are attracted to this binary because it seems to be part of a more intense strand in the poem, one that runs counter to the weary prospect of moving on toward a perhaps lonely ("how far *I've* come") middle-aged feeling. Burning goes with breaking and the smack of the jump rope, and even putting out, if we visualize putting out not just as fire extinguished but in terms of putting a cigarette out by pushing the burning end of it into something (the number 5 on the hopscotch court). The poem's language has a violent and passionate edge to it, even though the violent words are not always in a violent context (for example, the smack of the jump rope).

This is a rather melancholy poem in which, perhaps, the poetic voice is mourning the passing, the "putting out" of the passion of youth ("burning"). In the poem's more obvious binary—the opposition of childhood games to more "adult" ones—the same melancholy plays itself out, making the poem's refrain-like repetition of "how far I've come" ring with unhappy irony. The little blonde girl is an image of the speaker's own past self (because the poem talks about reminiscing), and the speaker mourns that little girl's (her own) passing into a more uncertain and less carefree state. It is 4:00 a.m. in Brooklyn Heights—just about the end of night, the darkest point perhaps before the beginning of morning, and windows in the poem are open, so things are not all bad. The friends make noise together, break bottles together, revisit hopscotch square 5 together, and contemplate moving on.

We couldn't, by the way, find any significant anomalies (step 5) in the poem. That in itself suggests how highly patterned the poem is around its basic strands and binaries.

▬ Try this 3.5: *Apply The Method to Something You Are Reading*

Try The Method on a piece of reading that you wish to understand better, perhaps a series of editorials on the same subject, an essay, one or more poems by the same author (because The Method is useful for reading across texts for common denominators), a collection of stories, a political speech, and so on. You can work with as little as a few paragraphs or as much as an entire article or chapter or book.

A Procedure for Finding and Querying Binaries

As should be evident, working with binaries is central to using The Method. But binaries are so pervasive a part of analysis that we've given them their own place in the Toolkit, and we take them up again in an upcoming chapter (Chapter 5, Analyzing Arguments).

In Chapter 5 we argue that writing and analyzing arguments is largely a matter of unearthing, rephrasing, and reevaluating the binary oppositions (this against that, on/off, dark/light, wild/domestic) that undergird them. Working with binaries is not the same thing as either/or thinking (right/wrong, good/bad, black/white, welfare state/free society). Either/or thinking is a problem because it reduces things to oversimplified extremes and reduces complex situations to only two choices. Working with binaries, however, is not about creating stark oppositions and weighing in heavily on one side or the other. It is about finding these oppositions and querying their accuracy.

In Chapter 5 there is a fuller discussion of a four-step procedure for working with binaries. This procedure should enhance your ability to understand and confront other people's arguments and your own. Here, in brief, are the four steps:

1. Locate a Range of Opposing Categories (Binaries)
2. Analyze and Define the Opposing Terms
3. Question the Accuracy of the Binary and Rephrase the Terms
4. Substitute "To What Extent?" for "Either/Or"

Step four is the move that we are recommending now. It is a tool for rephrasing either/or choices—either free enterprise or government control—into qualified claims, making things a matter of degree. The operative phrase is "to what extent" or "the extent to which." To what extent is the Supreme Court decision on allowing manufacturers to set minimum prices for retailers an evasion of government responsibility in favor of unregulated free enterprise?

▬ Try this 3.6: *Working with Binaries*

Write a few paragraphs in which you work with the binaries suggested by the following familiar expression: "School gets in the way of one's education." Keep the focus on working through the binaries implicit in the quotation. What other terms would you substitute for "school" and "education"? Coming up with a range of synonyms for each term will clarify what is at stake in the binary. Remember to consider the accuracy of the claim. To what extent, and in what ways, is the expression both true and false?

▃ Try this 3.7: *Fieldwork in Either/Or Thinking*

Locate some organizing contrasts in anything—something you are studying, something you've just written, something you saw on television last night, something on the front page of the newspaper, something going on at your campus or workplace, and so forth. Binaries pervade the way we think; therefore, you can expect to find them everywhere. Consider, for example, the binaries suggested by current trends in contemporary music or by the representation of women in birthday cards. Having selected the binaries you want to work with, pick one and transform the either/or thinking into more qualified thinking using the extent-to-which formula.

FREEWRITING

We have placed freewriting last in the Toolkit because it draws on the other writing strategies discussed in this chapter, notably paraphrasing and 10 on 1. Freewriting is a method of arriving at ideas by writing continuously about a subject for a limited period of time without pausing to edit, correct, bite your pen, or stare into space. The rationale behind this activity can be understood through a well-known remark by the novelist E.M. Forster (in regard to the "tyranny" of prearranging everything): "How do I know what I think until I see what I say?" Freewriting gives you the chance to see what you'll say.

The writer Anne Lamott writes eloquently (in *Bird by Bird*) about the censor we all hear as a nasty voice—actually a collection of nasty voices—in our heads that keep us from writing. These are the internalized voices of past critics whose comments have become magnified to suggest that we will never get it right. Freewriting allows us to tune out these voices long enough to discover what we might think.

This activity is sometimes known by the term *prewriting*. We prefer the terms *freewriting* or *exploratory* writing because prewriting implies something that happens before writing and that has no place in the final form. Good analytical writing, at whatever stage, has an exploratory feel. It shares its discovery process with the reader. And to a significant extent, the final draft re-creates for the reader the writer's experience of arriving at his or her key ideas.

This is not to say that writers should care only about the process of discovery and not about the final product, nor are we suggesting that writers should substitute freewriting and inconclusive thinking for carefully organized finished drafts. We are claiming, however, that writers have a much easier and more productive experience revising the final or penultimate draft if they spend more time doing various kinds of exploratory writing before moving to the final draft stage.

In freewriting, you write *without stopping* for a predetermined period of time, usually ten to twenty minutes. There aren't many rules to freewriting, just that it is important to keep your pen (or fingers on the keyboard) moving. Don't reread as you go. Don't pause to correct things. Don't cross things out. Just keep writing. To get to good writing, you first have to tolerate some chaos. In freewriting, especially if you engage in it frequently, you often surprise yourself with the quality of your own thinking, with the ideas you didn't really know you had and the many details you hadn't really noticed until you started writing.

■ **Try this 3.8:** *Descriptions from Everyday Life*

Spend a week describing things that you can observe in your everyday environment—whatever interests you on a particular day, or the same kind of thing over a period of days. Get the details of what you are describing on the page. If judgments and generalizations emerge, let them come, but don't stay on them long. Get back to the narration of detail as quickly as you can. At the end of the week, write a piece called either "What I learned in a week of looking at . . . " or come up with your own shaping title.

Passage-Based Focused Freewriting

Passage-based focused freewriting is a version of freewriting particularly suited for increasing your ability to learn from what you read. It prompts in-depth analysis of a representative example, on the assumption that you'll attain a better appreciation of the whole after you've explored how a piece of it works.

Passage-based focused freewriting resembles freewriting in encouraging you to leap associatively from idea to idea as they arise, and it differs from a finished essay, in which the sentences follow logically as you unfold your central idea. The passage-based version differs from regular freewriting, however, in adding the limitation of focus on a piece of text within which this associative thinking may occur.

Narrow the scope to a single passage, a brief piece of the reading (at least a sentence, at most a paragraph) to anchor your analysis. You might choose the passage in answer to one of the following questions:

- What one passage in the reading most needs to be discussed—is most useful for understanding the material—and why?
- What one passage seems puzzling, difficult to pin down, anomalous, or even just unclear—and how might this be explained?

One advantage of focused freewriting is that its impromptu nature encourages you to take chances, to think out loud on the page. It invites you to notice what you notice in the moment and take some stabs at what it might mean without having to worry about formulating a weighty thesis statement or maintaining consistency. It allows you to worry less about what you don't understand and instead start to work things out as you write.

There is no set procedure for such writing, but here are some guidelines:

1. Seek to understand before you judge. Focus on what the text is saying and doing and what it is inviting readers to think, not on your own agreement/ disagreement or like/dislike. Attend to the point of view it advances on the subject at hand, not to your point of view on that subject. Eventually you should arrive at your point of view about its point of view, but that generally comes later.

2. Choose a limited piece of concrete evidence to focus on. Select a passage that you find interesting, that you have questions about, perhaps one that you don't quite understand. That way your writing will have some work to do.

3. Contextualize the evidence. Where does the passage come from in the text? Of what larger discussion is it a part? Briefly answering these questions prevents you from taking things out of context.

4. Make observations about the evidence. Stay close to the data you've quoted. Paraphrase key phrases in the passage, teasing out the possible meanings of these words. Then reflect on what you've come to better understand through para- phrasing. Note: to encourage attention to the words and discourage overly gen- eral leaps, it is useful to write out the passage before you begin your freewriting (especially if you are being asked to do the freewriting in class, as is often the case in college writing). The act of copying often induces you to notice more about the particular features of your chosen passage.

5. Share your reasoning about what the evidence means. As you move from ob- servation to implication, remember that you need to explain how you know the data mean what you claim they mean.

6. Address how the passage is representative. Consider how the passage you've selected connects to broader issues in the reading. At various points in your freewriting feel free to move from your analysis of local details to address what, given what you now understand, the work as a whole may plausibly be "saying" about this or that issue or question. It's okay to work with the details for almost the entire time and then press yourself to an interpretive leap with the formula, "I'm almost out of time but my big point is . . ."

■■■ **Try this 3.9:**   *Doing a Passage-Based Focused Freewrite*

Select a passage from any of the material that you are reading and copy it at the top of the page. Then do a twenty-minute focused freewrite on it, using the guide- lines already stated. It is often productive to take the focused freewrite and type it, revising and further freewriting until you have filled the inevitable gaps in your thinking that the time limit has created. (One colleague of ours has students do this in a different font, so both can see how the thinking is evolving.) Eventually, you can build up, through a process of accretion, the thinking for an entire paper in this way.

Writers' Notebooks

Writers' notebooks (journals) are unlike a personal diary, in which you keep track of your days' activities and recount the feelings these occasioned; journals are for gen- erating and collecting ideas and for keeping track of your ongoing interactions with course materials. A journal can be, in effect, a collection of focused freewrites that you develop in response to the reading and lectures in a course.

The best way to get a journal to work for you is to experiment. You might try, for example, copying and commenting on statements from your reading or class meetings that you found potentially illuminating. Use the journal to write down the ideas, reactions, and germs of ideas you had during a class discussion or that you found running around in your head after a late night's reading. Use the journal to retain your first impressions of books or films or music or performances or whatever so that you can then look back at them and trace the development of your thinking.

If possible, write in your journal every day. As with freewriting, the best way to get started is just to start, see what happens, and take it from there. Also as with freewriting, the more you write, the more you'll find yourself noticing, and, thus, the more you'll have to say.

Passage-Based Focused Freewriting: An Example

Following is an example of a student's exploratory writing on an essay by the twentieth-century, African-American writer Langston Hughes. The piece is a twenty-minute reflection on two excerpts. Most notable about this piece, perhaps, is the sheer number of interesting ideas. That may be because the writer continually returns to the language of the original quotes for inspiration. She is not restricted by maintaining a single and consistent thread. It is interesting, though, that as the freewrite progresses, a primary focus (on the second of her two quotes) seems to emerge.

Passages from "The Negro Artist and the Racial Mountain" by Langston Hughes

"But jazz to me is one of the inherent expressions of Negro life in America; the eternal tom-tom beating in the Negro soul—the tom-tom of revolt against weariness in a white world, a world of subway trains, and work, work, work; the tom-tom of joy and laughter, and pain swallowed in a smile. Yet the Philadelphia clubwoman is ashamed to say that her race created it and she does not like me to write about it. The old subconscious 'white is best' runs through her mind. . . . And now she turns up her nose at jazz and all its manifestations—likewise almost everything else distinctly racial."

"We build our temples for tomorrow, strong as we know how, and we stand on top of the mountain, free within ourselves."

Langston Hughes's 1926 essay on the situation of the Negro artist in America sets up some interesting issues that are as relevant today as they were in Hughes's time. Interestingly, the final sentence of the essay ("We build our temples . . .") will be echoed some four decades later by the Civil Rights leader, Martin Luther King, but with a different spin on the idea of freedom. Hughes writes "we stand on top of the mountain, free within ourselves." King says, "Free at last, free at last, my God almighty, we're free at last." King asserts an opening out into the world—a freeing of black people, finally, from slavery and then another century of oppression.

Hughes speaks of blacks in a more isolated position— "on top of the mountain" and "within ourselves." Although the mountain may stand for a height from which the artist can speak, it is hard to be heard from the top of mountains. It is one thing to be free. It is another to be free within oneself. What does this phrase mean? If I am free within myself I am at least less vulnerable to those who would restrict me from without. I can live with their restrictions. Mine is an inner freedom. Does inner freedom empower artists? Perhaps it does. It may allow them to say what they want and not worry about what others say or think. This is one thing that Hughes seems to be calling for. But he is also worried about lack of recognition of Negro artists, not only by whites but by blacks. His use of the repeated phrase, tom-tom, is interesting in this respect. It, like the word "mountain," becomes a kind of refrain in the essay—announcing both a desire to rise above the world and its difficulties (mountain) and a desire to be heard (tom-tom and mountain as pulpit).

The idea of revolt, outright rebellion, is present but subdued in the essay. The tom-tom is a "revolt against weariness" and also an instrument for expressing "joy and laughter." The tom-tom also suggests a link with a past African and probably Native American culture—communicating by drum and music and dance. White culture in the essay stands for a joyless world of "work, work, work." This is something I would like to think about more, as the essay seems to link the loss of soul with the middle and upper classes, both black and white.

And so the essay seeks to claim another space among those he calls "the low down folks, the so-called common element." Of these he says " . . . they do not particularly care whether they are like white folks or anybody else. Their joy runs, bang! into ecstasy. Their religion soars to a shout. Work maybe a little today, rest a little tomorrow. Play awhile. Sing awhile. O, let's dance!" In these lines Hughes the poet clearly appears. Does he say then that the Negro artist needs to draw from those of his own people who are the most removed from middle class American life? If I had more time, I would start thinking here about Hughes's use of the words "race" and "racial." . . .

ASSIGNMENTS: Using the Toolkit

1. Pick a single scene from a film, a single photograph from a collection of a photographer's photographs, or some other single example that is interestingly representative of a larger subject. Do 10 on 1 with your scene or other representative example. Notice as much as you can about it. Then organize your observations using The Method: What details repeat? What is opposed to what? Use the results to generate a piece of writing.

2. Work with binaries to develop a short essay. You might consider, for example, some of the either/or categories that students tend to put each other in, or their teachers. Or look to current events in the world or in some more local arena, and find the binaries that seem to divide people or groups.

3. Find a subject to analyze using Notice and Focus and then The Method. Your aim here initially is not to write a formal paper but to do data-gathering on the page. After you have written the paragraph that is the final part of The Method, revise and expand your work into a short essay. Don't worry too much at this point about form (introductory paragraph, for example) or thesis. Just write at greater length about what you noticed and what you selected as most revealing or interesting or strange or significant, and why.

   You might use a story, essay, or poem by a writer you like, perhaps a painting or an artistic photograph. The Method could yield interesting results applied to the architecture on your campus, the student newspaper, campus clothing styles, or the latest news about the economy.

CHAPTER 4

Interpretation: What It Is, What It Isn't, and How to Do It

While Chapter 3, A Toolkit of Analytical Methods, provides a number of analytical methods (Paraphrase × 3, Notice and Focus, The Method, Working with Binaries, and Freewriting), this chapter offers only one—the interpretation-triggering question "So what?" This question, along with a variant we call Seems to Be about X . . . , takes you from observations to theories about the meaning of your data. Interpretation is the meaning-making phase of analysis.

Think of the analytical tools in this book as prompts or triggers. As you saw in Chapter 3, the words interesting, strange, significant, and revealing prompt different kinds of noticing. Each causes a particular spin or orientation on the way you look at your data. Similarly, when you employ the strategy we call ranking (naming one observation as more important than others), you have already pushed yourself toward interpretation. Habitually prompting your thinking with these words and phrases can train your attention, helping you to see features of your evidence that open up its meaning.

We begin this chapter with an example that demonstrates how the So what? question functions, along with revisiting the prompts interesting and strange. Then we step back from practice to theory and address the issues that interpretation typically raises. The chapter ends with an example that brings all the steps together, from observations to implications to conclusions.

To preview the theoretical discussion: just as the analytical frame of mind has to make way against its opposite, the anti-analytical mind-set, so too does interpretation. Here is a quick take on the premises underlying the pro-interpretation mind-set followed by examples of anti-interpretation claims.

Pro-Interpretation Premises

- *Everything means,* which is to say that everything in life calls on us to interpret, even when we are unaware of doing so.

- *Meaning is contextual,* which is to say that meaning-making always occurs inside of some social or cultural or other frame of reference.

Anti-Interpretation Thinking

- "Sometimes a cigar is just a cigar," which is a joke that psychoanalyst Sigmund Freud made about his own interpretive practice; that is, sometimes a thing simply is what it is and no more. (We'll demonstrate that a cigar is almost never just a cigar.)
- "You're just making that up," that is, "reading into" things and finding stuff that "isn't there." (This is a tenacious anti-interpretation attitude. We show that it is partially justified, but mostly not.)
- "I'm entitled to my opinion." (We spoke of this reflex in Chapter 2 in the context of overpersonalizing. Its anti-interpretive and anti-analytical power comes from the mistaken idea that meanings are entirely personal and thus that all interpretations are subjective and not susceptible to the rules of logic. This mind-set sounds attractively democratic—all meanings are created equal—but the fact is that some interpretations are better than others. We'll explain why this is so.)

And now, onto the chapter's primary formula for interpretation, So what?

PUSHING OBSERVATIONS TO CONCLUSIONS: ASKING SO WHAT?

The prompt for making the move from observation to implication and, ultimately, interpretation is So what?, which is shorthand for such questions as:

What does the observation imply?

Why does this observation matter?

Where does this observation get us?

How can we begin to generalize about the subject?

Asking So what?—or its milder cousin, And so?—is a calling to account, which is why, in conversation, its force is potentially rude. That is, the question intervenes rather peremptorily with a "Why does this matter?" It is thus a challenge to make meaning through a creative leap—to move beyond the patterns and emphases you've been observing in the data to tentative conclusions on what these observations suggest.

The peremptoriness of the So what? question can, we think, be liberating. Okay, take the plunge, it says. Start laying out possible interpretations. And, when you are tempted to stop thinking too soon, asking So what? will press you onward.

For example, let's say you make a number of observations about the nature of e-mail communication—it's cheap, informal, often grammatically incorrect, full of abbreviations ("IMHO"), and ephemeral (impermanent). You rank these and decide that its ephemerality is most interesting. So what? Well, that's why so many people use it, you speculate, because it doesn't last. So what that its popularity follows from its ephemerality? Well, apparently we like being released from the hard-and-fast rules of formal communication; e-mail frees us. So what? Well.

The repeated asking of this question causes people to push on from and pursue the implications of their first responses; it prompts people to reason in a chain, rather than settling prematurely for a single link.

Observation → So what? → Implication(s)

>At some point the So what? question will begin to trigger a move from implications to possible conclusions.

Implications → So what? → Conclusions(s)

FIGURE 4.1
So What?

In *step 1* of this process, you describe your evidence, paraphrasing key language and looking for interesting patterns of repetition and contrast.

In *step 2* you begin querying your own observations by making what is implicit explicit.

In the *final step* you push your observations and statements of implications to interpretive conclusions by again asking, So what? See Figure 4.1.

ASKING SO WHAT?: AN EXAMPLE

The following is the opening paragraph of a talk given by a professor of Political Science at our college, Dr. Jack Gambino, on the occasion of a gallery opening featuring the work of two contemporary photographers of urban and industrial landscapes. We have located in brackets our annotations of his turns of thought, as these pivot on "strange" and "So what?"

>If you look closely at Camilo Vergara's photo of Fern Street, Camden, 1988, you'll notice a sign on the side of a dilapidated building:
>
>Danger: Men Working
>
>W. Hargrove Demolition
>
>Perhaps that warning captures the ominous atmosphere of these very different kinds of photographic documents by Camilo Vergara and Edward Burtynsky: "Danger: Men Working." Watch out—human beings are at work! But the work that is presented is not so much a building-up as it is a tearing-down—the work of demolition. *[Strange: tearing down is unexpected; writer asks So what? and answers.]*Of course, demolition is often necessary in order to construct anew: old buildings are leveled for new projects, whether you are building a highway or bridge in an American city or a dam in the Chinese countryside. You might call modernity itself, as so many have, a process of creative destruction, a term used variously to describe modern art, capitalism, and technological innovation. The photographs in this exhibit, however, force us to pay attention to the "destructive" side of this modern

equation. *[Strange: photos emphasize destruction and not creation; writer asks So what? and answers.]* **What both Burtynsky and Vergara do in their respective ways is to put up a warning sign—they question whether the reworking of our natural and social environment leads to a sustainable human future. And they wonder whether the process of creative destruction may not have spun recklessly out of control, producing places that are neither habitable nor sustainable. In fact, a common element connecting the two photographic versions is the near absence of people in the landscape.** *[Writer points to supporting feature of evidence, which he will further theorize.]* **While we see the evidence of the transforming power of human production on the physical and social environment, neither Vergara's urban ruins nor Burtynsky's industrial sites actually show us "men working."** *[Writer continues to move by noticing strange absence of people in photographs of sites where men work.]* **Isolated figures peer suspiciously out back doors or pick through the rubble, but they appear out of place.** *[Writer asks a final So what? and arrives at a conclusion.]* **It is this sense of displacement—of human beings alienated from the environments they themselves have created—that provides the most haunting aspect of the work of these two photographers.**

The Gambino paragraph is a good example of how interpretive paragraphs are generated. Notice the pattern by which the paragraph moves: the observation of something strange, about which the writer asks and answers So what? several times until arriving at a final So what?—the point at which he decides what his observations ultimately mean. We call the final So what? in this chain of thinking "the ultimate So what" because it moves from implications to the writer's culminating point.

The Gambino paragraph is also a good example of the way paragraphs operate as smaller units or stages on the way to a longer paper. We'll say more in Chapter 10 about paragraph structure. For now, think of paragraphs as the building blocks of a piece of thinking in which *movement of mind* creates the structure (not the too-simple notion of topic sentence + evidence). Ideas evolve one paragraph at a time; there is no rule that says you can't write a paper in paragraph-length chunks and later line these up in a way that best reveals the big picture.

■ **Try this 4.1:** *Tracking the Interpretive Process in a Student Paper*

The following paper offers you an opportunity to further observe how a writer moves from observation to interpretation. We've inserted the phrase So what? at the places in the first four paragraphs where that prompt seems to be allowing the writer to draw out the implication of an observation. We have left the last three paragraphs unmarked so that you can supply the interpretive prompts wherever you see the writer moving from observations to implications and conclusions. Also watch for—and mark—places where the writer moves forward by seeking to explain some feature of the dance that she found strange.

Hua dan: The Dance of Values in the Beijing Opera

[1] Lanfang says in his autobiography that "The beautiful dance movements created by past artists are all based on gestures in real life, synthesized and accentuated to become art" . . . (36). In this quote Lanfang emphasizes a representation of life through "beautiful" movement. As he is a product of his culture, he is describing what his culture deems "beautiful." The female roles in the Beijing Opera, particularly the *Hua dan,* convey their own set of cultural values about femininity in Chinese culture.

[2] There is much posing and holding of shapes within the *Hua dan* role. *[So what?]* There is a gentle, poised focus in these moments. This allows the viewers time to take in the elegance of the shape, costumes, makeup, music, and artistry of the performer. The fruit of these efforts becomes evident and framed by the pausing. *[So what?]* The work the performers put in is valued in the pause.

[3] All the movements are very clear in their choices between making angles and using the full extension of the limbs, particularly the arms. The angular shapes give a sharp contrast to the extension of the arms and legs. Circular formations of the arms are seamlessly round and often repeated to emphasize their distinctness. *[So what?]* This exactness and clarity emphasizes the importance and power of the body. By paying such attention to particulars it gives greater emphasis to the powers held in making these shapes.

[4] There is much repetition and opening and closing in the movement. *[So what?]* Repetition can represent the large amount of time females spend on such activities. It can also give a sense of the time it actually takes for such actions in real life, such as sewing. The women do spend much time sewing, and this time is represented. It also takes consistency and dedication to complete such tasks multiple times, so these become valued characteristics.

[5] Rhythm is also an element of the very controlled female walking consisting of small, even steps. The feet barely leave the floor and don't extend into kicks or jumps, as do some of the male roles. Even in the *Hua dan* demonstration in the "Aspects of Peking Opera" video when a bounce was in the character's step and the eyes were alive, the flow of the walk remained consistent. The smallness of the steps could represent the female's place in society. They are petite and not flashy in their maneuvers. They complete their tasks without much fanfare. Keeping the feet low also limits the opening of the legs. Such protection and withholding represents a value in itself—the absence of overt sexual suggestion. Although the male characters may be more likely to overtly demonstrate their strength and power, it takes a great amount of control and focus for the women to execute their walks, so this convention is demonstrating the value of women keeping their struggles and work hidden.

[6] Although my viewing of Peking Opera is limited, it caught my eye to see the *Hua dan's* shoulders finally move in a flirtation demonstration in the "Aspects" video. This isolation and interruption of flow seemed out of character to all other demonstrated acts. All other actions were focused on creating lines and full range of motion. Breaking typically occurs only at the elbows and wrists. These shoulder shrugs break not only the lines but the flowing rhythm. Making flirtation stand out suggests that in the context of the opera, such coquettish moments are important for the audience both in terms of character and life off the stage. It also reminds the viewers that there are even more areas of the body that have not been used but are present within the character and performer.

VOICES FROM ACROSS THE CURRICULUM

Taking the Pressure Off

When writing about dance, the primary evidence is the dance itself and the theatrical accompaniments enhancing the work (sets, costumes, music, narrative, lights, etc.). Seeing and understanding how and what dance communicates is the main task of the dance writer. Because dance is often abstract and purposely open to multiple interpretations, students are usually terrified at the prospect of finding and interpreting evidence in support of a thesis. Typical first responses to analysis include

"I enjoy watching dance, but I have never looked for meaning or message."

"I don't know enough about dance to understand it."

My responses include, "Sit back, relax, and enjoy the dance—save analysis for later. Start your analysis by pretending you are discussing the performance with a friend who did not see it. As you tell him or her about the performance, you will naturally begin to gather evidence and analyze."

—Karen Dearborn, *Professor of Dance*

[7]   What are the recurring themes in all these observations? They lie in control, value of movement, and repetition. The "beauty" lies not only in the quality of the movement but in what it represents. The dainty representation of females, their modesty and strong work ethic, and care in their activities are of great importance, but so too is the slight pleasure in restricted flirtation. When combined, these qualities of movement create a carefully crafted portrayal of a polished female. It serves to represent not only a clear character but a beautiful and desirable female figure.

IMPLICATIONS VERSUS HIDDEN MEANINGS

Because implications (implicit meanings) are suggested by the language or details of a subject rather than explicitly stated, some people mistakenly believe that interpretation is a mysterious process. "Where do you get that?" they say, often suspiciously. Some people go further in their suspicion or outright rejection of interpretive thinking. They say things like "Why can't you just enjoy the movie?" or "Does everything have to mean something?"

Two familiar phrases reveal anxiety and even hostility toward what we named in the first chapter as one of the five analytical moves: Make the Implicit Explicit. The phrases are *hidden meanings* and *reading between the lines*. We say more about these later, but first we offer an exercise demonstrating that implicit meanings are really "there," which is to say that they are readily suggested by explicit language in the text even though they are not stated directly. Although it is true that people might not always agree on what is being implied by particular language or details, differences are usually small and can be negotiated because drawing out implications is a logical process.

■ Try this 4.2: *Inferring Implications from Observations*

Each of the following statements is rich in implication. Some are quite general observations; others are scientific facts, and others come to us as hypotheses from the social sciences. Write a list of as many plausible implications as you can think of for each of the statements. You might find it useful to do this exercise along with other people because part of its aim is to reveal the extent to which different people infer the same implications.

1. The sidewalk is disappearing as a feature of the American residential landscape. New housing developments have them only if a township requires them of the developer. (Here are a couple of implications to prime the pump: people don't walk anywhere anymore; builders lack much sense of social responsibility; current development practices are eliminating ways of life that involve anything except the car—and there are more.)

2. New house designs are tending increasingly toward open plans in which the kitchen is not separated from the rest of the house. New house designs continue to have a room called the living room, usually a space at the front of the house near the front door, but many (not all) also have a separate space called the family room, which is usually in some part of the house farther removed from the front door and closer to the kitchen.

3. "Good fences make good neighbors."—Robert Frost

4. In the female brain, there are more connections between the right hemisphere (emotions, spatial reasoning) and the left hemisphere (verbal facility). In the male brain, these two hemispheres remain more separate.

5. An increasing number of juveniles—people younger than eighteen—are being tried and convicted as adults, rather than as minors, in America, with the result that more minors are serving adult sentences for crimes they committed while still in their teens.

6. Neuroscientists tell us that the frontal cortex of the brain, the part that is responsible for judgment and especially for impulse control, is not fully developed in humans until roughly the age of twenty-one. What are the implications of this observation relative to observation 5?

7. Linguists have long commented on the tendency of women's speech to use rising inflection at the end of statements as if the statements were questions. An actual command form—Be home by midnight!—thus becomes a question instead. What are we to make of the fact that in recent years younger men (under thirty) have begun to end declarative statements and command forms with rising inflections?

8. Shopping malls and grocery stores rarely have clocks.

9. All data are neutral; they're neither good nor bad.

After you have made your list of implications for each item, consider how you arrived at them. On the basis of this experience, how would you answer the following questions? What is the difference between an idea being "hidden" and an idea being implied? What, in other words, is an implication? To what extent do you think most people would arrive at the same implications that you did?

═   ═   ═

As Try this 4.2 illustrates, the inferring of implications does require an act of mind. But the implications are neither hidden nor fancifully invented. The charge that the meaning is hidden implies an act of conspiracy on the part of either an author, who chooses to deliberately obscure his or her meaning, or on the part of readers, who conspire to "find" things lurking below the surface that other readers don't know about and are unable to see. A further assumption is that people probably know what they mean most of the time but, for some perverse reason, are unwilling to come out and say so.

"Reading between the lines" is a version of the hidden meaning theory in suggesting that we have to look for meanings elsewhere than in the lines of text themselves. At its most skeptical, reading between the lines means that an interpretation has come from nothing at all, from the white space between the lines, and therefore has been imposed on the material by the interpreter.

Proponents of these views of analysis are, in effect, committing themselves to the position that everything in life means what it says and says what it means. This position posits another related one: that meanings are always obvious and understood in the same way by everyone, and thus don't require interpretation (which is an example of "naturalizing our own assumptions" as discussed in Chapter 2). People who use the expressions *hidden meanings* and *reading between the lines* generally don't recognize that these phrases imply theories of interpretation, but they do.

It is probably safe to assume that most writers try to write what they mean and mean what they say. That is, they try to control the range of possible interpretations that their words could give rise to, but there is always more going on in a piece of writing (as in our everyday conversation) than can easily be pinned down and controlled. It is, in fact, an inherent property of language that it always means more than and thus other than it says.

Though we may not pause to take notice, we are continually processing what goes on around us for the indirect or suggested meanings it contains. If you observe yourself for a day, you'll find yourself interpreting even the most direct-seeming statements. There's an old cartoon about the anxiety bred by the continual demands of interpretation: a person saying "Good morning" causes the one addressed to respond, "What did she mean by that?"

The truth to which this cartoon points is that a statement can have various meanings, depending on various circumstances and how it is said. The relationship between words and meaning is always complex. As Marshall McLuhan, one of the fathers of modern communication theory, noted, communication always involves determining not just what is being said, but also "what kind of message a message is." Depending on tone and context, "Good morning" can mean a number of things.

THE LIMITS ON INTERPRETATION

As we said in the chapter opening, everything *means*, which is to say that everything in life calls on us to interpret, even when we are unaware of doing so. It is not the case, however, that things can mean whatever we want them to. There are powerful limits on interpretation because (1) meanings are bound by rules of logic and evidence, and (2) meanings always occur within one or more particular interpretive contexts.

To approach these claims, we need first to consider the elemental question of where meanings come from. The first thing to understand about meanings is that they are *made,* not ready-made in the subject matter. They are the product of a transaction between a mind and the world, between a reader and his or her materials. That is, the making of meaning is a process to which the observer and the thing observed both contribute. It is not a product of either alone.

If meanings aren't ready-made, there to be found in the subject matter, what's to prevent people from imposing meaning with wild abandon? To pursue this question, we ask that you revisit the photograph and discussion of the painting *Whistler's Mother* located at the end of Chapter 1. There we distinguished a summary—a focused description—of the painting from an interpretation that grew out of the summary. We interpreted such evidence as the figure of the mother being in profile and austerely dressed as signs that the painting is ultimately about her separateness from us, inviting us to contemplate her as an emblem of the mystery of self-sufficiency.

Plausible versus Implausible Interpretations

What if instead of our interpretation a person claimed that the painting is about death, with the black-clad mother mourning the death of a loved one, perhaps a person who lived in the house represented in the painting on the wall? It is true that black clothes often indicate mourning. This is a culturally accepted, recognized sign. But with only the black dress, and perhaps the sad facial expression (if it is sad) to go on, the mourning theory gets sidetracked from what is actually in the painting into story-telling. This points out one of the primary limits on the meaning-making process.

- Meanings must be reasoned from sufficient evidence if they are to be judged plausible. Meanings can always be refuted by people who find fault with your reasoning or can cite conflicting evidence.

Now what if another person asserted that Whistler's mother is an alien astronaut, for example, her long black dress concealing a third leg? Obviously, this interpretation would not win wide support, and for a reason that points out another of the primary limits on the meaning-making process.

- Meanings, to have value outside one's own private realm of experience, have to make sense to other people. The assertion that Whistler's mother is an alien astronaut is unlikely to be deemed acceptable by enough people to give it currency. This is to say that the relative value of interpretive meanings is socially (culturally) determined. Although people are free to say that things mean whatever they want them to mean, saying doesn't make it so. The mourning theory has more evidence than the alien astronaut theory, but it still relies too heavily on what is not there, on a narrative for which there is insufficient evidence in the painting itself.

Your readers' willingness to accept an interpretation is powerfully connected to their ability to see its *plausibility*—that is, how it follows from both the supporting details that you have selected and the language you have used in characterizing those details. The writer who can offer a plausible (not necessarily or obviously true, but believable) description of a subject's key features is likely to arrive at conclusions about possible meanings that others would share. Often the best that you can hope for with analytical conclusions is not that others will say, "Yes, that is obviously right," but "Yes, I can see where it might be possible and reasonable to think as you do."

Interpretive Contexts and Multiple Meanings

There are, however, other possible interpretations that would satisfy the two criteria of sufficient evidence and broad cultural acceptance. And it is valuable to recognize that evidence usually supports more than one plausible interpretation. Consider, for example, a reading of *Whistler's Mother* that a person might produce if he or she began with noticing the actual title, *Arrangement in Grey and Black: The Artist's Mother.* From this starting point, a person might focus observation on the disposition of color exclusively and arrive at an interpretation that the painting is about painting (which might then explain why there is also a painting on the wall). The figure of the mother then would have meaning only insofar as it contained the two colors mentioned in the painting's title, black and gray, and the painting's representational content (the aspects of life that it shows us) would be assigned less importance. This is a promising and plausible idea for an interpretation. It makes use of different details from previous interpretations that we've suggested, but it would also address some of the details already targeted (the dress, the curtain) from an entirely different context, focusing on the use and arrangement of color.

To generalize: two equally plausible interpretations can be made of the same thing. It is not the case that our first reading, focusing on the profile view of the mother and suggesting the painting's concern with mysterious separateness, is right, whereas the painting-about-painting (or aesthetic) view, building from the clue in the title, is wrong. They operate within different contexts.

An interpretive context is a lens. Depending on the context you choose—preferably a context suggested by the evidence itself—you will see different things. Regardless of how the context is arrived at, an important part of getting an interpretation accepted as plausible is to argue for the appropriateness of the interpretive context you use, not just the interpretation it takes you to.

Specifying an Interpretive Context: An Example

Notice how in the following analysis the student writer's interpretation relies on his choice of a particular interpretive context, post–World War II Japan. Had he selected another context, he might have arrived at some different conclusions about the same details. Notice also how the writer perceives a pattern in the details and how he queries his own observations (So what?) to arrive at an interpretation.

The series entitled "Kamaitachi" is a journal of the photographer Hosoe's desolate childhood and wartime evacuation in the Tokyo countryside. He returns years later to the areas where he grew up, a stranger to his native land, perhaps likening himself to the legendary Kamaitachi, an invisible sickle-toothed weasel, intertwined with the soil and its unrealized fertility. "Kamaitachi #8" (1956), a platinum palladium print, stands alone to best capture Hosoe's alienation from and troubled expectation of the future of Japan. *[Here the writer chooses the photographer's life as his interpretive context.]*

The image is that of a tall fence of stark horizontal and vertical rough wood lashed together, looming above the barren rice fields. Straddling the fence, half-crouched and half-clinging, is a solitary male figure, gazing in profile to the horizon. Oblivious to the sky above of dark and churning thunderclouds, the figure instead focuses his attentions and concentrations elsewhere. *[The writer selects and describes significant detail.]*

It is exactly this *elsewhere* that makes the image successful, for in studying the man we are to turn our attention in the direction of the figure's gaze and away from the photograph itself. He hangs curiously between heaven and earth, suspended on a makeshift man-made structure, in a purgatorial limbo awaiting the future. He waits with anticipation—perhaps dread?—for a time that has not yet come; he is directed away from the present, and it is this sensitivity to time that sets this print apart from the others in the series. One could argue that in effect this man, clothed in common garb, has become Japan itself, indicative of the post-war uncertainty of a country once-dominant and now destroyed. What will the future (dark storm clouds) hold for this newly-humbled nation? *[Here the writer notices a pattern of in-between-ness and locates it in an historical context in order to make his interpretive leap.]*

Remember that regardless of the subject you select for your analysis, you should directly address not just "What does this say?" but also, as this writer has done, *"What are we invited to make of it, and in what context?"*

INTENTION AS AN INTERPRETIVE CONTEXT

An interpretive context that frequently creates problems in analysis is intention. People relying on authorial intention as their interpretive context typically assert that the author—not the work itself—is the ultimate and correct source of interpretations. This is true of what a senator says about a bill he wishes passed. It is also true of what an artist says about her work.

FIGURE 4.2
The Dancers by Sarah Kersh. Pen-and-Ink Drawing, 6" × 13.75".

Look at the drawing titled *The Dancers* in Figure 4.2. What follows is the artist's statement about how the drawing came about and what it came to mean to her.

> This piece was created completely unintentionally. I poured some ink onto paper and blew on it through a straw. The ink took the form of what looked like little people in movement. I recopied the figures I liked, touched up the rough edges, and ended with this gathering of fairy-like creatures. I love how in art something abstract can so suddenly become recognizable.

In this case, interestingly, the artist initially had no intentions beyond experimenting with materials. As the work evolved, she began to arrive at her own interpretation of what the drawing might suggest. Most viewers would probably find the artist's interpretation plausible, but this is not to say that the artist must have the last word and that it is somehow an infraction for others to produce alternative interpretations.

Suppose the artist had stopped with her first two sentences. Even this explicit statement of her lack of intention would not prohibit people from interpreting the drawing in some of the ways that she later goes on to suggest. The artist's initial absence of a plan doesn't require viewers to interpret *The Dancers* as only ink on paper.

In any case, whenever an intention is ascribed to a person, an act, or a product, this intention contributes significantly to meaning; but the intention, whatever its source, does not outrank or exclude other interpretations. It is simply another context for understanding.

Why is this so? In our earlier discussion of personalizing, we suggested that people are not entirely free agents, immune to the effects of the culture they inhabit. It follows that when people produce things, they are inevitably affected by that culture in ways of which they are both aware and unaware. The culture, in other words, speaks through them. In the early 1960s, for example, a popular domestic sitcom entitled *Leave It to Beaver* portrayed the mother, June Cleaver, usually impeccably dressed in heels, dress, and pearls, doing little other than dusting the mantlepiece and making tuna fish sandwiches for her sons. Is the show then intentionally oppressing June by implying that the proper role for women is that of domestic helper? Well, in the context of post–women's movement thinking, the show's representation of Mrs. Cleaver might plausibly be read this way, but not as a matter of intention. But to conclude that *Leave It to Beaver* promoted a particular stereotype about women does not mean that the writers got together every week and asked, "How should we oppress June this week?" It is cultural norms asserting themselves here, not authorial intent.

It is interesting and useful to try to determine from something you are analyzing what its makers might have intended. But, by and large, you are best off concentrating on what the thing itself communicates as opposed to what someone might have wanted it to communicate.

What Is and Isn't "Meant" to Be Analyzed

What about analyzing things that were not intended to "mean" anything, like entertainment films and everyday things like blue jeans and shopping malls? Some people believe that it is wrong to bring out unintended implications. Let's take another example: Barbie dolls. These are just toys intended for young girls, people might say. Clearly, the intention of the makers of Barbie is to make money by entertaining children. Does that mean Barbie must remain outside of interpretive scrutiny for such things as her built-in earrings, high-heeled feet, and heavily marketed lifestyle?

What the makers of a particular product or idea intend is only a part of what that product or idea communicates. The urge to cordon off certain subjects from analysis on the grounds that they weren't meant to be analyzed unnecessarily excludes a wealth of information—and meaning—from your range of vision. It is right to be careful about the interpretive contexts we bring to our experience. It is less right—less useful—to confine our choice of context in a too literal-minded way to a single category. To some people, baseball is only a game and clothing is only there to protect us from the elements.

What such people don't want to admit is that things communicate meaning to others whether we wish them to or not, which is to say that the meanings of most things are socially determined. What, for example, does the choice of wearing a baseball cap to a staff meeting or to a class "say"? Note, by the way, that a communicative gesture such as the wearing of a hat need not be premeditated to communicate something to other people. The hat is still "there" and available to be "read" by others as a sign of certain attitudes and a culturally defined sense of identity—with or without intention.

Baseball caps, for example, carry different associations from berets or wool caps because they come from different social contexts. Baseball caps convey a set of attitudes associated with the piece of American culture they come from. They suggest, for example, popular rather than high culture, casual rather than formal, young— perhaps defiantly so, especially if worn backward—rather than old, and so on. The social contexts that make gestures like our choice of hats carry particular meanings are always shifting, but some such context is always present. As we asserted at the beginning of this chapter, everything means, and meaning is always contextual.

We can, of course, protest that the "real" reason for turning our baseball cap backward is to allow more light in, making it easier to see than when the bill of the cap shields our faces. This practical rationale makes sense, but it does not explain away the social statement that the hat and a particular way of wearing it might make.

Because meaning is, to a significant extent, socially determined, we can't entirely control what our clothing, our manners, our language, or even our way of walking communicates to others. This is one of the reasons that analysis makes some people suspicious and uneasy. They don't want to acknowledge that they are sending messages in spite of themselves, messages they haven't deliberately and overtly chosen.

We turn now to two common problems writers encounter in interpretation. These problems are so widespread that we have fancifully labeled them "schools."

THE FORTUNE COOKIE SCHOOL OF INTERPRETATION

The theory of interpretation that we call the Fortune Cookie School believes that things have a single, hidden, right meaning, and that if a person can only "crack" the thing, it will yield an extractable and self-contained message. There are several problems with this conception of the interpretive process.

First, the assumption that things have single hidden meanings interferes with open-minded and dispassionate observation. Adherents of the Fortune Cookie School look solely for clues pointing to *the* hidden message and, having found these clues, discard the rest, like the cookie in a Chinese restaurant once the fortune has been extracted. The fortune cookie approach forecloses on the possibility of multiple plausible meanings, each within its own context. When you assume that there is only one right answer, you are also assuming that there is only one proper context for understanding and, by extension, that anybody who happens to select a different starting point or context and who thus arrives at a different answer is necessarily wrong.

Most of the time, practitioners of the fortune cookie approach aren't even aware that they are assuming the correctness of a single context because they don't realize a fundamental truth about interpretations: they are always limited by contexts. In other words, we are suggesting that claims to universal truths are always problematic. Things don't just mean in some simple and clear way for all people in all situations; they always mean within a network of beliefs, from a particular point of view. The person who claims to have access to some universal truth, beyond context and point of view, is either naïve (unaware) or, worse, a bully—insisting that his or her view of the world is obviously correct and must be accepted by everyone.

THE ANYTHING GOES SCHOOL OF INTERPRETATION

At the opposite extreme from the single-right-answer Fortune Cookie School lies the completely relativist Anything Goes School. The problem with the anything goes approach is that it tends to assume that *all* interpretations are equally viable, that meanings are simply a matter of individual choice, irrespective of evidence or plausibility. Put another way, it overextends the creative aspect of interpretation to absurdity, arriving at the position that you can see in a subject whatever you want to see.

As we suggest throughout this book, it is simply not the case that meaning is entirely up to the individual. Some readings are clearly better than others: as we argued earlier, the aesthetic or separateness readings of *Whistler's Mother* are better than the mourning or, especially, alien astronaut interpretations. The better interpretations have more evidence and rational explanation of how the evidence supports the interpretive claims—qualities that make these meanings more public and negotiable.

In the field of logic there is a principle known as parsimony. This principle holds that "no more forces or causes should be assumed than are necessary to account for the facts" *(The Oxford English Dictionary)*. In other words, the explanation that both explains the largest amount of evidence (accounts for facts) and is the simplest (no more than necessary) is the best. There are limits to this rule as well: sometimes focusing on what appears to be an insignificant detail as a starting point can provide a revelatory perspective on a subject. But as rules go, parsimony is a useful one to keep in mind as you start sifting through your various interpretive leaps about a subject.

SEEMS TO BE ABOUT *X* BUT COULD ALSO BE (IS REALLY) ABOUT *Y*

This book's opening chapters have focused your attention on three prerequisites to becoming a more perceptive analytical thinker:

- Training yourself to observe more fully and more systematically—dwelling longer with the data before leaping to generalizations, using Paraphrase × 3, Notice and Focus (ranking), The Method, and working with binaries.
- Pushing yourself to make interpretive leaps by describing carefully and then querying your own observations by repeatedly asking, So what?
- Getting beyond common misconceptions about where meanings come from— that meanings are hidden, that they are read into something but are really not there (reading between the lines), that there are single right answers or that anything goes, that meanings ought to be controlled by a maker's intentions, that some things should not be analyzed because they weren't meant to be, and so forth.

A useful verbal prompt for acting on these principles is "seems to be about *X* but could also be (or is really) about *Y*." There are several reasons why this formula works to stimulate interpretation.

- The person who is doing the interpreting too often stops with the first answer that springs to mind as he or she moves from observation to implication, usually landing upon a cliché. If this first response becomes the *X*, then he or she is prompted by the formula to come up with other, probably less commonplace interpretations as the *Y*.
- Often a person who is interpreting will, in the data-gathering stage, collect statements of intention from spokespersons for the subject—what the book or ad or political speech or whatever is asking us to believe about itself. If we accept this information only as *X*, then the *Y* is a prompt that will more likely move us to analyze such statements more acutely.

In this context we can see how "Appears to Be about *X*. . .," like the other prompts in this book, defamiliarizes. When we begin to interpret something, we usually find that less obvious meanings are cloaked by more obvious ones, and so we are distracted from seeing them. In most cases, the less obvious and possibly unintended meanings are more telling and more interesting than the obvious ones we have been conditioned to see. But to get to these more interesting and less obvious meanings, we need to have assimilated two key elements of the interpretive methods offered in this chapter: (1) that there are multiple plausible interpretations because different interpretive contexts cause us to value different things in the evidence and (2) that intention does not control this process of meaning-making.

Why, you might ask, are less obvious meanings more likely to be more significant and telling? One reason is that this shift, particularly in the context of advertising or political language, is likely to orient us toward the *rhetoric* of the subject. We are focusing then on its means of persuading an audience. In the case of analyzing a work or art or an historical event, we are more likely to move beyond conventional generalizations. (See the discussion of rhetorical analysis in Chapter 6.)

Consider the following example:

A recent highly successful television ad campaign for Nike Freestyle shoes contains 60 seconds of famous basketball players dribbling and passing and otherwise handling the ball in dexterous ways to the accompaniment of court noises and hip-hop music. The ad seems to be about *X* (basketball or shoes) but could also be about *Y*. Once you've made this assertion, a rapid-fire (brainstormed) list might follow in which you keep filling in the blanks *(X* and *Y)* with different possibilities. Alternatively, you might find that filling in the blanks *(X* and *Y)* leads to a more sustained exploration of a single point. This is your eventual goal, but doing a little brainstorming first would keep you from shutting down the interpretive process too soon.

Here is one version of a rapid-fire list, any item of which might be expanded:

Seems to be about basketball but is really about dance.

Seems to be about selling shoes but is really about artistry.

Seems to be about artistry but is really about selling shoes.

Seems to be about basketball but is really about race.

Seems to be about basketball but is really about the greater acceptance of black culture in American media and society.

Seems to be about the greater acceptance of black culture in American media but is really about representing black basketball players as performing seals or freaks.

Seems to be about individual expertise but is really about working as a group.

Here is one version of a more sustained exploration of a single seems-to-be-about-*X* statement.

The Nike Freestyle commercial seems to be about basketball but is really about the greater acceptance of black culture in American media. Of course it is a shoe commercial and so aims to sell a product, but the same could be said about any commercial.

What makes the Nike commercial distinctive is its seeming embrace of African-American culture. The hip-hop sound track, for example, which coincides with the rhythmic dribbling of the basketball, places music and sport on a par, and the dexterity with which the players (actual NBA stars) move with the ball—moonwalking, doing 360s on it, balancing it on their fingers, heads, and backs—is nothing short of dance.

The intrinsic cool of the commercial suggests that Nike is targeting an audience of basketball lovers, not just African-Americans. If I am right, then it is selling blackness to white as well as black audiences. Of course, the idea that blacks are cooler than whites goes back at least as far as the early days of jazz and might be seen as its own strange form of prejudice. . . . In that case, maybe there is something a little disturbing in the commercial, in the way that it relegates the athletes to the status of trained seals. I'll have to think more about this.

Note: don't be misled by our use of the word *really* in this formula ("Seems to be about *X*, is really about *Y*") into thinking that there should be some single, hidden, right answer. Rather, the aim of the formula is to prompt you to think recursively, to come up, initially, with a range of landing sites for your interpretive leap, rather than just one. The prompt serves to get you beyond the obvious—for example, that the ad appears to be about basketball but is really about selling shoes.

■ **Try this 4.3:** *Apply the Formula "Seems to Be about* X, *but Could Also Be (Is Really) about* Y*"*

As we have been saying, this formula is useful for quickly getting past your first responses. An alternative version of this formula is "Initially I thought *X* about the subject, but now I think *Y*." Take any reading or viewing assignment you have been given for class, and write either version of the formula at the top of a page. Fill in the blanks several times, and then explain your final choice for *X* and *Y* in a few paragraphs. You might also try these formulae when you find yourself getting stuck while drafting a paper. Seems to Be about *X* . . . is a valuable revision as well as interpretive tool.

PUTTING IT ALL TOGETHER: INTERPRETATION OF A *NEW YORKER* COVER

A major point of this section is that interpretive contexts are suggested by the material you are studying; they aren't simply imposed. Explaining why you think a subject should be seen through a particular interpretive lens is an important part of making interpretations reasonable and plausible. Our discussion illustrates a writer's decision-making process in choosing an interpretive context, and how, once that context has been selected, the writer goes about analyzing evidence to test as well as support the usefulness of that context.

The example upon which we are focusing is a visual image, a cover from *The New Yorker* magazine (see Figure 4.3). The cover is by Ian Falconer and is entitled "The Competition"; it appeared on the October 9, 2000, issue.

Producing a close description of anything you are analyzing is one of the best ways to begin because the act of describing causes you to notice more and triggers analytical thinking. Here is our description of the *New Yorker* cover.

Description of a *New Yorker* Cover, Dated October 9, 2000

The picture contains four women, visible from the waist up, standing in a row in semi-profile, staring out at some audience other than us because their eyes look off to the side. All four gaze in the same direction. Each woman is dressed in a bathing suit and wears a banner draped over one shoulder in the manner of those worn in the swimsuit competition at beauty pageants. Three of the women are virtually identical. The banners worn by these three women show the letters *gia, rnia,* and *rida,* the remainder of the letters being cut off by the other women's shoulders, so that we have to fill in the missing letters to understand which state each woman represents.

FIGURE 4.3

The fourth woman, who stands third from the left in line, tucked in among the others who look very much alike, wears a banner reading *york*. This woman's appearance is different in just about every respect from the other three. Whereas they are blonde with long flowing hair, she is dark with her hair up in a tight bun. Whereas their mouths are wide open, revealing a wall of very white teeth, her mouth is closed, lips drawn together. Whereas their eyes are wide open and staring, hers, like her mouth, are nearly closed, under deeply arched eyebrows. The dark woman's lips, eyes, and hair are dark. She wears dark eye makeup and has a pronounced dark beauty mark on her cheek. Whereas the other three women's cheeks are high and round, hers are sharply angular. The three blonde women wear one-piece bathing suits in a nondescript gray color. The dark-haired woman, whose skin stands out in stark contrast to her hair, wears a two-piece bathing suit, exposing her midriff. Like her face, the dark-haired woman's breast, sticking out in half profile in her bathing suit, is pointed and angular. The other three women's breasts are round and quietly contained in their high-necked gray bathing suits.

Using The Method to Identify Patterns of Repetition and Contrast

As we discussed in Chapter 3, looking for patterns of repetition and contrast (that is, The Method) is one of your best means of getting at the essential character of a subject. It prevents you from generalizing, instead involving you in hands-on engagement with the details of your evidence. Our formula for looking for patterns, The Method, has five steps, which you should try to do one at a time so as not to rush to conclusions. You will find, however, that step 1, looking for things that repeat exactly, tends to suggest items for step 2, repetition of the same or similar kinds of words or details (strands), and that step 2 leads naturally to step 3, looking for binary oppositions and organizing contrasts. And so, in practice, noticing and listing the elements of strands tend to coincide with the discovery of binary oppositions.

Here are our partial lists of exact repetitions and strands and binary oppositions in the *New Yorker* cover:

Some details that repeat exactly:

Large, wide open, round eyes (3 pairs)

Long, blonde, face-framing hair (3)

Small, straight eyebrows (3 pairs)

Wide-open (smiling?) mouths with expanses of white teeth (3) (but individual teeth not indicated)

Banners (4) but each with different lettering

Round breasts (3)

States that end in *a* (3)

Some strands (groups of the same or similar kinds of details):

Lots of loose and flowing blonde hair/large, fully open, round eyes/large, open, rather round (curved) mouths:

Connecting logic = open, round

Skin uniformly shaded on three of the figures/minimal color and shading contrasts/ mouths full of teeth but just a mass of white without individual teeth showing:

Connecting logic = homogenous, undifferentiated, indistinct

Binary oppositions:

Blonde hair/black hair

Open mouths/closed mouth

Straight eyebrows/slanted (arched) eyebrows

Round breasts/pointed breast

Covered midriff/uncovered midriff

Notice that we have tried hard to stick with "the facts" here—concrete details in the picture. If we were to try, for example, to name the expression on the three blonde women's faces and the one on the black-haired woman (expressionless vs. knowing? vapid vs. shrewd? trusting vs. suspicious? etc.), we would move from data gathering— direct observation of detail—into interpretation. The longer you delay interpretation in favor of noticing patterns of like and unlike detail, the more thoughtful and better grounded your eventual interpretation will be.

Anomalies:

Miss New York

Pushing Observations to Conclusions: Selecting an Interpretive Context

As we argued throughout this chapter, the move from observations to conclusions depends on context. You would, for example, come up with different ideas about the significance of particular patterns of detail in the *New Yorker* cover if you were analyzing them in the context of the history of *The New Yorker* cover art than you might if your interpretive context was other art done by Ian Falconer, the cover's artist. Both of these possibilities suggest themselves, the first by the fact that the title of the magazine, *The New Yorker,* stands above the women's heads, and the second by the fact that the artist's last name, Falconer, runs across two of the women.

What other interpretive contexts might one plausibly and fairly choose, based on what the cover itself offers us? Consider the cover's date—October 9, 2000. Some quick research into what was going on in the country in the early fall of 2000 might provide some clues about how to read the cover in a *historical context*. November 2000 was the month of a presidential election. At the time the cover was published, the long round of presidential primaries, with presidential hopefuls courting various key states for their votes, had ended, but the last month of campaigning by the presidential nominees—Al Gore and George W. Bush—was in full swing.

You might wish to consider whether and how the cover speaks to the country's political climate during the Gore/Bush competition for the presidency. The banners, the bathing suits, and the fact that the women stand in a line staring out at some implied audience of viewers, perhaps judges, reminds us that the picture's narrative context is a beauty pageant, a competition in which women representing each of the states compete to be chosen the most beautiful of them all. Choosing to consider the cover in the context of the presidential campaign would be reasonable; you would not have to think you were imposing a context on the picture in an arbitrary and ungrounded way. Additionally, the Table of Contents identifies the title of Falconer's drawing as "The Competition."

Clearly, there is other information on the cover that might allow you to interpret the picture in some kind of political and or more broadly cultural context. A significant binary opposition is New York versus Georgia, California, and Florida. The three states having names ending in the same letter are represented by look-alike, virtually identical blondes. The anomalous state, New York, is represented by a woman, who, despite standing in line with the others, is about as different from them as a figure could be. *So what* that the woman representing New York looks so unlike the women from the other states? And why those states?

If you continued to pursue this interpretive context, you might want more information. Which presidential candidate won the primary in each of the states pictured? How were each of these states expected to vote in the election in November? When is the Miss America pageant held? Which state won the Miss America title in the time period before the cover was published? Since timing would matter in the case of a topical interpretive context, it would also be interesting to know when the cover art was actually produced and when the magazine accepted it. If possible, you could also try to discover whether other of the cover artist's work was in a similar vein. (He has a website.)

Making the Interpretation Plausible

As we have been arguing, the picture will "mean" differently, depending on whether we understand it in terms of American presidential politics in the year 2000, or in terms of American identity politics at the same point, specifically attitudes of and about New Yorkers, and *The New Yorker* magazine's place among these attitudes—and influence on them. As we have already observed, analytical thinking involves interpretation, and interpretive conclusions are tentative and open to alternative possibilities. An interpretive conclusion is not a fact but a theory. Interpretive conclusions stand or fall not so much on whether they can be proved right or wrong (or some combination of the two), but on whether they are demonstrably plausible.

What makes an interpretation plausible? Your audience might choose not to accept your interpretation for a number of reasons. They might, for example, be New Yorkers and, furthermore, inclined to think that New Yorkers are cool and that this is what the picture "says." They might be from one of the states depicted on the cover in terms of look-alike blondes and, further, inclined to think that New Yorkers are full of themselves and forever portraying the rest of the country as shallowly conformist and uncultured.

But none of these personal influences ultimately matters. What matters is that you share your evidence, show your reasons for believing that it means what you say it means, and do this well enough for a reader to find your interpretation reasonable (whether he or she actually believes it or not). Then you will have passed the plausibility test. Your interpretation will stand until another person offers an analysis with interpretive conclusions that seems more plausible than yours, pointing to more or better evidence, and arguing for the meaning of that evidence more convincingly.

Arriving at an Interpretive Conclusion: Making Choices

Let's try on one final interpretive context, and then see which of the various contexts (lenses) through which we have viewed the cover produces the most credible interpretation, the one that seems to best account for the patterns of detail in the evidence. Different interpretations will account better for some details than others—which is why it enriches our view of the world to try on different interpretations. Ultimately, you will have to decide which possible interpretation, as seen through which interpretive context, best accounts for what you think is most important and interesting to notice about your subject.

We will try to push our own interpretive process to a choice by selecting one interpretive context as the most revealing: *The New Yorker* magazine itself. The dark-haired figure wearing the New York banner stands, in a sense, for the magazine or, at least, for a potential reader—a representative New Yorker. What, then, does the cover "say" to and about New Yorkers and to and about the magazine and its readers?

Throughout this book we use the question So what? to prompt interpretive leaps. *So what* that the woman representing New York is dark when the other women are light, is closed (narrowed eyes, closed mouth, hair tightly pulled up and back) when the others are open (wide-open eyes and mouths, loosely flowing hair), is pointed and angular when the others are round, sports a bared midriff when the others are covered?

As with our earlier attempt to interpret the cover in the context of the 2000 presidential campaign, interpreting it in the context of other *New Yorker* covers would require a little research. How do *New Yorker* covers characteristically represent New Yorkers? What might you discover by looking for patterns of repetition and contrast in a set of *New Yorker* covers rather than just this one?

We are willing to bet that you would soon discover the magazine's droll awareness of its own heralding of New Yorkers as sophisticated, cultured, and cosmopolitan: it at once embraces and sends up the stereotype. How does the cover read in the context, for example, of various jokes about how New Yorkers think of themselves relative to the rest of the country, such as the cover depicting the United States as two large coastlines, east and west, connected by an almost nonexistent middle?

Armed with the knowledge that the covers are not only characteristically laughing at the rest of the country but also at New Yorkers themselves, you might begin to make explicit what is implicit in the cover.

Here are some attempts at making the cover speak. Does the cover "say" that New Yorkers are shrewder, less naïve (less open), warier than other Americans, but largely because they are also more worldly and smarter? Is the cover in some way a "dumb blonde" joke in which the dark woman with the pronounced beauty mark and calculating gaze participates in but also sets herself apart from some kind of national "beauty" contest? Are we being invited (intentionally or not) to invert the conventional value hierarchy of dark and light so that the dark woman—the sort that gets represented as the evil stepmother in fairy tales such as "Snow White"—becomes "the fairest of them all," and nobody's fool?

Let's end this sample analysis and interpretation with two possibilities— somewhat opposed to each other, but probably both "true" of what the cover communicates, at least to certain audiences (East and West Coast Americans, and readers of *The New Yorker*). At its most serious, the *New Yorker* cover may speak to American history in which New York has been the point of entry for generations of immigrants, the "dark" (literally and figuratively) in the face of America's blonde northern European legacy.

Within the context of other *New Yorker* covers, however, we might find ourselves gravitating to a less serious and perhaps equally plausible interpretive conclusion: that the cover is a complex joke. It appears to be saying, yes, America, we do think that we're cooler and more individual and less plastic than the rest of you, but we also know that we shouldn't be so smug about it.

ASSIGNMENTS: Write an Interpretive Essay

1. Build a paper from implications. Begin this assignment by making observations and drawing out implications for one of the topics below. Then use your list as the starting point for a longer paper.

   Having done the preceding exercise with inferring implications, you could now make up your own list of observations and pursue implications. Make some observations, for example, about the following, and then suggest the possible implications of your observations.

   • Changing trends in automobiles today
   • What your local newspaper chooses to put on its front page (or editorial page) over the course of a week
   • Shows (or advertisements) that appear on network television (as opposed to cable) during 1 hour of evening prime time
   • Advertisements for scotch whiskey in highbrow magazines

2. Analyze a magazine cover by researching an interpretive context. Choose a magazine that, like *The New Yorker,* has interesting covers. Write an analysis of one such cover by studying other covers from the same magazine. (Visit *The New Yorker* store website to access a wide range of covers,

including others by Ian Falconer.) Follow the model offered at the end of this chapter:

a. Apply The Method—looking for patterns of repetition and contrast—to the cover itself so that you arrive at key repetitions, strands, and organizing contrasts and begin to ponder a range of possible interpretive leaps to what they signify.

b. Use these data to suggest plausible interpretive contexts for the cover. Remember that interpretive contexts are not simply imposed from without; they're suggested by the evidence.

c. Then move to the other covers. Perform similar operations on them to arrive at an awareness of common denominators among the covers, and to analyze what those shared traits might reveal or make more evident in the particular cover you are studying. You will be trying to figure out how the magazine conceives of itself and its audience by the way that it characteristically represents its "face."

It might be illuminating to survey a range of covers by a single artist, such as Ian Falconer, who created the cover we analyze in the chapter. Or try Harry Bliss, who also creates covers and cartons for *The New Yorker* and is a children's illustrator. Work by both of these artists may be found on their websites.

CHAPTER 5

Analyzing Arguments

OUR MOST DIRECT ADVICE ON ANALYZING ARGUMENTS, and thus on learning to write them more effectively, can be found in this chapter. Here we show you how to unearth the essentially binary structure of arguments and how to uncover the unstated assumptions upon which arguments typically rest. Arguing with someone else's argument is usually as much a matter of addressing what is left unsaid—the assumptions underneath the argument that the arguer takes to be givens (obvious truths)—as confronting what is argued overtly.

THE ROLE OF BINARIES IN ARGUMENT

In human—and computerized—thinking, a binary is a pair of elements, usually in opposition to each other, as in off/on, yes/no, right/wrong, agree/disagree, and so on. Many ideas begin with a writer's noticing some kind of opposition or tension or choice within a subject—capital punishment either does or does not deter crime; a character in a novel is either a courageous rebel or a fool; a new environmental policy is either visionary or blind. As we note in earlier chapters, a major advantage of looking for binaries is that they help you determine what issues are at stake in your subject because binaries position you among competing choices. (See discussion of The Method in Chapter 3, A Toolkit of Analytical Methods.)

There is an old joke to the effect that there are two kinds of people: those who like binary thinking and those who do not. Part of the humor here lies in the recognition that we cannot help but think in binary terms. As the philosopher Herbert Marcuse says, "We understand that which is in terms of that which is not": light is that which is not dark; masculine is that which is not feminine; civilized is that which is not primitive. Creating opposing categories is fundamental to defining things. But as these examples may suggest, binaries are also dangerous because they can perpetuate what is called reductive thinking, especially if applied uncritically.

If you restrict yourself to thinking in binary terms, you can run into two problems. First, most subjects cannot be adequately considered in terms of only two options—either this or that, with nothing in between. Second, binaries often conceal value judgments: the category "primitive," as opposed to "civilized," is not a neutral description but a devaluation. Civilized, for example, is that which has rejected and moved beyond the primitive. Women, in this way of thinking, are an inverse of men: they are a category defined by unmanly traits. It is useful and necessary to construct binaries, but, as our examples reveal, it is dangerous to ignore the gray areas in between and the value judgments that binaries tend to conceal.

Often the trouble starts with the ways binaries are phrased. Two of the most common and potentially counterproductive ways of phrasing binaries are *either/or* and *agree/disagree*. In the vast majority of cases, there are more than two alternatives, but the either/or or agree/disagree phrasing prevents you from looking for them. And it does not acknowledge that both alternatives may have some truth to them. A new environmental policy may be both visionary and blind. And there may be more accurate categories than visionary and blind for considering the merits and demerits of the policy.

Framing an issue in either/or terms can be useful for stimulating a chain of thought, but it is usually not a good way to end one. Consider the either/or binary, "Was the Civil War fought over slavery or economics?" You could begin this way, but if you're not careful—conscious of the all-or-nothing force of binary formulations— you could easily get trapped in an overly dichotomized position; in this case, that economics caused the war and that slavery had nothing to do with it, or vice versa.

You can't analyze without binaries, but you need to be wary of putting everything into big, undifferentiated categories, labeled all black or all white, with nothing in between.

A PROCEDURE FOR REFORMULATING BINARIES IN ARGUMENT

We previewed this procedure in brief in our discussion of The Method in Chapter 3. Here we develop it in more detail.

Strategy 1: Locate a Range of Opposing Categories

The first step in using binaries analytically is to locate and distinguish them carefully. Consider, for example, the binaries contained in the following question: Does the model of management known as Total Quality Management (TQM) that is widely used in Japan work in the American automotive industry? The most obvious binary in this question is work versus not work. But there are also other binaries in the question— Japanese versus American, for example, and TQM versus more traditional and more traditionally American models of management. These binaries imply further binaries. Insofar as TQM is acknowledged to be a team-oriented, collaborative management model, the question requires a writer to consider the accuracy and relative suitability of particular traits commonly ascribed to Japanese versus American workers, such as communal and cooperative versus individualistic and competitive.

Strategy 2: Analyze and Define the Key Terms

Having located the various binaries, you should begin to analyze and define terms. What, for example, does it mean to ask whether TQM *works* in the American automotive industry? Does work mean "make a substantial profit"? Does work mean "produce more cars more quickly"? Does work mean "improving employee morale"? You would probably find yourself drowning in vagueness unless you carefully argued for the appropriateness of your definition of this key term.

Strategy 3: Question the Accuracy of the Binary

Having begun to analyze and define your terms, you would next need to determine how accurately they define the issues raised by your subject. You might consider, for example, the extent to which American management styles actually differ from the Japanese version of TQM. In the process of trying to determine if there are significant differences, you could start to locate particular traits in these management styles and in Japanese versus American culture that might help you formulate your binary more precisely. Think of the binary as a starting point—a kind of deliberate overgeneralization—that allows you to set up positions you can then test to refine.

Strategy 4: Substitute "To What Extent?" for "Either/Or"

The best strategy in using binaries productively is usually to locate arguments on both sides of the either/or choice that the binary poses and then choose a position somewhere between the two extremes. Once you have arrived at what you consider the most accurate phrasing of the binary, you can rephrase the original either/or question in the more qualified terms that asking "To what extent?" allows. Making this move does not release you from the responsibility of taking a stand and arguing for it.

So, in answer to a question such as "Was the Civil War fought over slavery or economics?" you would attempt to determine *the extent to which* each side of the binary—slavery and economics—could reasonably be credited as the cause of the war. To do so, you would first rephrase the question thus: To what extent did economics, rather than slavery, cause the Civil War? Rephrasing in this way might also enable you to see problems with the original binary formulation.

By analyzing the terms of the binary, you would come to question them and ultimately arrive at a more complex and qualified position to write about. Admittedly, in reorienting your thinking from the obvious and clear-cut choices that either/or formulations provide to the murkier waters of asking "To what extent?" your decision process is made more difficult. The gain, however, is that the to-what-extent mindset, by predisposing you to assess multiple and potentially conflicting points of view, will enable you to address more fairly and accurately the issues raised by your subject.

Applying these steps usually causes you to do one or more of the following:

1. Discover that you have not adequately named the binary and that another opposition would be more accurate.

2. Weight one side of your binary more heavily than the other, rather than seeing the issue as all or nothing.

3. Discover that the two terms of your binary are not really so separate and opposed after all but are actually parts of one complex phenomenon or issue (a move known as collapsing the binary).

Where might you end up if you approached our earlier sample topic (whether TQM works in the American automotive industry) by asking to what extent one side of the binary better suits available evidence, rather than arguing that one side is clearly the right choice and the other entirely wrong? You would still be arguing that one position on TQM in American industry is more accurate than the other, but you would inevitably arrive at more carefully qualified conclusions than the question might otherwise have led you to. You would most likely take care, for example, to suggest the danger of assuming that all American workers are rugged individualists and all Japanese workers are communal bees.

■ Try this 5.1: *Reformulating Binaries*

Apply the strategies for using binaries analytically to analyze the following statements (or questions), as we did with the TQM example. This does not mean that you must proceed step-by-step through the strategies, but, at the least, you should list all of the binaries you can find, isolate the key terms, and reformulate them. Even if the original formulation looks okay to you, assume that it is an overgeneralization that needs to be refined and rephrased.

1. It is important to understand why leaders act in a leadership role. What is the driving force? Is it an internal drive for the business or group to succeed, or is it an internal drive for the leader to dominate others?
2. Is nationalism good for emerging third-world countries?
3. The private lives of public figures should not matter in the way they are assessed by the public. What matters is how competently they do their jobs.
4. The Seattle sound of rock and roll known as Grunge was not original; it was just a rehash of Punk and New Wave elements.

UNCOVERING ASSUMPTIONS (REASONING BACK TO PREMISES)

All arguments ultimately rest on fundamental assumptions called givens—positions that you decide are not in need of argument because you assume the reader will "give" them to you as true. Often, however, these assumptions need first to be acknowledged and then argued, or at least tested. You cannot assume that their truth is self-evident. The failure to locate and examine unacknowledged assumptions (premises) is the downfall of many essays. The problem occurs because our categories—the mental boxes we've created over time—have become so fixed, so unquestioned, that we cease to be fully aware of them.

Everything you read has basic assumptions that underlie it. What are assumptions in this context? They are the basic ground of beliefs from which a position springs, its starting points or givens, its basic operating premises. *The Oxford English Dictionary* defines a premise—from a Latin word meaning "to put before"—as "a previous statement or proposition from which another statement is inferred or follows as a conclusion."

All arguments or articulations of point of view have premises—that is, they are based in a given set of assumptions, which are built upon to arrive at conclusions.

Often, though, the assumptions are not visible; they're implicit (which is why they need to be inferred). Usually writers are not hiding from readers the subterranean bases of their outlooks, which might be considered unethical. Rather, many writers (especially inexperienced ones) remain unaware of the premises that underlie their points of view. Similarly, most readers don't stop to think about the starting points of what they read, so they read only the tip of the proverbial iceberg.

The ability to uncover assumptions is a powerful analytical procedure to learn—it gives you insight into the roots, the basic givens that a piece of writing (or a speaker) has assumed are true. When you locate assumptions in a text, you understand the text better—where it's coming from and what else it believes that is more fundamental than what it is overtly declaring. You also find things to write about; uncovering assumptions offers one of the best ways of developing and revising your own work. Uncovering assumptions can help you understand why you believe *x*, or may reveal to you that two of your givens are in conflict with each other.

To uncover assumptions, you need to read "backward"—to ask what a reading must also already believe, given that it believes what it overtly claims. In other words, you need to imagine or reinvent the process of thinking by which a writer has arrived at a position.

Say you read a piece that praises a television show for being realistic but faults it for setting a bad example for the kids who watch it. What assumptions might we infer from such a piece?

- Television should attempt to depict life accurately (realistically).
- Television should produce shows that set good examples.
- Kids imitate or at least have their attitudes shaped by what they watch on television.
- Good and bad examples are clear and easily recognizable by everyone.

Note that none of these assumptions is self-evidently true; each would need to be argued for. And some of the assumptions conflict with others—for example, that shows should be both morally uplifting and realistic, given that in "real life" those who do wrong often go unpunished. These are subjects an analytical response to the piece (or a revision of it) could bring out.

VOICES FROM ACROSS THE CURRICULUM

What's Beneath the Question?

On some occasions, students find that they have confronted an issue that cannot be resolved by the deductive method. This can be exciting for them. Will cutting marginal tax rates cause people to work more? The answer is yes or no, depending on the premises underlying the work-leisure preferences incorporated into your model.

—James Marshall, *Professor of Economics*

UNCOVERING ASSUMPTIONS: A BRIEF EXAMPLE

Consider the common complaint that "Tax laws benefit the wealthy." No matter how you might develop this claim (moving it forward), you would get into trouble if you didn't also move backward to uncover the premises embedded in this thesis about the purpose of tax laws. The wording of this claim seems to conceal an egalitarian premise: the assumption that tax laws should not benefit anyone or, at least, that they should benefit everyone equally. But what is the purpose of tax laws? Should they redress economic inequities? Should they spur the economy by rewarding those who generate capital? You might go to the U.S. Constitution and/or legal precedents to resolve such questions, but our point here is that you would need to move your thesis back to this point and test the validity of the assumptions upon which it rests.

Regardless of the position you might adopt—attacking tax laws, defending them, showing how they actually benefit everyone, or whatever—you would risk arguing blindly if you failed to question what the purpose of tax law is in the first place. This testing of assumptions would, at the least, cause you to qualify and refine your thesis. (See Figure 5.1.)

A PROCEDURE FOR UNCOVERING ASSUMPTIONS

How do you actually go about uncovering assumptions? Here's a fairly flexible procedure, which we apply step-by-step to the claim "Tax laws benefit the wealthy."

1. Paraphrase the explicit claim. This activity gets you started interpreting the claim, and it may begin to suggest the claim's underlying assumptions. We might paraphrase the claim as "The rules for paying income tax give rich people monetary advantages" or "The rules for paying income tax help the rich get richer."

2. List the implicit ideas that the claim seems to assume to be true. Here are two: "Tax laws shouldn't benefit anybody" and "Tax laws should benefit those who need the benefit, those with the least money"(which, by the way, are mutually exclusive).

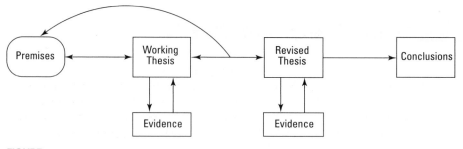

FIGURE 5.1
Reasoning Back to Premises

3. Determine the various ways that the key terms of the claim might be defined, as well as how the writer of the claim has defined them. This process of definition helps you see the key concepts upon which the claim depends. How does the writer intend *benefit*? Does he or she mean that tax laws benefit only the wealthy and presumably harm those who are not wealthy? Where is the line between wealthy and not wealthy drawn?

4. Try on an oppositional stance to the claim to see if this unearths more underlying assumptions. Regardless of your view on the subject, suppose for the sake of argument that the writer is wrong. This step allows you to think comparatively, helping you to see the claim more clearly, to see what it apparently excludes from its fundamental beliefs.

Knowing what the underlying assumption leaves out helps us see the narrowness upon which the claim may rest; we understand better its limits. Two positions that the claim appears to exclude are "Tax laws benefit the poor" and "Tax laws do not benefit the wealthy."

ANALYZING AN ARGUMENT: THE EXAMPLE OF "PLAYING BY THE ANTIOCH RULES"

Because the following essay originally appeared (in 1993) as a newspaper editorial (in *The New York Times*), it is less expository than much academic analytical writing. We have included it because it so clearly illustrates how a writer reasons forward to conclusions by reasoning backward to premises. The essay also illustrates how the strategies of refocusing binaries and qualifying claims operate in a finished piece of writing. As we have already noted, these strategies, which are so useful for analyzing arguments, are equally useful for producing them.

As you read this editorial on the controversial rules established at Antioch College (which, sadly, is closing its doors) to govern sexual conduct among its students, try to focus not only on the content of the argument, but also on its form; that is, how the writer moves from one phase of his thinking to the next. Toward this end, we have added our own summaries of what each paragraph of the editorial accomplishes. At the end of the editorial we sum up the writer's primary developmental strategies in a form you can apply to your own writing.

Playing by the Antioch Rules
By Eric Fassin

[1] A good consensus is hard to find, especially on sexual politics. But the infamous rules instituted last year by Antioch College, which require students to obtain explicit verbal consent before so much as a kiss is exchanged, have created just that. They have provoked indignation (this is a serious threat to individual freedom!) as well as ridicule (can this be serious?). Sexual correctness thus proves a worthy successor to political correctness as a target of public debate. *[The writer names the issue: the complaint that Antioch's rules threaten individual freedom.]*

[2]   Yet this consensus against the rules reveals shared assumptions among liberals, conserva- tives and even radicals about the nature of sex in our culture. *[The writer identifies members of an unlikely consensus and focuses on a surprising similarity.]*

[3]   The new definition of consent at Antioch is based on a "liberal" premise: it assumes that sexual partners are free agents and that they mean what they say—yes means yes, and no means no. But the initiator must now obtain prior consent, step by step, which in practice shifts the burden of clarification from the woman to the man. The question is no longer "Did she say no?" but "Did she say yes?" Silence does not indicate consent, and it becomes his responsibility to dispel any ambiguity. *[The writer identifies assump- tion of freedom underlying the rules.]*

[4]   The novelty of the rules, however, is not as great as it seems. Antioch will not exert more control over its students; there are no sexual police. In practice, you still do what you want—as long as your partner does not complain . . . the morning after. If this is censor- ship, it intervenes *ex post facto,* not *a priori. [The writer questions the premise that rules will actually control individual freedom more than current norms do.]*

[5]   In fact, the "threat" to individual freedom for most critics is not the invasion of privacy through the imposition of sexual codes, but the very existence of rules. Hence the suc- cess of polemicists like Katie Roiphe or Camille Paglia, who argue that feminism in recent years has betrayed its origins by embracing old-style regulations, paradoxically choosing the rigid 1950s over the liberating 1960s. Their advice is simply to let women manage on their own, and individuals devise their own rules. This individualist critique of feminism finds resonance with liberals, but also, strangely, with conservatives, who belatedly discover the perils of regulating sexuality. *[The writer locates an antiregulatory (laissez-faire) premise beneath the freedom premise.]*

[6]   But sexual laissez-faire, with its own implicit set of rules, does not seem to have worked very well recently. Since the collapse of established social codes, people play the same game with different rules. If more women are complaining of sexual violence, while more men are worrying that their words and actions might be misconstrued, who benefits from the absence of regulation? *[The writer attacks the laissez-faire premise for ineffectiveness.]*

[7]   A laissez-faire philosophy toward relationships assumes that sexuality is a game that can (and must) be played without rules, or rather that the invention of rules should be left to individual spontaneity and creativity, despite rising evidence that the rule of one's own often leads to misunderstandings. When acted out, individual fantasy always plays within preordained social rules. These rules conflict with the assumption in this culture that sex is subject to the reign of nature, not artifice, that it is the province of the individual, not of society. *[The writer uncovers an assumption beneath the laissez-faire premise: sex is natural and thus outside social rules.]*

[8]   Those who believe that society's constraints should have nothing to do with sex also agree that sex should not be bound by the social conventions of language. Indeed, this rebellion against the idea of social constraints probably accounts for the controversy over explicit verbal consent—from George Will, deriding "sex amidst semicolons," to Camille Paglia railing, "As if sex occurs in the verbal realm." As if sexuality were incompatible with words. As if the only language of sex were silence. For *The New Yorker,*

"the [Antioch] rules don't get rid of the problem of unwanted sex at all; they just shift the advantage from the muscle-bound frat boy to the honey-tongued French major." *[The writer develops the linguistic implications of the natural premise and questions the assumption that sex is incompatible with language.]*

[9] This is not very different from the radical feminist position, which holds that verbal persuasion is no better than physical coercion. In this view, sexuality cannot be entrusted to rhetoric. The seduction of words is inherently violent, and seduction itself is an object of suspicion. (If this is true, Marvell's invitation "To His Coy Mistress" is indeed a form of sexual harassment, as some campus feminists have claimed.) *[The writer develops a further implication: that the attack on rules masks a fear of language's power to seduce—and questions the equation of seduction with harassment.]*

[10] What the consensus against the Antioch rules betrays is a common vision of sexuality which crosses the lines dividing conservatives, liberals and radicals. So many of the arguments start from a conventional situation, perceived and presented as natural: a heterosexual encounter with the man as the initiator, and the woman as gatekeeper— hence the focus on consent. *[The writer redefines consensus as sharing the unacknowledged premise that conventional sex roles are natural.]*

[11] The outcry largely results from the fact that the rules undermine this traditional erotic model. Not so much by proscribing (legally), but by prescribing (socially). The new model, in which language becomes a normal form of erotic communication, underlines the conventional nature of the old one. *[The writer reformulates the claim about the anti-rules consensus: rules undermine attempts to pass off traditional sex roles as natural.]*

[12] By encouraging women out of their "natural" reserve, these rules point to a new definition of sexual roles. "Yes" could be more than a way to make explicit the absence of "no"; "yes" can also be a cry of desire. Women may express demands, and not only grant favors. If the legal "yes" opened the ground for an erotic "yes," if the contract gave way to desire and if consent led to demand, we would indeed enter a brave new erotic world. *[The writer extends the implication of the claim: rules could make sex more erotic rather than less free.]*

[13] New rules are like new shoes: they hurt a little at first, but they may fit tomorrow. The only question about the Antioch rules is not really whether we like them, but whether they improve the situation between men and women. All rules are artificial, but, in the absence of generally agreed-upon social conventions, any new prescription must feel artificial. And isn't regulation needed precisely when there is an absence of cultural consensus? *[The writer questions the standard by which we evaluate rules; the writer proposes reformulating the binary from artificial versus natural to whether rules will improve gender relations.]*

[14] Whether we support or oppose the Antioch rules, at least they force us to acknowledge that the choice is not between regulation and freedom, but between different sets of rules, implicit or explicit. They help dispel the illusion that sexuality is a state of nature individuals must experience outside the social contract, and that eroticism cannot exist within the conventions of language. As Antioch reminds us, there is more in eroticism and sexuality than is dreamt of in this culture. *[The writer culminates with his*

own idea: rules are good because they force us to acknowledge as a harmful illusion the idea that sex operates outside social conventions.]

Despite its brevity, this editorial covers a daunting amount of ground—an examination of "shared assumptions among liberals, conservatives and even radicals about the nature of sex in our culture" (paragraph 2). The writer, given his audience (readers of the Sunday *New York Times*), allows himself more breadth in both his topic and his claims than he would if he were writing an article on the same subject in an academic setting, where he would narrow his focus to supply more analysis of issues and evidence. The aim of editorials like this one is not only to inform or persuade but also to provoke and entertain. Nevertheless, the strategies that direct the thinking in this piece are, with some minor exceptions, the same as they would be in a more extended analytical piece. They are central strategies that you can apply to many sorts of writing situations, such as analyzing arguments and as a means of finding and developing your own ideas.

STRATEGIES FOR DEVELOPING AN ARGUMENT BY REASONING BACK TO PREMISES

1. *Set up a claim but delay passing judgment on it.* In the concluding sentence of paragraph 1, the word "target" suggests that the essay might attack Antioch's policy. In paragraph 2, however, the writer does not go on to demonstrate what is threatening and potentially ridiculous about Antioch's sexual contract, but neither does he yet offer his own conclusion on whether the views he has thus far described are right or wrong. Instead, he slows down the forward momentum toward judgment and begins to analyze what the consensus against the Antioch rules might mean—the "shared assumptions" it reveals "among liberals, conservatives, and even radicals about the nature of sex in our culture." In fact, the writer spends the first three-quarters of the essay trying on various answers to this question of meaning.

    (Note: a careful reader would recognize by tonal signals such as the exclamation mark in "serious threat to individual freedom!" that the opening paragraph has, in fact, begun to announce its position, albeit not overtly, by subtly overstating its opposite. It is not until later in the editorial, however, that we can clearly recognize that the writer is employing a common introductory strategy—defining the position you plan to argue against.)

2. *Decide what is really at issue by reasoning back to premises.* Rather than proceeding directly to a judgment on whether the Antioch rules threaten individual freedom, the writer carefully searches out the assumptions—the premises and givens—underlying the attacks on the rules. (This is a key step missing from most inadequately developed analyses and arguments.) He proposes, for example, that underneath the consensus' attack on the rules and its defense of individual freedom lies a basic premise about sex and society—that sexuality should not be governed by rules because it is natural rather than cultural: "These rules conflict with the assumption in this culture that sex is subject to the reign of nature, not artifice, that it is the province of the individual, not of society."

3. *Be alert for terms that create false dichotomies.* A false dichotomy (sometimes called a false binary) inaccurately divides possible views on a subject into two opposing camps, forcing a choice between black and white, when some shade of gray might be fairer and more accurate. When reading, or when writing an argument of your own, it is a good strategy to question any either/or dichotomy. Consider whether its opposing terms define the issue fairly and accurately before accepting an argument in favor of one side or the other.

Consider, too, how you might reject both choices offered by an either/or opposition to construct an alternative approach that is truer to the issues at hand. This is what the writer of the editorial does. He outlines and then rejects as a false dichotomy the consensus view that sexual behavior either is a province of individual freedom or is regulated by society:

False Dichotomies

Freedom vs. regulation

Natural vs. artificial

No rules vs. rules

The writer argues instead that much of what we perceive to be natural is in fact governed by social rules and conventions, such as the notion of men as sexual initiators and women as no-sayers and gatekeepers. He proposes that what is really at stake is a different dichotomy, a choice between two sets of rules, one implicit and one explicit:

Reformulated Dichotomies

Rules vs. other rules

Implicit vs. explicit

Not working vs. might work

Based on "no" vs. based on "yes"

The editorial concludes that we need to decide questions of sexual behavior—at Antioch and in the culture at large—by recognizing and evaluating the relative merits of the two sets of rules rather than by creating a false dichotomy between rules and no rules, between regulation and freedom.

4. *In your conclusion, return to the position that you set out to explore and restate it in the more carefully qualified way you arrived at in the body of your essay:* "The choice is not between regulation and freedom, but between different sets of rules." Clearly, the essay's conclusion does not simply repeat the essay's introductory claims, but it does respond to the way in which the essay began. Notice that virtually the entire essay has consisted of reasoning back to premises as a way of arriving at new ways of thinking.

▬ Try this 5.2: *Reasoning Back to Premises*

In the following excerpt from a student paper, the writer advances various claims based on premises that are not articulated. Analyze the excerpt using the procedure for uncovering assumptions detailed earlier. Find the places in the paragraph where the writer's operating assumptions—what he or she takes as givens—are left unsaid, and compile a list of these. First, try to find the premises that are articulated. On what premises, for example, does the writer base the argument that self-interest contributes to the health and growth of the economy as a whole?

> In all levels of trade, including individual, local, domestic, and international, both buyers and sellers are essentially concerned with their own welfare. This self-interest, however, actually contributes to the health and growth of the economy as a whole. Each country benefits by exporting those goods in which it has an advantage and importing goods in which it does not. Importing and exporting allow countries to focus on producing those goods that they can generate most efficiently. As a result of specializing in certain products and then trading them, self-interest leads to efficient trade, which leads to consumer satisfaction.

■ **Try this 5.3:** *Acknowledging Competing Premises*

In the following paragraph the writer has made his or her premises quite clear but has not acknowledged the possible validity of competing premises. (It is this same neglect of other possible positions that Fassin makes the substance of his editorial against the detractors of the Antioch rules; use him as a model). If the writer could become more self-conscious of reasoning back to premises, he or she would be more likely to discover these competing claims and either qualify the argument or overtly counter these competing claims.

> Field hockey is a sport that can be played by either men or women. All sports should be made available for members of both sexes. As long as women are allowed to participate on male teams in sports such as football and wrestling, men should be allowed to participate on female teams in sports such as field hockey and lacrosse. If women press for and receive equal opportunity in all sports, then it is only fair that men be given the same opportunity. If women object to this type of equal opportunity, then they are promoting reverse discrimination.

Examine the paragraph and lay out the writer's premises in your own words. First (1) Find at least two key assumptions that he or she wishes us to accept. Hint: the writer assumes, for example, that fairness ought to take precedence over other possible values in the selection of athletic teams. More generally, think about how he or she is defining other of her key terms. Then (2) formulate two assumptions that an audience who disagrees with the writer's point of view might hold.

THE PROBLEMS WITH DEBATE-STYLE ARGUMENT

Many of you will have been introduced to writing arguments through the debate model—writing pro or con on a given position, with the aim of defeating an imagined opponent and convincing your readers of the rightness of your position. But as the *American College Dictionary* says, "to argue implies reasoning or trying to understand; it does not necessarily imply opposition." It is this more exploratory, tentative, and dispassionate mode of argument that this book encourages you to practice.

To its credit, the debate model teaches writers to consider more than a single viewpoint, their opponent's as well as their own. But, unfortunately, it can also train them, even if inadvertently, to see the other side only as the opposition and to concentrate their energy only on winning the day. The problem with this approach is that it overemphasizes the bottom line—aggressively advancing a claim for *or* against some view—without first engaging in the exploratory interpretation of evidence that is so necessary to arriving at thoughtful arguments.

Thus, debate-style argument produces a frame of mind in which defending positions matters more than taking the necessary time to develop ideas worth defending. And, very possibly, it nourishes the mudslinging and opinionated mindset—attack first—that proliferates in editorials and television talk shows, not to mention the conversations you overhear in going about your life. We are not saying that people should forget about making value and policy decisions and avoid the task of persuading others. We are saying that too many of the arguments we all read, hear, and participate in every day are based on insufficient analysis.

In sum, adhering to the more restrictive, debate-style definition of argument can create a number of problems for careful analytical writers:

1. By requiring writers to be oppositional, it inclines them to discount or dismiss problems in the side or position they have chosen; they cling to the same static position rather than testing it as a way of allowing it to evolve.

2. It inclines writers toward either/or thinking rather than encouraging them to formulate more qualified (carefully limited, acknowledging exceptions, etc.) positions that integrate apparently opposing viewpoints.

3. It overvalues convincing someone else at the expense of developing understanding.

Analysis is an important corrective to narrow and needlessly oppositional thinking. A writer who is skeptical of global generalizations and of unexamined value judgments may sound timid and even confused compared with the insistent pronouncements of daytime talk shows and televised political debates. And because the argumentative habit of mind is so aggressively visible in our culture, most people never get around to experimenting with the more reflective and less combative approach that analysis embraces. But the effort you put into carefully formulating your ideas by qualifying them, checking for unstated assumptions, and acknowledging rather than ignoring problems in your position will make you a stronger writer and thinker.

SEEING THE TREES AS WELL AS THE FOREST: TOULMIN AND THE RULES OF ARGUMENT

At this point in our discussion, it will be helpful to digress slightly to talk about the systematic examination of evidence as it is described in the field of logic. Logic as a discipline has offered us various, sometimes conflicting rules of argument—procedures for locating and using evidence in the service of a claim and for determining when that use of evidence can be judged valid.

Philosophers have long quested for forms that might lend to human argument some greater clarity and certainty, more like what is possible with formulas in math. As our discussion of one particular debate within the discipline of philosophy demonstrates, however, the examination of evidence is necessarily an untidy process.

Probably the most common way of talking about logical argumentation goes back to the Greek philosopher Aristotle. At the heart of the Aristotelian model is the syllogism, which consists of three parts:

1. Major premise: a general proposition presumed to be true

2. Minor premise: a subordinate proposition also presumed to be true

3. Conclusion: a claim that follows logically from the two premises, if the argument has been properly framed

A frequently cited example of a syllogism is:

All men are mortal (major premise).

Socrates is a man (minor premise).

Therefore, Socrates is mortal (conclusion).

A premise is a proposition (assumption) upon which an argument is based and from which a conclusion is drawn. In the syllogism, if both of the premises are true and have been stated in the proper form (both containing a shared term), then theoretically the conclusion must also be true. In the example, if it is true that all men are mortal, and if it is true that Socrates is a man, then it must follow that Socrates is mortal.

The British philosopher Steven Toulmin offered a competing model of argument in his influential book, *The Uses of Argument* (1958). The Toulmin model can be seen as motivated by a desire to describe the structure of argument in a way that comes closer to what actually happens in practice when we try to take a position. The Toulmin model consists of:

1. Data: the evidence appealed to in support of a claim; data respond to the question "What have you got to go on?"

2. Warrant: a general principle or reason used to connect the data with the claim; the warrant responds to the question "How did you get there?" (from the data to the claim)

3. Claim: a conclusion about the data

Toulmin's model was motivated by his belief that the philosophical tradition of formal logic, with its many rules for describing and evaluating the conduct of arguments, conflicts with the practice and idiom (ways of phrasing) of arguers. To radically simplify Toulmin's case, it is that the syllogism does not adequately account for what really happens when thinkers try to frame and defend various claims.

Toulmin notes that the rules governing the phrasing of syllogistic arguments are very strict, as they must be if the form of an argument alone is to disclose its validity.

The Socrates syllogism cited above earns its validity on the basis of its form. But for Toulmin, the strictness of the rules necessary for guaranteeing formal validity leaves out the greater amount of uncertainty that is a part of reasoning about most questions, issues, and problems. A syllogism is designed to reveal its soundness through the careful framing and arrangement of its terms:

All men are mortal. (All x's are y.)

Socrates is a man. (Socrates is an x.)

Therefore, Socrates is mortal. (Socrates is y.)

But at what price, asks Toulmin, do we simplify our phrasing of complex situations in the world in order to gain this appearance of truth? In how many situations, he asks, can we say that "all x's are y"?

Toulmin observes, using his own argument structure as a case in point, that as soon as an argument begins to add information in support of its premises, the complexity and inevitable tentativeness of the argument become apparent, rather than its evident truth.

Here is one of Toulmin's examples of what must happen to the form of an argument when a person begins to add this supporting information, which he calls *backing*:

Data: Harry was born in Bermuda.

Warrant: The relevant statutes provide that people born in the colonies of British parents are entitled to British citizenship.

Claim: So, presumably, Harry is a British citizen.

The backing for the warrant would inevitably involve mentioning "the relevant statutes"—acts of Parliament, statistical reports, and so forth—to prove its accuracy. The addition of such information, says Toulmin, would "prevent us from writing the argument so that its validity shall be manifest from its formal properties alone" (*The Uses of Argument*, p. 123).

In other words, formal logic has evaluated an argument on the basis of a tightly structured form (such as the syllogism) that makes the argument's validity visible (manifest). But as soon as the form of the argument is made to include the greater amount of information that supports its accuracy and truth, it is no longer possible to evaluate the argument solely on the basis of its adherence to the required form. On this basis, Toulmin questions the tradition of guaranteeing the soundness of arguments solely on rules of form.

The advantage of understanding Toulmin's critique of syllogistic logic is that his model provides an antidote to the notion that there is a ready-made system for connecting evidence with claims that guarantees that an argument will always be right. To use an analogy, if the Aristotelian syllogism appears to offer us the promise of never mistaking the forest for the trees, Toulmin's revision of that model is to never let us forget that the forest is in fact made up of trees.

As a writer, you naturally want some guidelines and workable methods for selecting evidence and linking it to claims, and this book does what it can to provide them. But what you can't expect to find is a set of predetermined slots into which you can drop any evidence and find the truth. Rather, as Toulmin allows us to see, analyses and arguments cannot be separated from the complex set of details and circumstances that are part of life as we live it.

Clearly, the rules of argument are important for clarifying and testing our thinking. But an argument depends not only on whether its premises follow logically but on the quality of the thinking that produces those premises in the first place and painstakingly tests their accuracy. This is the job of analysis.

REFINING CATEGORICAL THINKING: TWO EXAMPLES

We have paused to extol Toulmin because his flexible and sensitive approach to argumentative context offers the way out of a problem that besets too many of the arguments we all encounter in our daily lives. That problem is categorical thinking, and, to be more precise, the rigidity to which categorical thinking is prone.

To generalize from particular experiences, we try to put those experiences into meaningful categories. Analytical thought is quite unthinkable without categories. But these can mislead us into oversimplification when the categories are too broad or too simply connected. This is especially the case with the either/or choices to which categorical thinking is prone: approve/disapprove, real/unreal, accurate/inaccurate, believable/unbelievable. The writer who evaluates leadership in terms of its selflessness/selfishness, for example, needs to pause to consider why we should evaluate leadership in these terms in the first place.

We will refer to the following two examples to illustrate how (1) qualifying your claims and (2) checking for the unstated assumptions upon which your claims depend can remedy the two primary problems created by categorical thinking: unqualified claims and overstated positions.

Example I: I think that there are many things shown on TV that are damaging for people to see. But there is no need for censorship. No network is going to show violence without the approval of the public, obviously for financial reasons. What must be remembered is that the public majority will see what it wants to see in our mass society.

Example II: Some members of our society feel that [the televised cartoon series] *The Simpsons* promotes wrong morals and values for our society. Other members find it funny and entertaining. I feel that *The Simpsons* has a more positive effect than a negative one. In relation to a real-life marriage, Marge and Homer's marriage is pretty accurate. The problems they deal with are not very large or intense. As for the family relationships, the Simpsons are very close and love each other.

The main problem with example I is the writer's failure to qualify his ideas, a problem that causes him to generalize to the point of oversimplification. Note the writer's habit of stating his claims absolutely (we have italicized the words that make these claims unqualified):

"there is *no* need for censorship"

"*no* network is going to show violence without"

"*obviously* for financial reasons"

"what *must* be remembered"

"the majority *will* see"

Such broad, pronouncement-like claims cannot be supported. The solution is to more carefully limit the claims, especially the key premise about public approval. The assertion that a commercial television industry will, for financial reasons, give the public "what it wants" is true to *an extent* (our key phrase for reformulating either/ors)—but it is not true as globally as the writer wishes us to believe.

Couldn't it also be argued, for example, that given the power of television to shape people's tastes and opinions, the public sees not just what it wants but what it has been taught to want? This complication of the writer's argument about public approval undermines the credibility of his global assertion that "there is no need for censorship."

Example II would appear to be more qualified than example I because it acknowledges the existence of more than one point of view. Rather than broadly asserting that the show is positive and accurate, she tempers these claims (as italics show): "I *feel* that *The Simpsons* has a *more* positive effect *than* a negative one"; "Marge and Homer's marriage is *pretty* accurate." These qualifications, however, are superficial.

Before she could convince us to approve of *The Simpsons* for its accuracy in depicting marriage, she would have to convince us that accuracy is a reasonable criterion for evaluating TV shows (especially cartoons) rather than assuming the unquestioned value of accuracy. Would an accurate depiction of the life of a serial killer, for example, necessarily make for a "positive" show? Similarly, if a fantasy show has no interest in accuracy, is it necessarily "negative" and without moral value?

When writers present a debatable premise as if it were self-evidently true, the conclusions built upon it cannot stand. At the least, the writer of example II needs to recognize her debatable premise, articulate it, and make an argument in support of it. She might also precede her judgment about the show with more analysis. Before deciding that the show is "more positive than negative" and thus does not promote "wrong morals and values for our society," she could analyze what the show says about marriage and how it goes about saying it.

Likewise, if the writer of example I had further examined his own claims before rushing to argue an absolute position on censorship, he would have noticed how much of the thinking that underlies them remains unarticulated and thus unexamined. It would also allow him to sort out the logical contradiction with his opening claim that "there are many things shown on TV that are damaging for people to see." If television networks will only broadcast what the public approves of, then apparently the public must approve of being damaged or fail to notice that it is being damaged. If the public either fails to notice it is being damaged or approves of it, aren't these credible arguments for rather than against censorship?

A BRIEF GLOSSARY OF COMMON LOGICAL ERRORS

This last section of the chapter returns briefly to the field of logic, which provides terms to shorthand certain common thinking errors. We mention six errors, all of which involve the root problem of oversimplification.

1. *Simple cause/complex effect.* The fallacy of simple cause/complex effect involves assigning a single cause to a complex phenomenon that cannot be so easily explained. A widespread version of this fallacy is seen in arguments that blame individual figures for broad historical events, for example, "Eisenhower caused America to be involved in the Vietnam War." Such a claim ignores the Cold War ethos, the long history of colonialism in Southeast Asia, and a multitude of other factors. When you reduce a complex sequence of events to a simple and single cause—or assign a simple effect to a complex cause—you will virtually always be wrong.

2. *False cause.* Another common cause/effect thinking error, false cause is produced by assuming that two events are causally connected when they aren't necessarily. One of the most common forms of this fallacy—known as *post hoc, ergo propter hoc* (Latin for "after this, therefore because of this")—assumes that because *A* precedes *B* in time, *A* causes *B*. For example, it was once thought that the sun shining on a pile of garbage caused the garbage to conceive flies.

   This error is the stuff that superstition is made of. "I walked under a ladder, and then I got hit by a car" becomes "Because I walked under a ladder, I got hit by a car." Because one action precedes a second one in time, the first action is assumed to be the cause of the second. A more dangerous form of this error goes like this:

   Evidence: A new neighbor moved in downstairs on Saturday. My television disappeared on Sunday.

   Conclusion: The new neighbor stole my TV.

   As this example also illustrates, typically in false cause some significant alternative has not been considered, such as the presence of flies' eggs in the garbage. Similarly, it does not follow that if a person watches television and then commits a crime, television watching necessarily causes crime; there are other causes to be considered.

3. *Analogy and false analogy.* An analogy is a means of understanding something relatively foreign in terms of something more familiar. When you argue by analogy you are saying that what is true for one thing will necessarily be true for something else that it in some way resembles. The famous poetic line "my love is like a red, red rose," is actually an argument by analogy. At first glance, this rather clichéd comparison seems too far-fetched to be reasonable. But is it a false analogy or a potentially enabling one? Past users of this analogy have thought the thorns, the early fading, the beauty, and so on, sufficient to validate the analogy between roses and women. Analogies, in short, are not bad

or illogical in themselves. In fact, they can be incredibly useful, depending on how you handle them.

The danger that arguing analogically can pose is that an inaccurate comparison, usually one that oversimplifies, prevents you from looking at the evidence. Flying to the moon is like flying a kite? Well, it's a little bit like that, but . . . in most ways that matter, sending a rocket to the moon does not resemble sending a kite into the air.

Another way that an analogy can become false is when it becomes overextended: there is a point of resemblance at one juncture, but the writer then goes on to assume that the two items compared will necessarily resemble each other in most other respects. To what extent is balancing your checkbook really like juggling? On the other hand, an analogy that first appears overextended may not be: how far, for example, could you reasonably go in comparing a presidential election to a sales campaign, or an enclosed shopping mall to a village main street?

When you find yourself reasoning by analogy, ask yourself two questions: (1) are the basic similarities greater and more significant than the obvious differences? and (2) am I overrelying on surface similarities and ignoring more essential differences?

4. *Equivocation.* Equivocation confuses an argument by slipping between two meanings for a single word or phrase. For example: "Only man is capable of religious faith. No woman is a man. Therefore, no woman is capable of religious faith." Here the first use of man is generic, intended to be gender neutral, while the second use is decidedly masculine. One specialized form of equivocation results in what are sometimes called *weasel words.* A weasel word is one that has been used so much and so loosely that it ceases to have much meaning (the term derives from the weasel's reputed practice of sucking the contents from an egg without destroying the shell). The word *natural,* for example, can mean good, pure, and unsullied, but it can also refer to the ways of *nature* (flora and fauna). Such terms (*love, reality,* and *experience* are others) invite equivocation because they mean so many different things to different people.

5. *Begging the question.* To beg the question is to argue in a circle by asking readers to accept without argument a point that is actually at stake. This kind of fallacious argument hides its conclusion among its assumptions. For example, "*Huckleberry Finn* should be banned from school libraries as obscene because it uses obscene language" begs the question by presenting as obviously true issues that are actually in question: the definition of obscenity and the assumption that the obscene should be banned because it is obscene.

6. *Overgeneralization.* An overgeneralization is an inadequately qualified claim. It may be true that some heavy drinkers are alcoholics, but it would be not fair to claim that all heavy drinking is or leads to alcoholism. As a rule, be wary of "totalizing" or global pronouncements; the bigger the generalization, the more likely it admits exceptions.

ASSIGNMENTS: Analyze or Produce an Argument

1. Locate the binaries in an editorial or other position piece and explore the extent to which these are adequate and inadequate ways of defining the subject. Once you have arrived at the essential claims of the piece, analyze these using the tools offered in this chapter. In particular, you should use the strategies for reformulating binaries in A Procedure for Reformulating Binaries in Argument and for unearthing premises in the A Procedure for Uncovering Assumptions sections. Remember to share your thinking, not just to present your conclusions, as you write your analysis.

2. Write an essay in which you reason back to the premises that underlie some idea or attitude of your own, preferably one that has undergone some kind of change in recent years (for example, your attitude toward the world of work, marriage, family life, community, religion, etc.). Take care not to substitute unanalyzed narrative for analysis. Even though you are working from your own experience, stay focused on analysis of your assumptions and binaries (which you can use the two procedures cited in the previous assignment option to produce).

3. Compose an argument of your own (it can be an editorial), using the chapter's Strategies for Developing an Argument by Reasoning Back to Premises. As you have seen, the editorial on the Antioch Rules is both a critique of the thinking in another argument and an argument in its own right. And so if you wish you may use an analysis of an existing argument to prompt your own.

CHAPTER 6

Topics and Modes of Analysis

THE FIRST UNIT OF THIS BOOK, The Analytical Frame of Mind, has sought to persuade you that analysis is worth the challenge—that you can unlearn less productive ways of thinking and take on fresh habits that will make you smarter. In this final chapter of Unit I, we offer concrete advice about how to succeed in creating writing that fulfills some of the most common basic writing tasks that you will be asked to produce at the undergraduate level and beyond.

A unifying element of the chapters in this unit is their focus on the stage of the composing process that rhetoricians call *invention*. This chapter takes up several of classical rhetoric's topics of invention, which are places (from the Greek *topoi*) from which a writer or orator might discover the things he or she needs to say. These topics include comparison/contrast and definition, to which we have added summary, reaction papers, and agree/disagree topics because these are such common forms in college and other writing settings. The chapter offers you strategies for making the best use of these topics as analytical tools.

The chapter opens by focusing on rhetorical analysis: an approach that we have been featuring from the opening pages, without labeling it as such. Rhetorical analysis is a concern for analytical thinkers because it focuses on *how* and *why* our responses are triggered and shaped by things in the world, from a sign we read on the subway to the language of a presidential speech.

Like analysis in general, rhetorical analysis asks what things mean, why they are as they are and do what they do. But rhetorical analysis asks these questions with one primary question always foregrounded: how does the thing achieve its effects on an audience? Rhetorical analysis asks not just what do I think, but *what am I being invited to think (and feel) and by what means?*

RHETORICAL ANALYSIS

To analyze the rhetoric of something is to determine how that something persuades and positions its readers or viewers or listeners. Rhetorical analysis is an essential skill because it reveals how particular pieces of communication seek to enlist our support and shape our behavior. Only then can we decide whether we should be persuaded to respond as we have been invited to respond.

Everything has a rhetoric: classrooms, churches, speeches, supermarkets, department store windows, Starbucks, photographs, magazine covers, your bedroom, this book. Intention, by the way, is not the issue. It doesn't matter whether the effect of a place or a piece of writing on its viewers (or readers) is deliberate and planned or not. What matters is that you can notice how the details of the thing itself encourage or discourage certain kinds of responses in the consumers of whatever it is you are studying. What, for example, does the high ceiling of a Gothic cathedral invite in the way of response from people who enter it? What do the raised platform at the front of a classroom and the tidy rows of desks secured to the floor say to the students who enter there?

If you are reading this book in a first-year college writing course, you may be asked to write a rhetorical analysis, often of a visual image of some kind, early in the semester. What follows is an exercise in rhetorical analysis that will help you better understand the aims and methods of this kind of analysis. We think it is easiest to start with analysis of visual rhetoric—the rhetoric, for example, of a typical classroom.

Rhetorical Analysis of a Place: A Brief Example

To get you started on a rhetorical analysis of a place, here is the beginning of one on the layout of our college campus. It was written as a freewrite and could serve as the basis for further observation.

The campus is laid out in several rows and quadrangles. It is interesting to observe where the different academic buildings are, relative to the academic departments they house. It is also interesting to see how the campus positions student housing. In a way, the campus is set up as a series of quadrangles—areas of space with four sides. One of the dormitories, for example, forms a quadrangle. Quadrangles invite people to look in—rather than out. They are enclosed spaces, the center of which is a kind of blank. The center serves as a shared space, a safely walled-off area for the development of a separate community. The academic buildings also form a quadrangle of sorts, with an open green space in the center. On one side of the quadrangle are the buildings that house the natural and social sciences. Opposite these—on the other side of a street that runs through the center of campus—are the modern brick and glass structures that house the arts and the humanities . . .

If you push these observations by asking "So what?," here are some of the rhetorical implications at which you might arrive:

- That the campus is inward-looking and self-enclosed
- That it invites its members to feel separate and safe
- That it announces the division of the sciences and the social sciences from the arts and humanities, so the campus layout arguably creates the sense of a divided community.

Rhetorical Analysis of an Advertisement: A Student Paper

This example is excerpted from a student's rhetorical analysis of a perfume advertisement that appeared in a magazine aimed at young women. The analysis was written in a course called Introduction to Communication. The writer's aim is not only to tell her readers what the advertisement "says" but to locate it in a social context. The student also uses secondary sources to provide an interpretive context (a lens) through which to see the rhetoric of the ad—its means of persuasion.

The visual imagery of advertisements offers instructive opportunities for rhetorical analysis because advertising is a form of persuasion. Advertisers attend to rhetoric by carefully targeting their audiences. This means advertisements are well suited to the questions that rhetorical analysis typically asks: how is the audience being invited to respond and by what means (in what context)? You'll notice that in the rhetorical analysis of the magazine ad, the writer occasionally extends her analysis to evaluative conclusions about the aims and possible effects (on American culture) of the advertisement. We've included the first five paragraphs of the essay along with a piece of its conclusion.

Marketing the Girl Next Door: A Declaration of Independence?

[1]   Found in *Seventeen* magazine, the advertisement for "tommy girl," the perfume manufactured by Tommy Hilfiger, sells the most basic American ideal of independence. Various visual images and text suggest that purchasing tommy girl buys freedom and liberation for the mind and body. This image appeals to young women striving to establish themselves as unbound individuals. Ironically, the advertisement uses traditional American icons as vehicles for marketing to the modern woman. Overall, the message is simple: American individualism can be found in a spray or nonspray bottle.

[2]   Easily, the young woman dominates the advertisement. She has the look of the all-American "girl next door." Her appeal is a natural one, as she does not rely on makeup or a runway model's cheekbones for her beauty. Freckles frame her eyes that ambitiously gaze skyward; there are no limits restricting women in capitalist America. Her flowing brown hair freely rides a stirring breeze. Unconcerned with the order of a particular hairstyle, she smiles and enjoys the looseness of her spirit. The ad tells us how wearing this perfume allows women to achieve the look of self-assured and liberated indifference without appearing vain.

[3]   The second most prevalent image in the advertisement is the American flag, which neatly matches the size of the young woman's head. The placement and size of the flag suggest that if anything is on her cloudless mind, it is fundamental American beliefs that allow for such self-determination. The half-concealed flag is seemingly continued in the young woman's hair. According to the ad, American ideals reside well within the girl as well as the perfume.

[4]   It is also noticeable that there is a relative absence of land surrounding the young woman. We can see glimpses of "fruited plains" flanking the girl's shoulders. This young woman is barely bound to earth, as free as the clouds that float beneath her head. It is this liberated image Americans proudly carry that is being sold in the product.

[5]   The final image promoting patriotism can be found in the young woman's clothing. The young woman is draped in the blue jean jacket, a classic symbol of American ruggedness and originality. As far as we can see, the jacket is spread open, supporting the earlier claim of the young women's free and independent spirit. These are the very same

ideals that embody American pride and patriotism. The ad clearly employs the association principle in linking the tommy girl fragrance with emotionally compelling yet essentially unrelated images of American nationalism and patriotism. [. . .]

[10] Yet in reality, this marketing of liberation is paradoxical; although this freeing message promotes rebellion and nonconformity, it actually supports the market economy and feeds into capitalism and conformity. When advertisers employ political protest messages to be associated with products, they imply that buying the product is a form of political action.

We now move to strategies for making your response to some traditional topics more analytical. Like the other thinking tools in this unit, each of these topics can aid in the invention stage of your writing.

SUMMARY

Summary and analysis go hand in hand; the primary goal for both is to understand rather than evaluate. Summary is a necessary early step in analysis because it provides perspective on the subject as a whole by explaining the meaning and function of each of that subject's parts. Within larger analyses—papers or reports—summary performs the essential function of contextualizing a subject accurately. It creates a fair picture of what's there.

Summarizing isn't simply the unanalytical reporting of information; it's more than just shrinking someone else's words. To write an accurate summary, you have to ask analytical questions, such as the following:

- Which of the ideas in the reading are most significant? Why?
- How do these ideas fit together?
- What do the key passages in the reading mean?

Summarizing is, then, like paraphrasing, a tool of understanding and not just a mechanical task.

When summaries go wrong, they are just lists, a simple "this and then this" sequence. Often lists are random, as in a shopping list compiled from the first thing you thought of to the last. Sometimes they are organized in broad categories: fruit and vegetables here, dried goods there. At best, they do very little logical connecting among the parts beyond "next." Summaries that are just lists tend to dollop out the information monotonously. They omit the *thinking* that the piece is doing—the ways it is connecting the information, the contexts it establishes, and the implicit slant or point of view.

Writing analytical summaries can teach you how to read for the connections, the lines that connect the dots. And when you're operating at that level, you are much more likely to have ideas about what you are summarizing.

Strategies for Making Summaries More Analytical

Strategy 1: Look for the Underlying Structure   Use The Method to find patterns of repetition and contrast. (See Chapter 3.) If you apply it to a few key paragraphs, you will find the terms that are repeated, and these will suggest strands,

Monthly Budget for the Fitzgerald Family, 1923

Monthly EXPENDITURE 1923

			TRIPS, PLEASURE + PARTIES	
TAXES	200	00		
RENT	300	00		
FOOD	200	00	House Liquor	80 00
			PLAZA	26 50
COAL + WOOD	35	00	ALABAMA	33 00
ICE	8	50	ATLANTIC CITY	10 00
GAS	27	00	THEATRE	20 00
LIGHT	14	50	BARBER	10 00
PHONE	25	00	HAIR DRESSING	15 00
WATER	5	00	CHARITY	4 00
			WILD PARTIES	100 00
SERVANTS	295	00	Taxis	15 00
			Gambling	33 00
DOCTORS	42	50	LUNCHES (N.Y.)	25 00
DRUG STORE	32	50	SUBWAY (ccl)	24 00
CLUB	105	50	Miscelaeneous Cash	276 00
NEWSPAPERS	5	00		
BOOKS	14	50		
FLOWERS	9	00		
AUTO	23	00		
PLUMBER	13	50		
ELECTRIC	1	50		
COMMUTATION	4	00		
SCOTTS CLOTHES	33	00		
Zelda's CLOTHES	100	00		
BABY'S CLOTHES	25	00		
HOUSEHOLD AND MISSCLANEUS CHARGES	81	00		
TYPING	12	00		
	1620	40		785 60
				1620.40
				2396.00

from F. Scott Fitzgerald's private papers
Yes, this is own handwriting (cool, no?)

A

Bookmark

without a name

which in turn make up organizing contrasts. This process works to categorize and then further organize information and, in so doing, to bring out its underlying structure.

Strategy 2: Select the Information That You Wish to Discuss on Some Principle Other Than General Coverage Use the Notice and Focus strategy to rank items of information in some order of importance. (See Chapter 3.) Let's say that you are writing a paper on major changes in the tax law or on recent developments in U.S. policy toward the Middle East. Rather than simply collecting the information, try to arrange it into hierarchies. What are the least or most significant changes or developments, and why? Which are most overlooked or most overrated or most controversial or most practical, and why? All of these terms—significant, overlooked, and so forth—have the effect of focusing the summary, guiding your decisions about what to include and exclude.

Strategy 3: Reduce Scope and Say More about Less Both The Method and Notice and Focus involve some loss of breadth; you won't be able to cover everything. But this is usually a trade-off worth making. Your ability to rank parts of your subject or choose a revealing feature or pattern to focus on gives you surer control of the material than if you just reproduce what is in the text. You can still begin with a brief survey of major points to provide context, before narrowing the focus. Reducing scope is an especially efficient and productive strategy when you are trying to understand a reading you find difficult or perplexing. It moves you beyond passive summarizing and toward having ideas about the reading.

   If, for example, you are reading Chaucer's *Canterbury Tales* and start cataloging what makes it funny, you are likely to end up with unanalyzed plot summary— a list that arranges its elements in no particular order. But narrowing the question to "How does Chaucer's use of religious commentary contribute to the humor of 'The Wife of Bath's Tale'?" reduces the scope to a single tale and the humor to a single aspect of humor. Describe those as accurately as you can, and you will begin to notice things.

Strategy 4: Get Some Detachment: Shift Your Focus from What? to How? and Why? Most readers tend to get too single-minded about absorbing the information. That is, they attend only to the *what*: what the reading is saying or is about. They take it all in passively. But you can deliberately shift your focus to how it says what it says, and why.

   If, for example, you were asked to discuss the major discoveries that Darwin made on *The Beagle*, you could avoid simply listing his conclusions by redirecting your attention to *how* he proceeds. You could choose to focus, for example, on Darwin's use of the scientific method, examining how he builds and, in some cases, discards hypotheses. Or you might select several passages that illustrate how Darwin proceeded from evidence to conclusion and then *rank* them in order of importance to the overall theory. Notice that in shifting the emphasis to Darwin's thinking—the how and why—you would not be excluding the what (the information component) from your discussion.

PERSONAL RESPONSE: THE REACTION PAPER

The biggest advantage of reaction papers is that they give you the freedom to explore where and how to engage your subject. They bring to the surface your emotional or intuitive response, allowing you to experiment with placing the subject in various contexts.

Another advantage of personal response questions is that they allow you to get some distance on your first impressions. If, as you reexamine your first reactions, you look for ways that they might not be accurate, you will often find places where you now disagree with yourself, in effect, stimulating you to think in new ways about the subject.

Personal response becomes a problem, however, when it distracts you from analyzing the subject. In most cases, when you are invited to respond personally, you are being asked for more than your endorsement or critique of the subject. If you find yourself constructing a virtual list—I agree with this point or I disagree with that point—you are probably doing little more than matching your opinions with the points of view encountered in a reading. In most cases, you misinterpret the intent of a personal response topic if you view it as an invitation to:

1. Assert your personal opinions unreflectively.
2. Substitute narratives of your own experience for careful consideration of the subject. In an academic setting, an opinion is more than simply an expression of your beliefs; it's a conclusion that you earn the rights to through a careful examination of evidence.

Strategies for Making Personal Responses More Analytical

Strategy 1: Trace Your Responses Back to Their Causes As we noted in Chapter 2, tracing your impressions back to their causes is the key to making personal response analytical—because you focus on the details that gave you the response rather than on the response alone.

Let's say, for example, that you are responding to an article on ways of increasing the numbers of registered voters in urban precincts. You find the article irritating; your personal experience working with political campaigns has taught you that getting out the vote is not as easy as this writer makes it seem. From that starting point, you might analyze one (to you) overly enthusiastic passage, concentrating on how the writer has not only overestimated what campaign workers can actually do but also condescends to those who don't register—assuming, perhaps, that they are ignorant rather than indifferent or disillusioned. Tracing your response back to its cause may help to defuse your emotional response and open the door to further investigation of the other writer's rationale. You might, for example, discover that the writer has in mind a much more long-term effect or that urban models differ significantly from the suburban ones of your experience.

Strategy 2: Assume That You May Have Missed the Point It's difficult to see the logic of someone else's position if you are too preoccupied with your own. Similarly, it is difficult to see the logic, or illogic, of your own position if you already assume it to be true.

Although an evaluative response (approve/disapprove) can sometimes spur analysis, it can also lead you to prejudge the case. If, however, you habitually question the validity of your own point of view, you will sometimes recognize the possibility of an alternative point of view, as was the case in the voter registration example. (See Figure 6.1.) Assuming that you have missed the point is a good strategy in all kinds of analytical writing. It causes you to notice details of your subject that you might not otherwise have registered.

Strategy 3: Locate Your Response within a Limiting Context Suppose you are asked in a religion course to write your religious beliefs. Although this topic would naturally lead you to think about your own experiences and beliefs, you would probably do best to approach it in some more limiting context. The reading in the course could provide this limit. Let's say that thus far you have read two modern religious thinkers, Martin Buber and Paul Tillich. Using these as your context, "What do I believe?" could become "How does my response to Buber and Tillich illuminate my own assumptions about the nature of religious faith?" An advantage of this move, beyond making your analysis less general, is that it would help you to get perspective on your own position.

Another way of limiting your context is to consider how one author or recognizable point of view that you have encountered in the course might respond to a single statement from another author or point of view. If you used this strategy to respond to the topic "Does God exist?" you might arrive at a formulation such as "How would Martin Buber critique Paul Tillich's definition of God?" Although this topic appears to exclude personal response entirely, it in fact does not. Your opinion would necessarily enter because you would be actively formulating something that is not already evident in the reading (how Buber might respond to Tillich).

Evaluative Personal Response: *"The article was irritating."* This response is too broad and dismissively judgmental. Make it more analytical by tracing the response back to the evidence that triggered it.

A More Analytical Evaluative Response: *"The author of the article oversimplifies the problem by assuming the cause of low voter registration to be voters' ignorance rather than voters' indifference."* Although still primarily an evaluative response, this observation is more analytical. It takes the writer's initial response ("irritating") to a specific cause.

A Nonevaluative Analytical Response: *"The author's emphasis on increased coverage of city politics in local/neighborhood forums such as the churches suggests that the author is interested in long-term effects of voter registration drives and not just in immediate increases."* Rather than simply reacting ("irritating") or leaping to evaluation ("oversimplifies the problem"), the writer here formulates a possible explanation for the difference between his or her point of view on voter registration drives and the article's.

FIGURE 6.1
Making Personal Response More Analytical

AGREE/DISAGREE

We offer here only a brief recap of this kind of topic because it is discussed at length in earlier chapters. Topics are frequently worded as agree/disagree, especially on essay exams, but the wording is potentially misleading because you are rarely being asked for as unqualified an opinion as agree or disagree.

In most cases, your best strategy in dealing with agree/disagree questions is to choose *neither* side. Instead, question the terms of the binary so as to arrive at a more complex and qualified position to write about. In place of choosing one side or the other, decide to what extent you agree and to what extent you disagree. You are still responsible for coming down more on one side than the other, but this need not mean that you have to locate yourself in a starkly either/or position. The code phrase for accomplishing this shift, as we've suggested in Chapter 5, is "the extent to which": "To what extent do you agree (or disagree)?"

COMPARISON/CONTRAST

Although comparison/contrast is meant to invite analysis, it is too often treated as an end in itself. The fundamental reason for comparing and contrasting is that you can usually discover ideas about a subject much more easily when you are not viewing it in isolation. When executed mechanically, however, without the writer pressing to understand the significance of a similarity or difference, comparison/contrast can suffer from pointlessness.

Comparison/contrast topics produce pointless essays if you allow them to turn into matching exercises—that is, if you match common features of two subjects but don't get beyond the equation stage *(a, b, c = x, y, z)*. Writers fall into this trap when they have no larger question or issue to explore and perhaps resolve by making the comparison. If, for example, you were to pursue the comparison of the representations of the Boston Tea Party in British and American history textbooks, you would begin by identifying similarities and differences. But simply presenting these and concluding that the two versions resemble and differ from each other in some ways would be pointless. You would need to press your comparisons with the So what? question (see Chapter 4) to give them some interpretive weight.

Strategies for Making Comparison/Contrast More Analytical

Strategy 1: Argue for the Significance of a Key Comparison   Rather than simply covering a range of comparisons, focus on a key comparison. Although narrowing the focus might seem to eliminate other important areas of consideration, in fact it usually allows you to incorporate at least some of these other areas in a more tightly connected, less list-like fashion. So, for example, a comparison of the burial rites of two cultures probably reveals more about them than a much broader but more superficial list of cultural similarities and differences. In the majority of cases, covering less is covering more.

You can determine which comparison is key by ranking. You are ranking whenever you designate one part of your topic as especially important or revealing. Suppose you are asked to compare General Norman Schwarzkopf's strategy in the first Persian Gulf War with General Douglas MacArthur's strategy in World War II. As a first move, you could limit the comparison to some revealing parallel, such as the way each man dealt with the media, and then argue for its significance above other similarities or differences. You might, for instance, claim that in their treatment of the media we get an especially clear or telling vantage point on the two generals' strategies. At this point you are on your way to an analytical point—for example, that because MacArthur was more effectively shielded from the media at a time when the media was a virtual instrument of propaganda, he could make choices that Schwarzkopf might have wanted to make but couldn't.

Strategy 2: Use One Side of the Comparison to Illuminate the Other Usually it is not necessary to treat each part of the comparison equally. It's a common misconception that each side must be given equal space. In fact, the purpose of your comparison governs the amount of space you'll need to give to each part. Often, you will be using one side of the comparison primarily to illuminate the other. For example, in a course on contemporary military policy, the ratio between the two parts would probably be roughly seventy percent on Schwarzkopf to thirty percent on MacArthur rather than fifty percent on each.

Strategy 3: Imagine How One Side of Your Comparison Might Respond to the Other This strategy, a variant of the preceding one, is a particularly useful way of helping you to respond to comparison/contrast topics more purposefully. This strategy can be adapted to a wide variety of subjects. If you were asked to compare Sigmund Freud with one of his most important followers, Jacques Lacan, you would probably be better off focusing the broad question of how Lacan revises Freud by considering how and why he might critique Freud's interpretation of a particular dream in *The Interpretation of Dreams*. Similarly, in the case of the Persian Gulf War example, you could ask yourself how MacArthur might have handled some key decision in the Persian Gulf War and why. Or you might consider how he would have critiqued Schwarzkopf's handling of that decision and why.

Strategy 4: Focus on Difference within Similarity (or Similarity within Difference) The typical move when you are asked to compare two subjects is to collect a number of parallel examples and show how they are parallel, which can lead to bland tallying of similarities without much analytical edge. In the case of obvious similarities, you should move quickly to significant differences within the similarity and the implications of these differences. In this way, you better define your subject, and you are more likely to offer your readers something that is not already clear to them. For example, the Carolingian and Burgundian Renaissances share an emphasis on education, but if you were asked to compare them, you could reveal the character of these two histori-cal periods more effectively by concentrating on the different purposes and origins of this emphasis on education.

A corollary of the difference within similarity formula is that you can focus on unexpected similarity rather than obvious difference. It is no surprise that President Bill Clinton's economic package differed from President Ronald Reagan's, but much could be written about the way that Clinton "out-Reaganed Bush" (as one politi-cal commentator put it) by appealing to voters with Reagan's brand of populist optimism—a provocative similarity within difference.

DEFINITION

Definition becomes meaningful when it serves some larger purpose. You define "rhythm and blues" because it is essential to any further discussion of the evolution of rock-and-roll music, or because you need that definition to discuss the British Invasion spearheaded by groups such as the Beatles, the Rolling Stones, and the Yard-birds in the late 1960s, or because you cannot classify John Lennon, Mick Jagger, or Eric Clapton without it.

Like comparison/contrast, definition can produce pointless essays if the writer gets no further than assembling information. Moreover, when you construct a sum-mary of existing definitions with no clear sense of purpose, you tend to list definitions indiscriminately. As a result, you are likely to overlook conflicts among the various definitions and overemphasize their surface similarities. Definition is in fact a site at which there is some contesting of authorities—different voices who seek to make their definition triumph.

Strategies for Making Definition More Analytical

Strategy 1: Test the Definition against Evidence One common form of definition asks you to apply a definition to a body of information. It is rare to find a perfect fit. Therefore, you should, as a general rule, use the data to assess the accuracy and the limitations of the definition, rather than simply imposing it on your data and ignoring or playing down the ways in which it does not fit. Testing the definition against evidence makes your definition evolve. The definition, in turn, serves as a lens to better focus your thinking about the evidence.

Suppose you were asked to define capitalism in the context of third-world economies. You might profitably begin by matching some standard definition of capitalism with specific examples from one or two third-world economies, with the express purpose of detecting where the definition does *and does not* apply. In other words, you would respond to the definition topic by assaying the extent to which (that phrase again!) the definition provides a tool for making sense of the subject.

Strategy 2: Use a Definition from One Source to Critique and Illuminate
Another As a general rule, you should attempt to identify the points of view
of the sources from which you take your definitions, rather than accepting
them as uncontextualized answers. It is essential to identify the particular slant
because otherwise you will tend to overlook the conflicting elements among various
definitions of a key term.

A paper on alcoholism, for example, will lose focus if you use all of the definitions available. If, instead, you convert the definition into a comparison and contrast
of competing definitions, you can more easily generate a point and purpose for your
definition. By querying, for example, whether a given source's definition of alcoholism is moral or physiological or psychological, you can more easily resolve the issue
of definition.

Strategy 3: Problematize as Well as Synthesize the Definition To explore
competing definitions of the same term requires you to attend to the difficulties of definition. In general, analysis achieves direction and purpose by locating
and then exploring a problem. You can productively make a problem out of
defining. This strategy is known as *problematizing,* which locates and then
explores the significance of uncertainties and conflicts. It is always a smart
move to problematize definitions to reveal complexity that less careful thinkers
might miss.

The definition of capitalism that you might take from Karl Marx, for
example, differs in its emphases from Adam Smith's. In this case, you would not only
isolate the most important of these differences but also try to account for the
fact that Marx's villain is Smith's hero. Such an accounting would probably
lead you to consider how the definition has been shaped by each of these
writers' political philosophies or by the culture in which each theory was
composed.

Strategy 4: Shift from What? to How? and Why? Questions It is no accident that
we earlier offered the same strategy for making summary more analytical: analytical
topics that require definition also depend on "why?" or "how?" questions, not "what?"
questions (which tend simply to call for information).

If, for example, you sought to define the meaning of darkness in Joseph
Conrad's *Heart of Darkness* and any two other modern British novels, you would do
better to ask why the writers find darkness such a fertile term than simply to
accumulate various examples of the term in the three novels. You might start
by isolating the single best example from each of the works, preferably ones
that reveal important differences as well as similarities. Then, in analyzing how
each writer uses the term, you could work toward some larger point that would
unify the essay. You might show how the conflicts of definition within Conrad's meta-
phor evolve historically, get reshaped by female novelists, change after World War I,
and so forth.

ASSIGNMENTS: Using the Topics and Modes of Analysis

1. Locate any magazine ad that you find interesting. Ask yourself, what is this a picture of? Use the student paper on the perfume ad as a kind of model for ways of thinking about the ad's rhetorical agenda. If you find yourself getting stuck, rephrase the question as, "What is this ad really about, and why did the advertiser choose this particular image or set of images? Strategies in this unit that might work well with this assignment are Seems to Be about X . . . (in Chapter 4) and Make the Implicit Explicit (see Chapters 1 and 4).

2. Analyze a *New Yorker* cover in more than one interpretive context. The cover we recommend is by Harry Bliss, dated August 1, 2005, and is entitled "King Kong." It depicts a large gorilla near the Empire State Building in New York squirting a crowd of overheated New Yorkers with a large green squirt gun. You can see this cover either on the artist's website or at *The New Yorker* store website (click on Browse by Artist; choose Harry Bliss.)

   One obvious context for the cover is the movie *King Kong,* which was about to come out in the latest Peter Jackson version. Another context is international terrorism in general, and probably 9/11 in particular, given that the gorilla (guerilla?) is perched near a prominent NYC architectural icon. Also, just before the cover was published, a bombing had occurred in the London underground.

   In your paper you should focus on how the cartoonist is negotiating both his contexts and his audience. How, in other words, does the rhetoric of the cover work in the context of current fears about international terrorism? Which details of the cover "speak" most interestingly in this regard—and what do they say?

3. Write two summaries of the same article or book chapter. Make the first one consecutive (the so-called "coverage" model)—that is, try to cover the piece by essentially listing the key points as they appear. Limit yourself to a typed page. Then rewrite the summary, doing the following:

   • Rank the items in order of importance according to some principle that you designate, explaining your rationale;

   • Eliminate the last few items on the list, or at most, give each a single sentence; and

   • Use the space you have saved to include more detail about the most important item or two.

   The second half of this assignment will probably require closer to two pages.

4. Write a paper in which you explore significant differences and similarities, using any item from the following list.

   List as many similarities and differences as you can: go for coverage. Then review your list and select the two or three most revealing similarities and the two or three most revealing differences. At this point, you are ready to write a few paragraphs in which you argue for the significance of a key difference or similarity. In so doing, you may find it interesting to focus on an *unexpected* similarity or difference—one that others might not initially notice. (We recommend trying the "unexpected" gambit.)

a. Accounts of the same event from two different newspapers or magazines or textbooks

b. Two CDs (or even songs) by the same artist or group

c. Two ads for the same kind of product

d. Graffiti in men's bathrooms versus graffiti in women's bathrooms

e. The political campaigns of two opponents running for the same or similar office

f. Courtship behavior as practiced by men and by women

g. Two breeds of dog

h. Two clothing styles as emblematic of socioeconomic class or a subgroup in your school, town, or workplace

i. Two versions of the same song by different artists

5. Write a comparative definition in which you seek out different and potentially competing definitions of the same term or terms.

Begin with a dictionary such as the *Oxford English Dictionary* (popularly known as the *OED*, available in most library reference rooms or online) that contains both historically based definitions tracking the term's evolution over time and etymological definitions that identify the linguistic origins of the term (its sources in older languages). Be sure to locate both the etymology and the historical evolution of the term or terms.

Then look up the term in one or preferably several specialized dictionaries. We offer a list of some of these in Chapter 16, Finding, Citing, and Integrating Sources, but you can also ask your reference librarian for pertinent titles. Generally speaking, different disciplines generate their own specialized dictionaries.

Summarize key differences and similarities among the ways the dictionaries have defined your term or terms. Then write a comparative essay in which you argue for the significance of a key similarity or difference, or an unexpected one.

Here is the list of words: hysteria, ecstasy, enthusiasm, witchcraft, leisure, gossip, bachelor, spinster, romantic, instinct, punk, thug, pundit, dream, alcoholism, aristocracy, atom, ego, pornography, conservative, liberal, entropy, election, tariff. Some of these words are interesting to look at together, such as ecstasy/enthusiasm or liberal/conservative or bachelor/spinster. Feel free to write on a pair instead of a single word.

UNIT II

Writing the Analytical Essay

CHAPTER 7

What Evidence Is and How It Works

> Most of what goes wrong in using a thesis is the result of a writer leaping too quickly to a generalization that would do as a thesis, and then treating evidence only as something to be mustered in support of that idea.

THIS CHAPTER IS ABOUT EVIDENCE—what it is, what it is meant to do, and how to recognize when you are using it well. The chapter's overall argument is that you should use evidence to test, refine, and develop your ideas, rather than just to prove that they are correct. The chapter begins by analyzing two common problems: claims without evidence (unsubstantiated claims) and evidence without claims (pointless evidence).

A claim is an assertion that you make about your evidence—an idea that you believe the evidence supports. The governing claim in a paper is the thesis. In analytical writing, the thesis is a theory that explains what some feature or features of a subject mean. When the material of your subject, your data, is used to demonstrate the truth or falsity of a particular claim, that material becomes evidence.

This chapter opens Unit II, which is about writing the thesis-driven essay. Unit I demonstrates how to make observations about data and reason to implications and conclusions, but it does not take this process to the point at which a writer settles on a formal claim (a thesis) and uses it to govern the development of an entire essay.

In this unit we demonstrate how to employ the analytical methods (tools) offered in Unit I—especially Notice and Focus, The Method, the So what? question, and Difference within Similarity—to find, formulate, and evolve a thesis.

This unit's approach to essay organization and the thesis may differ from what you're used to. *Writing Analytically* is most unlike other writing texts in its treatment of the thesis. We argue that the problem with much writing of the sort that people are taught to do in school is that it arrives prematurely at an idea that the writer then "proves" by attaching it to a number of examples—a pattern we call 1 on 10 (see Chapter 8). Textbooks about writing tend to present thesis statements as the finished products of an act of thinking—as inert statements that writers should march through their papers from beginning to end. As we show in Chapters 8 and 9, the relationship between thesis and evidence is far more fluid and dynamic. In most good writing, the thesis grows and changes in response to evidence, even in final drafts.

For now, though, we delay further discussion of the thesis to focus first on evidence—the stuff that generates thesis statements and responds to them.

THE FUNCTION OF EVIDENCE

A common assumption about evidence is that it is "the stuff that proves I'm right." Although this way of thinking about evidence is not wrong, it is much too limited. Corroboration (proving the validity of a claim) is one of the functions of evidence, but not the only one.

It helps to remember that the word *prove* actually comes from a Latin verb meaning "to test." The noun form of prove, *proof,* has two meanings: (1) evidence sufficient to establish a thing as true or believable and (2) the act of testing for truth or believability. When you operate on the first definition of proof alone, you are far more likely to seek out evidence that supports only your point of view, ignoring or dismissing other evidence that could lead to a different and possibly better idea. You might also assume that you can't begin writing until you have arrived at an idea you're convinced is right because only then could you decide which evidence to include. Both of these practices close down your thinking instead of leading you to a more open process of formulating and testing ideas.

The advantage to following the second definition of the word *proof*—in the sense of testing—is that you are better able to negotiate among competing points of view. Doing so predisposes your readers to consider what you have to say because you are offering them not the thoughts a person has had, but rather a person in the act of thinking. Writing well means sharing your thought process with your readers, telling them why you believe the evidence means what you say it does.

THE MISSING CONNECTION: LINKING EVIDENCE AND CLAIMS

Evidence rarely, if ever, can be left to speak for itself. The word *evident* comes from a Latin verb meaning "to see." To say that the truth of a statement is self-evident means that it does not need to be proved because its truth can be plainly seen by all. When a writer leaves evidence to speak for itself, he or she is assuming that it can be interpreted in only one way, and that readers necessarily will think as the writer does.

But the relationship between evidence and claims is rarely self-evident: that relationship virtually always needs to be explained. One of the five analytical moves discussed in Chapter 1 was making the implicit explicit. This move is critical for working with evidence. The thought connections that have occurred to you about what the evidence means will not automatically occur to others. (See Figure 7.1.) Persuasive writing always makes the connections between evidence and claim overt.

Writers who think that evidence speaks for itself often do very little with their evidence except put it next to their claims: "The party was terrible: there was no alcohol"—or, alternatively, "The party was great: there was no alcohol." Just juxtaposing the evidence with the claim leaves out the thinking that connects them, thereby

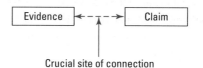

FIGURE 7.1
Linking Evidence and Claims

implying that the logic of the connection is obvious. But even for readers prone to agreeing with a given claim, simply pointing to the evidence is not enough.

Of course, before you can attend to the relationship between evidence and claims, you first have to make sure to include both of them. Let's pause to take a look at how to remedy the problems posed by leaving one out: unsubstantiated claims and pointless evidence.

"BECAUSE I SAY SO": UNSUBSTANTIATED CLAIMS

Problem: Making claims that lack supporting evidence.
Solution: Learn to recognize and support unsubstantiated assertions.

Unsubstantiated claims occur when a writer concentrates only on conclusions, omitting the evidence that led to them. At the opposite extreme, pointless evidence results when a writer offers a mass of detail attached to an overly general claim. Both of these problems can be solved by offering readers the evidence that led to the claim and explaining how the evidence led there. The word *unsubstantiated* means "without substance." An unsubstantiated claim is not necessarily false; it just offers none of the concrete "stuff" upon which the claim is based. When a writer makes an unsubstantiated claim, he or she has assumed that readers will believe it just because the writer put it out there.

Perhaps more important, unsubstantiated claims deprive you of details. If you lack some actual "stuff" to analyze, you can easily get stuck in a set of abstractions, which tend to overstate your position and leave your readers wondering exactly what you mean. The further away your language is from the concrete, from references to physical detail—things that you can see, hear, count, taste, smell, and touch—the more abstract it becomes.

DISTINGUISHING EVIDENCE FROM CLAIMS

To check your drafts for unsubstantiated assertions, you first have to know how to recognize them. It is sometimes difficult to separate facts from judgments, data from interpretations of the data. Writers who aren't practiced in this skill can believe that they are offering evidence when they are really offering only unsubstantiated claims. In your own reading and writing, pause once in a while to label the sentences of a paragraph as either evidence (E) or claims (C). What happens if we try to categorize the sentences of the following paragraph in this way?

The owners are ruining baseball in America. Although they claim they are losing money, they are really just being greedy. A few years ago, they even fired the commissioner, Fay Vincent, because he took the players' side. Baseball is a sport, not a business, and it is a sad fact that it is being threatened by greedy businessmen.

The first and last sentences of the paragraph are claims. They draw conclusions about as yet unstated evidence that the writer needs to provide. The middle two sentences are harder to classify. If particular owners have said publicly that they are losing money, the existence of the owners' statements is a fact. But the writer moves from evidence to unsubstantiated claims when he suggests that the owners are lying about their financial situation and are doing so because of their greed. Similarly, it is a fact that commissioner Fay Vincent was fired, but it is only an assertion that he was fired "because he took the players' side," an unsubstantiated claim. Although many of us might be inclined to accept some version of this claim as true, we should not be asked to accept his opinion as self-evident truth. What is the evidence in support of the claim? What are the reasons for believing that the evidence means what he says it does?

GIVING EVIDENCE A POINT: MAKING DETAILS SPEAK

> **Problem:** Presenting a mass of evidence without explaining how it relates to the claims.
> **Solution:** Make details speak. Explain how evidence confirms and qualifies the claim.

Your thinking emerges in the way that you follow through on the implications of the evidence you have selected. You need to interpret it for your readers. You have to make the details speak, conveying to your readers why they mean what you claim they mean.

The following example illustrates what happens when a writer leaves the evidence to speak for itself.

Baseball is a sport, not a business, and it is a sad fact that it is being threatened by greedy businessmen. For example, Eli Jacobs, the previous owner of the Baltimore Orioles, sold the team to Peter Angelos for one hundred million dollars more than he had spent ten years earlier when he purchased it. Also, a new generation of baseball stadiums have been built in the last two decades—in Baltimore, Chicago, Arlington (Texas), Cleveland, and most recently, in San Francisco, Milwaukee, Houston, and Philadelphia. These parks are enormously expensive and include elaborate scoreboards and luxury boxes. The average baseball players, meanwhile, now earn more than a million dollars a year, and they all have agents to represent them. Alex Rodriguez, the third baseman for the New York Yankees, is paid more than twenty million dollars a season. Sure, he continues to sets records for homers by a player at his age, but is any ballplayer worth that much money?

Unlike the previous example, which was virtually all claims, this paragraph, except for the opening claim and the closing question, is all evidence. The paragraph presents what we might call an evidence sandwich: it encloses a series of facts between two claims. (The opening statement blames greedy businessmen, presumably owners, and the closing statement appears to indict greedy, or at least overpaid, players.) Readers are left with two problems. First, the mismatch between the opening and concluding claims leaves it not altogether clear what the writer is saying that the evidence suggests. And second, he has not told readers why they should believe that the evidence means what he says it does. Instead, he leaves it to speak for itself.

If readers are to accept the writer's implicit claims—that the spending is too much and that it is ruining baseball—he will have to show how and why the evidence supports these conclusions. The rule that applies here is that evidence can almost always be interpreted in more than one way.

We might, for instance, formulate at least three conclusions from the evidence offered in the baseball paragraph. We might decide that the writer believes baseball will be ruined by going broke or that its spirit will be ruined by becoming too commercial. Worst of all, we might disagree with his claim and conclude that baseball is not really being ruined because the evidence could be read as signs of health rather than decay. The profitable resale of the Orioles, the expensive new ballparks (which, the writer neglects to mention, have drawn record crowds), and the skyrocketing salaries all could testify to the growing popularity rather than the decline of the sport.

How to Make Details Speak: A Brief Example

The best way to begin making the details speak is to take the time to look at them, asking questions about what they imply.

1. Say explicitly what you take the details to mean.
2. State exactly how the evidence supports your claims.
3. Consider how the evidence complicates (qualifies) your claims.

The writer of the baseball paragraph leaves some of his claims and virtually all of his reasoning about the evidence implicit. What, for example, bothers him about the special luxury seating areas? Attempting to uncover his assumptions, we might speculate that he intends it to demonstrate how economic interests are taking baseball away from its traditional fans because these new seats cost more than the average person can afford. This interpretation could be used to support the writer's governing claim, but he would need to spell out the connection, to reason back to his own premises. He might say, for example, that baseball's time-honored role as the all-American sport—democratic and grass-roots—is being displaced by the tendency of baseball as a business to attract higher box office receipts and wealthier fans.

The writer could then make explicit what his whole paragraph implies, that baseball's image as a popular pastime in which all Americans can participate is being tarnished by players and owners alike, whose primary concerns appear to be making money. In making his evidence speak in this way, the writer would be practicing step 3—using the evidence to complicate and refine his ideas. He would discover which specific aspect of baseball he thinks is being ruined, clarifying that the greedy businessmen to whom he refers include both owners and players.

Let's emphasize the final lesson gleaned from this example. When you focus on tightening the links between evidence and claim, the result is almost always a smaller claim than the one you set out to prove. This is what evidence characteristically does to a claim: it shrinks and restricts its scope. This process, also known as qualifying a claim, is the means by which a thesis develops.

Sometimes it is hard to give up on the large, general assertions that were your first response to your subject. But your sacrifices in scope are exchanged for greater accuracy and validity. The sweeping claims you lose ("Greedy businessmen are ruining baseball") give way to less resounding but also more informed, more incisive, and less judgmental ideas ("Market pressures may not bring the end of baseball, but they are certainly changing the image and nature of the game").

WHAT COUNTS AS EVIDENCE?

Thus far this chapter has concentrated on how to use evidence after you've assembled it. In many cases, though, a writer has to consider a more basic and often hidden question before collecting data: what counts as evidence?

This question raises two related concerns:

Relevance: In what ways does the evidence bear on the claim or problem that you are addressing? Do the facts really apply in this particular case, and if so, how?

Framing assumptions: In what ways is the evidence colored by the point of view that designated it as evidence? At what point do these assumptions limit its authority or reliability?

To raise the issue of framing assumptions is not to imply that all evidence is merely subjective, somebody's impressionistic opinion. We are implying, however, that even the most apparently neutral evidence is the product of some way of seeing that qualifies the evidence as evidence in the first place. In some cases, this way of seeing is embedded in the established procedure of particular disciplines. In the natural sciences, for example, the actual data that go into the results section of a lab report or formal paper are the product of a highly controlled experimental procedure. As its name suggests, the section presents the results of seeing in a particular way.

The same kind of control is present in various quantitative operations in the social sciences, in which the evidence is usually framed in the language of statistics. And in somewhat less systematic but nonetheless similar ways, evidence in the humanities and some projects in the social sciences are always conditioned by methodological assumptions. A literature student cannot assume, for example, that a particular fate befalls a character in a story because of events in the author's life (it is a given of literary study that biography may inform but does not explain a work of art). As the Voices from across the Curriculum sections make clear, evidence is never just some free-floating, absolutely reliable, objective entity for the casual observer to sample at random. It is always a product of certain starting assumptions and procedures that readers must take into account.

Questions of Relevance and Methodology

What counts as evidence? I try to impress upon students that they need to substantiate their claims with evidence. Most have little trouble with this. However, when I tell them that evidence itself is dependent upon methodology—that it's not just a question of gathering information, but also a question of how it was gathered—their eyes glaze over. Can we trust the source of information? What biases may exist in the way questions are posed in an opinion poll? Who counts as an authority on a subject? (No, Rush Limbaugh cannot be considered an authority on women's issues, or the environment, or, for that matter, anything else!) Is your evidence out of date? (In politics, books on electoral behavior have a shelf life only up to the next election. After two years, they may have severe limitations.)

Methodological concerns also determine the relevance of evidence. Some models of, say, democratic participation define as irrelevant certain kinds of evidence that other models might view as crucial. For instance, a pluralist view of democracy, which emphasizes the dominant role of competitive elites, views the evidence of low voter turnout and citizen apathy as a minor concern. More participatory models, in contrast, interpret the same evidence as an indication of the crisis afflicting contemporary democratic practices.

In addition to this question of relevance, methodology makes explicit the game plan of research: how did the student conduct his or her research? Why did he or she consider some information more relevant than others? Are there any gaps in the information? Does the writer distinguish cases in which evidence strongly supports a claim from evidence that is suggestive or speculative?

Finally, students need to be aware of the possible ideological nature of evidence. For instance, Americans typically seek to explain such problems as poverty in individualistic terms, a view consistent with our liberal heritage, rather than in terms of class structure, as a Marxist would. Seeking the roots of poverty in individual behavior simply produces a particular kind of evidence different from that which would be produced if we began with the assumption that class structure plays a decisive influence in shaping individual behavior.

—Jack Gambino, *Professor of Political Science*

Evidence is virtually never simply a matter of "the facts." It is no accident that one often hears the phrase "questions of evidence," because evidence is perennially subject to question—for its accuracy, its veracity, and so forth.

We are, to a significant degree, a society obsessed with evidence—from UFO watchers to conspiracy theorists to those who avidly follow the latest leaks in the press about the peccadilloes of the famous. This raises the question of the kinds of evidence that can be used to support claims.

KINDS OF EVIDENCE

The following survey of different types of evidence is not comprehensive, but we have tried to select the most common kinds.

Statistical Evidence

Statistics are a primary tool—a virtual language—for those writing in the natural and especially the social sciences. They have the advantage of greater objectivity, and, in the social sciences, of offering a broad view of a subject. Remember, though, that, like other forms of evidence, statistics do not speak for themselves; their significance must be overtly elucidated. Nor should it simply be assumed that statistics are valid representations of the reality they purport to measure. In baseball, the fielding average commonly assumed to indicate the best fielders measures errors against total chances, but it does not acknowledge that a superior fielder may get to more balls and commit errors on difficult plays that another, slower fielder with a higher average would never get to.

VOICES FROM ACROSS THE CURRICULUM

Interpreting the Numbers

So much is written about the advantages and limitations of empirical information that I hardly know where to begin. Briefly, if it is empirical, there is no guesswork or opinion (Skinner said, "The organism is always right"—that is, the data are always right). The limitations are that the collection and/or interpretation can be fraught with biases and error. For example, if I want to know if women still feel that there is gender discrimination in the workplace, I do not have to guess or intuit this (my own experiences are highly likely to bias my guesses): I can do a survey. The survey should tell me what women think (whether I like the answer or not). The limitations occur in how I conduct the survey and how I interpret the results. You might remember the controversy over the Hite Report on sexual activities (whom did she sample, and what kind of people answer those kinds of questions, and do they do so honestly?).

Despite the controversy over the problems of relying on empirical data in psychology, I think that it is the only way to find answers to many fascinating questions about humans. The patterns of data can tell us things that we have no other access to without empirical research. It is critically important for people to be aware of the limitations and problems, but then to go on and collect the data.

—Laura Edelman, *Professor of Psychology*

Anecdotal Evidence

An anecdote is a little story (a narrative), a piece of experience. The word comes from a Greek term meaning "things unpublished." Anecdotal evidence involves the close examination of particular instances, often including the writer's or researcher's own experience with whatever he or she is studying. So, for example, a historian wishing to understand the origins and development of the Latino community in a small East Coast American city might use as a large part of his or her evidence interviews conducted with local Latino residents.

Anecdotal evidence is in some ways at the opposite extreme from statistical evidence. Statistical research often attempts to locate broad trends and patterns by surveying large numbers of people and tries to arrive at reliable information by deliberately controlling the kind and amount of questions it asks. In fact, one of the most important tasks for someone using statistical research is the careful crafting of the questions to guarantee that they don't, for example, predispose the respondent to choose a particular response. By contrast, the kind of thinking based on anecdotal evidence is less concerned with verifiable trends and patterns than with a more detailed and up-close presentation of particular instances.

Given the difficulty of claiming that a single case (anecdote) is representative of the whole, researchers using anecdotal evidence tend to achieve authority through a large number of small instances, which begin to suggest a trend. Authority can also be acquired through the audience's sense of the analytical ability of the researcher, his or her skill, for example, at convincingly connecting the evidence with the claim. This is to say that an audience's assessment of the reasonableness of an argument is often influenced by its sense of the reasonableness of the arguer.

Authorities as Evidence

A common way of establishing support for a claim is to invoke an authority—to call in as evidence the thinking of an expert in the subject area you are writing about. The practice of invoking authorities as evidence can be heard in TV advertising ("three out of four doctors recommend . . . ," etc.) as well as in scholarly books and articles, in which a writer may offer as partial support for a claim the thinking of a better-known writer. Much academic writing consists of evaluating and revising views that people have come to believe are authoritative. The building of knowledge involves in large part the ongoing consideration of who or what will be accepted as authoritative.

Later in this book we devote a whole chapter to the matter of using authorities as evidence (Chapter 14). In that chapter we explain how to use—rather than just include and agree with—other writers on your subject. Calling in the support of an authority, an expert witness, can be very useful, but it's no substitute for logic: the fact that somebody has gotten a claim printed doesn't mean it's a good conclusion. Sharing the source's evidence and reasoning with your readers helps them to understand your use of the source.

Empirical Evidence

Empirical evidence is derived from experience, the result of observation and experiment, as opposed to theory. It is usually associated with the bodily senses; the word *empirical* means "capable of being observed, available to the senses"; the word comes from the Greek word for experience. Evidence from the sciences, for example, is heavily empirical. The scientific method is all about how to look at and evaluate physical evidence. But in the humanities, too, analyses are based on observation—of texts, of musical scores, of art works—not just on theories.

Experimental Evidence

Experimental evidence is a form of empirical evidence (capable of being observed). It is distinguished from other forms of evidence by the careful attention to procedure it requires. Evidence in the sciences is usually recorded in particular predetermined formats, both because methodology is important and because the primary test of validity in the sciences is that the experiment must be repeatable so that another experimenter can follow the same procedure and achieve the same results.

The concern with procedure is present throughout writing in the sciences, though, not just in the Methods section of a lab report. Scientific writing constantly begins by asking the question, "How do we know what we think we know?" And because experiments inevitably take a scientist into the unknown, it then asks, "On the basis of what we know, what else might be true, and how can we find out?" The concern with procedure in scientific writing is ultimately, then, a matter of clearly articulating the means of verifying and explaining what we think we know.

Textual Evidence

All of the examples we've presented are in some sense textual—they consist of words on the page. We are using the term *textual evidence* to designate instances in which the language itself is of fundamental importance, in which the emphasis lies on how things are worded. A primary assumption in analyzing textual evidence is that the meanings of words are never simple and unambiguous. That is, the meanings of particular words cannot be assumed; they must be explained, and those explanations must be argued for. Insofar as the actual language of a document counts, you are in the domain of textual evidence.

It's a mistaken assumption that only people in literary studies do textual analysis. Perhaps the profession that most commonly uses textual evidence is the law, which involves interpreting the language of contracts, wills, statutes, statements of intention, and so forth. Similarly, diplomats, accountants, people in business—all those who must rely on written documents to guarantee understanding—need to be adept at textual analysis. People in such fields as media studies, communications, and even public relations also engage in textual analysis when they examine visual images because the images themselves matter and mean in the same ways that words do in a verbal text.

VOICES FROM ACROSS THE CURRICULUM

Keeping the Evidence before You

A wonderful feature of "doing history" is that everything counts as evidence in uncovering lives, landscapes, institutions, and cultures of the past. The rings of an oak tree can play into a historical argument with as great a resonance as the crown jewels. The literary romance, the census record, the portrait, the peasant's stone bench are all matter for the historian. What, then, the student of history has to hone is the ability to distinguish types of evidence and to assess when and why certain categories of evidence are of legitimate use. [. . .] Students (and professional historians) sometimes prejudge too quickly the purview of a body of evidence and move away from it before the sources have yielded all they have to tell. Again, the qualities of patience and tenacity are crucial here. When a text does not immediately unveil a startling discovery, the tendency can sometimes be to cast a wider and wider net, lapsing into generalization or abstraction. Here is where a close summary of the nature of the evidence, the context for its production or presence (sometimes absence), and its audience can open the way to a lively and perceptive historical essay.

—Ellen Poteet, *Professor of History*

USING WHAT YOU HAVE

We've just talked about the different kinds of evidence, many of them distinguished by disciplinary community, but ultimately, the basic elements of argument and evidence always apply. Beneath the varieties of evidence, in other words, lie certain fundamental principles of application, principles that have occupied the bulk of this chapter.

It is time to return explicitly to an underlying principle first suggested, as a question, in the chapter's initial Voices from across the Curriculum: "Does the writer distinguish cases in which evidence strongly supports a claim from evidence that is suggestive or speculative?" Underneath this question lurks a messier one. Given that, depending on what you're trying to accomplish, there are different kinds of evidence, and different audiences to whom it is presented, how do you know if your evidence legitimately supports your claims?

A simple, but not very helpful, answer is that you don't. Nor should you really expect definitive assurance on this question. It is helpful to realize, though, that evidence is usually suggestive rather than conclusive. In the realm of analysis, there are precious few smoking guns and absolutely reliable eyewitnesses. (When there are, you have an open-and-shut case that probably does not need to be argued.) So you want to avoid thinking that a particular use of evidence is strong and good because the evidence is clearly true and factual, whereas another use of evidence is weak and inadequate because it's clearly untrue and not factual. Most analytical uses of evidence are a matter of making inferences, rather than arriving at obviously true claims from clearly factual information.

Most of the areas in which we dwell on evidence are those where the issue is not what is and isn't a fact, but rather what can fairly be made of the facts. Once we've proven a claim with a fact, we are not necessarily at a stopping point. So, for example, if you discover a mess on your rug with your dog nearby, the only dog in the house, chances are that the dog made the mess. But this simple move from fact to claim is probably not what will concern you most. You will quickly move on to more hypothetical questions about the facts, such as "Did she make the mess because she's lonely, inadequately trained, ill, or . . . ?" or "Why do dogs always choose the rug?" Questions of this kind and the hypotheses (tentative theories) we produce in answer to them are what most of our real thinking is about. Finding solid evidence—the facts—is only part of the problem. The larger question is always: what do the facts really tell us? But this question is the subject of the next several chapters.

We've shown in this chapter that there are different kinds of evidence. And we've suggested that the really interesting and important questions, at least for analytical writing, are to be found not in the facts but in our hypotheses about what the facts mean. Given these considerations, how do you know what kind of evidence to use and when you've done it right?

To a significant extent, the question of appropriateness depends on the kind of claim you are making (how broad, for example, and how conclusive) and the genre you are writing in. What could be appropriate and valid for writing a magazine profile of residents trying to rebuild a poor urban neighborhood might not be appropriate and valid for supporting policy decisions or sociological theories about people in such neighborhoods. The strength of such a profile, however, should not be underestimated because it may be rich in suggestion, in questions and angles of approach for further research.

Finally, whatever kind of evidence you're using, the emphasis rests on how you use what you have: how you articulate what it means and how carefully you link the evidence to your claims. When you find yourself asking, "How good is my argument?" here are two working criteria from the chapter:

1. Am I oversimplifying the implications of my evidence?

2. Does my use of evidence go beyond mere corroboration of an overly general claim?

Another and final guiding principle, perhaps the chapter's most important point, is: don't leave the evidence behind as you cast for what it means. Rather, think with the evidence; always keep it before you. Here is a good rule of thumb in this regard: if you find that as much as a paragraph has gone by with no reference to your evidence, you can suspect that you are moving off into a perhaps ungrounded and overly abstract discussion.

Your thoughts about the evidence should launch you into broader conceptualizations, but if you start to move too far afield, remember to return repeatedly to the source, to the evidence itself, to refresh your thinking and keep it honest.

ASSIGNMENT: Distinguishing Evidence from Claims

Take an excerpt from your own writing, at least two paragraphs in length—
perhaps from a paper you have already written or a draft you are working on—and
at the end of every sentence label the sentence as either evidence (E) or claim (C).
For sentences that appear to offer both, determine which parts of the sentence are
evidence and which are claim, and then decide which one, E or C, predominates.
What is the ratio of evidence to claim, especially in particularly effective or weak
paragraphs?

   As an alternative or a preface to the previous exercise, mark the following paragraph with Cs and Es. We have numbered the sentences for easier isolation and
discussion. A few of them—1 and 7, for example—are arguably quite tricky to
decide about: which part of the sentence is a claim, and which part evidence? Keep
in mind that you are making your decisions on the basis of the writer's use of the
sentences, not simply on their content. Is a secondary source's judgment that is
imported into an essay as support for the writer's point of view ultimately C or E,
for example?

[1] Though many current historians would argue that Andrew Jackson's treatment of the
     Native Americans was contrary to the ideals and precepts of the American Revolution,
     one must consider the legal and moral context of both Jackson and the time period in
     which he lived. (C)

[2] Jackson, both as a general and as a president, had no real love for the Native American
     populations in the southern and western United States. (C)

[3] As a military general he had defended the borders of the United States many times
     against Indian attacks and negotiated treaties with some of the tribes during the term of
     President James Monroe. (E)

[4] However, Jackson was also the archetype of the general American view of the Native
     Americans. (C)

[5] He described the Indians as barbarians and cruel savages in a letter to a fellow politician
     (Hollitz 172) and tried to convince President Monroe, during his negotiations with the
     Creek Indians, that Native Americans "are the subjects of the United States, inhabiting its
     territory and acknowledging its sovereignty" (Hollitz 174). (E)

[6] He subsequently argued that it was "absurd for the sovereign to negotiate with the
     subjects" (Hollitz 174). (E)

[7] Jackson and many of his contemporaries also saw the Indians only as a hindrance to
     America's exploitation of southern and western farmland and that they should be
     removed to facilitate American expansion. (C)

[8] This is clearly seen in a letter Jackson wrote to his wife in which he describes removing
     the natives of Alabama in terms of the fertile lands and wealth it will bring the United
     States as well as a secure southern border (Hollitz 173). (E)

[9]   They were subjects of American sovereignty. (E)

[10] In this sense, Jackson's policy of Indian removal was in line with the best wishes of the people that the ideals of the American Revolution were set aside for, the American citizens who wished for more fertile lands and safe borders. (c)

[11] Jackson was indeed providing for the citizens that he believed the Declaration of Independence encompassed. (6)

CHAPTER 8

Using Evidence to Build a Paper: 10 on 1 versus 1 on 10

IN THIS CHAPTER WE ARGUE for the importance of saying more about less. The phrase we use for this idea is 10 on 1. The concept of 10 on 1 was introduced in Chapter 3, A Toolkit of Analytical Methods, as a variant of Notice and Focus, an observation strategy. In this chapter, 10 on 1 is used to talk about essay structure as well as the analysis of selected data.

The phrase 10 on 1 stands for the principle that it is better to make ten observations or points about a single representative issue or example (10 on 1) than to make the same basic point about ten related issues or examples (1 on 10). Doing 10 on 1 teaches writers to narrow their focus and then analyze in depth, drawing out as much meaning as possible from their best examples.

The chapter opens with a critique of the ubiquitous high school format known as five-paragraph form, an organizational scheme that actively blocks sustained reflection about the meaning of evidence. The chapter then goes on to demonstrate the advantages of 10 on 1 as an alternative scheme both for writing and revising papers.

DEVELOPING A THESIS IS MORE THAN REPEATING AN IDEA (1 ON 10)

When the time comes to compose a formal paper with a thesis, it is very common for writers to abandon the wealth of data and ideas they have accumulated in the exploratory writing stage, panic, and revert to old habits: "Now I better have my one idea and be able to prove to everybody that I'm right." Out goes careful attention to detail. Out goes any evidence that doesn't fit. Instead of analysis, they substitute the kind of paper we call a *demonstration*. That is, they cite evidence to prove that a generalization is generally true. The problem with the demonstration lies with its too-limited notions of what a thesis and evidence can do in a piece of analytical thinking.

A paper produced by repeating a single unchanging idea generally follows the form we call 1 on 10: the writer makes a single and usually very general claim ("History repeats itself," "Exercise is good for you," etc.) and then proceeds to affix it to ten examples. (See Figure 8.1.) A writer who reasserts the same idea about each example is going to produce a list, not a piece of developed thinking. By contrast,

123

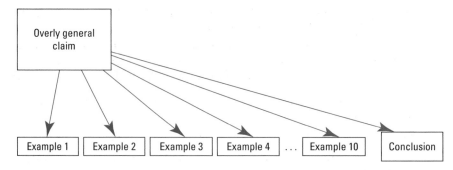

FIGURE 8.1

Doing 1 on 10   *The horizontal pattern of 1 on 10 (in which 10 stands arbitrarily for any number of examples) repeatedly makes the same point about every example. Its analysis of evidence is superficial.*

in nearly all good writing the thesis evolves by gaining in complexity and, thus, in accuracy as the paper progresses.

The 1 on 10 demonstration results from a mistaken assumption about the function of evidence, that it exists only to demonstrate the validity of (corroborate) a claim. Beyond corroborating claims, evidence should serve to test, develop, and evolve the thesis. This is one of the most important points of this chapter.

Admittedly, demonstrations have their place—short speeches, for example, in situations in which the audience has to follow a chain of thought in spite of interference from noise or other distractions. And it's also true that when a writer is trying to determine whether there is sufficient evidence to make a claim, it is useful to collect a group of related examples before focusing on the most interesting or revealing ones. If, for example, you were writing about the failure of faith in the biblical book of Exodus, you would do well to chart repeated instances of its failure to substantiate that it is a recurrent feature. But to get beyond this general demonstration, you would need to look more closely at a representative instance.

Where do writers get the idea that a thesis should be static? In most cases they learned it early in their writing careers as part of a stubbornly inflexible organizational scheme known as five-paragraph form.

WHAT'S WRONG WITH FIVE-PARAGRAPH FORM?

Perhaps the best introduction to what's wrong with five-paragraph form can be found in Greek mythology. On his way to Athens, the hero Theseus encounters a particularly surly host, Procrustes, who offers wayfarers a bed for the night but with a catch. If they do not fit his bed exactly, he either stretches them or lops off their extremities until they do. This story has given us the word *procrustean,* which the dictionary defines as "tending to produce conformity by violent or arbitrary means." Five-paragraph form is a procrustean formula that most students learn in high school. Although it has the advantage of providing a mechanical format that gives virtually any subject the appearance of order, it usually lops off a writer's ideas before they have the chance to form, or it stretches a single idea to the breaking point.

A complex idea is one that has many sides. To treat such ideas intelligently, writers need a form that does not require them to cut off all of those sides except the one that most easily fits the bed. Most of you will find the basic five-paragraph form familiar:

1. An introduction that ends with a thesis listing three points (the so-called tripartite thesis)
2. Three body paragraphs, each supporting one of the three points
3. A conclusion beginning "Thus, we see" or "In conclusion" that essentially repeats the thesis statement as it was in paragraph one.

Here is an example in outline form:

Introduction: The food in the school cafeteria is bad. It lacks variety, it's unhealthy, and it is always overcooked. In this essay I will discuss these three characteristics.

Paragraph 2: The first reason cafeteria food is bad is that there is no variety. (Plus one or two examples—no salad bar, mostly fried food, etc.)

Paragraph 3: Another reason cafeteria food is bad is that it is not healthy. (Plus a few reasons—high cholesterol, too many hot dogs, too much sugar, etc.)

Paragraph 4: In addition, the food is always overcooked. (Plus some examples—the vegetables are mushy, the mystery meat is tough to recognize, etc.)

Conclusion: Thus, we see . . . (Plus a restatement of the introductory paragraph.)

Most high school students write dozens of themes using this basic formula. They are taught to use five-paragraph form because it seems to provide the greatest good—a certain minimal clarity—for the greatest number of students. But the form does not promote logically tight and thoughtful writing. It is a meat grinder that can turn any content into sausages.

The two major problems it typically creates are easy to see.

1. The introduction reduces the remainder of the essay to *redundancy*. The first paragraph tells readers, in an overly general and list-like way, what they're going to hear; the succeeding three paragraphs tell the readers the same thing again in more detail, carrying the overly general main idea along inertly; and the conclusion repeats what the readers have just been told (twice). The first cause of all this redundancy lies with the thesis. As in the preceding example, the thesis (cafeteria food is bad) is too broad—an unqualified and obvious generalization—and substitutes a simple list of predictable points for a complex statement of idea.

2. The form arbitrarily divides content: why are there three points (or examples or reasons) instead of five or one? A quick look at the three categories in our example reveals how arbitrarily the form has divided the subject. Isn't overcooked food unhealthy? Isn't a lack of variety also conceivably unhealthy? The format invites writers to list rather than analyze, to plug supporting examples into categories without examining them or how they are related. Five-paragraph form,

as is evident in our sample's transitions ("first," "second," and "in addition"), counts things off but doesn't make logical connections. At its worst, the form prompts the writer to simply append evidence to generalizations without saying anything about it.

The subject, on the other hand, is not as unpromising as the format makes it appear. It could easily be redirected along a more productive pathway. (If the food is bad, what are the underlying causes of the problem? Are students getting what they ask for? Is the problem one of cost? Is the faculty cafeteria better? Why or why not?)

Now let's look briefly at the introductory paragraph from a student's essay on a more academic subject. Here we can see a remarkable feature of five-paragraph form— its capacity to produce the same kind of say-nothing prose on almost any subject.

Throughout the film *The Tempest,* a version of Shakespeare's play *The Tempest*, there were a total of nine characters. These characters were Calibano, Alonso, Antonio, Aretha, Freddy, the doctor, and Dolores. Each character in the film represented a person in Shakespeare's play, but there were four people who were greatly similar to those in Shakespeare, and who played a role in symbolizing aspects of forgiveness, love, and power.

The final sentence of the paragraph reveals the writer's addiction to five-paragraph form. It signals that the writer will proceed in a purely mechanical and superficial way, producing a paragraph on forgiveness, a paragraph on love, a paragraph on power, and a conclusion stating again that the film's characters resemble Shakespeare's in these three aspects. The writer is so busy demonstrating that the characters are concerned with forgiveness, love, and power that he or she misses the opportunity to analyze the significance of his or her own observations. Instead, readers are drawn wearily to a conclusion; they get no place except back where they began. Furthermore, the demonstration mode prevents the writer from analyzing connections among the categories. The writer might consider, for example, how the play and the film differ in resolving the conflict between power and forgiveness (focusing on difference within similarity), and to what extent the film and the play agree about which is the most important of the three aspects (focusing on similarity despite difference).

These more analytical approaches lie concealed in the writer's introduction, but they are never discovered because the five-paragraph form militates against sustained analytical thinking. Its division of the subject into parts, which is only one part of analysis, has become an end unto itself. The procrustean formula insists upon a tripartite list in which each of the three parts is separate, equal, and above all, inert.

Here are two quick checks for whether a paper of yours has closed down your thinking through a scheme such as five-paragraph form:

1. *Look at the paragraph openings.* If these read like a list, each beginning with an additive transition like "another" followed by a more or less exact repetition of your central point (another example is ..., yet another example is ...), you should suspect that you are not adequately developing your ideas.

2. *Compare the wording in the last statement of the paper's thesis (in the conclusion) with the first statement of it in the introduction.* If the wording at these

two locations is virtually the same, you know that your thesis has not responded adequately to your evidence.

ANALYZING EVIDENCE IN DEPTH: 10 ON 1

The practice called 10 on 1 focuses analysis on a representative example. In doing 10 on 1 you are taking one part of the whole, putting it under a microscope, and then generalizing about the whole on the basis of analyzing a single part.

- The phrase 10 on 1 means ten observations and implications about one representative piece of evidence (10 is an arbitrary number meaning many.)
- The phrase 1 on 10 means one general point attached to 10 pieces of evidence.

As a guideline, 10 on 1 leads you to draw out as much meaning as possible from your best example—a case of narrowing the focus and then analyzing in depth. (See Figure 8.2.) Eventually you will move from this key example to others that usefully extend and qualify your point, but first you need to let analysis of your representative example produce more thinking.

You can use 10 on 1 to accomplish various ends: (1) to locate the range of possible meanings your evidence suggests, (2) to make you less inclined to cling to your

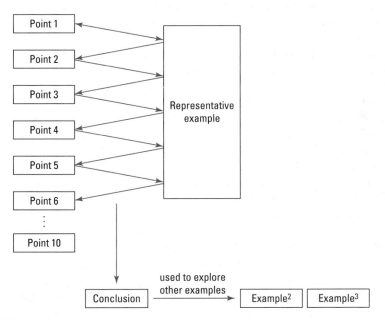

FIGURE 8.2
Doing 10 on 1 *The pattern of 10 on 1 (in which 10 stands arbitrarily for any number of points) successively develops a series of points about a single representative example. Its analysis of evidence is in depth.*

first claim, (3) to open the way for you to discover the complexity of your subject, and (4) to slow down the rush to generalization and thus help to ensure that when you arrive at a working thesis, it will be more specific and better able to account for your evidence.

Demonstrating the Representativeness of Your Example

Focusing on your single best example has the advantage of economy, cutting to the heart of the subject, but it runs the risk that the example you select might not in fact be representative. Thus, to be safe, you need to demonstrate its representativeness overtly. This means showing that your example is part of a larger pattern of similar evidence and not just an isolated instance. To establish that pattern it is useful to do 1 on 10—locating ten examples that share a trait—as a preliminary step, and then select *one* of these for in-depth analysis.

In terms of logic, the problem of generalizing from too little and unrepresentative evidence is known as an unwarranted inductive leap. The writer leaps from one or two instances to a broad claim about an entire class or category. Just because you see an economics professor and a biology professor wearing corduroy jackets, for example, you would not want to leap to the conclusion that all professors wear corduroy jackets. Most of the time, unwarranted leaps result from making too large a claim and avoiding examples that might contradict it.

10 on 1 and Disciplinary Conventions

In some cases, the conventions of a discipline appear to discourage doing 10 on 1. The social sciences in particular tend to require a larger set of analogous examples to prove a hypothesis. Especially in certain kinds of research, the focus of inquiry rests on discerning broad statistical trends over a wide range of evidence. But some trends deserve more attention than others, and some statistics similarly merit more interpretation than others. The best writers learn to choose examples carefully—each one for a reason—and to concentrate on developing the most revealing ones in depth.

For instance, proving that tax laws are prejudiced in particularly subtle ways against unmarried people might require a number of analogous cases along with a statistical summary of the evidence. But even with a subject such as this, you could still concentrate on some examples more than others. Rather than moving through each example as a separate case, you could use your analyses of these primary examples as lenses for investigating other evidence.

PAN, TRACK, AND ZOOM: USING 10 ON 1 TO BUILD A PAPER

How can 10 on 1 generate the form of a paper? The language of filmmaking offers a useful way for understanding the different ways that a writer can focus evidence. The writer, like the director of a film, controls the focus through different kinds of shots.

The pan—The camera pivots around a stable axis, giving the viewer the big picture. Using a pan, we see everything from a distance. Pans provide a context, some larger pattern, the "forest" within which the writer can also examine particular "trees." Pans establish the representativeness of the example the writer later examines in more detail, showing that it is not an isolated instance.

The track—The camera no longer stays in one place but follows some sequence of action. For example, whereas a pan might survey a room full of guests at a cocktail party, a track would pick up a particular guest and follow along as she walks across the room, picks up a photograph, proceeds through the door, and throws the photo in a trash can. Analogously, a writer tracks by moving in on selected pieces of the larger picture and following them to make telling connections among them.

The zoom—The camera moves in even closer on a selected piece of the scene, allowing us to notice more of its details. For example, a zoom might focus in on the woman's hand as she crumples the photograph she's about to throw away or on her face as she slams the lid on the trash can. A writer zooms in by giving us more detail on a particular part of his or her evidence and making the details say more. The zoom is the shot that enables you to do 10 on 1.

In a short paper (three to five pages), you might devote as much as 90 percent of your writing to exploring what one example (the 1—your zoom) reveals about the larger subject. Even in a paper that uses several examples, however, as much as 50 percent might still be devoted to analysis of and generalization from a single case. The remaining portion of the paper would make connections with other examples, testing and applying the ideas you arrived at from your single case. In-depth analysis of your best example thus creates a center from which you can move in two directions: (1) toward generalizations about the larger subject and (2) toward other examples, using your primary example as a tool of exploration.

This model, applicable across a wide variety of writing situations, can be reduced to a series of steps:

1. Use The Method or Notice and Focus to find a revealing pattern or tendency in your evidence. (See Chapter 3.)
2. Select a representative example.
3. Do 10 on 1 to produce an in-depth analysis of your example.
4. Test your results in similar cases.

Doing 10 on 1: A Brief Example (Tiananmen Square)

Note how the writer of the following discussion of the people's revolt in China in 1989 sets up his analysis. He first explains how his chosen example—a single photograph (shown in Figure 8.3) from the media coverage of the event—illuminates his larger subject. The image is of a Chinese man in a white shirt who temporarily halted a line of tanks on their way to quell a demonstration in Tiananmen Square in Beijing.

The tank image provided a miniature, simplified version of a larger, more complex revolution. The conflict between man and tank embodied the same tension found in the conflict between student demonstrators and the Peoples' Army. The man in the white shirt, like the students, displayed courage, defiance, and rebellious individuality in the face of power. Initially, the

©Jeff Widener/AP

FIGURE 8.3
Tiananmen Square, Beijing, 1989

peaceful revolution succeeded: the state allowed the students to protest; likewise, the tank spared the man's life. Empowered, the students' demands for democracy grew louder. Likewise, the man boldly jumped onto the tank and addressed the soldiers. The state's formerly unshakable dominance appeared weak next to the strength of the individual. However, the state asserted its power: the Peoples' Army marched into the square, and the tanks roared past the man into Beijing.

The image appeals to American ideology. The man in the white shirt personifies the strength of the American individual. His rugged courage draws on contemporary heroes such as Rambo. His defiant gestures resemble the demonstrations of Martin Luther King Jr. and his followers. American history predisposes us to identify strongly with the Chinese demonstrators: we have rebelled against the establishment, we have fought for freedom and democracy, and we have defended the rights of the individual. For example, *The New York Times* reported that President George [H. W.] Bush watched the tank incident on television and said, "I'm convinced that the forces of democracy are going to overcome these unfortunate events in Tiananmen Square." Bush represents the popular American perspective of the Chinese rebellion; we support the student demonstrators.

This analysis is a striking example of doing 10 on 1. In the first paragraph, the writer constructs a detailed analogy between the particular image and the larger subject of which it was a part. The analogy allows the writer not just to describe but also to interpret the event. In the second paragraph, he develops his focus on the image as an image, a photographic representation tailor-made to appeal to American viewing audiences. Rather than generalizing about why Americans might find the image appealing, he establishes a number of explicit connections (does 10 on 1) between the details of the image and typical American heroes. By drawing out the implications of particular details, he manages to say more about the significance of the American response to the demonstrations in China than a broader survey of those events would have allowed.

▇ Try this 8.1: *Doing 10 on 1 with Newspaper Visuals*

Search out photographs in the newspaper and do 10 on 1. Or alternatively, spend some time doing 10 on 1 on a comic strip. What perspectives emerge once you have restricted the focus? List details, but also list multiple implications. Remember to ask not just What do I notice? but What else do I notice? And not just What does it imply? but What else might it imply?

▇ Try this 8.2: *Doing 10 on 1 with a Reading*

Take a piece of reading—a representative example—from something you are studying and do 10 on 1. The key to doing 10 on 1 successfully is to slow down the rush to conclusions so that you can allow yourself to notice more about the evidence and make the details speak. The more observations you assemble about your data before settling on your main idea, the better that idea is likely to be. Remember that a single, well-developed paragraph from something you are reading can be enough to practice on, especially because you are working on saying more about less rather than less about more.

CONVERTING 1 ON 10 INTO 10 ON 1: A STUDENT PAPER (FLOOD STORIES)

The following student paper, about the recurrence of flood stories in religious texts and myth, shows what happens when a writer falls into doing 1 on 10. That is, rather than zooming in on representative examples to test and refine his ideas, he attaches the same underdeveloped point to each of his examples. Typical of the 1-on-10 pattern, the flood paper views everything from the same relatively unrevealing distance.

In the essay that follows, we have used boldface to track the "one" point—the as-yet-underdeveloped thesis idea—that the writer has attached to each of his examples (1 on 10). Brackets and ellipses [. . .] indicate where we have abridged the essay.

Flood Stories

[1] The **role of people,** as reflected in Genesis, Ovid's *Metamorphoses,* and the *Epic of Gilgamesh,* **is solely to please the gods.** Men, as the gods' subordinates, exist to do right in the gods' eyes **and make them feel more like gods;** for without men, whom could the gods be gods of? [. . .]

[2] In Genesis, for example, God created humans in his own image or likeness, and **when they displeased Him,** He destroyed them. If God could see wickedness in his creations, perhaps it was like seeing wickedness in himself. Further, the idea of having evidence of God being able to create an imperfect, "wicked" race of humans may have been a point God wasn't willing to deal with: "The Lord saw that the wickedness of man was great in the earth, and that every imagination of the thoughts of his heart was only evil continually. And the Lord was sorry that he had made man on the earth and it grieved

him to his heart." It seems as though **God had become unhappy with his creations** so they were to be destroyed. Like a toy a child no longer has use for, humankind was to be wasted.

[3]   Similarly, in Ovid's *Metamorphoses,* God made humanity and "fashioned it into the image of the all-governing gods." Again here, humans were made in the gods' image to serve as an everlasting monument of their glorification, to honor them and do good by them. In other words, **humans spent less time making the gods happy and therefore made them unhappy.** Some men even questioned the reality of the gods' existence and the strength of their power. Lyacon, for example, had a driving tendency to try to belittle the gods and make them look like fools. **The gods were very displeased** with this trend, and now the entire race had to be destroyed. A flood would be sent to wipe out the race of men. *[The writer then summarizes several examples in which the wicked are destroyed and a few upstanding citizens are preserved and arrives at the following conclusion.]* Thus, the justification of yet another flood to appease the gods' egos.

[4]   Further evidence of **humans as being a mere whim of the gods to make them happy** lies in the flood story in the *Epic of Gilgamesh.* It is obvious **the gods weren't concerned with humankind, but rather with their own comfort.** As the story goes, Enlil, the god of earth, wind, and air, couldn't bear the noise humans were making while he tried to sleep, so he gathered all the gods together, and thus they jointly decided to get rid of their grief of having all the humans around by destroying them. Ea [the god of wisdom], however, warned one man (Utnapishtim) of the flood to come. He told him to build a boat for himself and his wife and for the "seeds of all living creatures." [. . .]

[5]   Enlil later repented the harshness of his actions, deified Utnapishtim and his wife and then had the two live far away "on the distance of the rivers' mouths." It possibly **could have been belittling** to have Utnapishtim and his wife speaking to the new race of humans in terms of how rash and mindlessly the gods were capable of acting, so he immortalized them and had them live far out of the reach of human ears—"the secret of the gods."

[6]   It seems that the **main objective of the gods was to remain gods; for that is what made them happy. And humanity's role, then, was as the gods' stepping-stone to their happiness.** [. . .] Witnessing the fall of humankind, for the gods, was like witnessing imperfection in themselves, and thus their fall; anything causing these feelings didn't do the gods any good and therefore could be terminated without a second thought. **It was the job of human beings to make the gods happy,** and upon failure at this task, they could be "fired" (death), only to be replaced later—it wasn't a position which the gods could hold vacant for long. Thus were the great flood stories.

The essay starts with a pan on the "big picture." Panning on all three stories has allowed the writer to discover similarities among his blocks of evidence and to demonstrate that the examples he has chosen are representative of his generalization—his claim—that in all three flood stories men exist "solely to please the gods." The writer then constructs a series of tracks, summaries of each of the three stories that isolate some interesting parallels for readers to ponder. The problem is that, rather than allowing his tracks to set up zooms, the writer returns again and again to versions of his original pan. The result is a 1-on-10 paper in which the writer sees, in effect, only what he wants to see: opportunities to repeatedly match the evidence to his one governing claim.

What's wrong, one might ask, with showing how the evidence fits the claim? Isn't this what writers are supposed to do? The answer is that writers do want to use evidence to show that their claims have validity, but not in so general and redundant a way. As the final sentence of the essay demonstrates ("Thus were the great flood stories"), the writer never really arrives at a conclusion. To develop his central claim, the writer needs to devote much less space to repeating that claim, and more to actually looking at key pieces of evidence, zooming in on significant variations within the general pattern.

In his second paragraph, for example, the writer makes a claim about the God of Genesis that overlooks significant evidence. The claim is as follows: "God had become unhappy with his creations so they were to be destroyed. Like a toy a child no longer has use for, humankind was to be wasted." It is here that the writer allows the 1-on-10 pattern to rush his thinking and distract him from his evidence. The depiction of God as one who treats humans like toys may accurately describe Enlil, the god in *Gilgamesh* who, as we are later told, decides to get rid of humans because they make too much noise. But it does not so easily fit the God of Genesis, about whom the writer has just told us that "the wickedness of man . . . grieved him to his heart." Doesn't the grief that this evidence mentions suggest that God's decision to flood the earth was possibly ethical rather than childishly selfish and rash? And the statement from Genesis that "every imagination of the thoughts of [man's] heart was only evil continually" would seem to indicate that humans were not simply victims of divine prerogative, but rather that they deserved punishment.

The writer doesn't consider these other possible interpretations because his reliance on pans—the general pattern—has predisposed him to see his evidence only as another sign of the gods' egotism, their desire to remain happy at any cost. Pressed by the desire to match examples to his one governing idea, the writer is not allowing himself to really examine his evidence. Instead, he has attempted to squeeze that evidence into a pattern he has apparently superimposed from *Gilgamesh,* thereby neglecting potentially significant differences among his examples. Thus, he is not prepared to deal with potentially significant differences among his examples.

Revising the Draft Using 10 on 1 and Difference within Similarity

How might the writer make better use of the evidence he has collected, using the principle of looking for difference within similarity?

Revision Strategy 1. *Assume that the essay's answer—its conclusion about the evidence—does not yet go far enough.* Rather than having to throw out his thinking, the writer should consider, as is almost always the case in revision, that he hasn't refined his initial idea enough. As an interpretation of the evidence, it leaves too much unaccounted for.

Revision Strategy 2. *Find a "1" to use with 10 on 1—a piece of the evidence sufficiently revealing to be analyzed in more detail; then zoom in on it.* In the case of the writer of "Flood Stories," that 1 might be a single story, which he could examine in more detail. He could then test his claims about this story through comparison and contrast with the other stories. In the existing draft, the writer has not used comparison and contrast to refine his conclusion; he has just imposed the same conclusion on other stories. Alternatively, the 1 might be the single most interesting feature that the three stories share.

Revision Strategy 3. *To find the most revealing piece or feature of the evidence, keep asking, What can be said with some certainty about the evidence?* This question induces a writer to rehearse the facts to keep them fresh so that his or her first impressions don't "contaminate" or distort consideration of subsequent evidence.

If the writer were to apply these strategies, he might have a conversation with himself that sounded something like this:

"What can I say with some certainty about my evidence?"

"In all three of these stories, a first civilization created by a god is destroyed by the same means—a flood."

Notice that this is a factual description of the evidence rather than a speculation about it. You are always better off to report the facts in your evidence carefully and fully before moving to conclusions. (This is harder to do than you might think.)

"What else is certain about the evidence?"

"In each case the gods leave a surviving pair to rebuild the civilization rather than just wiping everybody out and inventing a new kind of being. Interestingly, the gods begin again by choosing from the same stock that failed the first time around."

Mulling over the evidence in this way, taking care to lay out the facts and distinguish them from speculation, can help you decide what evidence to zoom in on. One of the chief advantages of zooms is that they get you in close enough to your evidence to see the questions its details imply.

Revision Strategy 4. *Examine the evidence closely enough to see what questions the details imply and what other patterns they reveal.* So far, the writer has worked mostly from two quite general questions: Why did the gods decide to wipe out their creations? And why do the gods need human beings? But there are other questions his evidence might prompt him to ask. In each story, for example, the gods are disappointed by humankind, yet they don't invent submissive robots who will dedicate their lives to making the deities feel good about themselves. Why not? This question might cause the writer to uncover a shared feature of his examples (a pattern) that he has thus far not considered—the surviving pairs.

Revision Strategy 5. *Uncover implications in your zoom that can develop your interpretation further.* Having selected the surviving pairs for more detailed examination, what might the writer conclude about them? One interesting fact that the surviving pairs reveal is that the flood stories are not only descriptions of the end of a world but also creation accounts because they also tell us how a new civilization, the existing one, got started.

Revision Strategy 6. *Look for difference within similarity to better focus the thesis.* Given the recurrence of the survival pairs in the three stories, where might the writer locate a significant difference? One potentially significant difference involves the survival pair in the story of Gilgamesh, who are segregated from the new world and granted immortality. Perhaps this separation suggests that the new civilization will not be haunted by the painful memory of a higher power's intervention, leaving humans less fearful of what might happen in the future. This distinction could focus the argument in the essay; it does not distract from the writer's overall generalization but rather develops it.

Revision Strategy 7. *Constellate the evidence to experiment with alternative thesis options.* Notice how the hypothetical revision we've been producing has made use of looking for difference within similarity to explore alternative ways of connecting the evidence—a selected set of zooms—into an overall explanation. We call this activity constellating the evidence: like the imaginary lines that connect real stars into a recognizable shape, your thinking configures the examples into some larger meaning. In this case, instead of repeatedly concluding that the gods destroy humans when humans fail to make them happy, the writer might be on his way to a thesis about the relative optimism or skepticism of the way the flood stories represent change.

- Possible thesis #1: The flood stories propose the view that real change is necessarily apocalyptic rather than evolutionary.

- Possible thesis #2: The flood stories present qualified optimism about the possibility of new starts.

▬ **Try this 8.3:** *Describing Evidence*

Have a conversation with yourself (on paper) about some piece of evidence you are studying. Start with the question we proposed for the student writer of the flood stories essay: What can be said with some certainty about this evidence? What, in other words, is clearly true of the data? What can be reported as fact without going on to interpretation of the facts?

This distinction between fact and interpretation can be a tricky one, but it is also essential because if you can't keep your data separate from what you've begun to think about them, you risk losing sight of the data altogether. Press yourself to keep answering the same question—What can be said with some certainty about this evidence? or a variant of the question, such as What's clearly true of this evidence is . . .

You may find it helpful to do this exercise with a partner or in a small group. If you work in a small group, have one member record the results as these emerge. You might also try this exercise as a freewrite and then share your results with others by reading aloud your list of facts or putting them on a blackboard along with other people's results. Once you've assembled a list of what can fairly be stated as fact about your evidence, you are ready to start on some version of the question, What do these facts suggest? or What features of these data seem most to invite/require interpretation?

DOING 10 ON 1: A STUDENT PAPER *(GOOD BYE LENIN!)*

The following essay is an exploratory draft about a film, using a single scene to generate its thinking. As you read the essay, watch how the writer uses 10 on 1. Unlike "Flood Stories," in which the writer felt compelled to make all of his evidence fit a narrow thesis, here the writer repeatedly tests her tentative conclusions against the evidence until she arrives at a plausible *working thesis* that might organize the next draft.

Think of the working thesis as an ultimate So what?—the product of other, smaller interpretive leaps along the way. As we did in Chapter 4 we have written in the So what? prompt where the writer has used it to move from observation to implication to conclusions. Notice how the writer allows her evidence to complicate and stimulate her thinking rather than just confirm (corroborate) her general idea.

On the Edge: A Scene from *Good Bye Lenin!*

[1]   The movie shows us Alex and Lara's first date, which is to a sort of underground music club where the performers wear costumes made of plastic tubing and leather, and play loud hard-core rock music. At first, the musicians look surreal, as though they are part of a strange dream from which, at any moment, Alex will awake. The Western rock is real, though, as are the sci-fi costumes, and the scene moves forward to show Alex and Lara climbing a stairway out onto what looks like a fire escape and then through a window and into an apartment.

[2]   Here, Alex and Lara settle down into conversation. The young couple sits, hand in hand, and gazes together into the night sky; yet, as the camera pans away, we see that the apartment where the two have retreated is missing its façade. Inside, three walls are still decorated, complete with furniture, wallpaper, and even working lamps; yet, the two sit on the ledge of the fourth wall, which has crumbled away completely.

[3]   *[So what?]* On the surface, I think the movie invites us to read this as a visual representation of the new lives Alex, Lara, and the other characters face now that the wall has fallen. As a Westerner, at first I read this scene as a representation of the new relationship between Lara and Alex. In other words, I imagined the movie's placement of the couple on the ledge of a domestic space as a representation of where their lives were going together—toward some shared domestic life, toward living together, toward becoming a family. I also thought this was a clever representation of the collapse of communism—this wall has also fallen down.

[4]   *[Complicating evidence]* I don't think, however, that the movie lets us entertain this one romanticized reading of the scene for long—the image is too frightening. As the camera pans away, we see that this isn't a new Westernized apartment; this is an East German flat decorated in much the same way as Alex's home was only months before. The image is alarming; the wall here has been ripped down, *[So what?]* and we are

forced to ask, did the fall of communism violently blow apart domestic and daily living of East German people?

[5]   The movie allows us this dichotomy and, I think, fights to sustain it. On one hand, Alex and Lara would not be on this date if the wall hadn't come down, and yet the scene is more than just another representation of East Germany torn between Communism and the new Westernization. *[Working thesis]* The movie tries hard to remind us that the rapid Westernization of East Germany devastated while it liberated in other ways. This scene uses space to represent Alex and Lara's (and East Germany's) dilemma: Alex and Lara gaze out at the night sky but only because the wall has been blown apart. The exposed apartment is uninhabitable and yet the lights still work, the pictures are still hung, and a young couple leans against one another inside.

This draft is a really good example of a writer using evidence to complicate as well as support her claims. Her thinking evolves through successive complications; that is, she complicates a previous claim that was itself a complication. When the writer arrives at tentative answers, she tests them rather than just adding more evidence to prove that she is right.

■ **Try this 8.4:** *Marking Claims, Evidence, and Complications in a Draft*

As a check on the range of concepts that this and the previous chapter have introduced, mark the student draft as follows:

- *Mark claims—assertions made about the evidence—with the letter C.* Claims are ideas that the evidence seems to support. An example of a claim is in paragraph 4: "I don't think, however, that the movie lets us entertain this one romanticized reading of the scene for long."

- *Underline evidence.* The evidence is the pool of primary material (data)—details from the film, rather than the writer's ideas about it. An example of evidence is in paragraph 2: "The young couple sits, hand in hand, and gazes together into the night sky; yet, as the camera pans away, we see that the apartment where the two have retreated is missing its façade." This piece of evidence is the 1 of the 10 on 1. In effect, the whole draft goes after the range of possible implications that may be inferred from the image of the young couple sitting at the edge of an apartment that is missing one of its walls, presumably a result of war damage.

- *Circle complications.* Complications can be found both in the evidence a writer cites and in the claims a writer makes about it. Complicating evidence is evidence that does not fit the claims the writer has been making. For example, in paragraph 4: "As the camera pans away, we see that this isn't a new Westernized apartment; this is an East German flat decorated in much the same way as Alex's home was only months before. The image is alarming; the wall here has been ripped down." This evidence causes the writer to reconsider an earlier claim from paragraph 3, that the scene is about the couple moving "toward some shared domestic life, toward living together, toward becoming a family."

A TEMPLATE FOR ORGANIZING PAPERS USING 10 ON 1: AN ALTERNATIVE TO FIVE-PARAGRAPH FORM

Here is a template for writing papers using 10 on 1. It brings together much of the key terminology introduced in this chapter. Think of it not as a rigid format but as an outline for moving from one phase of your paper to the next. Unlike five-paragraph form, the template gives you room to think and to establish connections among your ideas.

1. In your introduction, start by noting (panning on) an interesting pattern or tendency you have found in your evidence. Explain what attracted you to it—why you find it potentially significant and worth looking at. This paragraph should end with a tentative theory (working thesis) about what this pattern or tendency might reveal or accomplish.

2. Zoom in on your representative example, some smaller part of the larger pattern and argue for the example's representativeness and usefulness in coming to a better understanding of your subject.

3. Do 10 on 1—analyze your representative example—sharing with your readers your observations (what you notice) and your tentative conclusions (answers to the So what? question). Then use complicating evidence to refine your claims.

4a. In a short paper you might at this point move to your conclusion, with its qualified, refined version of your thesis and brief commentary on what you've accomplished—that is, the ways in which your analysis has illuminated the larger subject.

4b. In a longer paper you would begin constellating—organizing the essay by exploring and elaborating the connections among your representative examples analyzed via 10 on 1. In the language of the film analogy, you would move from your initial zoom to another zoom on a similar case, to see the extent to which the thesis you evolved with your representative example needed further adjustment to better reflect the nature of your subject as a whole. This last move is a primary topic of our next chapter.

ASSIGNMENT: Writing a Paper Using 10 on 1

Write a paper in which you do 10 on 1 with a single representative example of something you are trying to think more carefully about. This could be a representative passage from a story or a representative story from a volume of stories by a single author. It could be a representative poem from a short volume of poetry or a representative passage from a nonfiction book or article. It could be a passage from a favorite columnist or a single representative song from a CD. It could be a single scene or moment or character from a film or play or other performance. It could be one picture or work of art that is representative of a larger exhibit.

Brainstorm your "1" on the page, making observations and asking So what? Draw out as much meaning as possible from your representative example. Go for depth. Then use this example as a lens for viewing similar examples. Use the template in the previous section as a model for organizing the paper.

CHAPTER 9

Making a Thesis Evolve

> If you think of an essay as an act of thinking, then the evolutions of the thesis record the history of your various changes in thinking as you confronted evidence.

THIS CHAPTER IS AT THE HEART of what we have to say about essay writing, especially about the function of thesis statements. The chapter argues that even in a final draft a thesis develops through successive complications; it doesn't remain static, as people tend to believe. Your ability to discover ideas and improve on them in revision, as we've argued in the preceding chapters, depends largely on your attitude toward evidence—on your ability to use it as a means of testing and developing your ideas rather than just (statically) confirming and reasserting them.

This chapter is built around two extended examples. The first demonstrates the process of finding and testing the adequacy of a thesis in an exploratory draft. The second shows how a thesis evolves in a later-stage piece of writing. Both use the chapter's primary strategy, six steps for making a thesis evolve. Like the template for organizing papers using 10 on 1 offered at the end of the previous chapter, the six steps guide writers to confront complicating evidence and use it to refine their claims.

WHAT A STRONG THESIS DOES

By way of definition, the thesis of an analytical paper is an idea about your subject, a theory that explains what some feature or features of your subject mean.

A strong thesis comes from carefully examining and questioning your subject to arrive at some point about its meaning that would not have been immediately obvious to your readers.

A weak thesis either makes no claim or makes a claim that does not need proving, such as a statement of fact or an opinion with which virtually all of your readers would most likely agree before reading your paper (for example, "Exercise is good for you").

There are two key concepts that this chapter will add to the discussions of evidence and thesis that occupy Chapters 7 and 8:

- First, a strong thesis moves, or in the language of this chapter's title, it evolves. To say that a thesis evolves is to say that it changes as a paper progresses; it is progressively reformulated.

- Second, the changes in the thesis are galvanized by its repeated encounters with evidence. Like an inert (unreactive) material, a weak thesis neither affects nor is affected by the evidence that surrounds it. By contrast, in nearly all good writing the thesis evolves by gaining in complexity, and thus, in accuracy as the paper progresses.

Weak thesis statements (poorly formulated and inadequately developed) are most easily detected not only by their repetitiveness, but by their predictability. The writer says the same thing again and again, drawing the same overgeneralized conclusion from each piece of evidence ("and so, once again we see that . . ."). As the discussion of the 1 on 10 approach to evidence in Chapter 8 illustrates, a thesis that functions as an inert formula closes down a writer's thinking rather than guiding and stimulating it.

Even in cases in which, in the practice of particular academic disciplines, the thesis itself cannot change, there is still movement between the beginning of the paper and the end. In the report format of the natural and social sciences, for example, the hypothesis as initially worded must be either confirmed or denied, but it still undergoes much conceptual development. Rather than simply being confirmed or rejected, its adequacy is considered from various angles, and alternatives are often proposed, along with alternative methodologies for testing the original hypothesis again.

The first step in finding a thesis is to recognize that one will not appear to you ready-made in the material you are analyzing. In other words, summarizing may help you to find an analytical thesis, but a restatement of some idea that is already clearly stated in your subject is not itself a thesis. The process of finding a thesis—an idea about the facts and ideas in your subject—begins only when you start to ask questions about the material, deliberately looking for a place where you detect some kind of problem to be solved.

Once you begin to ask questions, the evidence typically points in more than one direction. More often than not, when inexperienced writers face a situation in which evidence seems to be unclear or contradictory, they tend to make one of two unproductive moves: they either ignore the conflicting evidence, or they abandon the problem altogether and look for something more clear-cut to write about. Faced with evidence that complicates your thesis, the one thing not to do is run away. The complications you've encountered are an *opportunity* to make your thesis evolve, as the following example shows.

MAKING A THESIS EVOLVE: A BRIEF EXAMPLE (TAX LAWS)

The savvy writer actively seeks out complicating evidence, taking advantage of chances to bring out complications to make the thesis more fully responsive to evidence. Let's revisit a sample thesis from Chapter 5, "tax laws benefit the wealthy." If you were to seek out data that would complicate this overstated claim, you would soon encounter

FIGURE 9.1

Evolving Thesis Diagram   *A strong thesis evolves as it confronts and assimilates evidence; the evolved thesis may expand or restrict the original claim. The process may need to be repeated a number of times.*

evidence that would press you to make some distinctions that the initial formulation of this claim leaves obscure. You would need, for example, to distinguish different sources of wealth and then to determine whether all or just some wealthy taxpayers are benefited by tax laws.

Do people whose wealth comes primarily from investments benefit less (or more) than those whose wealth comes from high wages? Evidence might also lead you to consider whether tax laws, by benefiting the wealthy, also benefit other people indirectly. Both of these considerations would necessitate some reformulation of the thesis. By the end of the paper, the claim that tax laws benefit the wealthy would have evolved into a more carefully defined and qualified statement that would reflect the thinking you have done in your analysis of evidence. This, by and large, is what good concluding paragraphs do—they reflect back on and reformulate your paper's initial position in light of the thinking you have done about it. (See Figure 9.1.)

But, you might ask, isn't this reformulating of the thesis something a writer does before he or she writes the essay? Certainly some of it is accomplished in the early exploratory writing and note-taking stage. But your finished paper will necessarily do more than list conclusions. Your revision process will have weeded out various false starts and dead ends that you may have wandered into on the way to your finished ideas, but the main routes of your movement from a tentative idea to a refined and substantiated theory should remain visible for readers to follow. To an extent, all good writing reenacts the chains of thought that led you to your conclusions. (See the section Locating the Evolving Thesis in the Final Draft later in this chapter for further discussion of how much thesis evolution to include in your final draft.)

■ Try this 9.1: *Qualifying Overstated Claims*

Making a thesis evolve makes that thesis more accurate. To do so is almost always to qualify (limit) the claim. Using the model of inquiry in the treatment of the example "Tax laws benefit the wealthy," seek out complications in one of the overstated claims in the following list. These complications might include conflicting evidence (which you should specify) and questions about the meaning or appropriateness of key terms (which you should articulate). Illustrate a few of these complications and then reformulate the claim in language that is more carefully qualified and accurate.

Welfare encourages recipients not to work.

People who are religious are more moral than those who are not.

Herbal remedies are better than pharmaceutical ones.

The book is always better than the film.

Women are more sensitive than men.

We learn from the lessons of history.

THE RECIPROCAL RELATIONSHIP BETWEEN THESIS AND EVIDENCE: THE THESIS AS LENS

What we have said so far about the thesis does not mean that all repetition of ideas in an essay is bad or that a writer's concluding paragraph should have no reference to the way the paper began. One function of the thesis is to provide the connective tissue, so to speak, that holds together a paper's three main parts—beginning, middle, and end. Periodic reminders of your paper's thesis, its unifying idea, are essential for keeping both you and your readers on track.

As we've also argued, though, developing an idea requires more than repetition. It is in light of this fact that the analogy of thesis to connective tissue proves inadequate. A better way of envisioning how a thesis operates is to think of it as a camera lens. This analogy more accurately describes the relationship between the thesis and the subject it seeks to explain. Although the lens affects how we see the subject (which evidence we select, which questions we ask about that evidence), the subject we are looking at also affects how we adjust the lens.

Here is the principle that the camera lens analogy allows us to see: the relationship between thesis and subject is *reciprocal*. In good analytical writing, especially in the early, investigatory stages of writing and thinking, the thesis not only directs the writer's way of looking at evidence; the analysis of evidence should also direct and redirect (bring about revision of) the thesis. Even in a final draft, writers are usually fine-tuning their governing idea in response to their analysis of evidence. (See Figure 9.2.)

The enemy of good analytical writing is the fuzzy lens—imprecisely worded thesis statements. Very broad thesis statements, those that are made up of imprecise (fuzzy) terms, make bad camera lenses. They blur everything together and muddy important distinctions. If your lens is insufficiently focused, you are not likely to see much in your evidence. If you say, for example, that the economic situation today is bad, you will at least have some sense of direction, but the imprecise terms bad and economic situation don't provide you with a focus clear enough to distinguish significant detail in your evidence. Without significant detail to analyze, you can't develop your thesis,

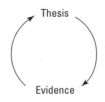

FIGURE 9.2

The Reciprocal Relationship between Thesis and Evidence   *Like a lens, the thesis affects the way a writer sees evidence. Evidence should also require the writer to readjust the lens.*

either by showing readers what the thesis is good for (what it allows us to understand and explain) or by clarifying its terms.

A writer's thesis is usually fuzzier in a paper's opening than it is in the conclusion. As we argued in our critique of five-paragraph form in Chapter 8, a paper ending with a claim worded almost exactly as it was in the beginning has not made its thesis adequately responsive to evidence. The body of the paper should not only substantiate the thesis by demonstrating its value in selecting and explaining evidence, but also bring the opening version of the thesis into better focus.

WHAT A GOOD THESIS STATEMENT LOOKS LIKE

One of the best and most common ways of bringing the thesis into focus is by pitting one possible point of view against another. Good ideas usually take place with the aid of some kind of back pressure, by which we mean that the idea takes shape by pushing against (so to speak) another way of seeing things. This is not the same as setting out to overturn and completely refute one idea in favor of another. In good thesis statements both ideas have some validity, but the forward momentum of the thesis comes from playing the preferred idea off the other one.

Look at the following two thesis statements, both taken from published essays.

- It may not seem like it, but "Nice Pants" is as radical a campaign as the original Dockers series.

- If opponents of cosmetic surgery are too quick to dismiss those who claim great psychological benefits, supporters are far too willing to dismiss those who raise concerns. Cosmetic surgery might make individual people happier, but in the aggregate it makes life worse for everyone.

Notice that there is tension in each, which results from the defining pressure of one idea against another potentially viable idea. In the first thesis sentence, for example, the primary idea is that the new advertising campaign for Dockers trousers is radical. The back pressure against which this idea takes shape is that this new campaign may not seem radical. The writer will demonstrate the truth of both of these claims, rather than overturning one and then championing the other.

The same can be said of the parts of the second thesis statement. One part of the thesis makes claims for the benefits of cosmetic surgery. The forward momentum of the thesis statement comes from the back pressure of this idea against the idea that cosmetic surgery will also make life worse for everyone. Notice that the thesis statement does not simply say, "Cosmetic surgery is bad." The writer's job is to demonstrate that the potential harm of cosmetic surgery outweighs the benefits, but the benefits won't be just summarily dismissed. Both of the two ideas are to some extent true. Neither idea, in other words, is "a straw man"—the somewhat deceptive argumentative practice of setting up a dummy position solely because it is easy to knock down. A straw man does not strengthen a thesis statement because it fails to provide genuine back pressure.

One final note: the tension between ideas in a thesis statement is frequently present as well in the sentence structure. You can more or less guarantee this necessary tension by starting your thesis statement with the word *although* or with the phrase "While it seems that " or with the "yes, but" or "if *X*, nonetheless *Y*" formulation.

■ **Try this 9.2:** *Spotting the Tension in Good Thesis Statements*

Find the tension in each of the following thesis statements. Decide which of the ideas is primary—the one you think the writer plans to support. Then locate the claim or claims in the thesis against which this primary claim will take shape.

1. Emphasis on the self in the history of modern thought may be an exaggeration, but the consequences of this vision of a self set apart have surely been felt in every field of inquiry.

2. We may join with the modern builders in justifying the violence of means—the sculptor's hammer and chisel—by appealing to ends that serve the greater good. Yet too often modern planners and engineers would justify the creative destruction of habitat as necessary for doubtful utopias.

3. The derogation of middlebrow, in short, has gone much too far. It's time to bring middlebrow out of its cultural closet, to hail its emollient properties, to trumpet its mending virtues. For middlebrow not only entertains, it educates—pleasurably training us to appreciate high art.

SIX STEPS FOR MAKING A THESIS EVOLVE

This is the central strategy of this chapter—a procedure not only for evolving a thesis but for shaping a draft. The remainder of the chapter offers two extended examples that apply the six steps. The first of these focuses on using the steps to find a thesis in an exploratory draft; the second focuses on how the thesis evolves as it encounters complicating evidence in a later draft. In both examples, you can see how the six steps build on the template for organizing papers using 10 on 1 that was offered at the end of Chapter 8. Both procedures use complicating evidence to refine claims. The template emphasizes moving to and from the analysis of a single representative example; the six steps offer a way of repeatedly testing the match between thesis and evidence. The former emphasizes evidence, the latter, thesis.

Here are the steps:

1. Formulate an idea about your subject. This working thesis should be some claim about the meaning of your evidence that is good enough to get you started.

2. See how far you can make this thesis go in accounting for evidence. Use the thesis to explain as much of your evidence as it reasonably can. Try it on.

3. Locate evidence that is not adequately accounted for by the thesis. You will need to look actively for such evidence because the initial version of the thesis will incline you to see only what fits and not to notice the evidence that doesn't fit.

4. Make explicit the apparent mismatch between the thesis and selected evidence. Explain how and why some pieces of evidence do not fit the thesis.

5. Reshape your claim to accommodate the evidence that hasn't fit. This will mean rewording your thesis to resolve or explain apparent contradictions.

6. Repeat steps 2, 3, 4, and 5 several times, until you are satisfied that the thesis statement accounts for your evidence as fully and accurately as possible. This is to say that the procedure for making a thesis evolve is recursive: it requires you to go over the same ground repeatedly, formulating successive versions of the thesis that are increasingly accurate in wording and idea.

As an overarching guideline, *acknowledge the questions that each new formulation of the thesis prompts you to ask.* The thesis develops through successive complications. Allowing your thesis to run up against potentially conflicting evidence ("but what about this?") enables you to build upon your initial idea, extending the range of evidence it can accurately account for by clarifying and qualifying its key terms.

EVOLVING A THESIS IN AN EXPLORATORY DRAFT: A STUDENT DRAFT ON *LAS MENINAS*

The example is a student writer's exploratory draft on a painting called *Las Meninas* (Spanish for "the ladies-in-waiting") by the seventeenth-century painter Diego Velázquez. We have, by the way, selected a paper on a painting because all of the student's data (the painting) is on one page where you can keep referring back to it, trying to share in the writer's thought process. The method of analysis used here will, however, work with anything, print or nonprint.

Look at the painting in Figure 9.3, and then read the student's draft. As you read, you will notice that much of the essay consists of list-like description, which leaves it somewhat unfocused. But careful description is a necessary stage in moving toward interpretations of evidence, especially in an exploratory draft in which the writer is not yet committed to any single position. Notice how the writer's word choice in her descriptions prompts various kinds of interpretive leaps. We have added in brackets our observations about how the writer's thinking is proceeding, and we have used underlining to track her various attempts at formulating a thesis.

As should be clear, we have incorporated into the six steps several of the observation and interpretation strategies from Unit I, especially Notice and Focus, The Method, Interesting and Strange from Chapter 3, A Toolkit or Analytical Methods; and So what? from Chapter 4, Interpretation: What It Is, What It Isn't, and How to Do It.

Velázquez's Intentions in *Las Meninas*

[1] Velázquez has been noted as being one of the best Spanish artists of all time. It seems that as Velázquez got older, his paintings became better. Toward the end of his life, he painted his masterpiece, *Las Meninas*. Out of all his works, *Las Meninas* is the only known self-portrait of Velázquez. There is much to be said about *Las Meninas*. <u>The painting is very complex, but some of the intentions that Velázquez had in painting *Las Meninas* are very clear.</u> *[The writer opens with background information and a broad working thesis (underlined).]*

SCALA/Art Resource, NY. Diego Rodrigues Velázquez. Las Meninas. 1656.

FIGURE 9.3
Las Meninas by Diego Velázquez, 1656   *Approximately 10′5″ × 9′. Museo del Prado, Madrid.*

[2]   First, we must look at the painting as a whole. The question that must be answered is, Who is in the painting? The people are all members of the Royal Court of the Spanish monarch Philip IV. In the center is the king's daughter, who eventually became Empress of Spain. Around her are her *meninas* or ladies-in-waiting. These *meninas* are all daughters of influential men. To the right of the *meninas* are dwarfs who are servants, and the family dog who looks fierce but is easily tamed by the foot of the little child. The more unique people in the painting are Velázquez himself, who stands to the left in front of a large canvas; the king and queen, whose faces are captured in the obscure mirror; the man in the doorway; and the nun and man behind the *meninas*. To analyze this painting further, the relationship between characters must be understood. *[The writer describes the evidence and arrives at an operating assumption— focusing on the relationship among characters.]*

[3]   Where is this scene occurring? Most likely it is in the palace. But why is there no visible furniture? Is it because Velázquez didn't want the viewers to become distracted from his true intentions? I believe it is to show that this is not just a painting of an actual event. This is an event out of his imagination. *[The writer begins pushing observations to tentative conclusions by asking So what?]*

[4]   Now, let us become better acquainted with the characters. The child in the center is the most visible. All the light is shining on her. <u>Maybe Velázquez is suggesting that she is the next light for Spain</u> and that even God has approved her by shining all the available light on her. Back in those days there was a belief in the divine right of kings, so this just might be what Velázquez is saying. *[The writer starts ranking evidence for importance and continues to ask, So what?; she arrives in the underlined sentence at a possible interpretation of the painter's intention.]*

[5]   The next people of interest are the ones behind the *meninas*. The woman in the habit might be a nun and the man a priest.

[6]   The king and queen are the next group of interesting people. They are in the mirror, which is to suggest they are present, but they are not as visible as they might be. Velázquez suggests that they are not always at the center where everyone would expect them to be. *[The writer continues using Notice and Focus and asking So what?; the writer has begun tackling evidence that might conflict with her first interpretation.]*

[7]   The last person and the most interesting is Velázquez. He dominates the painting along with the little girl. He takes up the whole left side along with his gigantic easel. But what is he painting? As I previously said, he might be painting the king and queen. But I also think he could be pretending to paint us, the viewers. The easel really gives this portrait an air of mystery because Velázquez knows that we, the viewers, want to know what he is painting. *[The writer starts doing 10 on 1 with her selection of the most significant detail.]*

[8]   The appearance of Velázquez is also interesting. His eyes are focused outward here. They are not focused on what is going on around him. It is a steady stare. Also interesting is his confident stance. He was confident enough to place himself in the painting of the royal court. <u>I think that Velázquez wants the king to give him the recognition he deserves by including him in the "family."</u> And the symbol on his vest is the symbol given to a painter by the king to <u>show that his status and brilliance have been appreciated by the monarch.</u> It is unknown how it got there. It is unlikely that Velázquez put it there himself. That would be too outright, and Velázquez was the type to give his messages subtly. Some say that after Velázquez's death, King Philip IV himself painted it to finally <u>give Velázquez the credit he deserved for being a loyal friend and servant.</u> *[The writer continues doing 10 on 1 and asking So what?; she arrives at three tentative theses (underlined).]*

[9]   I believe that Velázquez was very ingenious by putting his thoughts and feelings into a painting. He didn't want to offend the king who had done so much for him. It paid off for Velázquez because he did finally get what he wanted, even if it was after he died. *[The writer concludes and is now ready to redraft to tighten links between evidence and claims, formulate a better working thesis, and make this thesis evolve.]*

Characteristics of an Exploratory Draft

Although its thinking is still underdeveloped, this version of the student's paper is a good exploratory draft. The writer has begun to interpret details and draw plausible conclusions from what she sees, rather than just describing (summarizing) the scene depicted on the canvas or responding loosely to it with her unanalyzed impressions.

The paper is typical of an early draft in several ways:

- It is written more for the writer as a form of inquiry than for readers. The writer reports her thoughts as they occur, but she doesn't always explain how she arrived at them or how they connect to each other.

- A recognizable thesis doesn't emerge until near the end (in paragraph 8), probably at the point where the writer became able to formulate the idea her evidence has directed her to.

- The paper contains more than one potential thesis, ideas that are related but still inadequately connected. The writer appears not to be sufficiently aware that there are different ideas competing for control of the paper.

- The paper ignores the conflict between its various theses and some of its evidence.

- The writer tends to end paragraphs with promising observations and then walk away, leaving the observations undeveloped. Rather than draw out the implications of her observations, she halts her thinking too soon in order to move on to the next piece of evidence. As we illustrate later, the writer can remedy this problem by querying her observations with the question So what?

- Typically, first drafts contain undeveloped observations because they are not organized in a way that allows for development. See, for example, this writer's repeated return to paragraph openings using "next" and "also," which traps her into listing parallel examples rather than building connections among them. As a rule, the use of these terms (and "another") at points of transition traps writers in repetition, preventing them from seeing opportunities to advance their ideas. (See What's Wrong with Five-Paragraph Form? in Chapter 8.)

The purpose of the exploratory draft is to use writing as a means of arriving at a working thesis that your next draft can more fully evolve. Most writers find that potential theses emerge near the end of the exploratory draft—which is the case in the student draft (see the three claims that are underlined in paragraph 8).

What is especially good about the draft is that it reveals the writer's willingness to push on from her first idea (reading the painting as an endorsement of the divine right of kings, expressed by the light shining on the princess) by seeking out complicating evidence. This first idea does not account for enough of the evidence and is undermined by evidence that clearly doesn't fit, such as the small size and decentering of the king and queen, and the large size and foregrounding of the painter himself.

Rather than ignoring these potentially troublesome details, the writer instead zooms in on them, making the painter's representation of himself and of his employers the 1 for doing 10 on 1 (making a number of observations about a single representative piece of evidence and analyzing it in depth).

Now what? The writer is ready to rewrite the paper in order to choose and better define her thesis. She might first wish to step back a bit from her initial formulations by using The Method to again survey the details of the painting, looking for patterns of repetition and contrast.

Examples of exact or nearly exact *repetitions:*

The pictures in the background

The fact that both the dwarf and the painter, each on his own side of the painting, stare confidently and directly at the viewer

Examples of *strands* (repetition of the same or similar kind of detail):

Details having to do with family

Servants: dwarf, *meninas,* dog? painter?

Details having to do with art and the making of art: easel, brush, paintings on wall

Examples of organizing *contrasts*—binaries:

Royalty/commoners

Employers/servants

Large/small

Foreground/background

Central (prominent)/marginalized (less prominent)

Having used The Method to see the evidence anew, the writer would be ready to try the six steps for making the thesis evolve. She'd begin by noticing that, as is the case in most exploratory drafts, she has several potential thesis statements vying for control of the paper.

Applying the Six Steps to the Draft on *Las Meninas*

Step 1. Formulate a working thesis.

As a general rule, you should *assume the presence of multiple, often competing theses,* some of which you may not have yet detected. In the *Las Meninas* paper, as is often the case in early drafts, no single idea emerges clearly as the thesis. Instead, we get three related but not entirely compatible ideas vying for control of the paper (all in paragraph 8):

"I think that Velázquez wants the king to . . ."

Thesis 1: Give Velázquez "the recognition he deserves by including him in the 'family'."

Thesis 2: "[S]how that his [Velázquez's] status and brilliance [as an artist] have been appreciated."

Thesis 3: Give Velázquez "the credit he deserved for being a loyal friend and servant."

These three ideas about the painter's intentions could be made to work together, but at present the writer is left with an uneasy fit among them.

Step 2. See how far you can make each thesis go in accounting for evidence.

Each of the three potential thesis ideas explains some of the evidence. The writer should try on each one to see what it helps to explain.

Thesis 1: Painting as bid for inclusion in the family

Evidence: The painter's inclusion of himself with the family—the king, queen, and princess—in a fairly domestic scene

Thesis 2: Painting as bid for appreciation of painter's status and brilliance as an artist

Evidence: Prominence of easel and brush and painter himself in the painting; painter's confident stare and the apparent decentering of king and queen; painting set in artist's studio—his space

Thesis 3: Painting as bid for credit for being loyal friend and servant

Evidence: Painter's location of himself among other loyal servants at court (ladies in waiting, dog, and large dwarf)

Step 3. Locate evidence that is not adequately accounted for by each thesis.

Step 4. Make explicit the apparent mismatch between the thesis and selected evidence.

What happens when the writer begins to search for evidence that doesn't seem to be adequately accounted for by her various thesis formulations?

Thesis 1: Painting as bid for inclusion in the family

Evidence mismatches: Presence of painter among servants; foregrounding of servants in image and in painting's title *(The Ladies in Waiting)*—painter's large size (larger than king and queen) does not go with the idea of inclusion, and emphasis on servants does not go with inclusion in royal family

Thesis 2: Painting as bid for appreciation of painter's status and brilliance as an artist

Evidence mismatches: Prominence of other servants in the painting; emphasis on family as much as or more than on artist himself; if bidding for status, painter would not present himself as just one of the servants, nor might he give so much attention to the princess (and the king and queen's regard for her)

Thesis 3: Painting as bid for credit for being loyal friend and servant

Evidence mismatches: Painter's prominence; his confident stare; prominence of easel and brush; small size of king and queen (smaller than servants)—if painter wished to emphasize loyalty and service, his subordinate relationship to the more powerful at court, he would have made himself and the tools of his trade less important

Step 5. Choose the claim that seems to account for the most evidence and then re-shape that claim to better accommodate evidence that doesn't fit.

When you've found conflicting or inadequately explained evidence, try using it to evolve your existing thesis rather than beating a too-hasty retreat. The direction in which the writer's thinking is moving—that the painting asks for someone's strengths to be recognized—is not an entirely new start. The shift she is apparently making but not yet overtly articulating is from the painting as showcase of royal power to the painting as showcase of the painter's own power.

To better formulate this claim, the writer should query what she is emphasizing as the primary feature of her evidence: size, especially that of the king and queen versus the painter. She could do this by pushing her thinking with the question *So what?*

- *So what* that the king and queen are small, but the painter, princess, and dwarf (another servant) are all large and fairly equal in size and/or prominence?
- *So what* that there are size differences in the painting? What might large or small size mean?

Here are possible answers to the *So what?* questions:

- Perhaps the relative size and/or prominence of figures in the painting can be read as indicators of their importance or of what the painter wants to say about their importance.
- Perhaps the king and queen have been reduced so that Velázquez can showcase their daughter, the princess.
- Perhaps the size and physical prominence of the king and queen are relatively unimportant. In that case, what matters is that they are a presence, always over-seeing events (an idea implied but not developed by the writer in paragraph 6).
- Perhaps the painter is demonstrating his own ability to make the king and queen any size—any level of importance—he chooses. Although the writer does not overtly say so, the king and queen are among the smallest as well as the least visible figures.

Given these answers to the *So what?* questions, the writer should probably choose thesis 2—that the painting is a bid for recognition of the painter's status and brilliance as an artist—because this thesis explains more of the evidence than anything else the writer has come up with so far. It explains, for example, the painter's prominence and the relative insignificance of the monarchs: that the painter, in effect, creates their stature (size, power) in the world through his paintings. Framed in a mirror and appearing to hang on the wall, the king and queen are, arguably, suspended among the painter's paintings, mere reflections of themselves—or, rather, the painter's reflection of them.

Step 6. Repeat steps 2 through 5 as necessary.

The writer would probably want to concentrate on repeating Step 2, seeing how far she can go in making her revised thesis account for additional evidence.

Thesis: painting as bid for appreciation of painter's status and brilliance as an artist

Step 2 repeated. See how far you can make each thesis go in accounting for evidence.

Evidence:

- If the painter is demonstrating that he can make the members of the royal family any size he wants, then the painting not only is a bid for recognition but also can be seen as a playful though not-so-subtle threat: be aware of my power and treat me well, or else suffer the consequences. As artist, the painter decides how the royal family will be seen. The king and queen depend on the painter, as they do in a different way on the princess, with whom Velázquez makes himself equal in prominence, to extend and perpetuate their power.

- In subverting viewers' expectations both by decentering the monarchs and concealing what is on the easel, the painter again emphasizes his power, in this case, over the viewers (among whom might be the king and queen if their images on the back wall are mirror reflections of them standing, like us, in front of the painting). He is not bound by their expectations and in fact appears to use those expectations to manipulate the viewers: he can make them wish to see something he has the power to withhold.

- The large dwarf in the right-hand foreground is positioned in a way that links him with the painter. The dwarf arguably furthers the painting's message and does so, like much else in the painting, in the form of a loaded joke: the small ("dwarfed" by the power of others) are brought forward and made big.

Knowing When to Stop: How Much Revising Is Enough?

We emphasize before leaving this example that the version of the thesis that we have just proposed is not necessarily the "right" answer. Looked at in a different context, the painting might have been explained primarily as a demonstration of the painter's mastery of the tools of his trade—light, for example, and perspective. But our proposed revision of the thesis for the *Las Meninas* paper meets two important criteria for evaluating thesis statements:

1. It unifies the observations the writer has made.
2. It is capable of accounting for a wide range of evidence.

The writer has followed through on her original desire to infer Velázquez's intentions in the painting. As we argued in Chapter 4 (Interpretation: What It Is, What It Isn't, and How to Do It), whether or not Velázquez consciously intended to make his painting a tongue-in-cheek self-advertisement, there is clearly enough evidence to claim plausibly that the painting can be understood in this way.

How do you know when you've done enough reformulating of your thesis and arrived at the best possible idea about your evidence? Getting the thesis to account for (respond to) all rather than just some of your evidence does not mean that you need to discuss every detail of the subject. Writers (rather like trial lawyers) must take care not to ignore important evidence, especially if it would alter their "case," but no analysis can address everything—nor should it. Your job as a writer is to select those features of your subject that seem most significant and to argue for their significance. An analysis says to readers, in effect, "These are the details that best reveal the nature and meaning of my subject, or at least the part of the subject that I am trying to address."

EVOLVING A THESIS IN A LATER-STAGE DRAFT: THE EXAMPLE OF *EDUCATING RITA*

In this chapter's final example we again apply the six steps, but in this case we are using them to make a thesis evolve within the draft, rather than to select among various as yet unformed competitors for the role of thesis (as was the case with *Las Meninas*). The process of thesis evolution that we trace here would remain visible in the writer's final draft as a means of sharing her thought processes with her readers. By contrast, the writer of *Las Meninas* would probably not include in her final draft the competition among her three potential thesis statements—only the evolution of the "winning" one.

In the film *Educating Rita,* a working-class English hairdresser (Rita) wants to change her life by taking courses from a professor (Frank) at the local university, even though this move threatens her relationship with her husband (Denny), who burns her books and pressures her to quit school and get pregnant. Frank, she discovers, has his own problems: he's a divorced alcoholic who is bored with his life, bored with his privileged and complacent students, and bent on self-destruction. The film follows the growth of Frank and Rita's friendship and the changes it brings about in their lives. By the end of the film, each has left a limiting way of life behind and has set off in a seemingly more promising direction. She leaves her constricting marriage, passes her university examinations with honors, and begins to view her life in terms of choices; he stops drinking and sets off, determined but sad, to make a new start as a teacher in Australia.

Step 1. Formulate an idea about your subject, a working thesis.

> *Working thesis: Educating Rita* celebrates the liberating potential of education.

The film's relatively happy ending and the presence of the word *educating* in the film's title make this thesis a reasonable opening claim.

Step 2. See how far you can make this thesis go in accounting for evidence.

The working thesis seems compatible, for example, with Rita's achievement of greater self-awareness and independence. She becomes more articulate, which allows her to free herself from otherwise disabling situations. She starts to think about other kinds of work she might do, rather than assuming that she must continue in the one job she has always done. She travels, first elsewhere in England and then to the Continent. So the thesis checks out as viable: there is enough of a match with evidence to stick with and evolve it.

Steps 3 and 4. Locate evidence that is not adequately accounted for by the thesis, and ask So what? about the apparent mismatch between the thesis and selected evidence.

Some evidence reveals that the thesis as stated is not the whole picture. Rita's education causes her to become alienated from her husband, her parents, and her social class; at the end of the film she is alone and unsure about her direction in life.

In Frank's case, the thesis runs into even more problems. His boredom, drinking, and alienation seem to have been caused, at least in part, by his education rather than by his lack of it. He sees his book-lined study as a prison, not a site of liberation. Moreover, his profound knowledge of literature has not helped him control his life: he comes to class drunk, fails to notice or care that his girlfriend is having an affair with one of his colleagues, and asks his classes whether it is worth gaining all of literature if it means losing one's soul.

Step 5. Reshape your claim to accommodate the evidence that hasn't fit.

The idea that the film celebrates the liberating potential of education still fits a lot of significant evidence. Rita is arguably better off at the end of the film than at the beginning: we are not left to believe that she should have remained resistant to education, like her husband, Denny, whose world doesn't extend much beyond the corner pub. But the thesis also leaves some significant evidence unaccounted for. So the writer would need to bring out the complicating evidence—the film's seemingly contradictory attitudes about education—and then modify the wording of the thesis in a way that might resolve or explain these contradictions.

Education as represented by the film seems to be of two kinds: enabling and stultifying. The next step in the development of the thesis would be to elaborate on how the film seeks to distinguish enabling forms of education from debilitating ones (as represented by the self-satisfied and status-conscious behavior of the supposedly educated people at Frank's university).

Perhaps this difference is what the film is primarily interested in, not just education's potential to liberate.

Revised thesis: Educating Rita celebrates the liberating potential of enabling—in contrast to stultifying—education.

Step 6. Repeat steps 2 through 5.

Having refined the thesis in this way, the writer would then repeat the step of seeing what the new wording allows him or her to account for in the evidence. The revised thesis would foreground a contest in the film between two different kinds of and attitudes toward education. This thesis as lens would cause us to see Frank's problems as being less a product of his education than of the cynical and pretentious versions of education that surround him in his university life. It would also explain the film's emphasis on Frank's recovery of at least some of his idealism about education, for which Rita has provided the inspiration.

What else does this revised thesis account for in the evidence? What about Frank's emigration to Australia? If we can take Australia to stand for a newer world, one where education would be less likely to become the stale and exclusive property of a self-satisfied elite, then the refined version of the thesis would seem to be working well. In fact, given the possible thematic connection between Rita's working-class identity and Australia (associated, as a former frontier and English penal colony, with lower-class vitality as opposed to the complacency bred of class privilege), the thesis about the film's celebration of the contrast between enabling and stultifying forms of education could be sharpened further. It might be proposed, for example, that the film presents institutional education as desperately in need of frequent doses of "real life" (as represented by Rita and Australia)—infusions of working-class pragmatism, energy, and optimism—if it is to remain healthy and open, as opposed to becoming the oppressive property of a privileged social class. This is to say that the film arguably exploits stereotypical assumptions about social class.

> *Revised thesis: Educating Rita* celebrates the liberating potential of enabling education, defined as that which remains open to healthy doses of working-class, real-world infusions.

Steps 3 and 4 repeated. Locate evidence not adequately accounted for and ask So what?

At the end of the film, Frank and Rita walk off in opposite directions down long, empty airport corridors. Though promising to remain friends, the two do not become a couple. This closing emphasis on Frank's and Rita's alienation from their respective cultures, and the film's apparent insistence on the necessity of each going on alone, significantly qualifies the happiness of the "happy ending."

Having complicated the interpretation of the ending, the writer would again need to modify the thesis in accord with new observations. Does the film simply celebrate education if it also presents it as being, to some degree, incompatible with conventional forms of happiness? By emphasizing the necessity of having Frank and Rita each go on alone, the film may be suggesting that to be truly liberating, education—as opposed to its less honest and more comfortable substitutes—inevitably produces and even requires a certain amount of loneliness and alienation. Shown in Figure 9.4 are the successive revisions of the thesis.

Repeat Step 5. Reshape the claim.

> *Final version of thesis: Educating Rita* celebrates the liberating potential of enabling education (kept open to real-world, working-class energy) but also acknowledges its potential costs in loneliness and alienation.

Note: this last version of the thesis is the one that would appear in the writer's final paragraph, the product of qualifying and refining the paper's claim by repeatedly confronting and assimilating complicating evidence. In effect, the six steps have produced a reasonably complete draft in outline form.

▆ Try this 9.3: *Tracking a Thesis*

As should be clear now, various versions of the thesis recur throughout a piece of writing, usually with increasing specificity, complication, and grammatical complexity. The four evolutions of the thesis statement on *Educating Rita* illustrate this pattern of recurrence clearly. One of the best ways to teach yourself how and where to locate statements of the thesis in your own writing is to track the thesis in a piece of reading. Use a highlighter to mark the evolutions. Where in the essay do you find the thesis? How has it changed in each recurrence? In response to what complication?

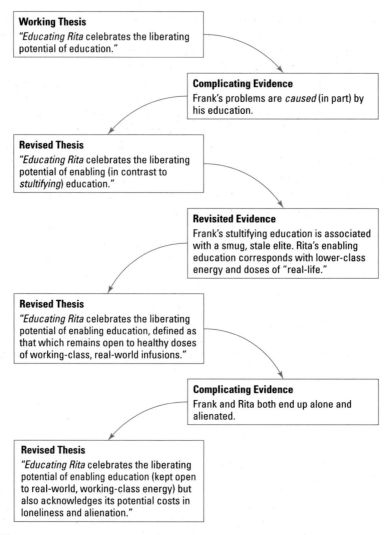

FIGURE 9.4

Successive Revisions of a Thesis   *An initial thesis about* Educating Rita *evolves through successive complications as it reexamines evidence in the film.*

LOCATING THE EVOLVING THESIS IN THE FINAL DRAFT

Having achieved a final version of a thesis, what next? Why wouldn't a writer just relocate the last and fullest statement of the thesis to his or her first paragraph and then prove it?

Usually it's neither possible nor desirable to encapsulate in the opening sentences what it will take the whole paper to explain. The position articulated in the fully evolved thesis is typically too complex to be stated intelligibly and concisely in the introduction. If you approach an essay as an act of thinking, then the evolutions of the thesis record the history of your various changes in thinking as you encounter evidence. If your readers get to see these, they are far more likely to go along with you, literally to follow your train of thought. Rather than imposing your conclusions, you are sharing your thought process with the reader, which is what good writing does.

Normally, you lead (usually at the end of the first paragraph or at the beginning of the second) with the best version of your thesis that you can come up with that will be understandable to your readers without a lengthy preamble. If you find yourself writing a page-long introductory paragraph to get to your initial statement of thesis, try settling for a simpler articulation of your central idea in its first appearance.

The first paragraph does not need to—and usually can't—offer your conclusion; it will take the body of your paper to accomplish that. It should, however, provide a quick look at particular details that set up the issue. Use these details to generate a theory, a working hypothesis, about whatever it is you think is at stake in the material. The rest of the paper tests and develops this theory.

The *Educating Rita* paper might open, for example, by using a version of the Seems-to-Be-about-*X* gambit (see Chapter 4), claiming that at first glance the film seems to celebrate the liberating potential of education. You could then lay out the evidence for this view and proceed to complicate it in the ways we've discussed.

Your concluding paragraph should offer the more carefully qualified and evolved version of your thesis that the body of your paper has allowed you to arrive at. Rather than just summarize and restate what you said in your introduction, the concluding paragraph leaves readers with what you take to be your single best insight. It should put what you have had to say into some kind of perspective. See Chapter 10 for a more extended discussion of organizational issues.

VOICES FROM ACROSS THE CURRICULUM

Recognizing Your Thesis

For an analytical or interpretive historical essay, *thesis* is a conventional term and one of much value. The thesis usually is that point of departure from the surfaces of evidence to the underlying significance, or problems, a given set of sources reveal to the reader and writer. In most cases, the thesis is best positioned up front, so that the writer's audience has a sense of what lies ahead and why it is worth reading on. I say *usually* and *in most cases* because the hard and fast rule should not take precedence over the inspirational manner in which a thesis can be presented. But the inspiration is not to be sought after at the price of the thesis itself. It is my experience, in fact, that if inspiration strikes, one realizes it only after the fact.

Recognizing a thesis can be extremely difficult. It can often be a lot easier to talk "about" what one is writing than to say succinctly what the thrust of one's discussion is. I sometimes ask students to draw a line at the end of a paper after they have finished it, and then write one, at most two sentences, saying what they most want to tell their readers. My comment on that post-script frequently is "Great statement of your thesis. Just move it up to your first paragraph where it could begin to develop."

—Ellen Poteet, *Professor of History*

ASSIGNMENT: Using the Six Steps for Making a Thesis Evolve

The chapter has modeled use of the six steps with a painting and a film. You could select one of these forms. Alternatively, you might use an episode of a television show or an advertisement or, for that matter, any subject that lends itself to fruitful analytical scrutiny.

Begin by formulating a variety of possible statements about the film or painting that could serve as a working thesis. These might be in answer to the question, What is the film/painting about? or What does it "say"? Or you might begin by using The Method to locate patterns of repetition and contrast and formulate a thesis to explain a pattern you have observed. In any case, you shouldn't worry that these initial attempts will inevitably be overstated and thus only partially true—you have to start somewhere. At this point you have completed step 1.

Then follow the remainder of the six steps for making the thesis evolve, listed again here in abbreviated form:

1. Formulate an idea about your subject, a working thesis.

2. See how far you can make this thesis go in accounting for evidence.

3. Locate evidence that is not adequately accounted for by the thesis.

4. Make explicit the apparent mismatch between the thesis and selected evidence, asking and answering So what?

5. Reshape your claim to accommodate the evidence that hasn't fit.

6. Repeat steps 2 through 5 several times.

Aim for a reasonably polished draft of four to six pages.

CHAPTER 10

Structuring the Paper: Forms and Formats

As NOTED IN EARLIER CHAPTERS, classical rhetoric divided the composing process into categories: invention, arrangement, and style. This book is interested in invention, in describing the acts of mind that go on in the observation and idea-generation phase of writing; but as Chapters 8 and 9 reveal, invention (the discovery of ideas) and arrangement (the ordering of ideas) aren't really separate. The way you learn to put a paper together affects and can drastically limit the kinds of ideas you are able to have, as is the case, for example, with the format called five-paragraph form (see Chapter 8).

The separation of invention from arrangement in classical rhetoric was largely a matter of convenience. Unfortunately, the consequence of treating invention and arrangement separately was that people began to dissociate rhetoric from the sense of finding and developing ideas and located it instead solely in the context of arranging ideas in ways most likely to persuade an audience. It is this reduced sense of rhetoric as arrangement minus invention that is largely responsible for the negative connotation that the word *rhetoric* has for many people today, as in "That was just empty rhetoric."

ROMANTICS VERSUS FORMALISTS

This split between invention and arrangement fuels a related conflict between *romantic* and *formalist* ways of thinking about organization. The formalist model (*formalist* being a dirty word to romantics) emphasizes writing as an act of communication with an audience, and so stresses the formal conventions that allow a reader to know what to expect and where to find things in the paper. The following Voice from across the Curriculum offers a nicely articulated argument for the formalist point of view.

The romantic model resists any kind of preconceived pattern for papers on the grounds that the content should naturally generate an appropriate form. Romantics tend to speak of form as organic, that is, like a plant, the parts of which grow according to an inherent logic rather than conforming to externally imposed rules.

The romantic assumption is attractive to those who value the intuitive and the semi-conscious side of writing. It is less attractive at 2:00 a.m. when you have a paper

VOICES FROM ACROSS THE CURRICULUM

In Defense of Formalism

Experimental Psychology uses a very rigid format. I explain to students the functions of the different sections for the reader. Once students start to read journal articles themselves, the functions of the sections become clear. Readers do not always want to read or reread the whole article. If I want to replicate someone's research, I may read just the "Methods" section to get the technical details I need. I may read just the "Results" section to get a sense of the numerical results I might expect. On the other hand, I may not care about the details of how the experiment was run. I might just want to know if it worked, in which case I would read the first few sentences of the "Discussion" section. The format lets me know exactly where to find whatever I might be looking for, without having to read through the whole article.

—Laura Edelman, *Professor of Psychology*

due the next day, but what you've produced is a meandering mass of stuff that no one but you (and possibly not even you!) could be expected to follow.

Clearly, both the romantic model and the formalist model have validity, but the split between these two orientations is exaggerated and misleading. The forms that romantics want to reject as artificial impositions on creativity need not be seen in this way. The mental processes that seem to come like magic to some people but not to others can in fact be described and thus learned and consciously employed. Becoming more aware of the forms that thinking takes neither kills ideas nor disables intuition. Instead it makes inroads into the problem of writer's block. It also levels the playing field, especially among students and teachers, by sharing the means of idea production.

Avoiding the unnecessary tension between the formalist and romantic views can be solved by training yourself to see both how form shapes content and how content shapes form. Ideally, forms and formats are not arbitrary, but set up meaningful relationships among ideas.

THE TWO FUNCTIONS OF FORMATS: PRODUCT AND PROCESS

Most of the writing (and thinking) we do is generated by some kind of format, even if we are not aware of it. Writers virtually never write in the absence of formal conventions. Accordingly, you should not regard most of the formats that you encounter simply as *prescriptive* (that is, strictly required) sets of artificial rules. Rather, try to think of them as descriptive accounts of the various *heuristics*—sets of questions and categories—that humans typically use to guide and stimulate their thinking.

The first step in learning to use formats productively is to recognize that they have two related but separate functions: product and process.

- *As sets of rules for organizing a final product,* formats make communication among members of a discipline easier and more efficient. By standardizing the means of displaying thinking in a discipline, the format enables readers to compare more readily one writer's work to that of others in the field because readers know where to look for particular kinds of information—the writer's methodology, for example, or his or her hypothesis or conclusions.

- *As guides and stimulants to the writing process,* formats offer writers a means of finding and exploring ideas. The procedures that formats contain seek to guide the writer's thinking process in a disciplined manner, prompting systematic and efficient examination of a subject. The notion of formats functioning as aids to invention—idea generation—goes back at least as far as Aristotle, whose *Rhetoric* defined twenty-eight general topics (such as considering causes and effects or dividing a subject into parts) that speakers might pursue to invent arguments.

Perhaps the biggest problem that formats can create for writers is *a premature emphasis on product*—on the form of the finished paper at the expense of process. When this happens, they tend to lose sight of *the logic* that formats provide for dividing the subject into parts, arranged in a particular order. The conventional format of the scientific paper, for example, stipulates the inclusion of a review of prior research, for instance, to induce writers to arrive at thoughtful connections between their own work and earlier experiments.

Using Formats Heuristically: A Brief Example

To lose sight of the heuristic value of formats is to become preoccupied with formats as disciplinary etiquette. The solution to this problem probably sounds easier than it is: you need to *find the spaces in a format that will allow it to work as a heuristic.* Consider how you might go about using even a highly specified organizational scheme like the following.

1. State the problem.
2. Develop criteria of adequacy for a solution.
3. Explore at least two inadequate solutions.
4. Explicate the proposed solution.
5. Evaluate the proposed solution.
6. Reply to anticipated criticisms.

The best reason not to ignore any of the six steps in this problem/solution format we've been looking at is that *the format does have a logic,* although it leaves that logic unstated. The purpose of including at least two inadequate solutions (step 3), for example, is to protect the writer against moving to a conclusion too quickly on the basis of too little evidence. The requirements that the writer evaluate the solution and reply to criticisms (steps 5 and 6) press the writer toward complexity, to prevent a one-sided and uncritical answer. In short, heuristic value in the format is there for a writer to use if he or she doesn't allow a premature concern with matters of form to take precedence over thinking. It would be a mistake, in other words, to assume that one must move through the six steps consecutively; the writer would only need to arrange his or her thinking in that order when putting together the final product.

CLASSICAL FORMS AND FORMATS

As we have been saying, the needs of an audience and the needs of the writer don't need to be separate. It's important to recognize that all organizational schemes are conventional—which is to say, they are agreed-upon protocols with social functions. But it's also important to recognize that these protocols embody ways of thinking capable of producing ideas in the first place.

General organizing formats have been around a long time. Some are very simple. Others are more elaborate. The simplest organizing scheme consists of three parts: introduction, body, and conclusion. The format of the classical oration has a more elaborate form:

- *Exordium,* introduction
- *Narratio,* statement of facts
- *Divisio,* outline of the points or steps in the argument
- *Confirmatio,* proof of the case
- *Confutatio,* refutation of opposing arguments
- *Peroratio,* conclusion

If you read or listen to (for example) political speeches, you will find that many of them follow this order. This is because the form of the classical oration is suited primarily to argument—to the kind of writing in which the writer makes a case for or against something and refutes opposing arguments. An analytical essay could be organized in this way, as an analytical argument wherein you make your case for a particular way of reading (interpreting) your data and argue against competing ways of reading it. But as we have been demonstrating throughout this book, analytical thinking does not fit well into formats calling for an up-front statement of a predetermined claim, which is then simply proven to be correct. And so we have offered some alternative organizational schemes that allow the space necessary for the recursive (back and forth) thinking that analytical writing involves. These forms include some of the elements of the classical oration but without its emphasis on proof and refutation.

WRITING ANALYTICALLY'S FORMS AND FORMATS

The invention strategies and analytical formulae this book has offered contain inherent organizational force. We revisit some of these briefly to suggest how they function as both stimuli to invention and as formats for organizing final drafts. All of the book's formats share the following traits:

1. In-depth analysis of a single representative example, which is then tested and extended by analysis of other examples

2. Evolution rather than repetition of a central claim through successive complication (progressive reformulation)

These formats make space for thinking to progress rather than forcing it into static and inflexible patterns. In this they differ from nonprogressing formats like five-paragraph form, which stubbornly substitute listing for thinking.

Pan, Track, and Zoom: Using 10 on 1 to Build a Paper

The *pan* gives the reader the big picture; pans provide context and establish the representativeness of the example the writer will examine in more detail (in the zoom).

The *track* moves to selected pieces of the larger picture and makes telling connections among them.

The *zoom* narrows the focus allowing the writer to draw out as much meaning as possible from a representative example. The zoom is the shot that enables you to do 10 on 1.

In a longer paper, you move from this key example to others that usefully extend and qualify your point, but only after the analysis of your representative example produces sufficient thinking. In practice, the moves can be in almost any order. You are the director of the film that is your paper. For example, **zoom → pan → track → zoom → pan,** or **pan → zoom → track → zoom → pan,** and so on. (Note that papers usually end with a pan, the big picture.)

Constellating

Constellating, like pan, track, and zoom, is a way of connecting your close analysis of representative examples (stars) to other telling evidence. Like the lines that connect stars into a recognizable shape, your thinking configures the examples into some larger meaning. The premise here is that there are many plausible patterns discernible in a pool of evidence.

A Template for Organizing Papers Using 10 on 1

1. Start by panning on an interesting pattern or tendency you have found in your evidence. Explain what attracted you to it—why you find it potentially significant and worth looking at. End this paragraph with a tentative theory (working thesis) about what this pattern or tendency might reveal or accomplish.

2. Zoom in on your representative example and argue for the example's representativeness and usefulness in coming to a better understanding of your subject.

3. Do 10 on 1—analyze your representative example, being sure to answer the So what? question. Then use complicating evidence to refine your claims.

4a. In a short paper, move to your conclusion: a qualified version of your thesis, your ultimate So what?, plus brief reflection on the implications of your discoveries. (See Chapter 11 on culmination and send-off.)

4b. In a longer paper, use your representative example as a lens to explore other examples (constellating). Use these additional examples to expand the range of your thesis and make it more accurate, and conclude as in 4a.

Six Steps for Making a Thesis Evolve

1. Formulate an idea about your subject, a working thesis.
2. See how far you can make this thesis go in accounting for evidence.
3. Locate evidence that is not adequately accounted for by the thesis.
4. Make explicit the apparent mismatch between the thesis and selected evidence, asking and answering So what?
5. Reshape your claim to accommodate the evidence that hasn't fit.
6. Repeat steps 2 through 5 several times.

As an overarching guideline, acknowledge the questions that each new formulation of the thesis prompts you to ask. The thesis develops through successive complications.

The Toolkit as Template

The templates we've just reviewed are the most explicit models for organizing papers. But in fact, all of the strategies the book has offered have the potential to function as formats. Here is an all-purpose pattern that combines strategies from Chapter 3 and Chapter 8:

1. Use The Method or Notice and Focus to find a revealing pattern or tendency in your evidence.
2. Select a representative example.
3. Do 10 on 1 to produce an in-depth analysis of your example.
4. Test your results in similar cases.

If the example involved a binary, a writer could use the procedure for reformulating binaries (Chapter 5) to organize her analysis:

Strategy 1: Locate a range of opposing categories

Strategy 2: Analyze and define the key terms

Strategy 3: Question the accuracy of the binary

Strategy 4: Substitute "to what extent?" for "either/or"

THE SHAPING FORCE OF THESIS STATEMENTS

As discussed in Chapter 9, a strong thesis usually contains *tension,* the balance of this against that. This tension is often evident in the actual sentence structure of the thesis statement. Many thesis statements begin with a grammatically subordinate idea that they go on to replace or outweigh with a more pressing claim: "Although X appears to account for Z, Y accounts for it better." This formula can also organize a paper, which proceeds by following the pattern predicted by the order of clauses in the thesis statement. The first part of the paper deals with the claims for X and then moves to a fuller embrace of Y.

The advantage of this subordinate construction (and the reason that so many theses are set up this way) is that the subordinate idea helps you define your own position by giving you something to define it against. The subordinate clause of a thesis helps you demonstrate that there is in fact an issue involved—that is, more than one possible explanation for the evidence you are considering—and thus a reason to be writing the paper in the first place. In practice, using this shape often leads you to arrive at some compromise position between the claims of X and Y. What appeared to be a *binary opposition*—not X but Y—emerges as a complex combination of the two.

A less effective thesis shape that can predict the shape of a paper is the list. This shape, in which a writer might offer three points and then devote a section to each, often leads to sloppier thinking than a shape having a thesis statement containing both subordinate and independent clauses because the list often does not sufficiently specify the connections among its various components. As a result, it fails to assert a relationship among ideas.

■ **Try this 10.1:** *Predicting Essay Shapes from Thesis Shapes*

It is a useful skill, both in reading and writing, to predict paper shapes from thesis shapes. For each of the theses below, what shape is predicted? That is, what will probably be discussed first, what second, and why? Which words in the thesis are especially predictive of the shape the paper will take?

1. The reforms in education, created to alleviate the problems of previous reforms, have served only to magnify the very problems they were meant to solve.

2. Joinville paints, though indirectly, a picture of military, social, and political gain having very little to do with religion and more to do with race hatred and the acquisition of material wealth.

3. Although women more readily cry in contemporary films, the men, by not crying, seem to win the audience's favor.

4. The complications that fuel the plots in today's romantic comedies arise because women and men express their sensitivity so differently; the resolutions, however, rarely require the men to capitulate.

THE SHAPING FORCE OF TRANSITIONS

A list, we have said, is a slack form of organization: overly loose, not identifying how this is related to that with the tension necessary to give a paper strength. The same criticism applies to transitions, the connective tissue among the parts of an essay. Although transitional wording such as "another example of" or "also" at the beginning of paragraphs does tell readers that a related point or example follows, it does not specify that relationship beyond piling on another "and."

If you find yourself relying on "another" and "also" at points of transition, force yourself to substitute other transitional wording that indicates more precisely the nature of the relationship with what has gone before in the paper. Language such as "similarly" and "by contrast" can sometimes serve this purpose. In many cases, however, some restatement of what has been said and its relation to what comes next is called for. Don't underestimate the amount of productive restating that goes on in papers—it's not necessarily redundant. It can be a saying again in different language for the purpose of advancing the writer's thinking further. A good transition reaches backward, telling where you've been, as the grounds for making a subsequent move forward.

The links between where you've been and where you're going are usually points in your writing at which thinking is taking place. Often this kind of transitional thinking requires you to concentrate on articulating *how* what has preceded connects to what follows—the logical links. This is especially the case in the evolving rather than the static model of thesis development, in which the writer continually *updates* the thesis as it moves through evidence.

It is useful to think of transitions as *directional indicators,* especially at the beginnings of paragraphs but also within them. *And,* for example, is a plus sign. It indicates that the writer will add something, essentially continuing in the same direction. The words *but, yet, nevertheless,* and *however* are among the many transitional words that alert readers to changes in the direction of the writer's thinking. They might indicate, for example, the introduction of a qualification, a potentially contradictory piece of evidence, an alternative point of view, and so forth. Note as well that some additive transitions do more work than *also* or *another.* The word *moreover* is an additive transition, but it adds emphasis to the added point. The transitional sequence *not only . . . but also* restates and then adds information in a way that clarifies what has gone before.

The first step toward improving your use of transitions (and thereby, the organization of your writing) is to become conscious of them. If you notice that you are beginning successive paragraphs with *another reason,* for example, you can probably conclude that you are listing rather than developing your ideas.

Finally, think of transitions as echoes in the service of continuity. If you study the transitions in a piece, you will usually find that they echo either the language or the ideas of something that precedes them as they point to what is ahead.

■ **Try this 10.2:** *Tracking Transitions*

As an exercise in becoming more conscious of how transitions shape thinking, track the transitions in a piece of writing. Take a few pages of something you are reading (preferably a complete piece, such as a short article) and circle or underline all of the directional indicators. Remember to check not only the beginnings of paragraphs but within them. Then, survey your markings. What do you notice now about the shape of the piece? Describe the shape. This exercise is also useful for expanding your repertoire of transitional words to use in your own writing. As an alternative, track the transitional wording in the next section of this chapter.

THE SHAPING FORCE OF COMMON THOUGHT PATTERNS: DEDUCTION AND INDUCTION

According to the usual definitions of the terms *deduction* and *induction,* you might expect that a fairly full fledged version of the thesis would appear at the beginning of a deductive paper but at the end of an inductive one. But as we go on to show, papers don't neatly fit these two abstract models of thinking. In practice, all writing combines the two patterns. In virtually all essays, the paper begins with some kind of organizing claim; this is not delayed until the end. And in virtually all essays, the opening claim is not simply repeated at the end but occurs there in its duly tested and evolved form. To clarify these claims we need to offer some definitions. (See Figure 10.1, A and B).

Deduction

As a thought process, deduction reasons from a general principle (assumed to be true) to the particular case. It introduces this principle up-front and then uses it to select and interpret evidence. For example, a deductive paper might state in its first paragraph that attitudes toward and rules governing sexuality in a given culture can be seen, at least in part, to have economic causes. The paper might then apply this principle, already assumed to be true, to the codes governing sexual behavior in several cultures or several kinds of sexual behavior in a single culture.

A good deductive argument is, however, more than a mechanical application or matching exercise of general claim and specific details that are explained by it. Deductive reasoning uses the evidence to draw out the implications—what logicians term *inferring the consequences*—of the claim. The general principle explains selected features of particular cases, and *reciprocally,* the evidence brings out implications in the principle.

Thus, the general principle stated at the beginning of the paper and the idea stated as the paper's conclusion are not the same. Rather, the conclusion presents the (evolved) idea that the writer has arrived at through the application of the principle.

Induction

An inductively organized paper typically begins, not with a principle already accepted as true, but with particular data for which it seeks to generate some explanatory principle.

Whereas deduction moves by applying a generalization to particular cases, induction moves from the observation of individual cases to the formation of a general principle. Because all possible cases can obviously never be examined—every left-handed person, for example, if one wishes to theorize that left-handed people

(A) Deduction

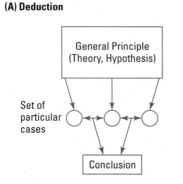

(B) Induction

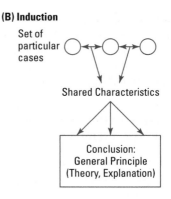

(C) Blend: Induction to Deduction

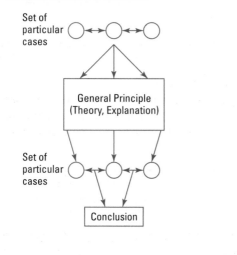

(D) Blend: Deduction to Induction

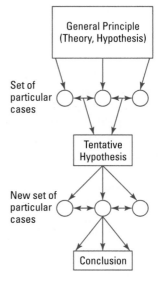

FIGURE 10.1

Deduction and Induction *Deduction (A) uses particular cases to exemplify general principles and analyze their implications. Induction (B) constructs general principles from the analysis of particular cases. In practice, analytical thinking and writing blend deduction and induction and start either with particular cases (C) or a general principle (D).*

are better at spatial thinking than right-handers—the principle (or thesis) arrived at through inductive reasoning always remains open to doubt.

Nevertheless, the thesis of an inductive paper is generally deemed acceptable if a writer can demonstrate that the theory is based on a reasonably sized sampling of representative instances. Suffice it to say that a child who arrives at the thesis that all orange food tastes bad on the basis of squash and carrots has not based that theory on an adequate sampling of available evidence.

The Overlap

In most cases induction and deduction operate in tandem (see Figure 10.1, C and D). Analysis by nature moves between the particular and the general, regardless of which comes first. Whether the overall shape of the analysis—its mode of progression—is primarily inductive or deductive, it still gains in complexity from beginning to end as it confronts evidence.

It's true that in some disciplines (philosophy, for example) the deductive pattern of argument prevails, but not exclusively. The analysis of evidence, though clearly designed to reflect a general principle, also leads to new formulations that modify the general principle in various ways.

THESIS SLOTS

Even in the most inductive forms of essay development, various formulations of the thesis guide readers through the essay. Here is a short list of the places in an essay that readers typically expect some version of the thesis to occur.

- The first articulation of the working thesis almost always occurs late in the opening paragraph or early in the second paragraph of a piece, after the writer has presented the problem or question that establishes the tension the thesis aims to resolve, and given some kind of context for it.

- Subsequent articulations of the thesis usually occur at points of transition, typically at paragraph openings following the analysis of complicating evidence. This kind of updating has the added benefit of providing unity to the essay, using the thesis as a kind of spine.

- The final statement of the thesis occurs in the concluding paragraph, or perhaps the penultimate one. It is usually offered in clear relationship to the terms offered in the introduction, so the reader is offered a last vision of where the essay has traveled.

NEGOTIATING DISCIPLINARY FORMATS

Especially in the natural sciences and psychology, the pattern of presentation for formal papers and reports is explicitly prescribed and usually mandatory. For example, the American Psychological Association (APA) issues a disciplinary style guide to which all writers seeking to publish in the field must adhere. In other disciplines, particularly in the humanities and other of the social sciences, the accepted patterns of organization are less rigidly defined. Nonetheless, writers in these fields also operate to a significant extent within established forms, such as those set forth by the Modern Language Association (MLA) handbook.

Because formats offer a means not only of displaying thinking in a discipline but also of shaping it, the format that a discipline tacitly or overtly requires conditions its members to think in particular ways. Learning to use the format that scientists use predisposes you to think like a scientist. Learning the differences among the various disciplines' formats can help you recognize differences in *epistemology* (ways of knowing).

A thesis functions differently depending on the academic discipline—whether it must be stated in full at the outset, for example, and what happens to it between the beginning of the paper and the end. The differences appear largest as you move back and forth between courses in the humanities and courses in the natural and certain of the social sciences.

Broadly speaking, papers in the humanities are inclined to begin inductively, and papers in the natural and social sciences deductively. The natural and social sciences generally use a pair of terms, *hypothesis* and *conclusion,* for the single term *thesis.* Because writing in the sciences is patterned according to the scientific method, writers in disciplines such as biology and psychology must report how the original thesis (hypothesis) was tested against empirical evidence and then conclude on this basis whether the hypothesis was confirmed.

The gap between this way of thinking about the thesis and the concept of an evolving thesis is not as large as it may seem. The scientific method is in sync with one of this book's main points, that something must happen to the thesis between the introduction and the conclusion so that the conclusion does more than reassert what was already asserted in the beginning.

Analogously, in a scientific paper, the hypothesis is tested against evidence, the results of which allow the writer to draw conclusions about the hypothesis's validity. Although the hypothesis does not change (or evolve), the testing of it qualifies the paper's central claim.

In the natural and social sciences, successive reformulations of the thesis are less likely to be recorded and may not even be expressly articulated. But, as in all disciplines, the primary analytical activity in the sciences is to repeatedly reconsider the assumptions upon which a conclusion is based.

VOICES FROM ACROSS THE CURRICULUM

Induction and Deduction in the Scientific Format

There are firm rules in organizing scientific writing. Papers are usually divided into four major sections: 1. Introduction: provides context and states the question asked and the hypothesis tested in the study; 2. Methodology: accurately describes experimental procedure; 3. Results: states the results obtained; 4. Discussion: analyzes and interprets results with respect to the original hypothesis; discusses implications of the results. As this organizational model should make clear, scientific papers are largely deductive with a shift to inductive reasoning in the discussion when the writer usually attempts to generalize or extend conclusions to broader circumstances.

—Richard Niesenbaum, *Professor of Biology*

Treating the Format Flexibly

Scientific format appears highly formulaic at first glance. Papers are generally broken into four sections: "Introduction" (What is this all about, what do we already know, why do we care?), "Experimental Procedures" (What did you actually do?), "Results" (What happened in your experiments?), and "Discussion" (What do you think it means, what are the remaining questions?). This breakdown is useful because it emphasizes the process of argument (introduction and results), providing evidence (results) and analysis (discussion). However, although this may seem different from writing in other disciplines, I think of it as a codification of basic analytical writing that is common in most disciplines.

A common mistake made by beginning and intermediate students is taking this breakdown too literally. In order to be comprehensible, the rules must be broken periodically. For example, results frequently must be referred to in the "Experimental Procedures" section in order to understand *why* the next procedure was performed. Similarly, the "Results" section frequently must include some discussion, so that the reader understands the immediate significance of the results, if not the broader implications. For example, the following sentences might appear in a "Results" section: "These data suggest that the p53 protein may function in repressing cell division in potential cancer cells. In order to test this possibility, we overexpressed p53 protein in a transformed cell line." The first sentence provides an interpretation of the results that is necessary to understand why the next experiment was performed.

—Bruce Wightman, *Professor of Biology*

THREE COMMON ORGANIZING STRATEGIES

The following organizational patterns are determined more by rhetorical considerations—the desired effect on an audience—than by their idea-generating potential. As you will see, however, each also has potential for shaping thought. The first two patterns, climactic order and comparison/contrast, are common in all forms of writing. The third pattern, which concerns locating refutations and concessions, is particular to composing arguments.

Climactic Order

Climactic order has to do with arranging the elements in a list from least important to most important. The idea is to build to your best points, rather than leading with them and thereby allowing the paper to trail off from your more minor and less interesting observations.

But what are your best points? A frequent mistake that writers commit in arranging their points climactically—and one that has much to do with the psychology of form—is to assume that the best point is the most obvious, the one with the most data attached to it and the one least likely to produce disagreement with readers. Such writers end up giving more space than they should to ideas that really don't need much development because they are already evident to most readers.

If you follow the principle of climactic order, you would begin with the most obvious and predictable points—and ones that, psychologically speaking, would get readers assenting—and then build to the more revealing and less obvious ones. So, for example, if the comparisons between film A and film B are fairly mundane but the contrasts are really provocative, you'd get the comparisons out of the way first and build to the contrasts, exploiting difference within similarity (see Chapter 6).

If, for example, there are three important reasons for banning snowmobiling in your town, you might choose to place the most compelling one last. If you were to put it first, you might draw your readers in quickly (a principle used by news stories) but then lose them as your argument seemed to trail off into less interesting rationales.

Comparison/Contrast

Chapter 6 discusses working comparatively as an invention strategy. We now want to address this subject from the perspective of organizing a paper. The first decision a writer has to make when arranging comparisons and contrasts is whether to address the two items being compared and contrasted *sequentially* in blocks or *point by point*. So, for example, if you are comparing subject A with subject B, you might first make all the points you wish to make about A and then make points about B by explicitly referring back to A as you go. The advantage of this format is that it allows you to use comparing and contrasting to figure out what you wish to say as you are drafting.

The disadvantage of this subject-A-then-subject-B format is that it can easily lose focus. If you don't manage to keep the points you raise about each side of your comparison parallel, you may end up with a paper comprised of two loosely connected halves. The solution is to make your comparisons and contrasts in the second half of the paper connect explicitly with what you said in the first half. What you say about subject A, in other words, should set the subtopics and terms for discussion of subject B.

The alternative pattern of organization for comparisons and contrasts is to organize by topic—not A and then B but A1 and B1, A2 and B2, A3 and B3, and so forth. That is, you talk about both A and B under a series of subtopics. If, for example, you were comparing two films, you might organize your work under such headings as directing, script, acting, special effects, and so forth.

The advantage of this format is that it better focuses the comparisons, pressing you to use them to think with. The disadvantage is that organizing in this way is sometimes difficult to manage until you've already done quite a bit of thinking about the two items you're comparing. The solution, particularly in longer papers, is sometimes to use both formats. You begin by looking at each of your subjects separately to make the big links and distinctions apparent and then focus what you've said by further pursuing selected comparisons one topic at a time.

Regardless of which format you adopt, the comparisons and contrasts will not really begin to take shape until you have done enough preliminary drafting to discover what the most significant similarities and differences are and, beyond that, whether the similarities or the differences are most important—whether, that is, your primary goal is to compare or to contrast.

Concessions and Refutations

In the language of argument, you *concede* whenever you acknowledge that a position at odds with your own does indeed have merit, even though you continue to believe that your position overall is the more reasonable one. To qualify as a concession, a competing point of view needs to be genuinely creditable—rather than only seemingly creditable until the writer lays out a means of opposing it. Another option is to argue against these views so as to *refute* their reasonableness.

It is a rule of thumb not to make your readers wait too long before you either concede or refute a view that you can assume has already occurred to them. If you delay too long, you may inadvertently suggest either that you are unaware of the competing view or that you are afraid to bring it up.

In the case of short and easily managed concessions and refutations, you can often house these within the first several paragraphs and, in this way, clear a space for the position you wish to promote. In the case of more complicated and potentially more threatening alternative arguments, you may need to express your own position clearly and convincingly first. But to avoid the rhetorical problem of appearing to ignore the threat, you probably need to give it a preliminary nod, telling readers that you will return to a full discussion of it later, once you have laid out your own position in some detail.

The placement of arguments has much to do with their relative complexity. Reasonably straightforward and easily explained concessions and refutations can often all be grouped in one place, perhaps as early as the second or third paragraph of a paper. The approach to concession and refutation in more complex arguments does not allow for such grouping. For each part of your argument, you probably need to concede and refute as necessary before moving to the next part of your argument and repeating the procedure.

STRUCTURING THE PARAGRAPH

Paragraphs serve both the writer and the reader. Paragraphing is a kindness to your reader because it divides your thinking into manageable bites. If you find a paragraph growing longer than half a page—particularly if it is your opening or second paragraph—search out a place to make a paragraph break. More frequent paragraphing provides readers with convenient resting points from which to relaunch themselves into your thinking.

Long paragraphs are daunting—rather like mountains—and they are easy to get lost in, for both readers and writers. When writers try to do too much in a single paragraph, they often lose the focus and lose contact with the larger purpose or point that got them into the paragraph in the first place. Remember that old high school rule about one idea to a paragraph? Well, it's not a bad rule, though it isn't exactly right because sometimes you need more space than a single paragraph can provide to lay out a complicated phase of your overall argument. In that case, just break wherever it seems reasonable to do so in order to keep your paragraphs from becoming ungainly.

When you draft, start a new paragraph whenever you feel yourself getting stuck— it's the promise of a fresh start. When you revise, use paragraphs as a way of cleaning up your thinking, dividing it into its most logical parts.

A short paragraph always provides emphasis, for which most readers will thank you.

Paragraph breaks are like turning a corner to a new view even when the thinking is continuous. They also force the writer to make transitions, overt connections among the parts of his or her thinking, and to state or restate key ideas. Paragraph indentations allow readers to scan essays, searching for connecting words and important ideas.

Paragraph breaks are a relief.

Paragraphing has two enemies: the writer who believes that the reader does not need paragraph breaks and the too-simple notion of the paragraph as claim plus supporting evidence. We now tackle the second of these.

The Topic Sentence Controversy

A long standing controversy of paragraph structure centers around the so-called topic sentence. Most scholars cite an 1866 textbook by Alexander Bain as the starting point for the argument about topic sentences. Bain's text included strict rules governing paragraph structure, including the nature and location of the topic sentence. More recently linguists and rhetoricians have taken different stands, including the idea that most paragraphs don't actually have topic sentences in the sense of a governing claim that organizes the paragraph. Others have argued that most paragraphs do have topic sentences, but that these don't necessarily occur, as commonly prescribed, in the first sentence.

In his influential essay, "A Generative Rhetoric of the Paragraph," Francis Christensen defined the word *topic* in topic sentences to mean simply "top sentence of the sequence . . . the one the other sentences depend from, the one they develop or amplify, the one they are a comment on" (*Notes Toward a New Rhetoric.* Harper & Row, 1967, p. 80).

Some Theories on Paragraph Structure

Christensen posits two kinds of paragraphs. In one, all of the sentences following the topic sentence are equal in weight, or as he puts it, "all children of the same mother" (61). He calls this structure coordinate. In the other, called subordinate, the relationship among ideas is more complex. Each sentence clarifies or comments on the one before it, as for example in this short sequence that he cites:

1. The process of learning is essential to our lives.
2. All higher animals seek it deliberately.

3. They are inquisitive and they experiment.

4. An experiment is a sort of harmless trial run . . . (60).

Each sentence in the coordinate structure relates back to the topic sentence, but in the subordinate structure each sentence generates the one that follows it. Christensen observes that in practice most paragraphs combine coordinate and subordinate sequences. His model has the advantage of reorienting writers to thinking about what the sentences in a paragraph *do*—rather than just what they *say*. That is, he gives us models for seeing paragraphs as movements of mind.

Other theories of the paragraph, such as Alton Becker's slot-filler approach, focus on essentially two acts of mind in relation to a paragraph's topic sentence: restriction (R) and illustration (I). Restriction limits the claim in some way, and illustration supplies examples in support of the claim. It is in fact quite useful to notice that sentences shrink and define claims rather than just supporting them. It is problematic, however, to think of development only in terms of idea plus illustration (claim plus proof).

In our model, we describe the movement of mind as follows: *Observation → so what? → implication → so what? → tentative conclusions.* This sequence differs from idea plus illustration because it contains more of the writer's thinking on how he or she derives the claim from evidence. Explicitly drawing out the implications of evidence differs from attaching examples to the idea they support.

We demonstrate our model of mental movement in two examples situated early in Chapter 4 ("Danger: Men Working" and "*Hua dan:* The Dance of Values in the Beijing Opera"), in which we annotate the way that two pieces of writing progress using the So what? question and the prompt "interesting." Not all paragraphs in an analytical paper move in this way, but a significant number of them do.

FINDING THE SKELETON OF AN ESSAY: AN EXAMPLE (SEPTEMBER 11TH: A NATIONAL TRAGEDY?)

We end this chapter with a skeletal version of an essay by one of our colleagues (available in the anthology version of this text). We have included only the first sentence of each paragraph, and in some cases the last, the working thesis as it appears at the end of paragraph 2, and the evolved thesis as it appears in the next to final paragraph. As you will see, each paragraph does begin with some kind of assertion. You will also see that writers allow themselves some flexibility on where they locate the working thesis and its later evolution. This way of looking at essays is a practice we recommend: it can teach you a lot about paragraphing and essay structure in a hurry.

September 11th: A National Tragedy?

By James Peck

Paragraph 1, sentence 1: Since the events of September 11th, I've been pursued by thoughts and images of tragedy.

Paragraph 1, last sentence: A voluminous literature theorizes the limits of tragic form, and I admit it rankles me to hear the word "tragic" used as a generic modifier for anything really bad that happens.

Paragraph 2, sentence 1: With the events of September 11th, however, I have found myself using the language of tragedy pretty indiscriminately.

Paragraph 2, last two sentences [Working thesis]: But I am coming to the conviction that tragedy offers a demanding, stark paradigm that at least accounts for some of the emotional force of these events and may even suggest some generative ways to think about them. Beyond simply capturing a bit of the devastation wrought by the attacks, can the form of tragedy help us narrate, image, or otherwise represent these horrors?

Paragraph 3, sentence 1: I acknowledge that it may seem frivolous, even blasphemous, to discuss these overwhelming and all too real events in a matrix borrowed from the relatively rarified topic of dramatic form.

Paragraph 4, sentence 1: I'm suggesting that the form of tragedy might accommodate some of the affective power of September 11th, and even point towards some of its moral claims.

Paragraph 5, sentence 1: I think this ought to be the tenor of our discourse in the wake of September 11th.

Paragraph 6, sentence 1: A tragic witnessing of September 11th must also preserve outrage at these callous acts.

Paragraph 7, sentence 1: Finally, a tragic witnessing of these events should squarely face some awful truths, dwell in the full weight of those truths, and try to see ourselves anew as a result of doing so.

Paragraph 8, sentence 1: The cornerstone of Aristotle's theory of tragedy is the dual principle of peripety and recognition.

Paragraph 9, sentence 1: I worry that my discussion may seem tasteless, or worse, coy.

Paragraph 10, sentence 1: I don't want to live in a melodrama.

Paragraph 11, sentence 1: It deeply worries me that the dominant national discourse in the aftermath of September 11th is melodramatic.

Paragraph 12, sentence 1: I'd like to close by evoking the function of tragedy in Athenian democracy.

Paragraph 13, sentence 1: Given this avowedly patriotic context, the most remarkable thing about the City Dionysia was its frank criticism of Athenian public life.

Paragraph 13, final sentence [The evolved thesis]: In this moment of national crisis, I think we would benefit from bringing the same questioning, restless, self-critical spirit to our own national conversation.

Paragraph 14 (entire): I hope we take seriously our casual language, and witness September 11th as a tragedy. Remember the dead. Pursue their killers. Interrogate ourselves.

ASSIGNMENTS: Finding Organizing Principles

1. Excerpt a skeletal version of an essay, using the model at the end of the chapter. Copy out the opening sentence of each paragraph, as well as sentences that state the essay's working thesis and its final form in or near the concluding paragraph. Your aim is to discern the shape of the thinking in the essay at a glance.

2. Study a group of like things inductively. You might, for example, use greeting cards aimed at women versus greeting cards aimed at men, a group of poems by

one author, or ads for one kind of product (jeans) or aimed at one target group (teenage girls).

Compile a set of significant details about the data, and then leap to a general claim about the group that you think is interesting and reasonably accurate. This generalization is your inductive principle. Then use the principle to examine deductively more data of the same kind, exploring its implications as you evolve it more accurately.

3. Infer the format of a published article. Assemble several articles from the same or a similar kind of journal or magazine. *Journal* is the name given to publications aimed at specialized, usually scholarly, audiences, as opposed to general or popular audiences. *Time, Newsweek,* and *The New Yorker* are called magazines rather than journals because they are aimed at a broader general audience. *Shakespeare Quarterly* is a journal; *Psychology Today* is a magazine.

Having found at least three journal or magazine articles, study them to focus on the following question: insofar as there appears to be a format that articles in this journal or magazine adhere to, what are its parts?

Write up your results. Cite particular language from at least two articles in support of your claims about the implicit format. In presenting your evidence, keep the focus on the underlying form, showing how the different articles proceed in the same or similar ways.

CHAPTER 11

Introductions and Conclusions

THIS CHAPTER ADDRESSES two perennial trouble-spots in all kinds of writing: introductions and conclusions. The chapter gives special attention to strategies for solving two particular problems: trying to do too much in the introduction and not doing enough in the conclusion.

As with other aspects of writing analytically, there are no absolute rules for writing introductions and conclusions, but there does seem to be a consensus across the disciplines that introductions should raise issues rather than settle them and that conclusions should go beyond merely restating what has already been said. Insofar as disciplinary conventions permit, in introductions, you should play an ace but not your whole hand; and in conclusions, don't just summarize—culminate.

INTRODUCTIONS AND CONCLUSIONS AS SOCIAL SITES

You have probably noticed that it is difficult to read attentively and do something else at the same time. Imagine, for instance, trying to read a book while playing a guitar. Depending on the difficulty of the reading matter and your powers of concentration, you might not be able even to listen to a guitar and read at the same time. When you read, you enter a world created of written language—a textual world—and to varying degrees, you leave the world "out there." Even if other people are around, we all read in relative isolation; our attention is diverted from the social and physical world upon which the full range of our senses normally operates.

In this context, place yourself in the position of the writer, rather than a reader, and consider the functions that the introduction and conclusion provide for a piece of writing. Your introduction takes the reader from a sensory world and submerges him or her into a textual one. And your conclusion returns the reader to his or her nonwritten reality. Introductions and conclusions mediate—they carry the reader from one way of being to another. They function as the most social parts of any written communication, the passageways in which you need to be most keenly aware of your reader.

At both sites, there is a lot at stake. The introduction gives the reader his or her first impression, and we all know how indelible that can be. The conclusion leaves the reader with a last—and potentially lasting—impression of the written world you have constructed.

Most of the difficulties in composing introductions and conclusions arise in deciding how you should deal with the thesis. How much of it should you put into the introduction? Should your conclusion summarize the thesis or extend it? The model of organization this book has been recommending—of evolving a thesis through successive encounters with evidence—may require a different kind of introduction and conclusion than you have been taught to write. It assumes, for example, that the introduction should not and cannot preview a paper's entire interpretation or argument.

As was discussed in Chapter 9, a fully evolved thesis is usually too complex and too dependent on the various reshapings that have preceded it to be stated succinctly but still coherently at the outset. But readers do need to know early on what your paper is attempting to resolve or negotiate. (See the section of Chapter 9 called Locating the Evolving Thesis in the Final Draft.)

WHAT INTRODUCTIONS DO: "WHY WHAT I'M SAYING MATTERS"

The introduction isolates a specific question or issue and explains why, in a specified context, this question or issue matters. The primary challenge in writing introductions lies in occupying the middle ground between saying too much too soon (overassertive prejudgment) and saying too little up-front (avoidance of taking a position).

The introduction should give your reader a quick (a third of a typed page or a half-page at most) sampling of some feature or features in your evidence that initially aroused your curiosity. A rule of thumb is *start fast*. Avoid unnecessary throat-clearing, and cut immediately to something interesting that you have observed and that your paper will put into context and explain. Your introduction is saying: "Look at this, reader; it is worth thinking about, and here's why."

As the Latin roots of the word suggest—*intro*, meaning "within," and *ducere*, meaning "to lead or bring"—an introduction brings the reader into a subject. Its length varies, depending on the scope of the writing project. An introduction may take a paragraph, a few paragraphs, a few pages, a chapter, or even a book. In most academic writing, one or two paragraphs is a standard length. In that space you should try to accomplish some or all of the following objectives:

- Define your topic—the issue, question, or problem—and say why it matters.
- Indicate your method of approach to the topic.
- Provide necessary background or context.
- Offer the working thesis (hypothesis) that your paper develops.

An objective missing from this list that you might expect to find there is the directive to engage the reader. Clearly, all introductions need to engage the reader, but this advice is too often misinterpreted as an invitation to be entertaining or cute. In academic writing, you don't need a gimmick to engage your readers; you can assume they care about the subject. You will engage them if you can articulate why your topic matters, doing so in terms of existing thinking in the field.

Especially in a first draft, the objectives just listed are not so easily achieved, which is why many writers wisely defer writing the polished version of the introduction until they have completed at least one draft of the paper. At that point, you usually have a clearer notion of why your subject matters and which aspect of your thesis to place first. Often the conclusion of a first draft becomes the introduction to the second draft.

In any case, the standard shape of an introduction is a *funnel*. It starts wide, providing background and generalization, and then narrows the subject to a particular issue or topic. Here is a typical example from an essay entitled "On Political Labels" by Christopher Borick.

One of the first things you should think about when you see or hear a political label is where it came from. Common political labels such as "liberal" or "conservative" have long histories that shed light on their contemporary use. It's important to recognize that a label's meaning differs from place to place and over time. A conservative in Texas may believe much differently from a conservative in New York, just as an American conservative varies in view points from a conservative in Norway. Similarly, someone calling herself a conservative in 2005 would significantly differ from someone calling himself a conservative in 1905 or even 1975. You may wonder, with such variation over time and place, how can we attach meaning to key political terms at all? While not always easy to see, at least part of the answer can be discovered through an examination of the history of the terms.

The paragraph begins with a generalization in the first sentence (about standard responses to the subject at hand) and funnels down in the last sentence to a qualified working thesis (that some of the meaning lies in the linguistic history of the terms themselves).

PUTTING AN ISSUE OR QUESTION IN CONTEXT

Rather than leaping immediately to the paper's issue, question, or problem, most effective introductions provide some broader context to indicate why the issue matters. Although the various models we offer here differ in small ways from discipline to discipline, the essential characteristics that they share suggest that most professors across the curriculum want the same things in an introduction: the locating of a problem or question within a context that provides background and rationale, culminating in a working thesis.

It is important for writers to be conscious of their choice of interpretive context, as we argue in Chapter 4. Things don't just "mean" in the abstract; they mean in particular contexts. Thus, to a significant extent, context shapes and determines what we see. Whether we are aware of it or not, we are always locating things in some context. An interpretive context is a lens through which we scrutinize what we are trying to understand. The best writers defend their choice of interpretive context and make their readers aware of it from the start.

Providing an Introductory Context

An introduction is not simply the statement of a thesis but also the place where the student needs to set a context, a framework that makes such a thesis statement interesting, timely, or in some other way important. It is common to see papers in political science begin by pointing out a discrepancy between conventional wisdom (what the pundits say) and recent political developments, between popular opinion and empirical evidence, or between theoretical frameworks and particular test cases. Papers, in other words, often begin by presenting *anomalies.*

I encourage students to write opening paragraphs that attempt to elucidate such anomalies by:

1. Stating the specific point of departure: are they taking issue with a bit of conventional wisdom? Popular opinions? A theoretical perspective? This provides the context in which a student is able to "frame" a particular problem, issue, and so forth.

2. Explaining why the wisdom/opinion/theory has become problematic or controversial by focusing on a particular issue, event, test case, or empirical evidence.

3. Formulating a brief statement of the tentative thesis/position to be pursued in the paper. This can take several forms, including the revising of conventional wisdom/theory/opinion, discarding it in favor of alternative conceptions, or calling for redefinition of an issue and question.

—Jack Gambino, *Professor of Political Science*

HOW MUCH TO INTRODUCE UP-FRONT: TYPICAL PROBLEMS

Introductions need to do a lot in a limited space. To specify a thesis and locate it within a larger context, suggest the plan or outline of the entire paper, and negotiate first relations with a reader—that's plenty to pack into a paragraph or two. In deciding how much to introduce up-front, you must make a series of difficult choices about what to include and exclude.

The danger is trying to turn the introduction into a miniature essay. Consider the three problems discussed next as symptoms of overcompression, telltale signs that you need to reconceive, and probably reduce, your introduction.

Digression

Digression results when you try to include too much background. If, for example, you plan to write about a recent innovation in video technology, you need to monitor the amount and kind of technical information you include in your opening paragraphs. You also should avoid starting at a point that is too far away from your immediate concerns, as in "From the beginning of time humans have needed to communicate."

As a general rule in academic writing, don't assume that your readers know little or nothing about the subject. Instead, use the social potential of the introduction to negotiate your audience, setting up your relationship with your readers and making clear what you are assuming they do and do not know.

Incoherence

Incoherence results when you try to preview too much of your paper's conclusion in the introduction. Such introductions move in too many directions at once, usually because the writer is trying to conclude before going through the discussion that makes the conclusion comprehensible. The language you are compelled to use in such cases tends to be too dense, and the connections between the sentences tend to be left out because there isn't enough room to include them. After having read the entire paper, your readers may be able to make sense of the introduction, but in that case, the introduction has not done its job.

The following introductory paragraph is incoherent, primarily because it tries to include too much. It neither adequately connects its ideas nor defines its terms.

Twinship is a symbol in many religious traditions. The significance of twinship will be discussed and explored in the Native American, Japanese Shinto, and Christian religions. Twinship can be either in opposing or common forces in the form of deities or mortals. There are several forms of twinship that show duality of order versus chaos, good versus evil, and creation versus destruction. The significance of twinship is to set moral codes for society and to explain the inexplicable.

Prejudgment

Prejudgment results when you appear to have already settled the question to be pursued in the rest of the paper. The problem here is logical. In the effort to preview your paper's conclusion at the outset, you risk appearing to assume something as true that your paper in fact needs to test. In most papers in the humanities and social sciences, in which the thesis evolves in specificity and complexity between the introduction and conclusion, writers and readers can find such assumptions prejudicial. Opening in this way can make the rest of the paper seem redundant. Even in the sciences, in which a concise statement of objectives, plan of attack, and hypothesis are usually required up-front, separate Results and Discussion sections are reserved for the conclusion.

VOICES FROM ACROSS THE CURRICULUM

Avoiding Strong Claims in the Introduction

I might be careful about how tentative conclusions should play in the opening paragraph, because this can easily slide into a prejudging of the question at hand. I would be more comfortable with a clear statement of the prevailing views held by others. For example, a student could write on the question, "Was Franklin Delano Roosevelt a Keynesian?" What purpose would it serve in an opening paragraph to reveal without any supporting discussion that FDR was or was not a Keynesian?

What might be better would be to say that in the public mind FDR is regarded as the original big spender, that some people commonly associate New Deal policies with general conceptions of Keynesianism, but that there may be some surprises in store as that common notion is examined.

In sum, I would discourage students from making strong claims at or near the beginning of a paper. Let's see the evidence first. We should all have respect for the evidence. Strong assertions, bordering on conclusions, too early on are inappropriate.

—James Marshall, *Professor of Economics*

USING PROCEDURAL OPENINGS

In the interests of clear organization, some academic disciplines require students to include in the introduction an explanation of how the paper will proceed. Such a general statement of method and/or intention is known as a *procedural opening*. Among the disciplines in which you are most likely to find this format are philosophy, political science, and sociology. The danger of procedural openings is that the writer avoids making a claim at all.

The statement of a paper's plan is not and cannot take the place of a thesis (an idea about the topic that the paper explores and defends). Consider the deficiencies of the following procedural opening.

In this paper I will first discuss the strong points and weak points in America's treatment of the elderly. Then I will compare this treatment with that in other industrial nations in the West. Finally, I will evaluate the various proposals for reform that have been advanced here and abroad.

This paragraph identifies the subject, but it neither addresses why the subject matters nor suggests the writer's approach. Nor does it provide background to the topic or suggest a hypothesis that the paper will pursue. In some kinds of essays, especially those that move (inductively) from specific observations to more general claims, there is little need for procedural openings, with their declaration of intention and method at the outset. As the following Voice from across the Curriculum reveals, however, there is real difference on this matter across disciplines.

Procedural Openings

I encourage students to provide a "road map" paragraph early in the paper, perhaps the second or third paragraph. (This is a common practice in professional journals.) The "road map" tells the reader the basic outline of the argument. Something like the following: "In the first part of my paper I will present a brief history of the issue. . . . This will be followed by an account of the current controversy. . . . Part III will spell out my alternative account and evidence. . . . I then conclude. . . ." I think such a paragraph becomes more necessary with longer papers.

—Jack Gambino, *Professor of Political Science*

GOOD WAYS TO BEGIN

All of the following ways to begin a paper enable you to play an ace, establishing your authority with your readers, without having to play your whole hand. They offer a starting position rather than a miniaturized version of the entire paper. Remember that the aim of the introduction is to answer the question, Why does what I'm about to say matter? What makes it especially interesting or revealing, and in what context? Here are a few methods of accomplishing this aim.

Challenge a Commonly Held View

This move provides you with a framework against which to develop your ideas; it allows you to begin with some back-pressure, which helps you define your position. Because you are responding to a known point of view, you have a ready way of integrating context into your paper. As the economics professor notes of the FDR example, until we understand what the prevailing view is on FDR, it is pointless to start considering whether he was a Keynesian.

Begin with a Definition

Beginning with a definition is a reliable way to introduce a topic, so long as that definition has some significance for the discussion to follow. If the definition doesn't do any conceptual work in the introduction, the definition gambit becomes a pointless cliché.

You are most likely to avoid cliché if you cite a source other than a standard dictionary for your definition. The reference collection of any academic library contains a range of discipline-specific lexicons that provide more precise and authoritative definitions than Webster ever could. A useful alternative is to quote a particular author's definition of a key term because you want to make a point about his or her particular definition: for example, "Although the *Dictionary of Economics* defines Keynesianism as *XYZ*, Smith treats only *X* and *Y* (or substitutes *A* for *Z*, etc.)."

Lead with Your Second-Best Example

Another versatile opening gambit, when disciplinary conventions allow, is to use your *second-best example* to set up the issue or question that you later develop in depth with your best example. This gambit is especially useful in papers that proceed inductively on the strength of representative examples. As you are assembling evidence in the outlining and prewriting stage, in many cases you will accumulate a number of examples that illustrate the same basic point. For example, several battles might illustrate a particular general's military strategy; several primaries might exemplify how a particular candidate tailors his or her speeches to appeal to the religious right; several scenes might show how a particular playwright romanticizes the working class; and so on.

Save the best example to receive the most analytical attention in your paper. If you were to present this example in the introduction, you would risk making the rest of the essay vaguely repetitive. A quick close-up of another example strengthens your argument or interpretation. By using a different example to raise the issues, you suggest that the phenomenon exemplified is not an isolated case and that the major example you eventually concentrate upon is indeed representative.

Exemplify the Topic with a Narrative

An occasional gambit in the humanities and social sciences, the narrative opening introduces a short, pertinent, and vivid story or anecdote that exemplifies a key aspect of a topic. Although generally not permissible in the formal reports assigned in the natural and social sciences, narrative openings turn up in virtually all other kinds of writing across the curriculum.

As the introduction funnels to its thesis, the readers receive a graphic sense of the issue that the writer will now develop nonnarratively. Nonnarrative treatment is necessary because by itself anecdotal evidence can be seen as merely personal. Storytelling is suggestive but usually does not constitute sufficient proof; it needs to be corroborated.

WHAT CONCLUSIONS DO: THE FINAL SO WHAT?

Like the introduction, the conclusion has a key social function: it escorts the readers out of the paper, just as the introduction has escorted them in. What do readers want as they leave the textual world you have taken them through? Think of the concluding paragraph as the site of the paper's final So what?, which, as you'll recall, is shorthand for "Where does this get us?" or "Why does this matter?"

Implicit here is the notion that conclusions always state (or restate) the thesis in its most fully evolved form (see Chapter 9). In addition, the conclusion usually makes all of the following moves:

- *It comes full circle.* That is, it creates a sense of closure by revisiting the way the paper began. Often it returns to some key phrase from the context established in the introduction and updates it.

- *It pursues implications.* That is, it reasons from the particular focus of the essay to broader issues, such as the study's practical consequences or applications, or future-oriented issues, such as avenues for further research. To unfold implications in this way is to broaden the view from the here and now of the paper by looking outward to the wider world and forward to the future.

- *It identifies limitations.* That is, it acknowledges restrictions of method or focus in the analysis, and qualifies the conclusion (and its implications) accordingly.

These moves are quite literally movements—they take the thinking in the essay, and the readers with it, both backward and forward. The backward thrust we call *culmination;* the forward thrust we call *send-off.*

When you culminate a paper, you bring together things that you have already said, establishing their connection and ascending to one final statement of your thinking. The word *culminate* is derived from the Latin *columen,* meaning "top or summit." To culminate is to reach the highest point, and it implies a mountain (in this case, of information and analysis) that you have scaled.

The climactic effects of culmination provide the basis for the send-off. The send-off is both social and conceptual, a final opening outward of the topic that leads the reader out of the paper with something further to think about. Here the thinking moves beyond the close analysis of data that has occupied the body of the paper into a kind of speculation that the writer has earned the right to formulate.

Simply put, you culminate with the best statement of your big idea, and your send-off gets you and the reader out of the paper.

VOICES FROM ACROSS THE CURRICULUM

Expanding Possibilities in the Conclusion

I tell my students that too many papers "just end," as if the last page or so were missing. I tell them the importance of ending a work. One could summarize main points, but I tell them this is not heavy lifting.

I believe the ending should be an expansion of possibilities, sort of like an introduction to some much larger "mental" paper out there. I sometimes encourage students to see the concluding section as an option to introduce ideas that can't be dealt with now. Sort of a "Having done this, I would want to explore boom, boom, boom if I were to continue further." Here the students can critique and recommend ("Having seen 'this,' one wonders 'that'").

—Frederick Norling, *Professor of Business*

VOICES FROM ACROSS THE CURRICULUM

Limiting Claims in the Conclusion

The conclusion does not appear simply as a restatement of a thesis, but rather as an attempt to draw out its implications and significance (the "So what?"). This is what I usually try to impress upon students. For instance, if a student is writing on a particular proposal for party reform, I would expect the concluding paragraph to consider both the significance of the reform and its practicality.

Professional papers often indicate the tentativeness of their conclusions by stressing the need for future research and indicating what these research needs might be. Although I haven't tried this, maybe it would be useful to have students conclude papers with a section entitled "For Further Consideration" in which they would indicate those things that they would have liked to have known but couldn't, given their time constraints, the availability of information, and lack of methodological sophistication. This would serve as a reminder of the tentativeness of conclusions and the need to revisit and revise arguments in the future (which, after all, is a good scholarly habit).

—Jack Gambino, *Professor of Political Science*

SOLVING TYPICAL PROBLEMS IN CONCLUSIONS

The primary challenge in writing conclusions, it should now be evident, lies in finding a way to culminate your analysis without claiming either too little or too much. There are a number of fairly common problems to guard against if you are to avoid either of these two extremes.

Redundancy

In Chapter 8 we lampooned an exaggerated example of the five-paragraph form for constructing its conclusion by stating "Thus, we see" and then repeating the introduction verbatim. The result is redundancy. It's a good idea to refer back to the opening, but it's a bad idea just to reinsert it mechanically. Instead, reevaluate what you said there in light of where you've ended up, repeating only key words or phrases from the introduction. This kind of selective repetition is a desirable way of achieving unity and keeps you from making one of two opposite mistakes—either repeating too much or bringing up a totally new point in the conclusion.

Raising a Totally New Point

Raising a totally new point can distract or bewilder a reader. This problem often arises out of a writer's praiseworthy desire to avoid repetition. As a rule, you can guard against the problem by making sure that you have clearly expressed the conceptual link between your central conclusion and any implications you may draw. An implication is not a totally new point but rather one that follows from the position you have been analyzing.

Similarly, although a capping judgment or send-off may appear for the first time in your concluding paragraph, it should have been anticipated by the body of your paper. Conclusions often indicate where you think you (or an interested reader) may need to go next, but you don't actually go there. In a paper on the economist Milton Friedman, for example, if you think that another economist offers a useful way of critiquing him, you probably should not introduce this person for the first time in your conclusion.

Overstatement

Many writers are confused over how much they should claim in the conclusion. Out of the understandable (but mistaken) desire for a grand (rather than a modest and qualified) culmination, writers sometimes overstate the case. They assert more than their evidence has proved or even suggested. Must a conclusion arrive at some comprehensive and final answer to the question that your paper has analyzed? Depending on the question and the disciplinary conventions, you may need to come down exclusively on one side or another. In a great many cases, however, the answers with which you conclude can be more moderate. Especially in the humanities, good analytical writing seeks to unfold successive layers of implication, so it's not even reasonable for you to expect neat closure. In such cases, you are usually better off qualifying your final judgments, drawing the line at points of relative stability.

Anticlimax

The end of the conclusion is a "charged" site because it gives the reader a last impression of your paper. If you end with a concession—an acknowledgement of a rival position at odds with your thesis—you risk leaving the reader unsettled and possibly confused. The term for this kind of letdown is *anticlimax*. In most cases, you will flub the send-off if you depart the paper on an anticlimax.

There are many forms of anticlimax besides ending with a concession. If your conclusion peters out in a random list or an apparent afterthought or a last-minute qualification of your claims, the effect is anticlimactic. And for many readers, if your final answer comes from quoting an authority in place of establishing your own, that, too, is an anticlimax.

At the beginning of this chapter we suggested that a useful rule for the introduction is to play an ace but not your whole hand. In the context of this card-game analogy, it is similarly effective to save an ace for the conclusion. In most cases, this high card provides an answer to some culminating So what? question—a last view of the implications or consequences of your analysis.

INTRODUCTIONS IN THE SCIENCES

The natural and social sciences both rely on a fairly tightly defined format for reports on research. The professors quoted in the Voices from across the Curriculum sections in the remainder of this chapter emphasize the importance of isolating a specific question or issue and locating it within a wider context. Notice, as you read these voices, how little the model for an introduction changes in moving from social science to natural science.

In the sciences, the introduction is an especially important and also somewhat challenging section of the report to compose because it requires a writer not merely to assemble but also to assimilate the background information and ideas that frame his or her hypothesis.

One distinctive feature of scientific papers is that a separate prefatory section called the *abstract* precedes the introduction. Authors also produce abstracts for papers in many other disciplines, but these are usually published separately—for example, in a bibliography, in a journal's table of contents, and so forth.

VOICES FROM ACROSS THE CURRICULUM

Introductions in the Sciences

A paper usually starts by making some general observation or a description of known phenomena and by providing the reader with some background information. The first paragraphs should illustrate an understanding of the issues at hand and should present an argument for why the research should be done. In other words, a context or framework is established for the entire paper. This background information must lead to a clear statement of the objectives of the paper and the hypothesis that will be experimentally tested. This movement from broad ideas and observations to a specific question or test starts the deductive scientific process.

—Richard Niesenbaum, *Professor of Biology*

VOICES FROM ACROSS THE CURRICULUM

Assimilating Prior Research

The introduction is one of the hardest sections to write. In the introduction, students must summarize, analyze, and integrate the work of numerous other authors and use that to build their own argument.

The task is to read each article and *summarize* it in their own words. The key is to analyze rather than just repeat material from the articles so as to make clear the connections among them. (It is important to note that experimental psychologists almost never use direct quotes in their writing. Many of my students have been trained to use direct quotation for their other classes, and so I have to spend time explaining how to summarize without directly quoting or plagiarizing the work that they have read.)

Finally, in the introduction the students must show explicitly how the articles they have summarized lead to the hypothesis they have devised. Many times the students see the connection as implicitly obvious, but I require that they explicitly state the relationships between what they read and what they plan to do.

—Laura Edelman, *Professor of Psychology*

VOICES FROM ACROSS THE CURRICULUM

Writing Conclusions in the Sciences

The conclusion occurs in a section labeled "Discussion" and, as specified by the *Publication Manual of the American Psychological Association,* is guided by the following questions:

What have I contributed here?

How has my study helped to resolve the original problem?

What conclusions and theoretical implications can I draw from my study?

In a broad sense, a particular research report should be seen as but one moment in a broader research tradition that *preceded* the particular study being written about and that will *continue after* this study is published. And so the conclusion should tie this particular study into both previous research considering implications for the theory guiding this study and (when applicable) practical implications of this study. One of the great challenges of writing a research report is thus to place this particular study within that broader research tradition. That's an analytical task.

—Alan Tjeltveit, *Professor of Psychology*

CONCLUSIONS IN THE SCIENCES: THE DISCUSSION SECTION

As is the case with introductions, the conclusions of reports written in the natural sciences and psychology are regulated by formalized disciplinary formats. Conclusions, for example, occur in a section entitled "Discussion." There the writer analyzes conclusions and qualifies them in relation to some larger experimental context, "the big picture."

First, specific results are interpreted (but not restated), and then their implications and limitations are discussed. At the end, the writer should rephrase the original research question and discuss it in light of the results presented. It is at this point that alternative explanations may be considered and new questions posed.

ASSIGNMENTS: Analyzing Introductions and Conclusions

1. Introductions and audience: compare and contrast introductory paragraphs from a popular magazine with those from an academic journal aimed at a more specialized audience. Select one of each and analyze them to determine what each author assumes the audience knows. Where in each paragraph are these assumptions most evident? If you write out your analysis, it should probably take about a page, but this exercise can also be done productively with other people in a small group.

2. Analyzing introductions: one of the best ways to learn about introductions is to gather some sample introductory paragraphs and, working on your own or in a small group, figure out how each one works and what it accomplishes.

Here are some particular questions you might pose:

- Why does the writer start in this way—what is accomplished?
- What kind of relationship does this opening establish with the audience and to what ends?
- How does the writer let readers know why what they are about to read is called for, useful, and necessary?
- Where and by what logic does the introduction funnel?

3. Analyzing conclusions: find some examples of concluding paragraphs from published writing. First, compare the conclusion with the introduction, looking for the way the conclusion comes full circle. Which elements of the introduction are repeated to accomplish this? Then look for the statement of the essay's thesis in its final, culminating form. Finally, locate the send-off by finding implications and limitations that the writer has noted as part of his or her final So what? On the basis of your findings, write a few paragraphs in which you describe the writer's approach to conclusions.

   At this point you will be ready to repeat this exercise with some of your own work. Only this time, rather than describing the writer's approach, write an improved version of one of your conclusions based on what you learned from your analysis.

CHAPTER 12

Recognizing and Fixing Weak Thesis Statements

THIS FINAL CHAPTER OF Unit II offers a brief review and parting check-up on writing the thesis-driven essay. It offers advice on how to recognize the difference between good thesis statements—statements that make claims that need proving—and weak thesis statements. The chapter consists largely of examples of weak thesis statements taken from actual student papers, followed by discussion of how to recognize and rethink and rephrase them.

Weak thesis statements have in common that they don't give the writer enough to do in his or her essay. Typically a weak thesis is an unproductive claim because it doesn't actually require further thinking or proof, as, for example, in the case of "The jean industry targets its advertisements to appeal to young adults" (probably a statement of fact that doesn't need proving) or "An important part of one's college education is learning to better understand others' points of view" (a piece of conventional wisdom that most people would already accept as true, and thus not in need of arguing).

Solutions? Be suspicious of your first responses to a subject. Privilege live questions over inert answers. Find ways to bring out the complexity of your subject. Look again at the What It Means to Have an Idea section in Chapter 2, which tells you to start with something puzzling that you want to figure out rather than with something you already believe to be clearly and obviously true. Look back as well to Chapter 9, which guides you to use evidence to complicate your claims and to compose thesis statements that contain inherent tension. When in doubt, do more exploratory writing to trigger better ideas.

FIVE KINDS OF WEAK THESIS STATEMENTS AND HOW TO FIX THEM

By way of review, a *strong thesis* makes a claim that (1) requires analysis to support and evolve it and (2) offers some point about the significance of your evidence that would not have been immediately obvious to your readers. By contrast, a *weak thesis* either makes no claim or makes a claim that does not need proving.

As a quick flash-forward, here are the five kinds of weak thesis statements—ones that:

1. Make no claim ("This paper examines the pros and cons of").
2. Are obviously true or a statement of fact ("Exercise is good for you").
3. Restate conventional wisdom ("Love conquers all").
4. Offer personal conviction as the basis for the claim ("Shopping malls are wonderful places").
5. Make an overly broad claim ("Individualism is good").

WEAK THESIS TYPE 1: THE THESIS MAKES NO CLAIM

Problem Examples

I'm going to write about Darwin's concerns with evolution in *The Origin of Species*.

This paper addresses the characteristics of a good corporate manager.

Both problem examples name a subject and link it to the intention to write about it, but they don't make any claim about the subject. As a result, they direct neither the writer nor the reader toward some position or plan of attack. Even if the second example were rephrased as "This paper addresses why a good corporate manager needs to learn to delegate responsibility," the thesis would not adequately suggest why such a claim would need to be argued or defended. *There is, in short, nothing at stake, no issue to be resolved.* (For more, see the discussion in Chapter 7 entitled Giving Evidence a Point.)

Solution: Raise specific issues for the essay to explore.

Solution Examples

Darwin's concern with survival of the fittest in *The Origin of Species* initially leads him to neglect a potentially conflicting aspect of his theory of evolution—survival as a matter of interdependence.

The very trait that makes for an effective corporate manager—the drive to succeed—can also make the leader domineering and, therefore, ineffective.

Some disciplines expect writers to offer statements of method and/or intention in their papers' openings. Generally, however, these openings also make a claim: for example, "In this paper I examine how Congressional Republicans undermined the attempts of the Democratic administration to legislate a fiscally responsible health care policy for the elderly," *not* "In this paper I discuss America's treatment of the elderly." (For further discussion of using overt statements of intention, see Chapter 11, Introductions and Conclusions.)

WEAK THESIS TYPE 2: THE THESIS IS OBVIOUSLY TRUE OR IS A STATEMENT OF FACT

Problem Examples

> The jean industry targets its advertisements to appeal to young adults.

> The flight from teaching to research and publishing in higher education is a controversial issue in the academic world. I will show different views and aspects concerning this problem.

A thesis needs to be an assertion with which it would be possible for readers to disagree.

In the second example, few readers would disagree with the fact that the issue is "controversial." In the second sentence of that example, the writer has begun to identify a point of view—that the flight from teaching is a problem—but her declaration that she will "show different views and aspects" is a broad statement of fact, not an idea. The phrasing of the claim is noncommittal and so broad that it prevents the writer from formulating a workable thesis. (For more, see Chapter 2 on the problems of generalizing.)

> **Solution**: Find some avenue of *inquiry*—a question about the facts or an issue raised by them. Make an assertion with which it would be possible for readers to disagree.

Solution Examples

> By inventing new terms, such as "loose fit" and "relaxed fit," the jean industry has attempted to normalize, even glorify, its product for an older and fatter generation.

> The "flight from teaching" to research and publishing in higher education is a controversial issue in the academic world. As I will attempt to show, the controversy is based to a significant degree on a false assumption, that doing research necessarily leads teachers away from the classroom.

WEAK THESIS TYPE 3: THE THESIS RESTATES CONVENTIONAL WISDOM

Problem Examples

> An important part of one's college education is learning to better understand others' points of view.

> "*I* was supposed to bring the coolers; *you* were supposed to bring the chips!" exclaimed ex-Beatle Ringo Starr, who appeared on TV commercials for Sun County Wine Coolers a few years ago. By using rock music to sell a wide range of products, the advertising agencies, in league with corporate giants such as Pepsi, Michelob, and Ford, have corrupted the spirit of rock and roll.

"Conventional wisdom" is a polite term for cultural cliché. Most clichés were fresh ideas once, but over time they have become trite, prefabricated forms of nonthinking. Faced with a phenomenon that requires a response, inexperienced writers sometimes resort to a small set of culturally approved "answers." Because conventional wisdom is so general and so commonly accepted, however, it doesn't teach anybody—including the writer—anything. Worse, because the cliché looks like an idea, it prevents the writer from engaging in a fresh exploration of his or her subject.

There is some truth in both of the preceding problem examples, but neither complicates its position. A thoughtful reader could, for example, respond to the advertising example by suggesting that rock and roll was highly commercial long before it colonized the airwaves. The conventional wisdom that rock and roll is somehow pure and honest while advertising is phony and exploitative invites the savvy writer to formulate a thesis that overturns these clichés. It could be argued that rock has actually improved advertising, not that ads have ruined rock—or, alternatively, that rock has shrewdly marketed idealism to gullible consumers. At the least, a writer committed to the original thesis would do better to examine what Ringo was selling—what he/wine coolers stand for in this particular case—than to discuss rock and advertising in such predictable terms.

> **Solution:** Seek to complicate—see more than one point of view on—your subject. Avoid conventional wisdom unless you can qualify it or introduce a fresh perspective on it.

Solution Examples

While an important part of one's college education is learning to better understand others' points of view, a persistent danger is that the students will simply be required to substitute the teacher's answers for the ones they grew up uncritically believing.

While some might argue that the presence of rock and roll soundtracks in TV commercials has corrupted rock's spirit, this point of view not only falsifies the history of rock but also blinds us to the ways that the music has improved the quality of television advertising.

WEAK THESIS TYPE 4: THE THESIS BASES ITS CLAIM ON PERSONAL CONVICTION

Problem Examples

Sir Thomas More's *Utopia* proposes an unworkable set of solutions to society's problems because, like communist Russia, it suppresses individualism.

Although I agree with Jeane Kirkpatrick's argument that environmentalists and business should work together to ensure the ecological future of the world, and that this cooperation is beneficial for both sides, the indisputable fact is that environmental considerations should always be a part of any decision that is made. Any individual, if he looks deeply enough into his soul, knows what is right and what is wrong. The environment should be protected because it is the right thing to do, not because someone is forcing you to do it.

Like conventional wisdom, personal likes and dislikes can lead inexperienced writers into knee-jerk reactions of approval or disapproval, often expressed in a moralistic tone. The writers of the preceding problem examples assume that their primary job is to judge their subjects, or testify to their worth, not to evaluate them analytically. They have taken personal opinions for self-evident truths. (See the Because I Say So section in Chapter 7, and Overpersonalizing in Chapter 2 for further discussion of why this is a problem.)

The most blatant version of this tendency occurs in the second problem example, which asserts, "Any individual, if he looks deeply enough into his soul, knows what is right and what is wrong. The environment should be protected because it is the right thing to do." Translation (only slightly exaggerated): "Any individual who thinks about the subject will obviously agree with me because my feelings and convictions feel right to me and therefore they must be universally and self-evidently true." Testing an idea against your own feelings and experience is not an adequate means of establishing whether something is accurate or true.

It is fine, of course, to write about what you believe and to consult your feelings as you formulate an idea. But the risk you run in arguing from your unexamined feelings and convictions is that you will continue to play the same small set of tunes in response to everything you hear. And without the ability to think from multiple perspectives, you are less able to defend your convictions against the ideas that challenge them because you won't really have examined the logic of your own beliefs—you just believe them.

> **Solution:** Try on other points of view honestly and dispassionately; treat your ideas as hypotheses to be tested rather than obvious truths. In the following solution examples, we have replaced opinions (in the form of self-evident truths) with ideas—theories about the meaning and significance of the subjects that are capable of being supported and qualified by evidence. (See the Opinions [versus Ideas] section in Chapter 2.)

Solution Examples

Sir Thomas More's *Utopia* treats individualism as a serious but remediable social problem. His radical treatment of what we might now call "socialization" attempts to redefine the meaning and origin of individual identity.

Although I agree with Jeane Kirkpatrick's argument that environmentalists and business should work together to ensure the ecological future of the world, her argument undervalues the necessity of pressuring businesses to attend to environmental concerns that may not benefit them in the short run.

WEAK THESIS TYPE 5: THE THESIS MAKES AN OVERLY BROAD CLAIM

Problem Examples

Violent revolutions have had both positive and negative results for man.

There are many similarities and differences between the Carolingian and the Burgundian Renaissances.

Othello is a play about love and jealousy.

Overly generalized theses avoid complexity. Such statements usually lead either to say-nothing theses or to reductive either/or thinking. Similar to a thesis that makes no claim, theses with overly broad claims say nothing in particular about the subject at hand and so are not likely to guide a writer's thinking beyond the listing stage. The necessity of limiting overly broad claims is an essential concern throughout this book: from the naming of overgeneralizing as a primary counterproductive habit of mind in Chapter 2 to the focus in Chapter 9 on using complicating evidence to qualify overstated claims. See especially Refining Categorical Thinking in Chapter 5, Analyzing Arguments.

One of the best ways to avoid drafting overly broad thesis statements is to sensitize yourself to the characteristic phrasing of such theses: "both positive and negative," "many similarities and differences," or "both pros and cons." Virtually everything from meatloaf to taxes can be both positive and negative.

Solution: Convert broad categories and generic claims to more specific, more qualified assertions; find ways to bring out the complexity of your subject.

Solution Examples

Although violent revolutions begin to redress long-standing social inequities, they often do so at the cost of long-term economic dysfunction and the suffering that attends it.

The differences between the Carolingian and Burgundian Renaissances outweigh the similarities.

Although *Othello* appears to attack jealousy, it also supports the skepticism of the jealous characters over the naïveté of the lovers.

■ **Try this 12.1:** *Revising Weak Thesis Statements*

You can learn a lot about writing strong thesis statements by analyzing and rewriting weak ones. For the following example, first identify which type of problem each thesis is. Then rewrite them, providing solutions as we have done. Revising will require you to add information and thinking—to come up with some interesting claims that most readers would not already have thought of.

VOICES FROM ACROSS THE CURRICULUM

Making the Thesis Specific

Not so good thesis/question: "What were Humphrey's and Weidman's reasons behind the setting of *With My Red Fires,* and of what importance were the set and costume design to the piece as a whole?"

Good thesis: "While Graham and Wigman seem different, their ideas on inner expression (specifically subjectivism versus objectivism) and the incorporation of their respective countries' surge of nationalism bring them much closer than they appear. "

What I like about the good thesis is that it moves beyond the standard "they are different, but alike" (which can be said about anything) to actually tell the reader what specific areas the paper will explore. I can also tell that the subject is narrow enough for a fairly thorough examination of one small slice of these two major choreographers' work rather than some overgeneralized treatment of these two historic figures.

—Karen Dearborn, *Professor of Dance*

1. In this paper I discuss police procedures in recent domestic violence cases.

2. The way that the media portrayed the events of April 30, 1975, when Saigon fell, greatly influenced the final perspectives of the American people toward the end result of the Vietnam War.

3. From cartoons in the morning to adventure shows at night, there is too much violence on television.

4. The songs of the punk rock group Minor Threat relate to the feelings of individuals who dare to be different. Their songs are just composed of pure emotion. Pure emotion is very important in music because it serves as a vehicle to convey the important message of individuality. Minor Threat's songs are meaningful to me because I can identify with them.

5. It is important to understand why leaders act in a leadership role. What is the driving force? Is it an internal drive for the business or group to succeed, or is it an internal drive for the leader to dominate over others?

HOW TO REPHRASE THESIS STATEMENTS: SPECIFY AND SUBORDINATE

Weak thesis statements can be quickly identified by their word choice and syntax (sentence structure). Each of the first three problem examples for Weak Thesis Type 5, for example, relies mostly on nouns rather than verbs; the nouns announce a broad heading, but the verbs don't do anything with or to the nouns. In grammatical terms, these thesis statements don't *predicate* (affirm or assert something about the subject of a proposition). Instead, they rely on anemic verbs like *is* or *are,* which function as equal signs that link general nouns with general adjectives rather than specify more complex relationships.

By replacing the equal sign with a more active verb, you can force yourself to advance some sort of claim, as in one of our solutions: "The differences between the Carolingian and Burgundian Renaissances *outweigh* the similarities." While this reformulation remains quite general, it at least begins to direct the writer along a more particular line of argument. Replacing *is* or *are* (verbs that function only as equal signs) with stronger verbs usually impels you to rank ideas in some order of importance and to assert some conceptual relation among them.

The best way to remedy the problem of overgeneralization is to move toward specificity in word choice, in sentence structure, and in idea. If you find yourself writing "The economic situation is bad," consider revising it to "The tax policies of the current administration threaten to reduce the tax burden on the middle class by sacrificing education and health care programs for everyone."

Here's the problem/solution in schematic form:

Broad Noun	+ Weak Verb	+ Vague, Evaluative Modifier
The economic situation	is	bad

Specific Noun	+ Active Verb	+ Specific Modifier
(The) tax policies (of the current administration)	threaten to reduce (the tax burden on the middle class)	by sacrificing education and health care programs for everyone

By eliminating the weak thesis formula—broad noun plus *is* plus vague evaluative adjective—a writer is compelled to qualify, or define carefully, each of the terms in the original proposition, arriving at a more particular and conceptually rich assertion.

A second way to rephrase overly broad thesis statements, in tandem with adding specificity, is to *subordinate* one part of the statement to another. The both-positive-and-negative and both-similarity-and-difference formulae are recipes for say-nothing theses because they encourage pointless comparisons. Given that it is worthwhile to notice both strengths and weaknesses—that your subject is not all one way or all another—what, then, can you do to convert the thesis from a say-nothing to a say-something claim? Generally, there are two strategies for this purpose that operate together. The first we have already discussed.

1. *Specify:* Replace the overly abstract terms—terms like *positive* and *negative* (or *similar* and *different*)—with something specific; *name* something that is positive and something that is negative instead.

2. *Subordinate:* Rank one of the two items in the pairing underneath the other. When you subordinate, you put the most important, pressing, or revealing side of the comparison in what is known as the main clause and the less important side in what is known as the subordinate clause, introducing it with a word like *while* or *although*. (See Glossary of Grammatical Terms in Chapter 19 for the definitions of main and subordinate clauses.)

In short, specify to focus the claim, and subordinate to qualify (further focus) the claim still more. This strategy produces the remedies to both the *Othello* and the violent revolution examples in Weak Thesis Type 5. As evidence of the refocusing work that fairly simple rephrasing accomplishes, consider the following version of the violent revolution example, in which we merely invert the ranking of the two items in the pair.

Although violent revolutions often cause long-term economic dysfunction and the suffering that attends it, such revolutions at least begin to redress long-standing social inequities.

(See the discussion entitled What a Good Thesis Statement Looks Like in Chapter 9.)

IS IT OKAY TO PHRASE A THESIS AS A QUESTION?

A question frequently asked about thesis statements is: Is it okay to phrase a thesis as a question? The answer is both yes and no. Phrasing a thesis as a question makes it more difficult for both the writer and the reader to be sure of the direction the paper takes because a question doesn't make an overt claim. Questions, however, can clearly imply claims. And many writers, especially in the early, exploratory stages of drafting, begin with a question, as we note in the discussion of What It Means to Have an Idea in Chapter 2.

As a general rule, use thesis questions cautiously, especially in final drafts. Although a thesis question often functions well to spark a writer's thinking, it can too often muddy the thinking by leaving the area of consideration too broad. Make sure that you do not let the thesis-question approach allow you to evade the responsibility of making some kind of claim. Especially in the drafting stage, a question posed overtly by the writer can provide focus, but only if he or she then proceeds to answer it with what would become a first statement of thesis.

▇ Try this 12.2: *Determining What the Thesis Requires You to Do Next*

Learning to diagnose the strengths and weaknesses of thesis statements is a skill that comes in handy as you read the claims of others and revise your own. A good question for diagnosing a thesis is *What does the thesis require the writer to do next?* This question should help you to figure out what the thesis actually wants to claim, which can then direct you to possible rephrasings that would better direct your thinking.

Using this question as a prompt, list the strengths and weaknesses of the following two thesis statements, and then rewrite them. In the first statement, just rewrite the last sentence (the other sentences have been included to provide context).

1. Many economists and politicians agree that, along with the Environmental Protection Agency's newest regulations, a global-warming treaty could damage the American economy. Because of the great expense that such environmental standards require, domestic industries would financially suffer. Others argue, however, that severe regulatory steps must be taken to prevent global warming, regardless of cost. Despite both legitimate claims, the issue of protecting the environment while still securing our global competitiveness remains critical.

2. Regarding promotion into executive positions, women are continually losing the race because of a corporate view that women are too compassionate to keep up with the competitiveness of a powerful firm.

ASSIGNMENT: "Love Is the Answer"—Analyzing Clichés

Clichés are not necessarily untrue; they just are not worth saying (even if you're John Lennon, who offered this sodden truism in one of his more forgettable tunes).

One of the best ways to inoculate yourself against habitually resorting to clichés to provide easy and safe answers to all the problems of the planet—easy because they fit so many situations generically, and safe because, being so common, they *must* be true—is to go out and collect them, and then use this data-gathering to generate a thesis. Spend a day doing this, actively listening and looking for clichés—from overheard conversations (or your own), from reading matter, from anywhere (talk radio and TV are exceptionally rich resources) that is part of your daily round.

Compile a list, making sure to write down not only each cliché but the context in which it is used. From this data, and applying what you have learned from the chapters in this unit, formulate a thesis and write a paper about one or more of the clichés that infect some aspect of your daily life. You might find it useful to use The Method to identify key shared traits among the clichés and/or among the contexts in which you have discovered them. And you might apply the advice provided under Weak Thesis Type 3 to work out alternative formulations to certain clichés to discover what that might teach us about the ways clichés function in given situations—how, for example, they do and don't fit the facts of the situation. If you can find a copy of Paul Muldoon's short poem, "Symposium," which is composed entirely of clichéd expressions, it might anchor an analysis or provide a lens for uncovering aspects of your data.

UNIT III

Writing the Researched Paper

CHAPTER 13

Reading Analytically

THIS BOOK IS ABOUT ANALYZING TWO KINDS OF SUBJECTS, one of which we might call the world (anything and everything you want to better understand), and the other we could call the world of reading—other people's ideas as these are developed in writing. This unit, Writing the Researched Paper, focuses specifically on writing about reading, using print sources to contextualize, ground, and stimulate your thinking.

One of the biggest differences between high school and college reading practices is that college students are expected to understand fairly sophisticated theoretical frameworks and apply these to other materials. The goal is to learn how to do things with readings rather than just passively registering the information contained in them.

Because analysis relies so heavily on reading, we address ways of negotiating what you read, directly or implicitly, throughout this book. In this chapter, though, we are focusing exclusively on how you can see more in what you read and do more with it. This chapter's strategies include:

- Becoming conversant instead of reading for the gist.
- Reading for the pitch, the complaint, and the moment.
- Uncovering the assumptions in a reading—where the piece is coming from.
- Reading with and against the grain.
- Using a reading as a model for writing.
- Applying a reading as a lens for examining something else.

The idea of using a reading as a lens takes us to the next chapter of this unit—Using Sources Analytically—where you will find a set of strategies that comprise what we call *the conversation model,* the goal of which is to put your sources into conversation with one another and to open ways for you, the writer, to enter the conversation.

The greatest enemies of reading analytically are reading for the gist and the transparent theory of language. Reading for the gist causes readers to leap to global (and usually unsubstantiated) impressions. Like the Fortune Cookie School of Analysis (see Chapter 4) wherein readers extract a single message and throw away the rest, reading for the gist inclines readers to attend only superficially to what they are reading. The transparent theory of language, which we discuss in Chapter 3, has a similar effect. It causes readers to treat words as clear windows rather than as the lenses they are. Failure to arrest attention on the words themselves (the window that focuses and frames what we see) causes readers to miss all but the vaguest impression of the ideas that the words embody.

HOW TO READ: WORDS MATTER

In a sense, the world is a text. As any child psychology textbook will tell you, as we acquire language, we acquire knowledge of the world. We can ask for things, say what's on our minds. This is not to say that everything is words, that words are the only reality. But to an enormous extent, we understand the world and our relation to it by working through language. Words matter: they are how we process the world.

As you have probably noticed, this book uses the word *reading* to mean *interpreting*. This usage goes back to the idea of the world as a text. This is not a new idea. The Puritans envisioned the world as a text in which God read their lives, and so, predictably, they started reading their lives too, reflecting on events that befell them, querying whether these were signs of salvation or damnation. (The stakes for being a good reader couldn't have been higher!) In short, reading for the Puritans meant gathering evidence and analyzing it to arrive at conclusions.

This more generalized notion of reading as interpretation remains with us today. For most of us a significant amount of that interpretation actually consists of the more literal act of reading—that is, moving our eyes along a line of printed words and processing what the words signify (reading comprehension, as the standardized tests call it). And so reading suggests two related activities: (1) reading in the literal sense of tackling words on the page, and (2) reading in the sense of gathering data that can be analyzed as primary evidence to produce ideas.

Considering how central both kinds of reading are in our lives, it's amazing how little we think about words themselves. We use words all the time, but often unthinkingly. We don't plan out our sentences before we utter them, for example, and the same goes for many of the ones that we write. Most of us live, however, as if there were a consensus about what words mean. We tend to assume that things mean simply or singly. Often—much more than you suspect—there isn't a consensus.

In previous chapters we put forth the notion that things have multiple meanings—that there are almost always multiple plausible interpretations. Similarly, all words have multiple meanings, and words mean differently depending on context. Consider the following examples of memorably silly headlines posted on the Internet: "Teacher Strikes Idle Kids," "Panda Mating Fails: Veterinarian Takes Over," "New Vaccines May Contain Rabies," "Local High School Drop-outs Cut in Half," and "Include Your Children When Baking Cookies" (or if you prefer, "Kids Make Nutritious Snacks"). Another posting included sentences such as "The bandage was wound around the wound" and "After a number of injections my jaw got number." English is often a nutty language, and we need to remember this fact whenever we start getting too complacent about the meanings of words being stable and obvious.

BECOMING CONVERSANT INSTEAD OF READING FOR THE GIST

Many readers operate under the mistaken impression that they are to read for the gist—for the main point, to be gleaned through a glancing speed-reading. Instead, the vast majority of writing tasks that you encounter in school and in the workplace require your *conversancy* with material that you have read. To become conversant means that:

1. After a significant amount of work with the material, you should be able to talk about it conversationally with other people, and answer questions about it without having to look everything up.

2. You should be able to converse with the material—to be in some kind of dialogue with it, to see the questions the material asks, and to pose your own questions about it.

Few people are able to really understand things they read or see without making the language of that material in some way their own—a goal most easily achieved by working closely with the language itself. We become conversant, in other words, by finding ways to actively engage material rather than moving passively through it.

Why bother to master information in this way when you can just Google it on your iPhone? It's all about what is actually in your head to think with and not just what's at your fingertips. The ancient Greek philosopher Plato speculated that the written word would damage civilization as he knew it. Writing, he argued, would eliminate people's need to remember things, and thus their capacity for assimilating information would decline. By analogy, the ready access we enjoy to information on the Internet has arguably further reduced our motivation to make the necessary effort to retain things in memory.

Why is this a problem? Why isn't it okay just to go look things up whenever you need them because information is now so easy to access? An insufficiently furnished mind—one crowded with whatever the loudest and most insistent voices in the culture are saying—doesn't allow for the same quality of thinking that a better furnished one would. Neuroscience is now telling us that what we put in our brains affects the way they work. The things we do and think actually change our brains, so it matters what we put in there.

And as learning theorists tell us, you can't learn passively; it requires an act of will and a set of activities that stir you into acquisition and assimilation mode. This is why skills such as note taking, paraphrasing, and outlining—all forms of summary—are not just empty mechanical tasks. They are the mind's means of acquiring material to think with.

THREE TOOLS TO IMPROVE YOUR READING: A REVIEW

The following three strategies combined can become the basis of your preparation for class discussion as well as writing about reading. The first move is to choose the single passage in the reading (and this can be as little as a sentence) to write about.

Paraphrase the key terms repeatedly. And then write a paragraph on what this process caused you to better understand. It's this last act of reflection that launches you into laying out the implications of the reading, allowing you to think with and about the material rather than just registering it passively.

- *Freewriting and passage-based focused freewriting:* Ask yourself: What is the single sentence that I think it is most important for us to discuss and why? The underlying assumption here is that readers gain a better appreciation of how the whole works when they've come to better understand a piece of it. A freewrite should target key phrases and paraphrase them, ask So what? about the details, and address how the passage is representative of broader issues in the reading.

- *Paraphrase × 3:* Paraphrasing inevitably discloses that what is being paraphrased is more complicated than it first appeared. Paraphrase is not summary; it's a mode of inquiry and the first step toward interpretation. (See Chapter 3.)

- *Ranking versus coverage:* Another means of combating passive registering of information is the strategy we call ranking. Once a reader has to decide which pieces of evidence are most interesting or most revealing or most significant, etc., he or she is propelled into thinking analytically rather than just recording information. This principle (ranking vs. neutral coverage) holds true for all of the standard modes of exposition, such as comparison/contrast, summary, and definition.

THE PITCH, THE COMPLAINT, AND THE MOMENT

In reading analytically, a useful premise to start from is that information is almost never neutral. There is no such thing as "just information." Every reading can be thought of in terms of the following three components:

- The *pitch:* what the piece wishes you to believe.
- The *complaint:* what the piece is reacting to or worried about.
- The *moment:* the historical and cultural context within which the piece is operating.

Here's a bit more on each.

The pitch: A reading is an argument, a presentation of information that makes a case of some sort, even if the argument is not explicitly stated. Look for language that reveals the position or positions the piece seems interested in having you adopt.

The complaint: A reading is a reaction to some situation, some set of circumstances, that the piece has set out to address, even though the writer may not come out and explicitly say so. An indispensable means of understanding someone else's writing is to figure out what seems to have caused the person to write the piece in the first place. Writers write, presumably, because they think something needs to be addressed. What? Look for language in the piece that reveals the writer's starting point. If you can find the position or situation he or she is worried about and possibly trying to correct, you will find it much easier to locate the argument, the position the piece asks you to accept.

The moment: A reading is a response to the world conditioned by the writer's particular moment in time. In your attempt to figure out not only what a piece says but where it is coming from (the causes of its having been written in the first place and the positions it works to establish), history is significant. When was the piece written? Where? What else was going on at the time that might have shaped the writer's ideas and attitudes?

■ Try this 13.1: *Locating the Pitch and the Complaint*

Take a passage of something you are reading, and look for language that reveals the position or positions the piece seems interested in having you adopt. It is easier to find the pitch if you first look for language that reveals the position or situation the writer is trying to correct. Type out the sentences that most fully articulate the pitch and the complaint. Then paraphrase them to enrich your sense of where the writer is coming from and where the piece is trying to take you.

UNCOVERING THE ASSUMPTIONS IN A READING

Uncovering assumptions is a primary and powerful move in reading analytically. We devoted an extended analysis to it at the end of Chapter 5. Because this move—also known as reasoning back to premises—is such an important tool in a reader's arsenal, we briefly revisit the topic here.

An assumption is the basic ground of belief from which a position springs, its starting points or givens. All arguments or articulations of point of view have underlying assumptions. All readings are built on assumptions. Often, assumptions are not visible; they are implicit, which is why you need to stop and take the time to infer them.

Sometimes a text deliberately hides its premises—a pro-Nazi website, for example, that is ostensibly concerned with the increasing disorder of society. Sometimes a source just neglects to divulge its premises and perhaps may not know them. In any case, when you locate assumptions in a text, you understand the text better—where it's coming from, what else it believes that is more fundamental than what it is overtly declaring.

Chapter 5 offers a step-by-step procedure for uncovering assumptions. The essential move is to ask, *Given its overt claim, what must this reading also already believe?* To answer this question you need to make inferences from the primary claims to the ideas that underlie them. In effect, you are working backwards, reinventing the chain of thinking that led the writer to the position you are now analyzing.

■ Try this 13.2: *What Must the Writer Also Already Believe?*

Here's a prime example of a statement that conceals a wealth of assumptions. In the reference application sent to professors at our college for students who are seeking to enter a student-teaching program, the professor is asked to rank the student from one to four (unacceptable to acceptable) on the following criterion: *The student uses his/her sense of humor appropriately.*

What must the writers of the recommendation form also already believe? Compile a list of their assumptions. Here are two hints that can help you do this:

- Do Paraphrase × 3 on the quotation (the explicit claim) to help you see the range of implicit ideas attached to it.
- Articulate what the claim is *not* saying because understanding that often brings into relief the underlying positions that it is "saying."

Want more practice? Locate a statement from anything you are reading that you find interesting or challenging. Paraphrase it. Then uncover assumptions, asking what must the text also already believe, given that it believes this. List at least three assumptions.

READING WITH AND AGAINST THE GRAIN

It is useful to think of both written and visual works as independent entities, independent, that is, of their authors, produced by authors but not ultimately controlled by them. The poet Emily Dickinson expresses this idea in a poem about words and about an author sending his or her words into the world. Dickinson writes (in poem #1212): "A word is dead/When it is said,/Some say./I say it just/Begins to live/That day."

If we allow ourselves to think in this way—that writing, once committed to the page and released into the world by its author, comes to have a life of its own—then we are at liberty to see what is going on in that life that may or may not have been part of the author's original intention. If we take this writing-as-a-living-creature analogy a step further, we might reasonably grant that a piece of writing (say, a book), like a person, has an unconscious. In other words, we can ask not only what the book knows, what it seems fully aware of, but also what the book is saying that it seems not to know it is saying.

You might now be saying to yourself, "Doesn't this strategy for thinking about writing take us back to the hidden meaning theory that you debunked in Chapter 4?" Well, not really. Surely you have had the experience of looking back on something you have written—something good, even if only a sentence or two—and wondering where it came from. You didn't plan to say it that way ahead of time; it just "came out." This suggests that writers and artists can never be fully in control of what they communicate, that words and images always, inescapably, communicate more than we intend. And so it does not follow that the writers and artists who have made such works have therefore deliberately hidden anything from us.

Instead, their work has revealed meanings that the writers and artists may not have intended to reveal and that they probably didn't know that they were revealing. Any of us who has had what we thought to be a perfectly clear and well-intentioned letter misinterpreted (or so we thought) by its recipient can understand this idea. When we look at the letter again we usually see what it said that we hadn't realized (at least not consciously) we were saying.

When we ask ourselves what a work (and, by implication, an author) might not be aware of communicating, we are doing what is called *reading against the grain*. When we ask ourselves what a work seems aware of, what its (and, by implication, its author's) conscious intentions are, we are *reading with the grain*.

Most good reading starts by reading with the grain, with trying to determine what the work and its author intend. This doesn't mean, as we discussed in Chapter 4, that an author's stated intentions get the last word on what his or her work can be taken to mean. But if we appreciate what authors and artists have to offer us, and if we respect them and the creative process, then we owe it to them and to ourselves to try to determine what they wished to say to us. This is known as a *sympathetic reading*, and generally speaking, you should always start this way, by trying to understand the piece on its own terms.

Both reading with the grain and reading against the grain require us to attend to implication. Communication of all kinds takes place both directly and indirectly. Some of what we mean is explicitly asserted and some—the indirect—must be inferred by readers. So, for example, in the classic novel *Jane Eyre,* the narrator Jane repeatedly remarks on her own plain appearance, with the implication that physical beauty is transient and relatively insignificant. The text is in fact obsessed with her plainness; almost every new character entering the novel reflects at some point on Jane's unattractiveness. Not that they don't like Jane—on the contrary, they esteem her greatly even as they acknowledge her lack of physical charms. Are we then to conclude that Jane and the novel believe that physical appearance does not matter? Probably not. Reading against the grain, we'd see the novel's very obsession with plainness as a symptom of how worried it is about the subject, how much it actually believes (but won't admit) looks matter.

Is reading against the grain—looking for what a work is saying that it might not know it is saying, that it might not mean to say—a hostile and potentially destructive activity? Some authors certainly think so because it is part of writing to wish to communicate to others what you want to communicate and thus to discourage readers from thinking something else instead. Many authors, however, also freely admit that writing is a somewhat scary as well as exhilarating process over which they have only tenuous control. Inquiring into intention often makes such writers nervous. They tend to think that the fewer questions asked about their creative process the less likely it will be for them to become paralyzed through self-consciousness. Writers in this second camp are more likely to agree that there are things in their writing—probably things worth finding—that they were not aware of. They just might prefer not to know what these are!

We can end this necessarily rather philosophical discussion of reading with and against the grain by returning to Dickinson's observation that the meaning of words is not fixed when they are put on paper. Her saying that a word "just begins to live that day" is an author's generous acknowledgement that a writer's works belong not just to the writer but to his or her readers. We cannot make of them what we will (as we argued in opposing the Anything Goes School of Interpretation in Chapter 4), but it is part of reading well to uncover ideas and assumptions that are not clearly and obviously evident as part of a writer's stated aims.

◼ Try this 13.3: *Appears to Be about X but Is Really about Y*

For obvious reasons, this strategy, introduced earlier, deserves another try here in the context of reading with and against the grain. Take a passage in anything you are reading and apply this formula to unearth attitudes and ideas in the reading that weren't immediately evident to you and that may not have been evident to the writer either. What, in other words, are some of the passage's implications that go somewhat against the grain of its apparent intention?

USING A READING AS A MODEL

Most of the critical activities that people do with readings involve assimilating and thinking about the information that is being conveyed to them. But to use a reading as a model is to focus instead on presentation. This represents a change in orientation for most readers, and it takes a little practice to learn how to do it. A useful guideline to remember is *look beyond content* (or subject matter). To focus on presentation is to focus on what a piece of writing *does* rather than just on what it says.

There are two primary reasons for using a reading as a model:

1. Most obviously, it can provide a way of approaching and organizing material that you might imitate.
2. Additionally, it can lead you to see features of a reading that you might otherwise overlook. We are, for the most part, seduced by the content of what we read, and so we do not see how the piece is behaving—how it sets us up, how it repeats certain phrases, how it is patterned. This is the analytical function of focusing on presentation rather than just on content.

If, for example, you were to do an analysis of programs designed to help smokers quit by using an analysis of programs designed to help drinkers quit, the latter might be used as a model for the former. And if the drinking cessation piece began with a long anecdote to phrase some central problem in program design, and you then began your piece with an analogous problem serving the same aim for your piece, that would represent still a closer use of a reading as a model.

To use a reading as a model, detach your attention from the pure information-assimilation mode to observe *how* the reading says *what* it says. Where does it make claims? What kind of evidence does it provide? Does the writer overtly reveal his or her premises? (See the section on uncovering assumptions earlier in this chapter.) How and when does he or she use metaphors or analogies?

And what about the overall organization of the piece you are reading? Not all reading proceeds in a straight narrative line from A to B to C. Some pieces are organized like quilts, a series of patches or vignettes operating as variations on a theme. Others favor a radial organization—locating some central issue or example in the center, and then spiraling out to connect it to other matters, then returning to it again and spiraling out again. A 10-on-1 analysis often takes this form, with the writer returning to the 1 for more details to explore.

Inexperienced writers sometimes resist using readings as models because they fear that imitation will suppress their ability to think for themselves. In practice this fear usually proves unfounded. Learning to see how other writers organize their thinking expands rather than closes down your range as both a reader and a writer.

APPLYING A READING AS A LENS

This final section of the chapter shows how to apply a reading to other material you are studying. Using a reading as a lens means literally looking at things as the reading does, trying to think in its terms.

When you put on a pair of glasses and look at something you know, you see it differently. In Chapter 2, we refer to this phenomenon as defamiliarizing. Defamiliarization is one function of using a reading as a lens. It allows us to see things anew.

Of course, the match between lens and new material is never perfect. Thus, you need to remember that whenever you apply the lens (A) to a new subject (B), you are taking A from its original context and using its ideas in different circumstances for different purposes.

As with using a reading as a model, when you use a reading as a lens you first need to separate its analytical method from the particular argument to which it leads. Not that the argument should be ignored, but your emphasis rests on *extracting the methodology* to apply it to your own analytical ends. For example, you can learn a lot about looking at spaces as described in an urban studies article on the relocation of the homeless in Los Angeles without necessarily focusing on either L.A. or the homeless. Most college campuses, for example, offer significant opportunities to observe the manipulation of public space either to encourage or deter use by certain populations.

The movement between lens and subject bears similarities with using a thesis to focus evidence. In Chapter 9, Making a Thesis Evolve, we explain that the relationship between thesis and evidence is reciprocal. The thesis causes you to see your evidence in a particular way, and your evidence in turn causes you to re-see parts of your thesis.

Your first goal when working with a reading as a lens, though, is to fully explore its usefulness for explaining features of your subject. We are not saying that you need to adopt a position of unquestioning reverence for all of the readings you'll be introduced to in college courses. But neither are we saying that your goal is to critique and dismiss other people's thinking solely on the grounds that it doesn't fit tidily with some subject you are considering. In the long run, the advance of knowledge is a product of patiently applying "old" ideas to new materials and of using the new materials to revise "old" ideas. In any event, what you typically do in college writing is not discover what's wrong with your lens, but discover which features in your evidence your lens doesn't seem to account for.

There are circumstances, however, in which evidence left fuzzy or unaccounted for by your reading-as-lens might appropriately be used to refocus the lens. Let's say, for example, that you have read a smart review essay on the representation of Black/White race relations in contemporary films in the 1970s, and you decide to use the review as a lens for exploring the spate of Black/White buddy films that emerged in the 1990s.

"Yes, but . . . ," you find yourself responding: there are places where the films appear to fit within the pattern that the article claims, but there are also exceptions to the pattern. What do you do? What *not* to do is either choose different films that "fit better" or decide that the article is wrong-headed. Instead, start with the "yes"—talk about how the film accords with the general pattern. Then focus on the "but"—the claims in the reading (the lens) that seem not to fit, or material in your subject not adequately accounted for by the lens.

Because cultural climates and trends are constantly shifting and reconfiguring themselves, particularly in popular culture, you will learn from examining the films how the original review might be usefully extended to account for phenomena that were not present when it was originally written. This move is a subject in our Chapter 14, Using Sources Analytically.

ASSIGNMENTS: Writing Analytically about Reading

1. Write a summary of a piece of writing using the following methods:
   a. Paraphrase × 3
   b. Ranking and reducing scope
   c. Attending to the pitch, the complaint, and the moment

2. Take a paragraph from an analytical essay you are reading in one of your courses or from a feature article from a newspaper or website such as Slate or aldaily .com—and do the following:

   • First, uncover assumptions by reasoning back to premises. Ask yourself, If the piece believes this, what must it also already believe? Answer that question and be sure to share your reasoning (why you think so).

   • Try reading against the grain. What, if anything, is the piece saying that it might not know it is saying?

3. Use a reading as a lens for examining a subject. For example, look at a piece of music or a film through the lens of a review that does not discuss the particular piece or film you are writing about. Or you might read about a particular theory of humor and use that as a lens for examining a comic play, film, story, television show, or stand-up routine.

4. Use a quotation as a lens: apply the following generalization about talk shows to a talk show of your choice: "These shows obviously offer a distorted vision of America, thrive on feeling rather than thought, and worship the sound-byte rather than the art of conversation." Alternatively, take any general claim you find in your reading and apply it to some other text or subject.

CHAPTER 14

Using Sources Analytically: The Conversation Model

THIS CHAPTER SHOWS YOU how to integrate secondary sources into your writing. That is often a daunting task because it requires you to negotiate with authorities who generally know more than you do about the subject at hand. Simply ignoring sources is a head-in-the-sand attitude, and, besides, you miss out on learning what people interested in your subject are talking about. But what role can you invent for yourself when the experts are talking? Just agreeing with a source is an abdication of your responsibility to present your thinking on the subject, but taking the opposite tack by disagreeing with a professor who has studied your subject and written books about it would also appear to be a fool's game. So what are you to do?

This chapter attempts to answer that question. It lays out the primary trouble spots that arise when writers use secondary materials, and it suggests remedies—ways of using sources as points of departure for your own thinking rather than using them as either The Answer or a whipping boy. We call this concept *conversing with sources*. In the next chapter we show how to use this model to arrange and revise researched papers that synthesize a range of sources. In this chapter we explain and illustrate the following strategies for analyzing sources.

SIX STRATEGIES FOR ANALYZING SOURCES

Strategy 1: Make Your Sources Speak

Strategy 2: Attend Carefully to the Language of Your Sources by Quoting or Paraphrasing

Strategy 3: Supply Ongoing Analysis of Sources (Don't Wait Until the End)

Strategy 4: Use Your Sources to Ask Questions, Not Just to Provide Answers

Strategy 5: Put Your Sources into Conversation with One Another

Strategy 6: Find Your Own Role in the Conversation

First, by way of definition, we use the terms *source* and *secondary source* interchangeably to designate ideas and information about your subject that you find in the work of other writers. Secondary sources allow you to gain a richer, more informed, and complex vantage point on your *primary sources.* Here's how primary and secondary sources can be distinguished: if you were writing a paper on the philosopher Nietzsche, his writing would be your primary source, and critical commentaries on his work would be your secondary sources. If, however, you were writing on the poet Yeats, who read and was influenced by Nietzsche, a work of Nietzsche's philosophy would become a secondary source of yours on your primary source, Yeats's poetry.

"SOURCE ANXIETY" AND WHAT TO DO ABOUT IT

Typically, inexperienced writers either use sources as answers—they let the sources do too much of their thinking—or ignore them altogether as a way of avoiding losing their own ideas. Both of these approaches are understandable but inadequate.

Confronted with the seasoned views of experts in a discipline, you may well feel that there is nothing left for you to say because it has all been said before or, at least, it has been said by people who greatly outweigh you in reputation and experience. This anxiety explains why so many writers surrender to the role of conduit for the voices of the experts, providing conjunctions between quotations. So why not avoid what other people have said? Won't this avoidance ensure that your ideas will be original and that, at the same time, you will be free from the danger of getting brainwashed by some expert?

The answer is no. If you don't consult what others have said, you run at least two risks: you waste your time reinventing the wheel, and you undermine your analysis (or at least leave it incomplete) by not considering information or acknowledging positions that are commonly discussed in the field.

By remaining unaware of existing thinking, you choose, in effect, to stand outside of the conversation that others interested in the subject are having. It is possible to find a *middle ground* between developing an idea that is entirely independent of what experts have written on a subject and producing a paper that does nothing but repeat other people's ideas. A little research—even if it's only an hour's browse in the reference collection of the library—almost always raises the level of what you have to say above what it would have been if you had consulted only the information and opinions that you carry around in your head.

A good rule of thumb for coping with source anxiety is to formulate a tentative position on your topic before you consult secondary sources. In other words, give yourself time to do some preliminary thinking. Try writing informally about your topic, analyzing some piece of pertinent information already at your disposal. That way you will have your initial responses written down to weigh in relation to what others have said.

THE CONVERSATION ANALOGY

Now, let's turn to the major problem in using sources—a writer leaving the experts he or she cites to speak for themselves. In this situation, the writer characteristically makes a generalization in his or her own words, juxtaposes it to a quotation or other reference from a secondary source, and assumes that the meaning of the reference is self-evident. This practice not only leaves the connection between the writer's thinking and his or her source material unstated but also substitutes mere repetition of someone else's viewpoint for a more active interpretation. The source has been allowed to have the final word, with the effect that it stops the discussion and the writer's thinking.

First and foremost, then, you need to do something with the reading. Clarify the meaning of the material you have quoted, paraphrased, or summarized and explain its significance in light of your evolving thesis.

It follows that the first step in using sources effectively is to reject the assumption that sources provide final and complete answers. If they did, there would be no reason for others to continue writing on the subject. As in conversation, we raise ideas for others to respond to. Accepting that no source has the final word does not mean, however, that you should shift from unquestioning approval to the opposite pole and necessarily assume an antagonistic position toward all sources. Indeed, a habitually antagonistic response to others' ideas is just as likely to bring your conversation with your sources to a halt as is the habit of always assuming that the source must have the final word.

Most people would probably agree on the attributes of a really good conversation. There is room for agreement and disagreement, for give and take, among a variety of viewpoints. Generally, people don't deliberately misunderstand each other, but a significant amount of the discussion may go into clarifying one's own as well as others' positions. Such conversations construct a genuinely collaborative chain of thinking: Karl builds on what David has said, which induces Jill to respond to Karl's comment, and so forth.

There are, of course, obvious differences between conversing aloud with friends and conversing on paper with sources. As a writer, you need to construct the chain of thinking, orchestrate the exchange of views with and among your sources, and give the conversation direction. A good place to begin in using sources is to recognize that you need not respond to everything another writer says, nor do you need to come up with an entirely original point of view—one that completely revises or refutes the source. You are using sources analytically, for example, when you note that two experiments (or historical accounts, or whatever) are similar but have different priorities or that they ask similar questions in different ways. Building from this kind of observation, you can then analyze what these differences imply.

WAYS TO USE A SOURCE AS A POINT OF DEPARTURE

There are many ways of approaching secondary sources, but these ways generally share a common goal: to use the source as a point of departure. Here is a partial list of ways to do that.

- Make as many points as you can about a single representative passage from your source, and then branch out from this center to analyze other passages that speak to it in some way. (See 10 on 1; Pan, Track, and Zoom; and Constellating in Chapter 8.)

- Use Notice and Focus to identify what you find most strange in the source (see Chapter 3); this helps you cultivate your curiosity about the source and find the critical distance necessary to thinking about it.

- Use The Method to identify the most significant organizing contrast in the source (see Chapter 3); this helps you see what the source itself is wrestling with, what is at stake in it.

- Apply an idea in the source to another subject. (See Applying a Reading as a Lens in Chapter 13.)

- Uncover the assumptions in the source, and then build upon the source's point of view, extending its implications. (See Uncovering the Assumptions in a Reading in Chapter 13.)

- Agree with most of what the source says, but take issue with one small part that you want to modify.

- Identify a contradiction in the source, and explore its implications, without necessarily arriving at a solution.

In using a source as a point of departure, you are in effect using it as a stimulus to have an idea. If you quote or paraphrase a source with the aim of conversing rather than allowing it to do your thinking for you, you will discover that sources can promote rather than stifle your ability to have ideas. Try to think of sources not as answers but as voices inviting you into a community of interpretation, discussion, and debate.

VOICES FROM ACROSS THE CURRICULUM

Evaluating Sources in the Sciences

One of the problems with trying to read critical analyses of scientific work is that few scientists want to be in print criticizing their colleagues. That is, for political reasons scientists who write reviews are likely to soften their criticism or even avoid it entirely by reporting the findings of others simply and directly.

What I want from students in molecular biology is a critical analysis of the work they have researched. This can take several forms.

First, *analyze* what was done. What were the assumptions (hypotheses) going into the experiment? What was the logic of the experimental design? What were the results?

Second, *evaluate* the results and conclusions. How well do the results support the conclusions? What alternative interpretations are there? What additional experiments could be done to strengthen or refute the argument? This is hard, no doubt, but it is what you should be doing every time you read anything in science or otherwise.

Third, *synthesize* the results and interpretations of a given experiment in the context of the field. How does this study inform other studies? Even though practicing scientists are hesitant to do this in print, everyone does it informally in journal clubs held usually on a weekly basis in every lab all over the world.

—Bruce Wightman, *Professor of Biology*

SIX STRATEGIES FOR ANALYZING SOURCES

Many people never get beyond like/dislike responses with secondary materials. If they agree with what a source says, they say it's good, and they cut and paste the part they can use as an answer. If the source somehow disagrees with what they already believe, they say it's bad, and they attack it or—along with readings they find hard or boring—discard it. As readers they have been conditioned to develop a point of view on a subject without first figuring out the conversation (the various points of view) that their subject attracts. They assume, in other words, that their subject probably has a single meaning—a gist—disclosed by experts, who mostly agree. The six strategies that follow offer ways to avoid this trap.

Strategy 1: Make Your Sources Speak

Quote, paraphrase, or summarize *in order to* analyze—not in place of analyzing. Don't assume that either the meaning of the source material or your reason for including it is self-evident. Stop yourself from the habit of just stringing together citations for which you provide little more than conjunctions. Instead, explain to your readers what the quotation, paraphrase, or summary of the source means. What elements of it do you find interesting, revealing, or strange? Emphasize how those affect your evolving thesis.

In making a source speak, focus on articulating how the source has led to the conclusion you draw from it. Beware of simply putting a generalization and a quotation next to each other (juxtaposing them) without explaining the connection. Instead fill the crucial site between claim and evidence with your thinking. Consider this problem in the following paragraph from a student's paper on political conservatism.

Edmund Burke's philosophy evolved into contemporary American conservative ideology. There is an important distinction between philosophy and political ideology: philosophy is "the knowledge of general principles that explain facts and existences." Political ideology, on the other hand, is "an overarching conception of society, a stance that is reflected in numerous sectors of social life" (Edwards 22). Therefore, conservatism should be regarded as an ideology rather than a philosophy.

The final sentence offers the writer's conclusion—what the source information has led him to—but how did it get him there? The writer's choice of the word *therefore* indicates to the reader that the idea following it is the result of a process of logical reasoning, but this reasoning has been omitted. Instead, the writer assumes that the reader will be able to connect the quotations with his conclusion. The writer needs to make the quotation speak by analyzing its key terms more closely. What is "an overarching conception of society," and how does it differ from "knowledge of general principles"? More important, what is the rationale for categorizing conservatism as either an ideology or a philosophy?

Here, by contrast, is a writer who makes her sources speak. Focus on how she integrates analysis with quotation.

Stephen Greenblatt uses the phrase "self-fashioning" to refer to an idea he believes developed during the Renaissance—the idea that one's identity is not created or born but rather shaped, both by one's self and by others. The idea of self-fashioning is incorporated into an attitude to- ward literature that has as its ideal what Greenblatt calls "poetics of culture." A text is examined with three elements in mind: the author's own self, the cultural self-fashioning process that created that self, and the author's reaction to that process. Because our selves, like texts, are "fashioned," an author's life is just as open to interpretation as that of a literary character.

   If this is so, then biography does not provide a repository of unshakeable facts from which to interpret an author's work. Greenblatt criticizes the fact that the methods of literary inter- pretation are applied just to art and not to life. As he observes, "We wall off literary symbolism from the symbolic structures operative elsewhere, as if art alone were a human creation" (Begley 37). If the line between art and life is indeed blurred, then we need a more complex model for understanding the relationship between the life and work of an author.

In this example, the writer shows us how her thinking has been stimulated by the source. At the end of the first paragraph and the beginning of the second, for example, she not only specifies what she takes to be the meaning of the quotation but also draws a conclusion about its implications (that the facts of an author's life, like his or her art, require interpretation). And this manner of proceeding is habitual: the writer repeats the pattern in the second paragraph, moving beyond what the quotation says to explore what its logic suggests.

Strategy 2: Attend Carefully to the Language of Your Sources by Quoting or Paraphrasing

Rather than generalizing broadly about ideas in your sources, you should spell out what you think is significant about their key words. In those disciplines in which it is permis- sible, *quote sources if the actual language that they use is important to your point.* This practice helps you represent the view of your source fairly and accurately. In situations in which quotation is not allowed—such as in the report format in psychology—you still need to attend carefully to the meaning of key words to arrive at a summary or paraphrase that is not overly general. As we have been saying, paraphrasing provides an ideal way to begin interpreting because the act of careful rephrasing usually illuminates attitudes and assumptions implicit in a text. It is almost impossible not to have ideas and not to see the questions when you start paraphrasing.

   Another reason that quoting and paraphrasing are important is that your analysis of a source nearly always benefits from attention to the way the source represents its position. Although focusing on the manner of presentation matters more with some sources than with others—more with a poem or a scholarly article in political science than with a paper in the natural sciences—the information is never wholly separable from how it is expressed. If you are going to quote *Newsweek* on Pakistan, for example, you will be encountering not "the truth" about American involvement in Pakistan but rather one particular representation of the situation—in this case, one crafted to meet or shape the expectations of mainstream popular culture. Similarly, if you quote President Bush on terrorism, what probably matters most is that the president chose particular words to represent—and promote—the government's position. It is not neutral information. The person speaking and the kind of source in which his or her words appear usually acquire added significance when you make note of these words rather than just summarizing them.

Strategy 3: Supply Ongoing Analysis of Sources (Don't Wait Until the End)

Unless disciplinary conventions dictate otherwise, analyze *as* you quote or paraphrase a source, rather than summarizing everything first and leaving your analysis for the end. A good conversation does not consist of long monologues alternating among the speakers. Participants exchange views, query, and modify what other speakers have said. Similarly, when you orchestrate conversations with and among your sources, you need to integrate your analysis into your presentation of them.

In supplying ongoing analysis, you are much more likely to explain how the information in the sources fits into your unfolding presentation, and your readers are more likely to follow your train of thought and grasp the logic of your organization. You will also prevent yourself from using the sources simply as an answer. A good rule of thumb in this regard is to force yourself to ask and answer So what? at the ends of paragraphs. In laying out your analysis, however, take special care to distinguish your voice from the sources'. (For further discussion of integrating analysis into your presentation of sources, see the commentary on the sample research papers in Chapter 15.)

Strategy 4: Use Your Sources to Ask Questions, Not Just to Provide Answers

Use your selections from sources as a means of raising issues and questions. Avoid the temptation to plug in such selections as answers that require no further commentary or elaboration. You will no doubt find viewpoints you believe to be valid, but it is not enough to drop these answers from the source into your own writing at the appropriate spots. You need to *do* something with the reading, even with those sources that seem to have said what you want to say.

VOICES FROM ACROSS THE CURRICULUM

Bringing Sources Together

Avoid serial citation summaries; that is, rather than discussing what Author A found, then what Author B found, then what Author C found, and so forth, *integrate* material from all of your sources. For instance, if writing about the cause and treatment of a disorder, discuss what all authors say about cause, then what all authors say about treatment, and so forth, addressing any contradictions or tensions among authors.

—Alan Tjeltveit, *Professor of Psychology*

As long as you consider only the source in isolation, you may not discover much to say about it. Once you begin considering it in other contexts and with other sources, you may begin to see aspects of your subject that your source does not adequately address. Having recognized that the source does not answer all questions, you should not conclude that the source is "wrong"—only that it is limited in some ways. Discovering such limitations is in fact advantageous because it can lead you to identify a place from which to launch your own analysis.

It does not necessarily follow that your analysis will culminate in an answer to replace those offered by your sources. Often—in fact, far more often than many writers suspect—it is enough to discover issues or problems and raise them clearly. Phrasing explicitly the issues and questions that remain implicit in a source is an important part of what analytical writers do, especially with cases in which there is no solution, or at least none that can be presented in a relatively short paper. Here, for example, is how the writer on Stephen Greenblatt's concept of self-fashioning concludes her essay:

It is not only the author whose role is complicated by New Historicism; the critic also is subject to some of the same qualifications and restrictions. According to Adam Begley, "it is the essence of the new-historicist project to uncover the moments at which works of art absorb and refashion social energy, an endless process of circulation and exchange" (39). In other words, the work is both affected by and affects the culture. But if this is so, how then can we decide which elements of culture (and text) are causes and which are effects? If we add the critic to this picture, the process does indeed appear endless. The New Historicists' relationship with their culture infuses itself into their assessment of the Renaissance, and this assessment may in turn become part of their own self-fashioning process, which will affect their interpretations, and so forth . . .

Notice that this writer incorporates the quotation into her own chain of thinking. By paraphrasing the quotation ("In other words"), she arrives at a question ("how then") that follows as a logical consequence of accepting its position ("but if this is so"). Note, however, that she does not then label the quotation right or wrong. Instead, she tries to figure out to what position it might lead and to what possible problems.

By contrast, the writer of the following excerpt, from a paper comparing two films aimed at teenagers, settles for plugging in sources as answers and consequently does not pursue the questions implicit in her quotations.

In both films, the adults are one-dimensional caricatures, evil beings whose only goal in life is to make the kids' lives a living hell. In *Risky Business,* director Paul Brickman's solution to all of Joel's problems is to have him hire a prostitute and then turn his house into a whorehouse. Of course, as one critic observes, "the prostitutes who make themselves available to his pimply faced buddies are all centerfold beauties: elegant, svelte, benign and unquestionably healthy (after all, what does V.D. have to do with prostitutes?)" (Gould 41)—not exactly a realistic or legal solution. Allan Moyle, the director of *Pump Up the Volume,* provides an equally unrealistic solution to Mark's problem. According to David Denby, Moyle "offers self-expression as the cure to adolescent funk. Everyone should start his own radio station and talk about his feelings" (59). Like Brickman, Moyle offers solutions that are neither realistic nor legal.

This writer is having a hard time figuring out what to do with sources that offer well-phrased and seemingly accurate answers (such as "self-expression is the cure to adolescent funk"). She settles for the bland conclusion that films aimed at teenagers are not "realistic"—an observation that most readers would already recognize as true. But unlike the writer of the previous example, she does not ask herself, If this is true, then what follows? Some version of the So what? question might have led her to inquire how the illegality of the solutions is related to their unrealistic quality. So what, for example, that the main characters in both films are not marginalized as criminals and made to suffer for their illegal actions, but rather are celebrated as heroes? What different kinds of illegality do the two films apparently condone, and how might these be related to the different decades in which each film was produced? Rather than use her sources to think with, to clarify or complicate the issues, the writer has used them to confirm a fairly obvious generalization.

Strategy 5: Put Your Sources into Conversation with One Another

Rather than limiting yourself to agreeing or disagreeing with your sources, aim for conversation with and among them. Although it is not wrong to agree or disagree with your sources, it is wrong to see these as your only possible moves. This practice of *framing the discussion* typically locates you either for or against some well-known point of view or frame of reference; it's a way of sharing your assumptions with the reader. You introduce the source, in other words, to succinctly summarize a position that you plan to develop or challenge in a qualified way. This latter strategy—sometimes known as straw man because you construct a dummy position specifically to knock it down—can stimulate you to formulate a point of view, especially if you are not accustomed to responding critically to sources.

As this boxing analogy suggests, however, setting up a straw man can be a dangerous game. If you do not fairly represent and put into context the straw man's argument, you risk encouraging readers to dismiss your counterargument as a cheap shot and to dismiss you for being reductive. On the other hand, if you spend a great deal of time detailing the straw man's position, you risk losing momentum in developing your own point of view.

In any case, if you are citing a source to frame the discussion, the more reasonable move is both to agree *and* disagree with it. First, identify shared premises; give the source some credit. Then distinguish the part of what you have cited that you intend to develop or complicate or dispute. This method of proceeding is obviously less combative than the typically blunt straw man approach; it verges on conversation.

In the following passage from a student's paper on Darwin's theory of evolution, the student clearly recognizes that he needs to do more than summarize what Darwin says, but he seems not to know any way of conversing with his source other than indicating his agreement and disagreement with it.

The struggle for existence also includes the dependence of one being on another being to survive. Darwin also believes that all organic beings tend to increase. I do not fully agree with Darwin's belief here. I cannot conceive of the fact of all beings increase in number. Darwin goes on to explain that food, competition, climate, and the location of a certain species contribute to its survival and existence in nature. I believe that this statement is very valid and that it could be very easily understood through experimentation in nature.

This writer's use of the word "here" in his third sentence is revealing. He is tagging summaries of Darwin with what he seems to feel is an obligatory response—a polite shake or nod of the head: "I can't fully agree with you there, Darwin, but here I think you might have a point." The writer's tentative language lets us see how uncomfortable, even embarrassed, he feels about venturing these judgments on a subject that is too complex for this kind of response. It's as though the writer moves along, talking about Darwin's theory for a while, and then says to himself, "Time for a response," and lets a particular summary sentence trigger a yes/no switch. Having pressed that switch, which he does periodically, the writer resumes his summary, having registered but not analyzed his own interjections. There is no reasoning in a chain from his own observations, just random insertions of unanalyzed agree/disagree responses.

Here, by contrast, is the introduction of an essay that uses summary to frame the conversation that the writer is preparing to have with her source.

In *Renaissance Thought: The Classic, Scholastic and Humanist Strains,* Paul Kristeller responds to two problems that he perceives in Renaissance scholarship. The first is the haze of cultural meaning surrounding the word "humanism": he seeks to clarify the word and its origins, as well as to explain the apparent lack of religious concern in humanism. Kristeller also reacts to the notion of humanism as an improvement upon medieval Aristotelian scholasticism.

Rather than leading with her own beliefs about the source, the writer emphasizes the issues and problems she believes are central in it. Although the writer's position on her source is apparently neutral, she is not summarizing passively. In addition to making choices about what is especially significant in the source, she has also located it within the conversation that its author, Kristeller, was having with his own sources—the works of other scholars whose view of humanism he wants to revise ("Kristeller responds to two problems").

As an alternative to formulating your opinion of the sources, try constructing the conversation that you think the author of one of your sources might have with the author of another. How might they recast each other's ideas, as opposed to merely agreeing or disagreeing with those ideas? Notice how, farther on in the paper, the writer uses this strategy to achieve a clearer picture of Kristeller's point of view:

Unlike Kristeller, Tillyard [in *The Elizabethan World Picture*] also tries to place the seeds of individualism in the minds of the medievals. "Those who know most about the Middle Ages," he claims, "now assure us that humanism and a belief in the present life were powerful by the 12th century" (30). Kristeller would undoubtedly reply that it was scholasticism, lacking the humanist emphasis on individualism, that was powerful in the Middle Ages. True humanism was not evident in the Middle Ages.

In Kristeller's view, Tillyard's attempts to assign humanism to medievals are not only unwarranted, but also counterproductive. Kristeller ends his chapter on "Humanism and Scholasticism" with an exhortation to "develop a kind of historical pluralism. It is easy to praise everything in the past that appears to resemble certain favorable ideas of our own time, or to ridicule and minimize everything that disagrees with them. This method is neither fair nor help-ful" (174). Tillyard, in trying to locate humanism within the medieval world, allows the value of humanism to supersede the worth of medieval scholarship. Kristeller argues that there is inher-ent worth in every intellectual movement, not simply in the ones that we find most agreeable.

Kristeller's work is valuable to us primarily for its forthright definition of humanism. Tillyard has cleverly avoided this undertaking: he provides many textual references, usually with the companion comment that "this is an example of Renaissance humanism," but he never overtly and fully formulates the definition in the way that Kristeller does.

As this excerpt makes evident, the writer has found something to say about her source by putting it into conversation with another source with which she believes her source, Kristeller, would disagree ("Kristeller would undoubtedly reply"). Although it seems obvious that the writer prefers Kristeller to Tillyard, her agreement with him is not the main point of her analysis. She focuses instead on foregrounding the problem that Kristeller is trying to solve and on relating that problem to different attitudes toward history. In so doing, she is deftly orchestrating the conversation between her sources. Her next step would be to distinguish her position from Kristeller's. Having used Kristeller to get perspective on Tillyard, she now needs somehow to get perspective on Kristeller. The next strategy addresses this issue.

Strategy 6: Find Your Own Role in the Conversation

Even in cases in which you find a source's position entirely congenial, it is not enough simply to agree with it. This does not mean that you should feel compelled to attack the source but rather that you need to find something of your own to say about it.

In general, you have two options when you find yourself strongly in agreement with a source. You can (1) apply it in another context to qualify or expand its implica-tions. Or you can (2) seek out other perspectives on the source in order to break the spell it has cast upon you. To break the spell means that you will necessarily become somewhat disillusioned but not that you will then need to dismiss everything you previously believed.

How, in the first option, do you take a source somewhere else? Rather than focus-ing solely on what you believe your source finds most important, locate a lesser point, not emphasized by the reading, that you find especially interesting and develop it fur-ther. This strategy will lead you to uncover new implications that depend upon your source but lie outside its own governing preoccupations. In the preceding humanism example, the writer might apply Kristeller's principles to new geographic (rather than theoretical) areas, such as Germany instead of Italy.

The second option, researching new perspectives on the source, can also lead to uncovering new implications. Your aim need not be simply to find a source that dis-agrees with the one that has convinced you and then switch your allegiance because this move would perpetuate the problem from which you are trying to escape. Instead, you would use additional perspectives to gain some critical distance from your source. An ideal way of sampling possible critical approaches to a source is to consult book reviews on it found in scholarly journals. Once the original source is taken down from the pedestal through additional reading, there is a greater likelihood that you will see how to distinguish your views from those it offers.

You may think, for example, that another source's critique of your original source is partly valid and that both sources miss things that you could point out; in effect, you *referee* the conversation between them. The writer on Kristeller might play this role by asking herself: "So what that subsequent historians have viewed his objective—a disinterested historical pluralism—as not necessarily desirable and in any case impossible? How might Kristeller respond to this charge, and how has he responded already in ways that his critics have failed to notice?" Using additional research in this way can lead you to situate your source more fully and fairly, acknowledging its limits as well as its strengths.

In other words, this writer, in using Kristeller to critique Tillyard, has arrived less at a conclusion than at her next point of departure. A good rule to follow, especially when you find a source entirely persuasive, is that if you can't find a perspective on your source, you haven't done enough research.

ASSIGNMENTS: Conversing with Sources

1. Make one source speak to another. Choose two articles or book chapters by different authors or by the same author at different points in his or her career. The aim of the assignment is to give you practice in getting beyond merely reacting and generalizing, and instead, participating in your sources' thinking.

    Keep in mind that your aim is not to arrive at your opinion of the sources, but to construct the conversation that you think the author of one of your sources might have with the author of another. How might they recast each other's ideas, as opposed to merely agreeing or disagreeing with those ideas? It's useful to confine yourself to thinking as impartially as you can about the ideas found in your two sources.

2. Use passage-based freewriting to converse with sources. Select a passage from a secondary source that appears important to your evolving thinking about a subject you are studying, and do a passage-based, focused freewrite on it. You might choose the passage in answer to the question "What is the one passage in the source that I need to discuss, that poses a question or a problem or that seems, in some way difficult to pin down, anomalous or even just unclear?" Copy the passage at the top of the page, and write without stopping for 20 minutes or more. Paraphrase key terms as you repeatedly ask So what? about the details.

3. Apply a brief passage from a secondary source to a brief passage from a primary source, using the passage from the secondary source as a lens (see Chapter 13). Choose the secondary source passage first—one that you find particularly interesting, revealing, or problematic. Then locate a corresponding passage from the primary source to which the sentence from the first passage can be connected in some way. Copy both passages at the top of the page, and then write for 20 minutes. You should probably include paraphrases of key phrases in both— not just the primary text—but your primary goal is to think about the two together, to allow them to interact.

CHAPTER 15

Organizing and Revising the Research Paper: Two Sample Essays

IN THE PREVIOUS TWO CHAPTERS we have offered a range of strategies for analyzing sources, for putting them into conversation with one another, and for finding your own voice in that conversation. In this chapter we offer and analyze two research papers written by college students. The first is still in need of revision. The second is a good example of a finished draft.

A SAMPLE RESEARCH PAPER AND HOW TO REVISE IT: THE FLIGHT FROM TEACHING

This paper is a synthesis of sources on the tension between research and teaching among college faculty. In the paper the student attempts to negotiate among competing positions while also arriving at her own position. The problem of the paper, in brief, is that the writer raises but does not adequately deal with points of view in her sources that disagree with one another as well as her own. Our revision suggestions show how the writer might have more effectively brought her sources into conversation and thus discovered that the assertion she offers as her conclusion is in fact an evasion that needs to be reconsidered.

Revision suggestions follow the essay. Our ongoing analysis of the student's text appears inside the essay in brackets.

The Flight from Teaching

[1] The "flight from teaching" (Smith 6) in higher education is a controversial issue of the academic world. The amount of importance placed on research and publishing is the major cause of this flight. I will show different views and aspects concerning the problem plaguing our colleges and universities, through the authors whom I have consulted. *[The introductory paragraph needs to be revised to eliminate prejudgment. Calling the issue controversial implies that there are different points of view on the subject. The writer, however, offers only one and words it in a way that suggests she has already leaped to a premature conclusion. Instead, she needs to better frame the issue and then replace the*

*procedural opening (see Chapter 11) with a more hypothetical working
thesis that will enable her to explore the subject.]*

[2]   Page Smith takes an in-depth look at the "flight from teaching" in *Killing the Spirit*. Smith's
views on this subject are interesting, because he is a professor with tenure at UCLA.
Throughout the book, Smith stresses the sentiment of the student being the enemy, as
expressed by many of his colleagues. Some professors resent the fact that the students take
up their precious time—time that could be better used for research. Smith goes on about
how much some of his colleagues go out of their way to avoid their students. They go as
far as making strange office hours to avoid contact. Smith disagrees with the hands-off approach being taken by the professors: "There is no decent, adequate, respectable education,
in the proper sense of that much-abused word, without personal involvement by a teacher
with the needs and concerns, academic and personal, of his/her students. All the rest is
'instruction' or 'information transferal,' 'communication technique,' or some other impersonal and antiseptic phrase, but it is not teaching and the student is not truly learning"
(7). *[The writer summarizes and quotes one of her sources but does not
analyze or offer any perspective on it.]*

[3]   Page Smith devotes a chapter to the ideal of "publish or perish," "since teaching is shunned
in the name of research." Smith refutes the idea that "research enhances teaching" and that
there is a "direct relationship between research and teaching" (178). In actuality, research
inhibits teaching. The research that is being done, in most cases, is too specialized for the
student. As with teaching and research, Smith believes there is not necessarily a relationship between research and publication. Unfortunately, those professors who are devoted to
teaching find themselves without a job and/or tenure unless they conform to the requirements of publishing. Smith asks, "Is not the atmosphere hopelessly polluted when professors are forced to do research in order to validate themselves, in order to make a living, in
order to avoid being humiliated (and terminated)?" (197). Not only are the students and
the professors suffering, but also as a whole, "Under the publish-or-perish standard, the
university is perishing" (180). *[The writer continues her summary of her source,
using language that implies but does not make explicit her apparent agreement with it. She appears to use the source to speak for her but has not
clearly distinguished her voice from that of her source. See, for example,
the third sentence and the last sentence of the paragraph. Is the writer only
reporting what Smith says or appropriating his view as her own?]*

[4]   Charles J. Sykes looks at the "flight from teaching" in *Profscam: Professors and the
Demise of Higher Education*. Sykes cites statistics to show the results of the reduction of
professors' teaching loads enabling them time for more research. The call to research
is the cause of many problems. The reduced number of professors actually teaching increases both the size of classes and the likelihood that students will find at registration
that their courses are closed. Students will also find they do not have to write papers,
and often exams are multiple choice, because of the large classes. Consequently, the
effects of the "flight from teaching" have "had dramatic ramifications for the way under-
graduates are taught" (40). *[The writer summarizes another of her sources
without analysis of its reasoning and again blurs the distinction between
the source's position and her own.]*

[5]   E. Peter Volpe, in his chapter "Teaching, Research, and Service: Union or Coexistence?" in the book *Whose Goals for American Higher Education?,* disagrees strongly that there is an overemphasis on research. Volpe believes that only the research scholar can provide the best form of teaching because "Teaching and research are as inseparable as the two faces of the same coin" (80). The whole idea of education is to increase the student's curiosity. When the enthusiasm of the professor, because of his or her research, is brought into the classroom, it intensifies that curiosity and therefore provides "the deepest kind of intellectual enjoyment" (80). Volpe provides suggestions for solving the rift between students and professors, such as "replacing formal discourse by informal seminars and independent study programs" (81). He feels that this will get students to think for themselves and professors to learn to communicate with students again. Another suggestion is that the government provide funding for "research programs that are related to the education function" (82). This would allow students the opportunity to share in the research. In conclusion, Volpe states his thesis to be, "A professor in any discipline stays alive when he carries his enthusiasm for discovery into the classroom. The professor is academically dead when the spark of inquiry is extinguished within him. It is then that he betrays his student. The student becomes merely an acquirer of knowledge rather than an inquirer into knowledge" (80). *[Here the writer summarizes a source that offers an opposing point of view. It is good that she has begun to represent multiple perspectives, but as with the preceding summaries, there is not yet enough analysis. If she could put Volpe's argument into active conversation with those of Sykes and Smith, she might be able to articulate more clearly the assumptions her sources share and to distinguish their key differences. How, for example, do the three sources differ in their definitions of research and of teaching?]*

[6]   The "flight from teaching" is certainly a problem in colleges and universities. When beginning to research this topic, I had some very definite opinions. I believed that research and publication should not play any role in teaching. Through the authors utilized in this paper and other sources, I have determined that there is a need for some "research" but not to the extent that teaching is pushed aside. College and universities exist to provide an education; therefore, their first responsibility is to the student. *[Here the writer begins to offer her opinion of the material, which she does, in effect, by choosing sides. She appears to be compromising— "there is a need for some 'research' but not to the extent that teaching is pushed aside"—but as her last sentence shows, she has in fact dismissed the way that Volpe complicates the relationship between teaching and research.]*

[7]   I agree with Smith that research, such as reading in the professor's field, is beneficial to his or her teaching. But requiring research to the extent of publication in order to secure a tenured position is actually denying education to both the professors and their students. I understand that some of the pressure stems from the fact that it is easier to decide tenure by the "tangible" evidence of research and publication. The emphasis on "publish or perish" should revert to "teach or perish" (Smith 6). If more of an effort is required to base tenure upon teaching, then that effort should be made. After all, it is

the education of the people of our nation that is at risk. *[The writer continues to align herself with one side of the issue, which she continues to summarize but not to raise questions about.]*

[8]   In conclusion, I believe that the problem of the "flight from teaching" can and must be addressed. The continuation of the problem will lead to greater damage in the academic community. The leaders of our colleges and universities will need to take the first steps toward a solution. *[The writer concludes with a more strongly worded version of her endorsement of the position of Smith and Sykes on the threat of research to teaching. Notice that the paper has not really evolved from the unanalyzed position it articulated in paragraph 2.]*

STRATEGIES FOR WRITING AND REVISING RESEARCH PAPERS

In our analysis of this student research paper, we offer suggestions that are keyed to our Six Strategies for Analyzing Sources in Chapter 14:

Strategy 1: Make Your Sources Speak

Strategy 2: Attend Carefully to the Language of Your Sources by Quoting or Paraphrasing

Strategy 3: Supply Ongoing Analysis of Sources (Don't Wait Until the End)

Strategy 4: Use Your Sources to Ask Questions, Not Just to Provide Answers

Strategy 5: Put Your Sources into Conversation with One Another

Strategy 6: Find Your Own Role in the Conversation

Be Sure to Make Clear Who Is Talking

When, for example, the writer refers to the professors' concern for their "precious time" in paragraph 2 or when she writes that "In actuality, research inhibits teaching" in paragraph 3, is she simply summarizing Smith or endorsing his position? You can easily clarify who's saying what by inserting attributive tag phrases such as "in Smith's view" or "in response to Smith, one might argue that." Remember that your role is to provide explanation of and perspective on the ideas in your source—not, especially early on, to cheerlead for it or attack it.

Analyze as You Go Along Rather Than Saving Analysis for the End (Disciplinary Conventions Permitting) (see Strategy 3)

It is no coincidence that a research paper that summarizes its sources and delays discussing them, as "The Flight from Teaching" does, should have difficulty constructing a logically coherent and analytically revealing point of view. The organization of this research paper interferes with the writer's ability to have ideas about her material because the gap is too wide between the presentation and analysis of her sources. As a result, readers are left unsure how to interpret the positions she initially summarizes, and her analysis, by the time she finally gets to it, is too general.

Quote *in Order to* Analyze: Make Your Sources Speak (see Strategy 1)

Even if the language you quote or paraphrase seems clear in what it means to you, the aim of your analysis is to put what you have quoted or paraphrased into some kind of frame or perspective. Quoting is a powerful form of evidence, but recognize that you can quote *very* selectively—a sentence or even a phrase will often suffice. After you quote, you usually need to paraphrase in order to discover and articulate the implications of the quotation's key terms. *As a general rule, you should not end a discussion with a quotation but rather with some point you want to make about the quotation.*

The following sentence from the second paragraph of "The Flight from Teaching" demonstrates the missed opportunities for analysis that occur when a quotation is allowed to speak for itself.

Smith disagrees with the hands-off approach being taken by the professors: "There is no decent, adequate, respectable education, in the proper sense of that much-abused word, without personal involvement by a teacher with the needs and concerns, academic and personal, of his/her students"(7).

This sentence is offered as part of a neutral summary of Smith's position, which the writer informs us "disagrees with the hands-off approach." But notice how Smith's word choices convey additional information about his point of view. The repetition of "personal" and the quarrelsome tone of "much-abused" suggest that Smith is writing a polemic—that he is so preoccupied with the personal that he wishes to restrict the definition of education to it. The writer may agree with Smith's extreme position, but the point is that if she attends to his actual language, she will be able to characterize that position much more accurately.

By contrast, notice how the writer of the following passage quotes *in order to* analyze the implications of the source's language:

If allegations that top levels of U.S. and British governments acted covertly to shape foreign policy are truthful, then this scandal, according to Friedman, poses serious questions concerning American democracy. Friedman explains, "The government's lack of accountability, either to Congress or to the public, was so egregious as to pose a silent threat to the principles of American democracy" (286). The word "principles" is especially important. In Friedman's view, without fundamental ideals such as a democracy based on rule by elected representatives *and* the people, where does the average citizen stand? What will happen to faith in the government, Friedman seems to be asking, if elected representatives such as the president sully that respected office?

By emphasizing Friedman's word choice ("principles"), this writer uses quotation not only to convey information but also to frame it, making a point about the source's point of view.

Try Converting Key Assertions in the Source into Questions (see Strategy 4)

When you are under the spell of a source, its claims sound more final and unquestionably true than they actually are. So, a useful habit of mind is to experiment with rewording selected assertions as questions. Consider, for example, what the writer of

"The Flight from Teaching" might have discovered had she tried converting the following conclusions (in paragraph 4) drawn from one of her sources into questions.

The call to research is the cause of many problems. The reduced number of professors actually teaching increases both the size of classes and the likelihood that students will find at registration that their courses are closed. Students will also find they do not have to write papers, and often exams are multiple choice because of the large classes.

Some questions: Is it only professors' desire to be off doing their own research that explains closed courses, large class sizes, and multiple-choice tests? What about other causes for these problems, such as the cost of hiring additional professors or the pressure universities put on professors to publish in order to increase the status of the institution? We are not suggesting that the writer should have detected these particular problems in the passage but rather that she needs, somewhere in the paper, to raise questions about the reasoning implicit in her sources.

By *querying how your sources are defining, implicitly and explicitly, their key terms,* you can gain perspective on the sources, uncovering their assumptions. Consider in this context the writer's own fullest statement of her thesis.

Through the authors utilized in this paper and other sources, I have determined that there is a need for some 'research' but not to the extent that teaching is pushed aside. Colleges and universities exist to provide an education; therefore, their first responsibility is to the student (paragraph 6).

More questions: What do she and her sources mean by research and what do they mean by teaching? To what extent can the writer fairly assume that the primary purpose of universities is and should be "to provide an education"? Can't an education include being mentored in the skills that university teachers practice in their own research? And isn't teaching only one of a variety of contributions that universities make to the cultures they serve?

Get Your Sources to Converse with One Another, and Actively Referee the Conflicts among Them (see Strategies 5 and 6)

By doing so, you will often find the means to reorganize your paper around issues rather than leave readers to locate these issues for themselves as you move from source to source. Both looking for difference within similarity and looking for similarity despite difference are useful for this purpose. (See Chapter 6.)

The organizing contrast that drives "The Flight from Teaching" is obviously that between teaching and research, but what if the writer actively sought out an unexpected similarity that spanned this binary? For example, Smith asserts that "research inhibits teaching" (paragraph 3), whereas Volpe contends that "only the research scholar can provide the best form of teaching because 'teaching and research are as inseparable as the two faces of the same coin'" (paragraph 5). But both sides agree that educating students is the "first responsibility" of colleges and universities, despite differing radically on how this responsibility is best fulfilled. Given this unexpected similarity, the writer could then explore the significance of the difference—that Smith believes professors' research gets in the way of excellent teaching, whereas Volpe believes research is essential to it. If the writer had brought these sources into dialogue, she could have discovered that the assertion she offers as her conclusion is, in fact, inaccurate, even an evasion.

By way of conclusion, we would like to emphasize that the strategies we've offered share a common aim: to get you off the hot seat of judging the experts when you are not an expert. Most of us are more comfortable in situations in which we can converse amicably rather than judge and be judged. Think of that as you embark on research projects, and you will be far more likely to learn and to have a good time doing it.

A GOOD SAMPLE RESEARCH PAPER: HORIZONTAL AND VERTICAL MERGERS WITHIN THE HEALTHCARE INDUSTRY

What does an effective analytical research paper look like? Look at the following piece, which demonstrates the analytical skills we discuss in this unit. We include brief commentary at the ends of selected paragraphs, but for the most part, you should notice how the writer uses her sources to focus questions, analyzing as she goes along. Also, note her habitual use of complicating evidence to evolve the conversation she is having with her sources.

Horizontal and Vertical Mergers within the Healthcare Industry

[1] The United States healthcare industry is constantly changing, as new ideas and strategies are developed to make healthcare more accessible and affordable for a greater number of people. Mergers within the industry are one of the new influential methods of altering the relationship between buyers and sellers of healthcare. Mergers distort the traditional roles of physicians, hospitals, and patients, but do so with an emphasis on cost-cutting, more efficient management, and better quality of care. Whether these mergers actually succeed in their outward goals is debatable; many studies have shown that these acquisitions seldom fully meet their objectives. Mergers are business deals, occurring in every market. But the healthcare market is unique in that its product, a necessity, often becomes an economic luxury—not everyone can afford the costs of medical coverage or care. *[The introduction opens with a clear premise—constant change—and rapidly limits the focus to mergers as one cause of change. The writer raises but does not prematurely resolve the question of mergers' successes and ends the paragraph by distinguishing what is at stake in her topic.]*

[2] The first distinct type of acquisition is known as a horizontal merger. It describes the joining of two hospital systems into one. Some simple examples of horizontal mergers include the transaction between Memorial Health System and Adventist Health System, both located in Florida: the four-hospital Memorial purchased the thirty-two-hospital Adventist in late August, 2000. Another example is the purchase of St. Mary Medical Hospital by Trinity Health, in separate parts of Michigan, completed in July 2000. In this case, the new hospital system was renamed St. Mary Mercy Hospital.[1] There are advantages and disadvantages to horizontal mergers, which will be explored, but a hospital system's main objectives in merging include reducing managerial costs, combining marketing efforts, pooling capital, and reducing excess equipment. *[Having used*

a panning shot to establish context in the first paragraph, the writer now tracks one kind of merger and suggests that further debate is to come.]

[3]   A vertical merger, however, is one in which a company is bought by another company within the same "supply chain"—that is, a firm might purchase its merchandise supplier.[2] In healthcare economies, this applies to suppliers and buyers of healthcare services, such as hospitals and HMOs, or hospitals and physicians. There are several complications to vertical mergers, especially apparent when the level of competition between the two merging entities is explored. Esther Gal-Or's article, "The Profitability of Vertical Mergers Between Hospitals and Physician Practices," will be used to illustrate these complications. *[The writer begins to foreground a complication that she will develop into an organizing contrast in the next paragraph, that between private profit and public good.]*

[4]   The selling point for all horizontal and vertical mergers is the expected increase in efficiency under the new system. But mergers benefit the merging parties immensely; are their public goals of efficiency and, in turn, lowered costs, really being achieved? In their article, "Are Multihospital Systems More Efficient?" economists Dranove, Durkac, and Shanley write that although "the conventional wisdom is that [horizontal mergers] will generate efficiencies in the production of services, surprisingly little systematic evidence exists to support this view."[3] By studying local Californian hospital systems in the 1980's and 1990's, the three researchers found that "the benefits of horizontal integration stem from greater efficiencies in marketing hospital systems . . . than from efficiencies in the production of services." *[The writer uses sources to frame questions. She then cites sources offering slightly different answers to the question of efficiency.]*

[5]   Using data from the California Office of Statewide Health Planning and Development, the researchers selected eleven hospital systems that met their requirements for inclusion in the study. After investigating costs per admission, administrative costs, price/cost margins, and limitations, the research "[challenged the idea] that horizontally integrated hospitals generate production efficiencies." More specifically, the study showed that the multihospital systems did not consistently reduce high-tech services, or have lower patient costs. In fact, the study concluded that "integrated hospital systems are more likely than their nonintegrated hospital counterparts to have unusually high administrative costs" and that they had "unusually high price/cost margins and operating profits."[4] These findings raise questions as to why hospitals merge if a merger does not provide a substantial increase in the method of operation's efficiency. If it actually results in higher costs for consumers in certain instances, what benefit does a merger bring? *[The writer again uses her sources to focus relevant questions. Notice how she moves beyond what one of her sources says to query what it suggests.]*

[6]   The instance is similar with vertical mergers. Many times, the joining of a hospital and HMO plan or hospital and physician practice does not result in the expected lowered costs and higher quality care for consumers. In her article "The Profitability of Vertical Mergers Between Hospitals and Physician Practices," Esther Gal-Or outlines her complex and thorough study of vertical mergers. Gal-Or details several different facets of the vertical merger: there are possible restrictions that these new systems face, all of which jeopardize their original

intent for efficiency. She also notes the importance of the competition between the two, writing

> When the degree of competitiveness [between the hospital and physician practice] is comparable, a vertical merger enhances the bargaining position of both merging parties vis-à-vis insurers. In contrast, when one provider's market is much more competitive than the other a vertical merger may reduce the joint profits of the merged entity.[5]

Therefore, the success of a vertical merger depends upon the relationship between the two merging parties. *[Here the writer leads with similarity despite difference to get her to her next source, which she briefly summarizes before zooming on a selected piece. Her final sentence draws a conclusion from the quotation, though more analysis of it might have enriched the conversation.]*

[7] Two examples noted in Gal-Or's study show the types of vertical mergers that are changing U.S. healthcare today. One of these is Allina Health System, a Minnesota-based system that covers over 25% of the state's residents through its HMO and PPO plans. A 1994 merger between a hospital chain and a health plan, Allina is continuing to acquire more hospitals and physician practices. Blue Cross of Western Pennsylvania, another example in the article, has also been purchasing physician practices.[6] Gal-Or's study eventually finds that when "two providers' markets are characterized by comparable degrees of competitiveness . . . both the merging hospital and the merging physician can negotiate higher rates with insurers. . . .Consumers are obviously worse off, as a result, since the higher rates translate to higher premia charged by insurers."[7] This offers a major criticism of vertical mergers because consumers are surely not looking to raise the cost of their premiums. These mergers, especially with the evidence provided in this article, seem to benefit the suppliers of healthcare but only at the financial expense of the patients. *[Using representative examples from her source, the writer interprets significant detail to draw a conclusion.]*

[8] By contrast, in a study entitled "What Types of Hospital Mergers Save Consumers Money," four researchers studied 3,500 United States hospitals from 1986–1994, including 122 horizontal mergers. Their study found that the mergers saved consumers by approximately 7%, which may show that vertical mergers (which also accounted for a large section of the systems studied) do reduce costs to consumers.[8] *[The paper pauses here to introduce complicating evidence, which leads to a brief concession (see Chapter 10). Note how the writer qualifies it with her choice of the word "may."]*

[9] Mergers, especially between hospitals, also provoke an interesting ethical dilemma. Special interest groups like Planned Parenthood and the American Civil Liberties Union (ACLU) have recently argued that these mergers are being treated as business contracts between two "sellers" and that the emphasis on providing better coverage for all has been disregarded. They argue that mergers aim not to help consumers, but to reduce internal costs and therefore raise profits for the hospitals. There are two aspects of hospital mergers that most concern these groups: first, the acquisition between religious and non-religious health facilities, resulting in religiously restrictive hospital systems, and, second, the possibility of a system becoming the only option for patients in rural communities. The ACLU recently released the following:

Many nonsectarian hospitals have recently been merging with religiously controlled hospitals. As a condition of the merger . . . these hospitals observe religious prohibitions against providing certain health services. The most publicized and significant prohibitions are found in the *Ethical and Religious Directives for Catholic Health Care Services.* . . . The *Directives* bar Catholic health care facilities from providing tubal ligation, vasectomy, abortion, in vitro fertilization, contraception, and emergency contraception in the case of rape.[9]

[Notice the evolving conversation, as the writer shifts from economic issues to the ethics these issues entail. Also note her habitual focus on complication, citing the "aspects that most concern."]

[10] In many instances, even when a Catholic hospital is acquired by a non-religious facility, the terms of the agreement include the system's adherence to these Catholic provisions. A statement from Planned Parenthood notes, "a Catholic hospital, or an HMO contracted with a Catholic hospital, is a community's only provider—leaving women with little or no access to reproductive health services."[10] For some, the decision to choose a hospital is religiously motivated; for others, especially women, they believe it is a personal right to have access to these reproductive health services. The ACLU and Planned Parenthood, however, feel strongly that it is a patient's right to choose whether or not to use these specific services. They also feel that mergers between hospitals jeopardize that right by creating a system in which certain services may not be available, regardless of patient preference. *[The conversation continues to evolve as the writer introduces new complicating evidence ("the second ethical issue") and analyzes its implications. Notice as well the diverse range of sources she has brought to bear.]*

[11] This argument is closely related to the second ethical issue against horizontal hospital mergers. In more rural communities, where there may be few options from which medical care consumers can choose, mergers create a monopolistic environment. The ACLU states that "low-income women and women in rural areas with few choices in medical care are the most vulnerable . . . Women who live in rural communities frequently have little choice. . . ."[11] This is detrimental to consumer choice because mergers in rural communities most likely create only one hospital system. A dissatisfied consumer in this situation does not have the power to switch medical suppliers; the power is taken away from the consumer and the seller has the ultimate control over the cost, type, and quality of care. Mergers in rural communities greatly resemble a monopolistic market force, and for this reason, are often the targets of antitrust cases against the new hospital system.

[12] The issue of antitrust violations frequently arises regarding mergers in the healthcare industry. This, too, is a criticism of the acquisitions. The majority of the antitrust cases in the United States involve horizontal mergers because, often, they produce one hospital system that borders closely on the definition of a monopoly. But there have also been antitrust questions raised regarding vertical mergers. The Marshfield Clinic case, from 1996, shows some of the questions. The Marshfield Clinic was a physician-owned clinic in Wisconsin that had vertically integrated with its HMO. But in the merger, the clinic had also excluded Blue Cross/Blue Shield HMO coverage from its services. Eventually, the courts found in favor of the Marshfield Clinic because its HMO obviously did not have the power to eliminate Blue Cross/Blue Shield from the healthcare market. *[As has been*

the case throughout the paper, the writer continues to focus on the important questions raised by her representative examples.]

[13] The most recent development in the antitrust cases of hospital mergers is the influential lobby groups, petitioning state governments on behalf of the hospital systems to exempt mergers within the medical industry from antitrust laws. The state of Maine lately encountered such a request. The 565-bed Maine Medical Center, in an effort to merge with two other hospitals, successfully lobbied the state government in 1996 to pass legislation exempting hospitals from state antitrust laws. Since the enactment of the Maine law, nearly twelve other states have also passed laws to free multihospital systems from antitrust regulations.[12] These laws have significant implications for the future of horizontal hospital mergers. They create a safer environment for mergers to occur: without antitrust laws, hospitals can freely merge and even assume a monopolistic form that jeopardizes the market of healthcare. *[As the paper approaches its end, the writer cites the "most recent" developments and opens out the conversation to "significant implications for the future."]*

[14] The advantages for horizontal and vertical mergers seem clear—by combining efforts, and creating one system, a multihospital facility should manage its administrative duties more efficiently, provide a higher level of care, and lower costs for its patients. Mergers should make the healthcare industry more successfully directed. The ultimate aim of any improvement or change in the industry should be to make better healthcare more accessible to a broader number of Americans. It appears as though horizontal and vertical mergers have the opposite effect on the industry. Their failure to provide a more efficient means of business and the way multihospital systems capitalize on reduced costs by simply earning a larger profit show that these mergers serve the providers, not the consumers. Additionally, multihospital systems jeopardize choices in care for those patients who would want specific services (which might not be available from a large system, religiously controlled). They also create a monopoly for consumers geographically distant from other choices. The horizontal and vertical mergers within the medical care market have not met expectations; instead, they reduce medical choices for consumers, do not guarantee increased efficiency, and create additional profits for the hospitals, physicians, and insurance companies involved. *[The paper concludes by coming full circle—back to change—and focusing on an unexpected similarity between horizontal and vertical mergers that leads the writer to take a stand in the debate that the paper's sources have been staging.]*

End Notes

1. "Mergers & Acquisitions," *Business Watch:* July 2000, p. 63.
2. Ibid, 1.
3. Dranove, Durkac, Shanley. "Are Multihospital Systems More Efficient?"
   Health Affairs: Volume 15, 1996.
4. Ibid, 102.
5. Gal-Or, Esther. "The Profitability of Vertical Mergers Between Hospitals and Physician Practices. *Journal of Health Economics:* October 1999, p. 623.
6. Ibid, 624.

7. Ibid, 625.
8. "Which Types of Hospital Mergers Save Consumers Money?" *Health Affairs:* Volume 16, p. 62–74.
9. "Hospital Mergers: The Threat to Reproductive Health Services." www.aclu.org.
10. "Opposing Dangerous Hospital Mergers." www.plannedparenthood.org.
11. "Hospital Mergers: The Threat to Reproductive Health Services." www.aclu.org.
12. "Smaller Hospitals Quicker to Use Maine Merger Law." *Modern Healthcare:* October 7, 1996.

GUIDELINES FOR WRITING THE RESEARCHED PAPER

Here are some guidelines stated in economical list form that are drawn from the strategies offered in this and the previous two chapters (Unit III).

1. Avoid the temptation to plug in sources as answers. Aim for a *conversation* with them. Think of sources as voices inviting you into a community of interpretation, discussion, and debate.

2. Quote, paraphrase, or summarize *in order to* analyze. Explain what you take the source to mean, showing the reasoning that has led to the conclusion you draw from it.

3. Quote sparingly. You are usually better off centering your analysis on a few quotations, analyzing their key terms, and branching out to aspects of your subject that the quotations illuminate.

4. Don't underestimate the value of close paraphrasing. You will almost invariably begin to interpret a source once you start paraphrasing its key language.

5. Locate and highlight what is at stake in your source. Which of its points does the source find most important? What positions does it want to modify or refute, and why?

6. Look for ways to develop, modify, or apply what a source has said, rather than simply agreeing or disagreeing with it.

7. If you challenge a position found in a source, be sure to represent it fairly. First, give the source some credit by identifying assumptions you share with it. Then, isolate the part that you intend to complicate or dispute.

8. Look for sources that address your subject from different perspectives. Avoid relying too heavily on any one source.

9. When your sources disagree, consider playing mediator. Instead of immediately agreeing with one or the other, clarify areas of agreement and disagreement among them.

ASSIGNMENTS: Exercises in Researched Writing

1. Here are a series of exercises organized in ascending order of complexity that go into writing a researched paper. You can practice these one at a time and then put them together.

   a. Compose an analytical summary of a single source (try ranking).

   b. Write about a primary source using a single secondary source as a lens.

   c. Compose a comparative analytical summary of two sources (try difference within similarity or similarity despite difference).

   d. Write a synthesis that brings together three or more sources, using them to raise questions and allowing each to help you complicate positions in the others (as the paper on mergers in health care does).

2. Here are a set of writing assignments, each using a strategy discussed in this and the preceding chapter.

   a. Practice making quotations speak by using paraphrase as a means of uncovering assumptions and bringing out implications. Use this method to zoom in on how sources define key terms.

   b. Practice putting two or more sources in conversation with one another: figure out how each source might see and recast the other's ideas. Construct and referee a conversation among your sources.

   c. Practice finding your voice in the conversation: take a source and apply it to another context, or locate a point it makes but does not dwell on and develop it further.

CHAPTER 16

Finding, Citing, and Integrating Sources

Featuring a Guided Tour of Research Methodology
by Reference Librarian Kelly Cannon

THIS CHAPTER SHIFTS ATTENTION to more technical matters associated with writing the researched paper. Although conventional library research has obviously changed a lot since the advent of computers, many of the basic strategies remain the same. More than just mechanically gathering information, research continues to be a primary means of discovering the ongoing conflicts about a subject and having ideas about it. Engaging the information sparks thinking, not just arranging.

The core of this chapter is a discussion of research methods written by a reference librarian at our college, Kelly Cannon. It offers a wealth of insider's tips for making more productive use of your research time, especially online and with databases. Among the featured topics are the following:

- How to assess a web page, including how to find out more about its author's credentials.
- How to search databases by subject heading in addition to keyword.
- Where to find full-text databases in different disciplines.
- The best subject-specific databases by discipline.
- A "Fool-Proof Recipe for Great Research—Every Time."
- Where to find citation guides on the Internet.

The chapter also offers sections on the following topics:

- How to cite secondary sources in MLA and APA style (a brief guide).
- How to integrate source material smoothly into your own prose while clearly distinguishing it from your comments about it.
- How to recognize and avoid plagiarism.
- How to compose abstracts of sources.

GETTING STARTED

The problem with doing research in the Information Age is that there is so much information available. How do you know which information is considered respectable in a particular discipline and which isn't? How can you avoid wasting time with source materials that have been effectively refuted and replaced by subsequent thinking? A short answer to these questions is that you should start not in the stacks but in the reference room of your library or with its electronic equivalent.

If you start with specialized dictionaries, abstracts, and bibliographies, you can rapidly gain both a broad perspective on your subject and a summary of what particular sources contain. This is the purpose of the reference room: it offers sources that review and summarize material for you in shorthand forms. In any case, you should take care not to get bogged down in one author's book-length argument until you've achieved a wider view of how other sources treat your subject.

It is also helpful to be aware that reference sources use agreed-upon keywords for different subjects. Thus, don't be surprised if the subject headings you enter initially yield nothing. Always check first at the reference desk for the *Library of Congress Subject Headings* to see what headings might be appropriate for your subject. It will tell you, for example, that fraternities and sororities are listed not under "fraternities and sororities" but rather under "Greek letter organizations."

Ask your reference librarian to direct you to the printed and online *indexes, bibliographies, specialized dictionaries,* and compilations of *abstracts* that are pertinent to your subject or discipline. An index offers a list of titles directing you to scholarly journals; often this list is sufficient to give you a clearer idea of the kinds of topics about which writers in the field are conversing. Here are a few index titles, indicating the range of what's available: *Applied Science and Technology Index, Art Index, Biography Index, Business Periodicals Index, Education Index, General Science Index, Humanities Index, Literary Criticism Index, New York Times Index, Philosopher's Index, Religion Index, Reader's Guide to Periodical Literature,* and *Social Sciences Index.*

Compilations of abstracts and annotated bibliographies provide more information—anywhere from a few sentences to a few pages that summarize each source. (See the section on abstracts and how to write them at the end of this chapter.) Here are a few commonly used titles: *Abstracts of English Studies, Chemical Abstracts, Communication Abstracts, Dissertation Abstracts, Historical Abstracts, MLA (Modern Language Association) International Bibliography, Psychological Abstracts, Monthly Catalog of United States Government Publications, Sociological Abstracts.*

Specialized dictionaries and encyclopedias are sometimes extraordinarily useful in sketching the general terrain for a subject, and they often include bibliographical leads as well. Here are some titles, ranging from the expected to the eccentric: *Dictionary of the History of Ideas, Dictionary of Literary Biography, Encyclopedia of American History, Encyclopedia of Bioethics, Encyclopedia of Crime and Justice, Encyclopedia of Economics, Encyclopedia of Native American Religions, Encyclopedia of Philosophy, Encyclopedia of Psychology, Encyclopedia of Unbelief, Encyclopedia of World Art, Encyclopedic Dictionary of Mathematics, Macmillan Encyclopedia of Computers, Encyclopedia of Medical*

History, McGraw Hill Encyclopedia of Science and Technology, New Grove Dictionary of Music and Musicians, Oxford English Dictionary.

Most of the indexes just listed also include book reviews. The *Reader's Guide to Periodical Literature* locates reviews as well as articles in popular—general audience—publications such as *Time* and *Newsweek.* For a broader range of titles, you might also consult *Book Review Index, Book Review Digest,* and *Subject Guide to Books in Print.* Indexes organized by discipline are more likely to take you to sources reviewed in academic journals; consult with your reference librarian for the indexes most pertinent to your subject.

Periodicals and journals offer an effective next step in finding sources once you've surveyed your topic in digest form. These are generally more up to date than either reference materials or books. Most library reference rooms have either a booklet that lists all of the periodicals and journals to which the library subscribes or a means of accessing a list of such holdings through the electronic catalogue. There are thousands of specialized journals available. If an index or bibliography refers you to a journal that your library does not hold, the library can usually get it for you (sometimes for a small fee) through a service known as interlibrary loan. Now many articles and reviews can be downloaded electronically; see the next section, Electronic Research: Finding Quality on the Web.

VOICES FROM ACROSS THE CURRICULUM

Tips for Starting Your Research

A useful research technique is to begin with indexes that will take you to specialized periodicals rather than beginning with books. Most scholarly journals have an index in the last issue for each year. Listed alphabetically by author, subject, or title are articles for a given year. Also, you may want to use any number of indexes. Here you look up a key word or phrase (of your choosing), and the index tells you when, what, where, and so forth for the word/phrase. Some of the key indexes are: *Social Science Index, Wall Street Journal Index* (for *WSJ* stories), *New York Times Index* (for *NYT* stories), and the *Public Affairs Information Service.*

A critical part of the bibliographic effort is to find a topic on which there are materials. Most topics can be researched. The key is to choose a flexible keyword/phrase and then try out different versions of it. For example, a bibliography on "women in management" might lead you to look up *women, females, business* (women in), *business* (females in), *gender in the workplace, sexism and the workplace, careers* (of men, of women, in business), *women and CEOs, women in management, affirmative action and women, women in corporations, female accountants,* and so forth. Be imaginative and flexible. A little bit of time with some of the indexes, listed earlier, will provide you with a wealth of sources.

—Frederick Norling, *Professor of Business*

VOICES FROM ACROSS THE CURRICULUM

Choosing Reputable Sources

Use quality psychological references. That is, use references that professional psychologists use and regard highly. *Psychology Today* is not a good reference; *Newsweek* and *Reader's Digest* are worse. And don't even think about the *National Enquirer*. APA journals, such as the *Journal of Abnormal Psychology,* on the other hand, are excellent.

In looking for reference material, be sure to search under several headings. For example, look under *depression, affective disorders,* and *mood disorders.*

Books (e.g., *The Handbook of Affective Disorders*) are often very helpful, especially for giving a general overview of a topic. Books addressing a professional audience are generally preferable to those addressing a general, popular audience.

Finally, references should be reasonably current. In general, the newer, the better. For example, with rare exceptions (classic articles), articles from before 1970 are outdated and so should not be used.

—Alan Tjeltveit, *Professor of Psychology*

Three Rules of Thumb for Getting Started

- *A half-hour spent with a reference librarian can save you a half a day wandering randomly though the stacks.*
- *Start in the present and work backward.* Usually the most current materials include bibliographical citations that can help you identify the most important sources in the past. Along the same lines, you are usually better off starting with journal articles rather than books because they are more current.
- *The reliability of the source is always an issue, but what's most important is knowing its slant.* The evidence is *always* qualified by the frame. For example, *Newsweek* can be a useful source if you want evidence about popular understanding of a subject or issue, but in this case, the fact that the material comes from *Newsweek* and thus represents a position aimed at a mainstream, nonacademic audience provides the central reason for citing it.

ELECTRONIC RESEARCH: FINDING QUALITY ON THE WEB

By Kelly Cannon, Reference Librarian

The Internet has dramatically altered public access to information. But the quality of information has also changed; it is almost as easy to publish on the web as it is to surf it. A general caveat might well be Reader Beware.

Take as an example *Martinlutherking.org* (www.martinlutherking.org). This site appears prominently in any web search for information about Martin Luther King, Jr. The website is visually appealing, claiming to include "essays, speeches, sermons, and more." But who created the site? As it turns out, after a little digging (see Tips #1 and #2 later in the chapter), the site is sponsored by Stormfront, Inc. (http://stormfront.org), an organization out of West Palm Beach, Florida, serving "those courageous men and women fighting to preserve their White Western culture, ideals and freedom of speech." This author is concealed behind the work, a ghost writer of sorts. While the site is at one's fingertips, identifying the author is a challenge, more so than in the world of print publications, where author and publisher are located on the same pages as the title. For those websites with no visible author, no publishing house, no recognized journal title, no peer-review process, and no library selection process (the touchstones of scholarship in the print world), seemingly easy Internet research is now more problematic: the user must discern for him- or herself what is and is not authoritative information.

Understanding Domain Names

But how is the user to begin evaluating a web document? Fortunately, there are several clues to assist you through the Internet labyrinth. One clue is in the web address itself. For example, the *Internet Movie Database* has www.imdb.com as its web address (also known as URL, or uniform resource locator). One clue lies at the very end of the URL in what is known as the domain name, in this case the abbreviation ".com." Websites ending in .com are commercial, often with the purpose of marketing a product. Sites ending in .org generally signal nonprofits, but many have a veiled agenda, whether it is marketing or politics. Like the .coms, .org addresses are sold on a first-come first-served basis. (The organization that oversees the many vendors of .com and .org domain names is The Internet Corporation for Assigned Names and Numbers, or ICANN [www.icann.org/].)

On the other hand, .edu and .gov sites may indicate less bias, as they are ostensibly limited exclusively to educational and government institutions, and they are often the producers of bonafide research. In particular, .gov sites contain some of the best information on the Internet. This is in part because the U.S. government is required by an act of Congress to disseminate to the general public a large portion of its research. The U.S. government, floated as it is by tax dollars, provides the high-quality, free websites reminiscent of the precommercial Internet era. This means that government sites offer high-quality data, particularly of a statistical nature. Scholars in the areas of business, law, and the social sciences can benefit tremendously, without subscription fees, from a variety of government databases. Prime examples are the legislative site known as *Thomas* (http://thomas.loc.gov) and data gathered at the website of the Census Bureau (www.census.gov).

Print Corollaries

But a domain name can be misleading; it is simply one clue in the process of evaluation. Another clue, perhaps more significant, is the correlation between a website and the print world. Many websites offer print corollaries, and some have print equivalents. For example, Johns Hopkins University Press now publishes all its journals, known and respected for years by scholars, in both print and electronic formats. Many college and university libraries subscribe to these Johns Hopkins journals electronically, collectively known as *Project Muse* (http://muse .jhu.edu). In this case, the scholar can assume that the electronic form of the journal undergoes the same editorial rigor as the print publication because they are identical in content.

Web Classics

Building a reputation of high quality takes time. But the Internet has been around long enough now that some publications with no pre-web history have caught the attention of scholars who turn to these sites regularly for reliable commentary on a variety of subject areas.

These high-quality sites can best be found by tapping into scholarly web directories such as the *Librarians' Index to the Internet* (http://lii.org) and *intute* (www .intute.ac.uk) that work like mini search engines but are managed by humans who sift through the chaff, including in these directories only what they deem to be gems.

The student looking specifically for free, peer-reviewed journals original to the web can visit a highly specific directory called the *Directory of Open Access Journals* (www.doaj.org), listing several hundred journals in a variety of subject areas. Many libraries have begun to link to these journals to promote their use by students and faculty.

Then there are gems that compare to highbrow magazines or newspapers such as *The New Yorker*. Two celebrated examples are *Salon.com* (http://salon.com) and *Slate* (http://slate.com), both online literary reviews. Once tapped into, these sites do a good job of recommending other high-quality websites. Scholars are beginning to cite from these web-based publications just as they would from any print publication of long-standing reputation.

An excellent site for links to all kinds of interesting articles from journals and high-level general interest magazine is Arts and Letters Daily.com (http://aldaily.com), sponsored by *The Chronicle of Higher Education*. You should also be aware of websites run by special interest organizations, such as the American Academy of Poets (http:// poets.org), which offers bibliographic resources, interviews, reviews, and the like.

Wikipedia, Google, and Blogs

Three tools have in recent years dramatically altered the nature of web-based research. First and foremost, the search engine Google, through a proprietary search algorithm, has increased the relevance and value of search results. Relevance in Google is determined by text-matching techniques, while value is determined by a unique "PageRank" technology that places highest on the list those results that are most often linked to other websites.

However, the determination of value is by no means foolproof. Google's ranking of value assesses less a website's authoritativeness than its popular appeal. For example, a recent search on "marijuana" yielded as its top result a private website promoting the use of marijuana and selling marijuana paraphernalia. This site could be useful in any number of ways in a research paper (i.e., as a primary resource reflecting public perceptions and use of marijuana in the United States). That it appears first suggests Google's algorithm of popularity over authoritativeness. This is not necessarily a bad thing, just something to be aware of. It is a little like picking a pebble off the ground. Its value is not inherent: responsibility rests with the user to discover its value. Finding information in Google is never the challenge. Discerning appropriateness and authoritativeness is the bigger task.

High on the list of most search results in Google is Wikipedia. Is this an authoritative source? Certainly Wikipedia has revolutionized the way web pages are authored. The world is the author of every entry. That is the beauty and the hazard, and the secret, to its broad scope and thus to its popularity. Anyone can write and edit in Wikipedia. In this way, Wikipedia is infinitely democratic. All opinions count equally, for better or worse—while authority languishes. Consequently, Wikipedia is likely to contribute little to a scholarly research project. In fact, it could detract from an assertion of authority. In short, use Wikipedia entries judiciously. Like any encyclopedia, Wikipedia will be viewed by the informed reader as introductory, not as the hallmark of thorough research.

Just as Wikipedia invites all of us to be writers, so too do blogs. But unlike Wikipedia, blogs typically reveal the identity or at least the assumed identity of the author and are written by a closed group of people, often one individual. As such, over time the identity and politics of the author(s) show through. In the best tradition of the World Wide Web, blogs have extended the sphere of publication, inviting everyone to be published authors, possibly achieving popularity and authority on a topic no matter how narrow by being at the right place at the right time, with access to the right information written in a voice of confidence. Blogs invite outside comment, but lack the formal structure of a peer review. As such, use blogs sparingly in academic research, being attentive to the credentials of the author(s), and to the wider acceptance of a particular blog in the scholarly community.

Asking the Right Questions

In the end, it is up to the individual user to evaluate each website independently. Here are some critical questions to consider:

Question: Who is the author?

Response: Check the website's home page, probably near the bottom of the page.

Question: Is the author affiliated with any institution?

Response: Check the URL to see who sponsors the page.

Question: What are the author's credentials?

Response: Check an online database, available through your local library, like *Academic Search* (www.epnet.com) or *LexisNexis Academic* (www .lexisnexis.com) to see if this person is published in journals or books.

Question: Has the information been reviewed or peer-edited before posting?

Response: Probably not, unless the posting is part of a larger publication; if so, the submission process for publication can be verified at the publication home page.

Question: Is the page part of a larger publication?

Response: Try the various links on the page to see if there is an access point to the home page of the publication. Or try the backspacing technique mentioned later in the chapter.

Question: Is the information documented properly?

Response: Check for footnotes or methodology.

Question: Is the information current?

Response: Check the "last update," usually printed at the bottom of the page.

Question: What is the purpose of the page?

Response: Examine content and marginalia.

Question: Does the website suit your purposes?

Response: Review what the purpose of your project is. Review your information needs: primary vs. secondary, academic vs. popular. And always consult with your instructor.

Subscriber-Only Databases

An organized and indexed collection of discreet pieces of information is called a *database.* Two examples of databases are a library's card catalogue and online catalogue. The World Wide Web is full of databases, though they are often restricted to subscribers. Subscription fees can be prohibitive, but fortunately for the average researcher, most college and university libraries foot the bill. The names of these databases are now well known, and arguably contain the most thoroughly reviewed (i.e., scholarly) full text available on the web: *Academic Search* from Ebsco (www.epnet.com), *Expanded Academic* from Gale (www.cengage.com/gale), *Proquest Direct* from ProQuest (www. proquest.com), and *Omnifile* from Wilson (www.hwwilson.com). Inquire at your library to see if you have access to these databases.

Each of these databases contains its own proprietary search engine, allowing refinement of searches to a degree unmatched by search engines on the Internet at large. Why? For one, these databases are exclusive rather than inclusive, as the Internet is. More is not better in an information age. The fact that information is at your fingertips, and sometimes "in your face," can be a problem. Well-organized databases are shaped and limited by human hands and minds, covering only certain media types or subject areas.

Second, databases allow searching by subject heading, in addition to keyword searching. This means that a human has defined the main subject areas of each entry, consequently allowing the user much greater manipulation of the search. For example, if I enter the words "New York City" in a simple keyword search, I will retrieve everything that simply mentions New York City even once; the relevance will vary tremendously. On the other hand, if subject headings have been assigned, I can do a subject search on New York City and find only records that are devoted to my subject. This may sound trivial, but in the age of information overload, precision searching is a precious commodity.

Although there is no foolproof way to a perfect database search, here is a point that will save you hours of frustration: consult with the most frequent users of research databases—reference librarians. Ask them (a) which databases they would use for your research topic and (b) how they would construct a search.

Indexes of Scholarly Journals

Up until now, we've only addressed electronic information that is full text. There may come a time when most secondary information needed for research is available online and as full text, but because of copyright and other restrictions, much scholarly information is still available only in print. This almost always implies a slight delay in retrieving the information; although full-text databases and the Internet promise instant gratification, more traditional modes of research necessitate either document delivery (fax or mail) or a visit to the library or other holding institution where a copy of the item can be retrieved. As individual journals begin to publish online (bypassing print altogether), the access to scholarly material may improve, but for now print copies remain the norm.

What has improved tremendously—with few exceptions—is the indexing of scholarly journals. Even if the journals themselves are not readily available in an electronic format, the indexing is available electronically. These electronic indexes provide basic bibliographic information and sometimes an abstract (summary) of the article or book chapter. When professors refer to bibliographic research, they probably mean research done with indexes. These indexes are available in any of three formats—print, CD-ROM, or online—depending on the academic institution. Inquire at your library about index availability.

Many academic institutions now subscribe to the following indexes online: *MLA* (literary criticism), *ERIC* (education), *PsycInfo* (psychology), *Historical Abstracts* (non-U.S. history), *Sociological Abstracts* (sociology), *Biological Abstracts* (biology), and a host of others. Note that these indexes are specific to particular subject areas. Their coverage is not broad, but deep and scholarly. These are the indexes to watch for when seeking the most scholarly information in your area of study. If a professor asks students to support their papers with scholarly secondary research, these indexes provide that kind of information. Although the full text is often not included, the indexing provides information sufficient to track down the complete article, whether it is in the library or available through interlibrary loan or other document delivery service.

These indexes are a great aid in evaluating the scholarly merit of a publication, as they usually eliminate any reference that isn't considered scholarly by the academy. For example, *MLA* only indexes literary criticism that appears in peer-reviewed journals and academically affiliated books. So, consider the publications that appear in these indexes to have the academic "Good Housekeeping" seal of approval.

■ **Try this 16.1:** *Tuning in to Your Research Environment*

Every university and college is different, each with its own points of access to information. Following are some exercises to help you familiarize yourself with your own scholarly environment.

Exercise #1: Go to your library's reference desk and get a list of all the scholarly journal indexes that are available electronically at your school. Then get a list of all online, full-text databases that are available to you.

Exercise #2: Go to your library's reference desk and get a list of all the journals that the library subscribes to electronically. Then get a list of all journals that are available at your library either in print or electronically in your major area of study.

Exercise #3: Ask the reference librarian about web access in general for your major area of study. What tips can the library give you about doing electronic research at your academic institution? Are there any special databases, web search engines/directories, or indexes that you should consult in your research?

Exercise #4: Try out some or all of the full-text databases available on your campus. Now try the same searches in a scholarly index. What differences do you see in the quality/scope of the information?

Who's Behind That Website?

Tip #1: Backspacing "Backspacing" a URL can be an effective way to evaluate a website. It may reveal authorship or institutional affiliation. To do this, place the cursor at the end of the URL and then backspace to the last slash and press Enter. Continue backspacing to each preceding slash, examining each level as you go.

Tip #2: Using WHOIS *WHOIS* (www.networksolutions.com/whois/index.jsp) is an Internet service that allows anyone to find out who's behind a website.

Tip #3: Beware of the ~ in a Web Address Many educational institutions allow the creation of personal home pages by students and faculty. While the domain name remains .edu in these cases, the fact that they are personal means that pretty much anything can be posted and so cannot assure academic quality.

Tip #4: Phrase Searching Not finding relevant information? Trying using quotation marks around key phrases in your search string. For example, search in *Google* for this phrase, enclosed in quotation marks: "whose woods these are I think I know."

Tip #5: Title Searching Still finding irrelevant information? Limit your search to the titles of web documents. A title search is an option in several search engines, among them *Yahoo* (advanced search) (http://search.yahoo.com) and *Google* (advanced search) (www.google.com).

Tip #6: Wikipedia Discussion Tabs Use Wikipedia to full advantage by clicking on the discussion tabs located at the top of Wikipedia entries. The discussion tabs expose the often intense debates that rage behind the scenes on topics like marijuana, genocide, and Islam. The discussion tabs are an excellent source for locating paper topics because they highlight ongoing sources of controversy—those areas worthy of additional writing and research. To find the most controversial topics at any given moment, visit Wikipedia's Controversial Issues page (http://en.wikipedia.org/wiki/Wikipedia:List_of_controversial_issues).

Tip #7: Full Text The widest selection of previously published full text (newspapers, magazines, journals, book chapters) is available in subscription databases via the web. Inquire at your library to see if you have access to *LexisNexis Academic* (www.lexisnexis.com), *Omnifile* (www.hwwilson.com), *Academic Search* (www.epnet.com), *ProQuest Direct* (www.proquest.com), *Expanded Academic* (www.galegroup.com), or other full-text databases.

The leading free full-text site is *LookSmart's FindArticles* (http://findarticles.com). This database of "hundreds of thousands of articles from more than 300 magazines and journals, dating back to 1998" can be searched by all magazines, magazines within categories, or specific magazine.

For the full text of books, try the *IPL Online Texts* directory (www.ipl.org/div/subject/browse/hum60.60.00), pointing to the major digital text archives.

For more of the best full-text sites on the web, search on the term "full-text" in the *Librarians' Index to the Internet* (http://lii.org).

Tip #8: Archives of Older Published Materials Full text for newspapers, magazines, and journals published prior to 1990 is difficult to find on the Internet. One subscription site that your library may offer is *JSTOR* (www.jstor.org), an archive of scholarly full-text journal articles dating back in some cases into the late 1800s. *LexisNexis Academic* (www. lexisnexis.com), also a subscription service, includes the full text of popular periodicals such as *The New York Times* as far back as 1980.

Two free sites offer the full text of eighteenth- and nineteenth-century periodicals from Great Britain and the U.S. respectively: *Internet Library of Early Journals* (www.bodley.ox.ac.uk/ilej) and *Nineteenth Century in Print* (http://memory.loc.gov/ammem/ndlpcoop/moahtml/snchome.html).

Use interlibrary loan or another document delivery service like *IngentaConnect* (www.ingentaconnect.com) to have a copy of the print version of older titles sent to you. Electronic indexing (no full text) for older materials is readily available, back as early as 1900, sometimes earlier. Inquire at your library.

Tip #9: Best Sites, Free or Subscription, for Quantity and Quality of Scholarly Information across the Disciplines Following are a few of the sites most relied upon by academic librarians. For the subscription databases, you will need to inquire at your library for local availability.

A Foolproof Recipe for Great Research—Every Time

First, search at least one of these multidisciplinary subscription databases; check your library's website for availability.

- *Academic Search Elite/Premier* (EBSCOhost) for journals
- *Expanded Academic* (Gale) for journals
- *Omnifile* (WilsonWeb) for journals
- *Proquest* for journals
- *WorldCat* (OCLC FirstSearch) for books

   Second, search subject-specific databases. These too are mostly subscription databases; check your library's website for availability.

- Anthropology: *Anthropological Abstracts*
- Art: *Art Abstracts*
- Biology: *Biological Abstracts, Biosis*
- Business: *ABI Inform, Business Source Elite/Premier, Business & Company Resource Center, Dow Jones, LexisNexis*
- Chemistry: *SciFinder Scholar, Science Citation Index Expanded (ISI)*
- Communication: *Communication and Mass Media, Communication Abstracts*
- Computer Science: *INSPEC*
- Economics: *EconLit*
- Education: *ERIC* (free)
- Film Studies: *MLA*
- Geography/Geology: *GeoBase*
- History: *America History and Life, Historical Abstracts*
- Language, Literature: *MLA, LION (Literature Online)*
- Law: *LexisNexis, WestLaw*
- Mathematics: *MathSciNet*
- Medicine: *PubMed* (free)
- Music: *RILM*
- Philosophy: *Philosopher's Index*
- Physics: *INSPEC*
- Political Science: *PAIS*
- Psychology: *PsycInfo*
- Religion: *ATLA Religion*
- Sociology: *Sociological Abstracts*

Third, visit these not-to-be-missed free websites and meta-sites:

- Anthropology: *Anthropological Index Online* http://aio.anthropology.org.uk/cgi-bin/uncgi/search_bib_ai/anthind, *Anthropology Resources on the Internet* www.anthropology-resources.net
- Art: *ArtCyclopedia* www.artcyclopedia.com
- Biology: *Biology Browser* www.biologybrowser.org, *Agricola* http://agricola.nal.usda.gov
- Business: *EDGAR* www.sec.gov/edgar.shtml, *Hoover's Online* www.hoovers.com/free
- Chemistry: *Chemdex.org* www.chemdex.org, *World of Chemistry* http://scienceworld.wolfram.com/chemistry
- Communication: *Television News Archive: Vanderbilt University* http://tvnews.vanderbilt.edu
- Computer Science: *CompInfo* www.compinfo-center.com
- Economics: *Intute: Economics* www.intute.ac.uk/socialsciences/economics
- Education: *Educator's Reference Desk* http://eduref.org
- Film Studies: *Film Studies Resources* www.lib.berkeley.edu/MRC/filmstudies/index.html
- Geography/Geology: *GeoSource* www.library.uu.nl/geosource
- History: *American Memory* http://memory.loc.gov/ammem/index.html
- Language, Literature: *Online Literary Criticism Collection* www.ipl.org/div/litcrit
- Law: *FindLaw* www.findlaw.com
- Mathematics: Mathworld http://mathworld.wolfram.com, *MathSearch* www.maths.usyd.edu.au/MathSearch.html
- Medicine: *BioMed Central* www.biomedcentral.com
- Music: *Online Resources for Music Scholars* http://hcl.harvard.edu/research/guides/music/resources/index.html
- Philosophy: *Stanford Encyclopedia of Philosophy* http://plato.stanford.edu
- Physics: *World of Physics* http://scienceworld.wolfram.com/physics
- Political Science: *Intute: Politics* www.intute.ac.uk/socialsciences/politics, *THOMAS* http://thomas.loc.gov
- Psychology: *Intute: Psychology* www.intute.ac.uk/socialsciences/psychology/
- Religion: *Religion Online* http://www.religion-online.org/, *Hartford Institute for Religion Research* www.hartfordinstitute.org
- Sociology: *Intute: Sociology* www.intute.ac.uk/socialsciences/sociology

Citation Guides on the Web

The two most common styles of documentation are those established by the Modern Language Association (MLA) and the American Psychological Association (APA). These associations each provide examples of basic citations of electronic and print resources at their websites; you will find the MLA at www.mla.org/publications/style and APA at http://apastyle.apa.org

   Also, many writing centers have made available citation guides at their websites. One recommended site is by the writing center of Purdue University (http://owl.english .purdue.edu/handouts/research/index.html).

   For citation examples not given at these websites, it is advisable to consult the associations' printed manuals—*Publication Manual of the American Psychological Association* or the *MLA Handbook for Writers of Research Papers*—in their most recent editions.

A Librarian's Brief Guidelines to Successful Research

1. Consult with your professor to determine what types of resources are most appropriate for the project at hand.

2. Consider whether you need scholarly or popular sources or a mixture of both.

3. Consider whether you need primary or secondary works or a mixture of both.

4. With the assistance of a reference librarian, find which search tools will direct you to the most relevant resources.

5. Range widely. Try a new search tool with each new research project.

6. Begin early, in case interlibrary loan is needed to obtain research owned only by other libraries.

7. Examine bibliographies at the end of the articles and books you've already found. Remember that one quality source can, in its bibliography, point to many other resources.

PLAGIARISM AND THE LOGIC OF CITATION

It is impossible to discuss the rationale for citing sources without reference to plagiarism, even though the primary reason for including citations is not to prove that you haven't cheated. It's essential that you give credit where it's due as a courtesy to your readers. Along with educating readers about who has said what, citations enable them to find out more about a given position and to pursue other discussions on the subject. Nonetheless, plagiarism is an important issue: academic integrity matters. And because the stakes are very high if you are caught plagiarizing, we think it necessary to pause in order to discuss how to avoid it.

In recent years there has been a significant rise in the number of plagiarism cases nationally. Many commentators blame the Internet, with its easily accessible, easy to cut-and-paste information, for increasing the likelihood of plagiarism. Others cite a lack of clarity about what plagiarism is and why it is a serious problem. So, let's start by clarifying.

Most people have some idea of what plagiarism is. You already know that it's against the rules to buy a paper from an Internet "paper mill" or to download others' words verbatim and hand them in as your own thinking. And you probably know that even if you change a few words and rearrange the sentence structure, you still need to acknowledge the source. By way of formal definition, plagiarism (as one handbook puts it) gives "the impression that you have written or thought something that you have in fact borrowed from someone else" (Joseph Gibaldi, *MLA Handbook for Writers of Research Papers,* fifth edition. New York: MLA, 1999, p. 30). It is a form of theft and fraud. Borrowing from someone else, by the way, also includes taking and not acknowledging words and ideas from your friends or your parents. Put another way, any assignment with your name on it signifies that you are the author—that the words and ideas are yours—with any exceptions indicated by source citations and, if you're quoting, by quotation marks.

Knowing what plagiarism is, however, doesn't guarantee that you'll know how to avoid it. Is it okay, for example, to cobble together a series of summaries and paraphrases in a paragraph, provided you include the authors in a bibliography at the end of the paper? Or how about if you insert a single footnote at the end of the paragraph? The answer is that both are still plagiarism because your reader can't tell where your thinking starts and others' thinking stops. As a basic rule of thumb, "Readers must be able to tell as they are reading your paper exactly what information came from which source and what information is your contribution to the paper" (Christine A. Hult, *Researching and Writing Across the Curriculum.* Boston: Allyn and Bacon, 1996, p. 203). More on this later.

Why Does Plagiarism Matter?

A recent survey indicated that 53 percent of Who's Who High Schoolers thought that plagiarism was no big deal (Sally Cole and Elizabeth Kiss, "What Can We Do About Student Cheating?" *About Campus,* May–June 2000, p. 6). So why should institutions of higher learning care about it? Here are two great reasons:

- Plagiarism poisons the environment. Students who don't cheat become alienated by students who do and get away with it, and faculty can become distrustful of students and even disillusioned about teaching when constantly driven to track down students' sources. It's a lot easier, by the way, than most students think for faculty to recognize language and ideas that are not the student's own. And now there are all those search engines provided by firms like Turnitin.com that have been generated in response to the Internet paper-mill boom. Who wants another cold war?

- Plagiarism defeats the purpose of going to college, which is learning how to think. You can't learn to think by just copying others' ideas; you need to learn to trust your own intelligence. Students' panic about deadlines and their misunderstandings about assignments sometimes spur plagiarism. It's a good bet that your professors would much rather take requests for help and give extra time on assignments than have to go through the anguish of confronting students about plagiarized work.

So, plagiarism gets in the way of trust, fairness, intellectual development, and, ultimately, the attitude toward learning that sets the tone for a college or university community.

Frequently Asked Questions (FAQs) about Plagiarism

Is it still plagiarism if I didn't intentionally copy someone else's work and present it as my own; that is, if I plagiarized it by accident?
Yes, it is still plagiarism. Colleges and universities put the burden of responsibility on students for knowing what plagiarism is and then making the effort necessary to avoid it. Leaving out the quotation marks around someone else's words or omitting the attribution after a summary of someone else's theory may be just a mistake—a matter of inadequate documentation—but faculty can only judge what you turn in to them, not what you intended.

If I include a list of works consulted at the end of my paper, doesn't that cover it?
No. A works-cited list (bibliography) tells your readers what you read but leaves them in the dark about how and where this material has been used in your paper. Putting one or more references at the end of a paragraph containing source material is a version of the same problem. The solution is to cite the source at the point that you quote or paraphrase or summarize it. To be even clearer about what comes from where, also use what are called in-text attributions. See the next FAQ on these.

What is the best way to help my readers distinguish between what my sources are saying and what I'm saying?
Be overt. Tell your readers in the text of your paper, not just in citations, when you are drawing on someone else's words, ideas, or information. Do this with phrases like "According to *X*" or "As noted in *X*"—called in-text attributions.

Are there some kinds of information that I do not need to document?
Yes. Common knowledge and facts you can find in almost any encyclopedia or basic reference text generally don't need to be documented (that is, John F. Kennedy became president of the United States in 1960). This distinction can get a little tricky because it isn't always obvious what is and is not common knowledge. Often, you need to spend some time in a discipline before you discover what others take to be known to all. When in doubt, cite the source.

If I put the information from my sources into my own words, do I still need to include citations?

Yes. Sorry, but rewording someone else's idea doesn't make it your idea. Paraphrasing is a useful activity because it helps you better understand what you are reading, but paraphrases and summaries have to be documented and carefully distinguished from ideas and information you are representing as your own.

If I don't actually know anything about the subject, is it okay to hand in a paper that is taken entirely from various sources?

It's okay if (1) you document the borrowings and (2) the assignment called for summary. Properly documented summarizing is better than plagiarizing, but most assignments call for something more. Often comparing and contrasting your sources will begin to give you ideas so that you can have something to contribute. If you're really stumped, go see the professor.

You can also reduce the risk of plagiarism if you consult sources after—not before—you have done some preliminary thinking on the subject. If you have become somewhat invested in your own thoughts on the matter, you will be able to use the sources in a more active way, in effect, making them part of a dialogue.

Is it plagiarism if I include things in my paper that I thought of with another student or a member of my family?

Most academic behavior codes, under the category called "collusion," allow for students' cooperative efforts only with the explicit consent of the instructor. The same general rule goes for plagiarizing yourself—that is, for submitting the same paper in more than one class. If you have questions about what constitutes collusion in a particular class, be sure to ask your professor.

What about looking at secondary sources when my professor hasn't asked me to? Is this a form of cheating?

It can be a form of cheating if the intent of the assignment was to get you to develop a particular kind of thinking skill. In this case, looking at others' ideas may actually retard your learning process and leave you feeling that you couldn't possibly learn to arrive at ideas on your own. Professors usually look favorably on students who are willing to take the time to do extra reading on a subject, but it is essential that, even in class discussion, you make it clear that you have consulted outside sources. To conceal that fact is to present others' ideas as your own. Even in class discussion, if you bring up an idea you picked up on the Internet, be sure to say so explicitly.

HOW TO CITE SOURCES

In general, you will be expected to follow a formalized style of documentation. The two most common are the MLA style, which uses the author-work format, and the APA style, which uses the author-date format. Most writing handbooks (compilations of the rules of grammar and punctuation, available at most bookstores) contain detailed accounts of documentation styles. In addition, you can access various web-sites that provide most (though not all) of this information. (See Citation Guides on the Web earlier in this chapter.)

The various styles differ in the specific ways that they organize the bibliographical information, but all of them share the following characteristics:

1. They place an extended citation for each source, including the author, the title, the date, and the place of publication, at the end of the paper. These end-of-text citations are organized in a list, usually alphabetically.

2. They insert an abbreviated citation within the text, located within parentheses directly following every use of the source. Usually this in-text citation consists of the author's name and either the page (in MLA) or date (in APA). In-text citations indicate in shorthand form in the body of your paper the source you are using and direct your readers to the complete citation located in a list of references at the end of the paper or report.

3. They distinguish among different kinds of sources—providing slightly differing formulas for citing books, articles, encyclopedias, government documents, interviews, and so forth.

4. They have particular formats for citing electronic sources of various kinds, such as CD-ROMs, the Internet, and online journals and databases. These citations replace the publication information typically provided for text references to printed material with what is called an *availability statement,* which provides the method of accessing the source. This statement should provide the information sufficient to retrieve the source.

You have probably already discovered that some professors are more concerned than others that students obey the particulars of a given documentation style. Virtually all faculty across the curriculum agree, however, that *the most important rule for writers to follow in documenting sources is formal consistency.* That is, all of your in-text citations should follow the same abbreviated format, and all of your end-of-text citations should follow the same extended format.

Once you begin doing most of your writing in a particular discipline, you may want to purchase or access on the Internet the more detailed style guide adhered to by that discipline. Because documentation styles differ not only from discipline to discipline but also even from journal to journal within a discipline, you should consult your professor about which documentation format he or she wishes you to use in a given course.

Here are a few basic examples of in-text and end-of-text citations in both MLA and APA form, followed by a brief discussion of the rules that apply.

Single Author, MLA Style

In-text citation: The influence of Seamus Heaney on younger poets in Northern Ireland has been widely acknowledged, but Patrick Kavanagh's "plain-speaking, pastoral" influence on him is "less recognized" (Smith 74).

"(Smith 74)" indicates the author's last name and the page number on which the cited passage appears. If the author's name had been mentioned in the sentence—had the sentence begun "According to Smith"—you would include only the page number in the citation. Note that there is no abbreviation for "page," that there is no intervening punctuation between name and page, and that the parentheses precede the period or other punctuation. If the sentence ends with a direct quotation, the parentheses come after the quotation marks but still before the closing period. Also note that no punctuation occurs between the last word of the quotation ("recognized") and the closing quotation mark.

End-of-text book citation: Douglas, Ann. *Terrible Honesty: Mongrel Manhattan in the 1920s.* New York: Farrar, Straus, and Giroux, 1995.

End-of-text article citation: Cressy, David. "Foucault, Stone, Shakespeare and Social History." *English Literary Renaissance* 21 (1991): 121–33.

MLA style stipulates an alphabetical list of references (by author's last name, which keys the reference to the in-text citation). This list is located at the end of the paper on a separate page and entitled "Works Cited."

Each entry in the Works Cited list is divided into three parts: author, title, and publication data. Each of these parts is separated by a period from the others. Titles of book-length works are italicized, unless your instructor prefers underlining. (Underlining is a means of indicating italics.) Journal citations differ slightly: article names go inside quotations, no punctuation follows the titles of journals, and a colon precedes the page numbers.

Single Author, APA Style

In-text citation: Studies of students' changing attitudes towards the small colleges that they attend suggest that their loyalty to the institution declines steadily over a four-year period, whereas their loyalty to individual professors or departments increases "markedly, by as much as twenty-five percent over the last two years" (Brown, 1994, p. 41).

For both books and articles, include the author's last name, followed by a comma, and then the date of publication. If you are quoting or referring to a specific passage, include the page number as well, separated from the date by a comma and the abbreviation "p." (or "pp.") followed by a space. If the author's name has been mentioned in the sentence, include only the date in the parentheses immediately following the author's name.

In-text citation: Brown (1992) documents the decline in students' institutional loyalty.

End-of-text book citation: Tannen, D. (1991). *You just don't understand: Women and men in conversation.* New York: Ballantine Books.

End-of-text article citation: Baumeister, R. (1987). How the self became a problem: A psychological review of historical research. *Journal of Personality and Psychology, 52,* 163–176.

APA style requires an alphabetical list of references (by author's last name, which keys the reference to the in-text citation). This list is located at the end of the paper on a separate page and entitled "References." Regarding manuscript form, the first line of each reference is not indented, but all subsequent lines are indented three spaces.

In alphabetizing the references list, place entries for a single author before entries that he or she has co-authored, and arrange multiple entries by a single author by beginning with the earliest work. If there are two or more works by the same author in the same year, designate the second with an "a," the third a "b," and so forth, directly after the year. For all subsequent entries by an author after the first, substitute three hyphens followed by a period [---.] for his or her name. For articles by two or more authors, use commas to connect the authors, and precede the last one with a comma and an ampersand (&).

The APA style divides individual entries into the following parts: author (using initials only for first and middle names), year of publication (in parentheses), title, and publication data. Each part is separated by a period from the others. Note that only the first letter of the title and subtitle of books is capitalized (although proper nouns would be capitalized as necessary).

Journal citations differ from those for books in a number of small ways. The title of a journal article is neither italicized (nor underlined) nor enclosed in quotation marks, and only the first word in the title and subtitle is capitalized. The name of the journal is italicized (or underlined), however, and the first word and all significant words are capitalized. Also, notice that the volume number (which is separated by a comma from the title of the journal) is italicized (or underlined) to distinguish it from the page reference. Page numbers for the entire article are included, with no "p." or "pp.," and are separated by a comma from the preceding volume number. If the journal does not use volume numbers, then p. or pp. is included.

HOW TO INTEGRATE QUOTATIONS INTO YOUR PAPER

An enormous number of writers lose authority and readability because they have never learned how to correctly integrate quotations into their own writing. The following guidelines should help.

1. **Acknowledge sources in your text, not just in citations.** *When you incorporate material from a source, attribute it to the source explicitly in your text—not only in a bibliography.* In other words, when you introduce the material, *frame* it with a phrase such as "according to Marsh" or "as Cartelli argues."

   Although it is not required, you are usually much better off making the attribution overtly, even if you have also cited the source within parentheses or with a footnote at the end of the last sentence quoted, paraphrased, or summarized. If a passage does not contain an attribution, your readers will not know that it comes from a source until they reach the citation at the end. Attributing up-front clearly distinguishes what one source says from what another says and, perhaps more important, what your sources say from what you say. Useful verbs for introducing attributions include the following: notes, observes, argues, comments, writes, says, reports, suggests, and claims. Generally speaking, by the way, you should cite the author by last name only—as "Cartelli," not as "Thomas Cartelli" or "Mr. Cartelli."

2. **Splice quotations onto your own words.** *Always attach quotations to some of your own language; don't let them sit in your text as independent sentences with quotation marks around them.* You can normally satisfy this rule with an

attributive phrase—commonly known as a tag phrase—that introduces the quotation.

According to Paul McCartney, "All you need is love."

Note that the tag phrase takes a comma before the quote.

Alternatively you can splice quotations into your text with a setup: a statement followed by a colon.

Patrick Henry's famous phrase is one of the first that American schoolchildren memorize: "Give me liberty, or give me death."

The colon, you should notice, usually comes at the end of an independent clause (that is, a subject plus verb that can stand alone), at the spot where a period normally goes. It would be incorrect to write "Patrick Henry is known for: 'Give me liberty, or give me death.'"

The rationale for this guideline is essentially the same as that for the previous one: if you are going to move to quotation, you first need to identify its author so that your readers will be able to put it in context quickly.

Spliced quotations frequently create problems in grammar or punctuation for writers. Whether you include an entire sentence (or passage) of quotation or just a few phrases, you need to take care to integrate them into the grammar of your own sentence.

One of the most common mistaken assumptions is that a comma should always precede a quotation, as in "A spokesperson for the public defender's office demanded, 'an immediate response from the mayor.'" The sentence structure does not call for any punctuation after "demanded."

3. **Cite sources after quotations.** *Locate citations in parentheses following the quotation and before the final period.* The information about the source appears at the end of the sentence, with the final period coming after the closing parenthesis.

A recent article on the best selling albums in America claimed that "Ever since Elvis, it has been pop music's job to challenge the mores of the older generation" (Hornby 168).

Note that there is normally *no punctuation* at the end of the quotation itself, either before or after the closing quotation mark. A quotation that ends either in a question mark or an exclamation mark is an exception to this rule because the sign is an integral part of the quotation's meaning.

As Hamlet says to Rosencrantz and Guildenstern, "And yet to me what is this quintessence of dust?" (IIii.304–05).

See the section entitled How to Cite Sources earlier in this chapter for the appropriate formats for in-text citations.

4. **Use ellipses to shorten quotations.** *Add ellipses to indicate that you have omitted some of the language from within the quotation.* Form ellipses by entering three

dots (periods) with spaces in between them, or use four dots to indicate that the deletion continues to the end of the sentence (the last dot becomes the period). Suppose you wanted to shorten the following quotation from a recent article about Radiohead by Alex Ross:

The album "OK Computer," with titles like "Paranoid Android," "Karma Police," and "Climbing Up the Walls," pictured the onslaught of the information age and a young person's panicky embrace of it (Ross 85).

Using ellipses, you could emphasize the source's claim by omitting the song titles from the middle of the sentence:

The album "OK Computer" . . . pictured the onslaught of the information age and a young person's panicky embrace of it (Ross 85).

In most cases, the gap between quoted passages should be short, and in any case, you should be careful to preserve the sense of the original. The standard joke about ellipses is apposite here: a reviewer writes that a film "will delight no one and appeal to the intelligence of invertebrates only, but not average viewers." An unethical advertiser cobbles together pieces of the review to say that the film "will delight . . . and appeal to the intelligence of . . . viewers."

5. **Use square brackets to alter or add information within a quotation.** Sometimes it is necessary to change the wording slightly inside a quotation to maintain fluency. Square brackets indicate that you are altering the original quotation. Brackets are also used when you insert explanatory information, such as a definition or example, within a quotation. Here are a few examples that alter the original quotations previously cited.

   According to one music critic, the cultural relevance of Radiohead is evident in "the album 'OK Computer' . . . [which] pictured the onslaught of the information age and a young person's panicky embrace of it" (Ross 85).

   Popular music has always "[challenged] the mores of the older generation," according to Nick Hornby (168).

   Note that both examples respect the original sense of the quotation; they have changed the wording only to integrate the quotations gracefully within the writer's own sentence structure.

HOW TO PREPARE AN ABSTRACT

There is one more skill essential to research-based writing that we need to discuss: how to prepare an abstract. The aim of the nonevaluative summary of a source known as an abstract is to represent a source's arguments as fairly and accurately as possible, not to critique them. Learning how to compose an abstract according to the conventions of a given discipline is a necessary skill for academic researched writing. Because abstracts differ in format and length among disciplines, you should sample some in the reference section of your library or via the Internet to provide you with models to imitate. Some abstracts, such as those in *Dissertation Abstracts,* are very brief—less than 250 words. Others may run as long as two pages.

Despite disciplinary differences, abstracts by and large follow a generalizable format. The abstract should begin with a clear and specific explanation of the work's governing thesis (or argument). In this opening paragraph, you should also define the work's purpose, and possibly include established positions that it tries to refine, qualify, or argue against. What kind of critical approach does it adopt? What are its aims? On what assumptions does it rest? Why did the author feel it necessary to write the work—that is, what does he or she believe the work offers that other sources don't? What shortcomings or misrepresentations in other criticism does the work seek to correct?

You won't be able to produce detailed answers to all of these questions in your opening paragraph, but in trying to answer some of them in your note-taking and drafting, you should find it easier to arrive at the kind of concise, substantive, and focused overview that the first paragraph of your abstract should provide. Also, be careful not to settle for bland, all-purpose generalities in this opening paragraph. And if you quote there, keep the selections short, and remember that quotations don't speak for themselves.

In summary, your aim in the first paragraph is to define the source's particular angle of vision and articulate its main point or points, including the definition of key terms used in its title or elsewhere in its argument.

Once you've set up this overview of the source's central position(s), you should devote a paragraph or so to the source's *organization* (how it divides its subject into parts) and its *method* (how it goes about substantiating its argument). What kind of secondary material does the source use? That is, how do its own bibliographic citations cue you to its school of thought, its point of view, its research traditions?

Your concluding paragraph should briefly recount some of the source's conclusions (as related to, but not necessarily the same as, its thesis). In what way does it go about culminating its argument? What kind of significance does it claim for its position? What final qualifications does it raise? The following model is a good example of an abstract:

Abstract of "William Carlos Williams," An Essay
By Christopher MacGowan in The Columbia History of American Poetry, *pp. 395–418, Columbia University Press, 1993*

MacGowan's is a chronologically organized account of Williams' poetic career and of his relation to both modernism as an international movement and modernism as it affected the development of poetry in America. MacGowan is at some pains both to differentiate Williams from some features of modernism (such as the tendency of American writers to write as well as live away from their own cultural roots) and to link Williams to modernism. MacGowan argues, for example, that an essential feature of Williams's commitment as a poet was to "the local—to the clear presentation of what was under his nose and in front of his eyes" (385).

But he also takes care to remind us that Williams was in no way narrowly provincial, having studied in Europe as a young man (at Leipzig), having had a Spanish mother and an English father, having become friendly with the poets Ezra Pound and H. D. while getting his medical degree at the University of Pennsylvania, and having continued to meet important figures in the literary and art worlds by making frequent visits to New York and by traveling on more than one occasion to Europe (where Pound introduced him to W. B. Yeats, among others). Williams corresponded with Marianne Moore, he continued to write to Pound and to show Pound some of his work, and he wrote critical essays on the works of other modernists. MacGowan reminds us that Williams also translated Spanish works (ballads) and so was not out of contact with European influences.

Williams had a long publishing career—beginning in 1909 with a self-published volume called *Poems* and ending more than fifty years later with *Pictures from Brueghel* in 1962. What MacGowan emphasizes about this career is not only the consistently high quality of work, but also its great influence on other artists (he names those who actually corresponded with Williams and visited with him, including Charles Olson, Robert Creeley, Robert Lowell, Allen Ginsberg, and Denise Levertov). MacGowan observes that Williams defined himself "against" T. S. Eliot—the more rewarded and internationally recognized of the two poets, especially during their lifetimes—searching for "alternatives to the prevailing mode of a complex, highly allusive poetics," which Williams saw as Eliot's legacy (395). MacGowan depicts Williams as setting himself "against the international school of Eliot and Pound—Americans he felt wrote about root-lessness and searched an alien past because of their failure to write about and live within their own culture" (397).

GUIDELINES FOR FINDING, CITING, AND INTEGRATING SOURCES

1. Citing sources isn't just about acknowledging intellectual or informational debts; it's also a courtesy to your readers, directing them how to find out more about the subjected cited.

2. Before you settle in with one author's book-length argument, use indexes and bibliographies and other resources to achieve a broader view.

3. Given that the accessibility of Internet research has made it more difficult to distinguish reliable and authoritative information from fraudulent information, domain names ending in .edu and .gov usually offer more reliable choices than the standard .com.

4. When professors direct you to do bibliographic research, they usually are referring to research done with indexes; these are available in print, online, and CD-ROM formats.

5. In evaluating a website about which you don't know much, try "backspacing" a URL to trace back to its authorship or institutional affiliation. Place the cursor at the end of the URL, backspace to the last slash, and press enter.

6. Tell your readers in the text of your paper, not just in citations, when you are using someone else's words, ideas, or information; rewording someone else's idea doesn't make it your idea.

7. Avoid sacrificing your authority by incorrectly splicing quotation into your own discussions. For example, always attach a quotation to some of your own lan-

guage; never let it stand as its own sentence in your text. Attribution—"According to Dickson"—before the quote fulfills this function nicely.

8. One of the best ways of getting to know an important source during the research process is to compose an abstract of it, from 250 words to two pages. A good abstract aims to summarize the governing argument, organization and method as fairly and accurately as possible.

ASSIGNMENTS: A Research Sequence

The traditional sequence of steps for building a research paper—or for any writing that relies on secondary materials—is *summary, comparative analysis, and synthesis.* The following sequence of four exercises addresses the first two steps as discrete activities. (You might, of course, choose to do only some of these exercises.)

1. *Compose a relatively informal prospectus,* in which you formulate your initial thinking on a subject before you do more research. Include what you already know about the topic, especially what you find interesting, particularly significant, or strange. This exercise will help deter you from being overwhelmed by and absorbed into the sources you later encounter.

2. *Conduct a "what's going on in the field" search, and create a preliminary list of sources.* This exercise is ideal for helping you to find a topic or, if you already have one, to narrow it. The kinds of bibliographic materials you consult for this portion of the research project depend on the discipline within which you are writing. Whatever the discipline, start in the reference room of your library with specialized indexes (such as the *Social Sciences Index* or the *New York Times Index*), book review indexes, specialized encyclopedias and dictionaries, and bibliographies (print version or CD-ROM) that give you an overview of your subject or topic. If you have access to databases through your school or library, you should also search them. (See the section in this chapter entitled Electronic Research: Finding Quality on the Web.)

    The "what's going on in the field" search has two aims:

    •   To survey materials in order to identify trends—the kinds of issues and questions that others in the field are talking about (and, thus, find important)

    •   To compile a bibliography that includes a range of titles that interest you, that could be relevant to your prospective topic, and that seem to you representative of research trends associated with your subject (or topic)

    You are not committed at this point to pursuing all of these sources but rather to reporting what is being talked about. You might also compose a list of keywords (such as Library of Congress headings) that you have used in conducting your search. If you try this exercise, you will be surprised how much value there is in exploring indexes *just for titles,* to see the kinds of topics people are currently conversing about. And you will almost surely discover how *narrowly* focused most research is (which will get you away from global questions).

Append to your list of sources (a very preliminary bibliography) a few paragraphs of informal discussion of how the information you have encountered (the titles, summaries, abstracts, etc.) has affected your thinking and plans for your paper. These paragraphs might respond to the following questions:

a. In what ways has your "what's going on in the field" search led you to narrow or shift direction in or focus your thinking about your subject?

b. How might you use one or more of these sources in your paper?

c. What has this phase of your research suggested you might need to look for next?

3. *Write an abstract of an article (or book chapter)* from your "what's going on" exercise that you think you might use in your final paper. Use the procedure offered in the preceding section, "How to Prepare an Abstract." Aim for two pages in length. If other members of your class are working on the same or similar subjects, it is often extremely useful for everyone to share copies of their abstracts. Remember that your primary concern should lie with representing the argument and point of view of the source as fairly and accurately as possible.

Append to the end of the abstract a paragraph or two that addresses the question, "How has this exercise affected your thinking about your topic?" Objectifying your own research process in this way helps move you away from the cut-and-paste–provide-only-the-transitions mode of writing research papers.

4. *Write a comparative summary of two reviews of a single source.* Most writers, before they invest the significant time and energy required to study a book-length source, take the much smaller amount of time and energy required to find out more about the book. Although you should always include in your final paper your own analytical summary of books you consult on your topic, it's extremely useful also to find out what experts in the field have to say about the source.

Select from your "what's going on" list one book-length source that you've discovered is vital to your subject or topic. As a general rule, if a number of your indexes, bibliographies, and so forth, refer you to the same book, it's a good bet that this source merits consultation.

Locate two book reviews on the book, and write a summary that compares the two reviews. Ideally, you should locate two reviews that diverge in their points of view or in what they choose to emphasize. Depending on the length and complexity of the reviews, your comparative summary should require two or three pages.

In most cases, you will find that reviews are less neutral in their points of view than are abstracts, but they always do more than simply judge. A good review, like a good abstract, should communicate the essential ideas contained in the source. It is the reviewer's aim also to locate the source in some larger context, by, for example, comparing it to other works on the same subject and to the research tradition the book seeks to extend, modify, and so forth. Thus, your summary should try to encompass how the book contributes to the ongoing conversation on a given topic in the field.

Append to your comparative summary a paragraph or two answering the question, "How has this exercise affected your thinking about your topic?"

Obviously, you could choose to do a comparative summary of two articles, two book chapters, and so forth, rather than of two book reviews. But in any event, if you use books in your research, you should always find a means of determining how these books are received in the relevant critical community.

The next step, if you were writing a research paper, would involve the task known as *synthesis,* in which you essentially write a comparative discussion that includes more than two sources. Many research papers start with an opening paragraph that synthesizes prevailing, perhaps competing, interpretations of the topic being addressed. Few good research papers consist only of such synthesis, however. Instead, writers use synthesis to frame their ideas and to provide perspective on their own arguments; the synthesis provides a platform or foundation for their own subsequent analysis.

It is probably worth adding that bad research papers fail to use synthesis as a point of departure. Instead, they line up their sources and agree or disagree with them. To inoculate you against this unfortunate reflex, review the section in Chapter 14 entitled Six Strategies for Analyzing Sources, especially Strategy 6: Find Your Own Role in the Conversation. See also Comparison/Contrast in Chapter 6 and the section about organizing comparison/contrast in Chapter 10.

UNIT IV

Grammar and Style

CHAPTER 17

Style: Choosing Words for Precision, Accuracy, and Tone

THIS FIRST CHAPTER ON STYLE ADDRESSES WORD CHOICE, also known as diction, and its effect on style. The chapter seeks to make you more self-conscious about the kinds of words you habitually use and to expand your range of choices. Chapter 18 attempts to do the same with sentence shapes (syntax). The unit's final chapter moves from stylistic questions—a matter of choice—to common grammatical errors, a matter of correct versus incorrect forms. For this chapter and the next, we'll be asking you to think rhetorically: that is, in terms of appropriate choices for particular contexts rather than right versus wrong.

Most people simply don't pay attention to words. They use words as if their sounds were inaudible, their shapes were invisible, and their meanings were single and self-evident. One goal of this chapter is to interest you in words themselves—as *things* with particular qualities, complex histories, and varied shades of meaning.

A key concept throughout this unit is that style is not merely decorative. It is often mistakenly assumed that style is separate from meaning and in that sense largely cosmetic. From this perspective, paying close attention to style seems finicky, or worse, cynical—a way of dressing up the content to sell it to readers or listeners. The problem with this perspective is that it subscribes to what we have earlier referred to as *the transparent theory of language.* This is the idea that meaning exists outside of language—that we somehow see *through* words to meaning and can then address that meaning without addressing the words that embody it. In the transparent theory of language, words are merely pointers to get past.

Another key concept of this unit is that simplicity does not necessarily equal clarity. This chapter targets the unexamined cultural bias in favor of "straight talk." The assumption seems to be that people who use too many words, especially big ones, are needlessly complicating what would otherwise be obvious to anyone's common sense. *Not so.* (Those imperious arbiters of style, Strunk and White, are sometimes correct when they say in *The Elements of Style*—"Never use six words when three will do" —but not always.) Strunk and White also say, for example, never to use the "not un-" formation. So they summarily rule that it is always better

271

to say "I am happy" rather than "I am not unhappy." The second sentence, however, does not mean the same thing as the first. The difference is not just a matter of words but of meaning. This chapter seeks to persuade you that a matter of words is always a matter of meaning.

NOT JUST ICING ON THE CAKE: STYLE IS MEANING

Getting the style right is not as simple as proofreading for errors in grammar or punctuation. Proofreading occurs in the relatively comfortable linguistic world of simple right and wrong. Stylistic considerations, by contrast, take place in the more exploratory terrain of *making choices* among more and less effective ways of formulating and communicating your meaning.

You may have been taught that you should always avoid the first-person *I* in academic writing, steer clear of jargon, and never start a sentence with *and* or *but*. There are occasions when all three rules, and others like them, should be rejected. These are matters of usage, not hard-and-fast rules of grammar. This chapter seeks to persuade you that all writing is *contextual,* its appropriateness dependent on the rhetorical situation.

And what is style? Well, it's not just icing on the cake—cosmetic, a matter of polishing the surface. Broadly defined, *style* refers to all of a writer's decisions in selecting, arranging, and expressing what he or she has to say. Many factors affect your style: your aim and sense of audience, the ways you approach and develop a topic, the kinds of evidence you choose, and, particularly, the kinds of syntax (word order) and diction (word choice) you characteristically select.

In this sense, style is personal. The foundations of your style emerge in the dialogue you have with yourself about your topic. When you revise for style, you consciously reorient yourself toward communicating the results of that dialogue to your audience. Stylistic decisions, then, are a mix of the unconscious and conscious, of chance and choice. You don't simply impose style onto your prose; it's not a mask you don or your way of icing the cake. Revising for style is more like sculpting. As a sculptor uses a chisel to "bring out" a shape from a block of walnut or marble, a writer uses style to bring out the shape of the conceptual connections in a draft of an essay. This bringing out demands a certain detachment from your own language. It requires that you become aware of your words as words and of your sentences as sentences.

It is commonly assumed that "getting the style right" is a task that begins at the editing stage of producing a paper, as part of polishing the final draft. This assumption is only partly true. Most writers do delay a full-fledged stylistic revision until a late stage of drafting, but that doesn't mean that they totally ignore stylistic questions as they draft. The decisions you make about how to phrase your meaning inevitably exert a powerful influence on the meaning you make.

If stylistic considerations are not merely cosmetic, then it follows that rethinking the way you have said something can lead you to rethink the substance of what you have said.

How Style Shapes Thought: A Brief Example

How does the difference in sentence structure affect the meaning of the following two sentences?

Draft: The history of Indochina is marked by colonial exploitation as well as international cooperation.

Revision: The history of Indochina, *although* marked by colonial exploitation, testifies to the possibility of international cooperation.

In the draft, the claim that Indochina has experienced colonial exploitation is equal in weight to the claim that it has also experienced international cooperation. But the revision ranks the two claims. The "although" clause makes the claim of exploitation secondary to the claim of cooperation. The first version of the sentence would probably lead you to a broad survey of foreign intervention in Indochina. The result would likely be a static list in which you judged some interventions to be "beneficial" and others "not beneficial." The revised sentence redirects your thinking, tightens your paper's focus to prioritize evidence of cooperation, and presses you to make decisions, such as whether the positive consequences of cooperation outweigh the negative consequences of colonialism. In short, the revision leads you to examine the dynamic relations between your two initial claims.

Rethinking what you mean is just as likely to occur when you attend to word choice. Notice how the change of a single word in the following sentences could change the entire paper.

Draft: The president's attitude toward military spending is ambiguous.

Revision: The president's attitude toward military spending is ambivalent.

In the draft, the use of the word "ambiguous" (meaning "open to many interpretations") would likely lead to a paper on ways that the president's decisions are unclear. If the president's policies aren't unclear—hard to interpret—but are conflicted over competing ways of thinking, then the writer would want the word "ambivalent." This recognition would lead not only to reorganizing the final draft but also to refocusing the argument, building to the significance of this ambivalence (that the president is torn between adopting one of two stances) rather than to the previous conclusion (that presidential policy is incoherent).

MAKING DISTINCTIONS: SHADES OF MEANING

The nineteenth-century English statesman Benjamin Disraeli once differentiated between *misfortune* and *calamity* by using these words in a sentence describing his political rival William Gladstone: "If Mr. Gladstone fell into the Thames, it would be a misfortune; but if someone dragged him out, it would be a calamity." Misfortune and calamity might mean the same thing to some people, but in fact the two words allow a careful writer to discriminate fine shades of meaning.

One of the best ways to get yourself to pay attention to words as words is to practice making subtle distinctions among related words. The "right" word contributes accuracy and precision to your meaning. The "wrong" word, it follows, is inaccurate or imprecise. The most reliable guide to choosing the right word and avoiding the wrong word is a dictionary that includes not only concise definitions but also the origin of words (known as their *etymology*). A dicey alternative is a thesaurus (a dictionary of synonyms, now included in most word processing software). A thesaurus can offer you a host of choices, but you run a fairly high risk of choosing an inappropriate word because the thesaurus lists words as synonyms that really have different shades of meaning and connotation.

Many of the most common diction errors happen because the writer has not learned the difference between similar terms that actually have different meanings. A common error of this kind is use of the word "notorious" when what the writer means to say is "famous." A *notorious* figure is widely but unfavorably known, whereas a *famous* person is usually recognized for accomplishments that are praiseworthy. Referring to a famous person as notorious—a rather comic error—could be an embarrassing mistake.

A slightly less severe version of getting the wrong word occurs when a writer uses a word with a shade of meaning that is inappropriate or inaccurate in a particular context. Take, for example, the words *assertive* and *aggressive.* Often used interchangeably, they don't really mean the same thing—and the difference matters. Loosely defined, both terms mean forceful. But assertive suggests being bold and self-confident, whereas aggressive suggests being eager to attack. In most cases, you compliment the person you call assertive but raise doubts about the person you call aggressive (whether you are giving a compliment depends on the situation: aggressive is a term of praise on the football field but less so if used to describe an acquaintance's behavior during conversation at the dinner table).

One particularly charged context in which shades of meaning matter involves the potentially sexist implications of using one term for women and another for men. If, for example, in describing a woman and a man up for the same job, the employer were to refer to the woman as *aggressive* but the man as *assertive,* his diction would deservedly be considered sexist. It would reveal that what is perceived as poised and a sign of leadership potential in a man is being construed as unseemly belligerence in a woman. The sexism enters when word choice suggests that what is assertive in a man is aggressive in a woman.

Word Histories and the *OED*

In choosing the right shade of meaning, you will get a sharper sense for the word by knowing its etymological history—the word or words from which it evolved. In the preceding example, *aggressive* derives from the Latin *aggressus,* meaning "to go to or approach"; and *aggressus* is itself a combination of *ad,* a prefix expressing motion, and *gradus,* meaning "a step." An aggressive person, then, is "coming at you." *Assertive,* on the other hand, comes from the Latin *asserere,* combining *ad* and *serere,* meaning "to join or bind together." An assertive person is "coming to build or put things together"—certainly not to threaten.

The best dictionary for pursuing word histories, by the way, is the *Oxford English Dictionary,* which commonly goes by its initials, *OED.* Available in every library reference collection and usually online at colleges and universities as well, it provides examples of how every word has been used over time.

■ **Try this 17.1:** *Tracing Word Histories*

One of the best ways to get yourself to pay attention to words as words is to practice making fine distinctions among related words, as we did with aggressive and assertive. The following exercise will not only increase your vocabulary but also acquaint you with that indispensable reference work for etymology, the *OED.*

Look up one of the following pairs of words in the *OED.* Write down the etymology of each word in the pair, and then, in a paragraph for each, summarize the words' linguistic histories—how their meanings have evolved across time. (The *OED*'s examples of how the word has been used over time will be helpful here.)

ordinal/ordinary

explicate/implicate

tenacious/stubborn

induce/conducive

enthusiasm/ecstasy

adhere/inhere

monarchy/oligarchy

overt/covert

What's Bad about "Good" and "Bad"

Broad evaluative terms such as *good* and *bad* can seduce you into stopping your thinking while it is still too general and ill-defined—a matter discussed at length in the section of Chapter 2 called The Judgment Reflex. If you train yourself to select more precise words whenever you encounter *good* and *bad* in your drafts, not only will your prose become clearer but also the search for new words will probably start you thinking again, sharpening your ideas. If, for example, you find yourself writing a sentence such as "The subcommittee made a *bad* decision," ask yourself *why* you called it a bad decision. A revision to "The subcommittee made a shortsighted decision" indicates what in fact is bad about the decision and sets you up to discuss why the decision was myopic, further developing the idea.

Be aware that often evaluative terms are disguised as neutrally descriptive ones—*natural,* for instance, and *realistic.* Realistic according to whom, and defined by what criteria? Something is natural according to a given idea about nature—an assumption—and the same goes for *moral.* These are not terms that mean separately from a particular context or ideology (that is, an assumed hierarchy of value). Similarly, in a sentence such as "Society disapproves of interracial marriage," the broad and apparently neutral term *society* can blind you to a host of important distinctions about social class, about a particular culture, and so on.

Concrete and Abstract Diction

At its best, effective analytical prose uses both concrete and abstract words. Simply defined, concrete diction brings things to life by offering readers words that play on their senses. *Telephone, eggshell, crystalline, azure, striped, kneel, flare,* and *burp* are examples of concrete diction. You need concrete language whenever you are describing what happens or what something looks like—in a laboratory experiment, in a military action, in a painting or film sequence. The language of evidence consists of concrete diction. It allows us to see for ourselves the basis of a person's convictions in the stuff of lived experience.

By contrast, abstract diction refers to words that designate concepts and categories. *Virility, ideology, love, definitive, desultory, conscientious, classify,* and *ameliorate* are examples of abstract diction. So are *democracy, fascism, benevolence,* and *sentimentality.* Abstract words give us the language of ideas. We cannot do without abstract terms, and yet writing made up only of such words loses contact with experience, with the world that we can apprehend through our senses.

The line between abstract and concrete is not always as clear as these examples may suggest. You may recall the ladder of abstraction that we discuss in the section entitled Generalizing in Chapter 2. There we propose that abstract and concrete are not hard-and-fast categories so much as a continuum, a sliding scale. Word A (for example, machine) may be more abstract than word B (computer) but more concrete than word C (technology).

Concrete and abstract diction need each other. Concrete diction illustrates and anchors the generalizations that abstract diction expresses. Notice the concrete language used to define the abstraction *provinciality* in this example.

There is no cure for *provinciality* like traveling abroad. In America the waiter who fails to bring the check promptly at the end of the meal we rightly convict for not being watchful. But in England, after waiting interminably for the check and becoming increasingly irate, we learn that only an ill-mannered waiter would bring it without being asked. We have been rude, not he.

In the following example, the abstract terms *causality, fiction,* and *conjunction* are integrated with concrete diction in the second sentence.

According to the philosopher David Hume, *causality* is a kind of *fiction* that we ascribe to what he called "the constant *conjunction* of observed events." If a person gets hit in the eye and a black semicircle develops underneath it, that does not necessarily mean the blow caused the black eye.

A style that omits concrete language can leave readers lost in a fog of abstraction that only tangible details can illuminate. The concrete language helps readers see what you mean, much in the way that examples help them understand your ideas. Without the shaping power of abstract diction, however, concrete evocation can leave you with a list of graphic but ultimately pointless facts. The best writing integrates concrete and abstract diction, the language of showing and the language of telling (explaining).

■ **Try this 17.2:** *Two Experiments with Abstract and Concrete Diction*

1. Compose a paragraph using only concrete diction and then one using only abstract diction. Compare results with another person who has done the same task, as this can lead to an interesting discussion of kinds of words, where they reside on the ladder of abstraction, and why.

2. Rewrite the sentences listed below, substituting more concrete language and/or more precise abstractions. Support any abstractions you retain with appropriate detail. Just for the challenge, try to rewrite so that your sentences include no abstract claims; that is, use only concrete details to convey the points.

It was a great party; everybody had fun.

It was a lousy party; everybody disliked it.

The book was really boring.

The film was very interesting.

His morals were questionable.

Social Security is not an entitlement.

He became extraordinarily angry.

Latinate Diction

One of the best ways to sensitize yourself to the difference between abstract and concrete diction is to understand that many abstract words are examples of what is known as Latinate diction. This term describes words in English that derive from Latin roots, words with such endings as –tion, –ive, –ity, –ate, and –ent. (Such words are designated by an *L* in the etymological section of dictionary definitions.) Taken to an extreme, Latinate diction can leave your meaning vague and your readers confused. This is not because there is something dubious about words that come into English from Latin. A large percentage of English words have Latin or Greek roots, words like *pentagon* (Greek for five sides), *anarchy* (Latin for without order), and *automobile* (Latin for self-moving).

The problem with Latinate diction lies in the way it is sometimes used. Latin endings such as –tion make it too easy for writers to construct sentences made up of a high percentage of vague nouns, as in the following example.

The examination of different perspectives on the representations of sociopolitical anarchy in media coverage of revolutions can be revelatory of the invisible biases that afflict television news.

This sentence actually makes sense, but the demands it makes upon readers will surely drive off most of them before they have gotten through it. Reducing the amount of Latinate diction can make it more readable.

Because we tend to believe what we see, the political biases that afflict television news coverage of revolutions are largely invisible. We can begin to see these biases when we focus on how the medium reports events, studying the kinds of footage used, for example, or finding facts from other sources that the news has left out.

Although the preceding revision retains a lot of Latinate words, it provides a ballast of concrete, sensory details that allows readers to follow the idea. Although many textbooks on writing argue against using Latinate terms where shorter, concrete terms (usually of Anglo-Saxon origin) might be used instead, such an argument seems needlessly limiting in comparison with the advantages offered by a thorough mixture of the two levels of diction. It's fine to use Latinate diction; just don't make it the sole staple of your verbal diet.

CHOOSING WORDS: SOME RHETORICAL CONSIDERATIONS

We don't wish to make too firm a distinction between writing to make things clear and writing that is considerate of the needs of an audience beyond just clarity. And yet it is the case that when you begin to imagine the response of an audience, an actual listener to or reader of your prose, some additional considerations do come into play. The most important of these is tone.

Tone

Tone is the *implied attitude* of a piece of language toward its subject and audience. Whenever you revise for style, your choices in syntax and diction affect the tone. There are no hard-and-fast rules to govern matters of tone, and your control of it depends on your sensitivity to the particular context—your understanding of your own intentions and your readers' expectations.

Let's consider, for example, the tonal implications of the warning signs in the subways of London as compared with New York.

London: Leaning out of the window may cause harm.

New York: Do not lean out of the window.

Initially, you may find the English injunction laughably indirect and verbose in comparison with the shoot-from-the-hip clarity of the American sign. But that is to ignore the very thing we are calling *style*. The American version appeals to authority, commanding readers what not to do without telling them why. The English version, by contrast, appeals to logic; it is more collegial toward its readers and assumes they are rational beings rather than children prone to misbehave.

In revising for tone, you need to ask yourself if the attitude suggested by your language is appropriate to the aim of your message and to your audience. Your goal is to keep the tone *consistent* with your rhetorical intentions. The following paragraph, from a college catalogue, offers a classic mismatch between the overtly stated aim and the tonal implications:

> The student affairs staff believes that the college years provide a growth and development process for students. Students need to learn about themselves and others and to learn how to relate to individuals and groups of individuals with vastly different backgrounds, interests, attitudes and values. Not only is the tolerance of differences expected, but also an appreciation and a celebration of these differences must be an outcome of the student's experience. In addition, the student must progress toward self-reliance and independence tempered by a concern for the social order.

The explicit content of this passage—*what* it says—concerns tolerance. The professed point of view is student-friendly, asserting that the college exists to allow students "to learn about themselves and others" and to support the individual in accord with the "appreciation . . . of . . . differences." But note that the implicit tone—*how* the passage goes about saying *what* it says—is condescending and intolerant. Look at the verbs. An imperious authority lectures students about what they "*need* to learn," that tolerance is "*expected*," that "celebration . . . *must* be an outcome," and that "the student *must* progress" along these lines. Presumably, the paragraph does not intend to adopt this high-handed manner, but its deafness to tone subverts its desired meaning.

▬ Try this 17.3: *Analyzing Tone-Deaf Prose*

Using the example from the college catalogue as a model, locate and bring to class examples of tonal inconsistency or inappropriateness that you encounter in your daily life. If you have difficulty finding examples, try memos from those in authority at your school or workplace, which often contain excruciating examples of officialese. Type one of your passages, and underneath it compose a paragraph of analysis in which you single out particular words and phrases and explain how the tone is inappropriate. Then rewrite the passage to remedy the problem.

Formal and Colloquial Styles: Who's Writing to Whom, and Why Does It Matter?

How you say something is always a significant part of *what* you say. To look at words as words is to focus on the *how* as well as the *what*. Imagine that you call your friend on the phone, and a voice you don't recognize answers. You ask to speak with your friend, and the voice responds, "With whom have I the pleasure of speaking?" By contrast, what if the voice instead responds, "Who's this?" What information do these two versions of the question convey, beyond the obvious request for your name?

The first response—"With whom have I the pleasure of speaking?"—tells you that the speaker is formal and polite. He is also probably fastidiously well educated: he not only knows the difference between "who" and "whom" but also obeys the etiquette that outlaws ending a sentence with a preposition ("Whom have I the pleasure of speaking *with*?"). The very formality of the utterance, however, might lead you to label the speaker pretentious. His assumption that conversing with you is a "pleasure" suggests empty flattery. On the other hand, the second version—"Who's this?"—while also grammatically correct, is less formal. It is more direct but also terse to a fault; the speaker does not seem particularly interested in treating you politely.

The two hypothetical responses represent two different levels of style. Formal English obeys the basic conventions of standard written prose, and most academic writing is fairly formal. An informal style—one that is conversational and full of slang—can have severe limitations in an academic setting. The syntax and vocabulary of written prose aren't the same as those of speech, and so attempts to import the language of speech into academic writing can result in your communicating less meaning with less precision. Let's look at one brief example:

Internecine quarrels within the corporation destroyed morale and sent the value of the stock plummeting.

The phrase "internecine quarrels" may strike some readers as a pretentious display of formal language, but consider how difficult it is to communicate this concept economically in more colloquial (talk-like, conversational) terms. "Fights that go on between people related to each other" is awkward; "brother against brother" is sexist and a cliché; and "mutually destructive disputes" is acceptable but long-winded and less precise.

It is arguably a part of our national culture to value the simple and the direct as more genuine and democratic than the sophisticated, which is supposedly more aristocratic and pretentious. This "plain-speaking" style, however, can hinder your ability to develop and communicate your ideas. In the case of internecine, the more formal diction choice actually communicates more, and more effectively, than the less formal equivalents.

When in doubt about how your readers will respond to the formality or informality of your style, you are usually better off opting for some version of "With whom have I the pleasure of speaking?" rather than "Who's this?" The best solution usually lies somewhere in between: "May I ask who's calling?" would protect you against the imputation of either priggishness or piggishness.

What generalizations about style do these examples suggest?

- There are many ways of conveying a message.
- The way you phrase a message constitutes a significant part of its meaning.
- Your phrasing gives your reader cues that suggest your attitude and your ways of thinking.
- There are no transparent (absolutely neutral) delivery systems.
- All stylistic decisions depend on your sensitivity to context—who's talking to whom about what subject and with what aims.

The last of these generalizations concerns what is called the *rhetorical situation*. *Rhetoric* is the subject that deals with how writers and speakers behave in given situations and, more specifically, how they can generate language that produces the effects they desire on a particular audience. Obviously, as you make stylistic choices, you need to be aware of the possible consequences of making certain statements to a certain audience in a certain fashion.

▰ **Try this 17.4:** *Analyzing Effective Tone*

Find an example of tone that you think is just about perfect for the message and audience. Type it, and underneath discuss why it succeeds. Be as specific as you can about how the passage functions stylistically. Talk about particular phrasings and the match between what is being said and how it is said. Factor into your discussion the relationship between levels of style in the example and its presumed audience.

The Person Question

The person question concerns which of the three basic forms of the pronoun you should use when you write. Here are the three forms, with brief examples.

First person: I believe Heraclitus is an underrated philosopher.

Second person: You should believe that Heraclitus is an underrated philosopher.

Third person: He or she believes that Heraclitus is an underrated philosopher.

Which person to use is a stylistic concern because it involves a writer's *choices* as regards to level of formality, the varying expectations of different audiences, and overall tone.

As a general rule, in academic writing you should discuss your subject matter in the third person and avoid the first and second person. There is logic to this rule: most academic analysis focuses on the subject matter rather than on you as you respond to it. If you use the third person, you keep the attention where it belongs.

The First Person Pronoun "I": Pro and Con

Using the first-person "I" can throw the emphasis on the wrong place. Repeated assertions of "in my opinion" actually distract your readers from what you have to say. Omit them except in the most informal cases. You might, however, consider using the first person in the drafting stage if you are having trouble bringing your own point of view to the forefront. In this situation, the "I" becomes a strategy for loosening up and saying what you really think about a subject rather than adopting conventional and faceless positions. In the final analysis, though, most analytical prose is more precise and straightforward in the third person. When you cut "I am convinced that" from the beginning of any claim, what you lose in personal conviction you gain in concision and directness by keeping the focus on the main idea in a main clause.

Are there cases when you should use "I"? Contrary to the general rule, some professors actually prefer the first-person pronoun in particular contexts, as noted in the accompanying Voices from across the Curriculum section.

VOICES FROM ACROSS THE CURRICULUM

Using the First-Person *I* in Academic Writing

Avoid phrases like *"The author* believes (or will discuss)." Except in the paper's abstract, *"I* believe (or will discuss)" is okay, and often best.

—Alan Tjeltveit, *Professor of Psychology*

I prefer that personal opinion or voice (for example, "I this," or "I that") appear throughout. I like the first person. No "the author feels" or "this author found that," please! Who is the author? Hey, it's you!

—Frederick Norling, *Professor of Business*

The biggest stylistic problem is that students tend to be too personal or colloquial in their writing, using phrases such as the following: "Scientists all agree," "I find it amazing that," "The thing that I find most interesting." Students are urged to present data and existing information in their own words, but in an objective way. My preference in writing is to use the active voice in the past tense. I feel this is the most direct and least wordy approach: "I asked this," "I found out that," "These data show."

—Richard Niesenbaum, *Professor of Biology*

Note that these are not blanket endorsements; they specify a limited context within which "I" is preferred. The biology professor's cautioning against using an overly personal and colloquial tone is also probably the consensus view.

Although a majority of professors may prefer the first-person "I think" to the more awkward "the writer (or 'one') thinks," we would point out that, in the service of reducing wordiness, you can often avoid both options. For example, in certain contexts and disciplines, the first-person-plural, we, is acceptable usage: "The president's speech assumes that *we* are all dutiful but disgruntled taxpayers." The one case in which the first person is particularly appropriate occurs when you are citing an example from your own experience. Otherwise, if you are in doubt about using I or we, avoid these first-person pronouns.

The Second Person Pronoun "You": Pro and Con

As for the second person, proceed with caution. Using "you" is a fairly assertive gesture. Many readers will be annoyed, for example, by a paper about advertising that states, "When you read about a sale at the mall, you know it's hard to resist." Most readers resent having a writer airily making assumptions about them or telling them what to do. Some rhetorical situations, however, call for the use of "you." Textbooks, for example, use "you" frequently because it creates a more direct relationship between authors and readers. Yet, even in appropriate situations, directly addressing readers as "you" may alienate them by ascribing to them attitudes and needs they may not have.

The conventional argument for using the first and second person is that "I" and "you" are personal and engage readers. It is not necessarily the case, however, that the third person is therefore impersonal. Just as film directors put their stamps on films by the way they organize the images, move among camera viewpoints, and orchestrate the sound tracks, so writers, even when writing in the third person, have a wide variety of resources at their disposal for making the writing more personal and accessible for their audiences. See, for example, the discussion of the passive voice in Chapter 18.

Using and Avoiding Jargon

Many people assume that all jargon—the specialized vocabulary of a particular group—is bad: pretentious language designed to make most readers feel inferior. Many writing textbooks attack jargon in similar terms, calling it either polysyllabic balderdash or a specialized, gate-keeping language designed by an in-group to keep others out.

Yet, in many academic contexts, jargon is downright essential. It is conceptual shorthand, a technical vocabulary that allows the members of a group (or a discipline) to converse with one another more clearly and efficiently. Certain words that may seem odd to outsiders in fact function as connective tissue for a way of thought shared by insiders. The following sentence, for example, although full of botanical jargon, is also admirably cogent:

In angiosperm reproduction, if the number of pollen grains deposited on the stigma exceeds the number of ovules in the ovary, then pollen tubes may compete for access to ovules, which results in fertilization by the fastest growing pollen tubes.

We would label this use of jargon acceptable because it is written, clearly, *by* insiders *for* fellow insiders. It might not be acceptable language for an article intended for readers who are not botanists, or at least not scientists.

The problem with jargon comes when this insiders' language is directed at outsiders as well. The language of contracts offers a prime example of such jargon at work.

The Author hereby indemnifies and agrees to hold the Publisher, its licensees, and any seller of the Work harmless from any liability, damage, cost, and expense, including reasonable attorney's fees and costs of settlement, for or in connection with any claim, action, or proceeding inconsistent with the Author's warranties or representations herein, or based upon or arising out of any contribution of the Author to the Work.

Run for the lawyer! What does it mean to "hold the Publisher . . . harmless"? To what do "the Author's warranties or representations" refer? What exactly is the author being asked to do here—release the publisher from all possible lawsuits that the author might bring? We might label this use of jargon obfuscating; although it may aim at precision, it leaves most readers bewildered. Although nonprofessionals are asked to sign them, such documents are really written by lawyers for other lawyers.

As the botanical and legal examples suggest, the line between acceptable and obfuscating jargon has far more to do with the audience to whom the words are addressed than with the actual content of the language. Because most academic writing is addressed to insiders, students studying a particular area need to learn its jargon. Using the technical language of the discipline is a necessary skill for conversing with others in that discipline. Moreover, by demonstrating that you can "talk the talk," you will validate your authority to pronounce an opinion on matters in the discipline.

Here are two guidelines that can help you in your use of jargon: (1) when addressing *insiders,* use jargon accurately ("talk the talk"); and (2) when addressing *outsiders*—the general public or members of another discipline—either define the jargon carefully or replace it with a more generally known term, preferably one operating at the same level of formality. As the anecdote in the following Voices from across the Curriculum illustrates, questions of jargon—which are also questions of tone—are best resolved by considering the particular contexts for given writing tasks.

ASSIGNMENT: Style Analysis

Write a paper that analyzes the style of a particular group or profession (for example, sports, advertising, bureaucracy, show business, or music reviewing). Or as an alternative, adopt the voice of a member of this group, and write a parody that critiques or analyzes the language practices of the group. If you choose the latter, be aware that there is always a risk in parody of belittling in an unduly negative way a style that is not your own.

Obviously, you will first need to assemble and make observations about a number of samples of the style that you are analyzing or parodying. Use The Method to help

---

VOICES FROM ACROSS THE CURRICULUM

When to Use and Not Use Jargon

I worked for the Feds for many years before seeking the doctorate. My job required immense amounts of writing: reports, directives, correspondence, and so forth. But, on a day-to-day basis for almost seven years I had to write short "write-ups" assessing the qualifications of young people for the Peace Corps and VISTA programs. I'd generate "list-like," "bullet-like" assessments: "Looks good with farm machinery, has wonderful volunteer experience, would be best in a rural setting, speaks French." But I had to conclude each of these assessments with a one-page narrative. Here I tended to reject officious governmentese for a more personal style. I'd write as I spoke. Rather than "Has an inclination for a direction in the facilitation of regulation," I'd write "Would be very good directing people on projects." I'd drop the "-tion" stuff and write in "speak form," not incomplete sentences, but in what I call "candid, personal" style. I carry this with me today.

—Frederick Norling, *Professor of Business*

you uncover the kinds of words that are repeated, the most common strands, and so forth. Look at the level of formality, the tone, the use of concrete and abstract diction, and the predilection for Latinate as opposed to Anglo-Saxon words. Who's writing to whom about what, and so what that the writing adopts this style? Also, see the assignments at the end of Chapter 18.

CHAPTER 18

Style: Shaping Sentences for Precision and Emphasis

THE GOAL OF THIS CHAPTER is to enable you to see the stylistic choices available to you as you fashion and revise your sentences. The fundamental unit of composition is the sentence. Every sentence has a shape, and once you can recognize the shape of a sentence, you can recast it to make it more graceful, logical, and emphatic.

Recasting sentences is not just a stylistic practice but a thinking practice. The way a sentence is structured reveals a way of thinking. Casting and recasting sentences in different words and in different shapes helps you experiment with the way you arrive at ideas.

Toward this end, we need to take you through some basic grammatical categories, such as coordinate and subordinate sentence forms. We are venturing into grammar, though, not to enter the domain of right and wrong, of correctness and error, but to help you expand your range of stylistic choices.

HOW TO RECOGNIZE THE FOUR BASIC SENTENCE TYPES

Given that the sentence is the fundamental unit of composition, you will benefit immensely, both in composing and in revising your sentences, if you can identify and construct the four basic sentence types. We will supply the necessary grammatical terminology as we go, but you can also consult the Glossary of Grammatical Terms at the end of Chapter 19. (In particular, see entries for the following terms: *clause, conjunction, conjunctive adverb, coordination, direct object, phrase, preposition, subject, subordination,* and *verbals.*)

Every sentence is built upon the skeleton of its independent clause(s), the subject and verb combination that can stand alone. Consider the following four sentences:

Consumers shop.

Consumers shop; producers manufacture.

Consumers shop in predictable ways, so producers manufacture with different target groups in mind.

Consumers shop in ways that can be predicted by such determinants as income level, sex, and age; consequently, producers use market research to identify different target groups for their products.

Certainly these four sentences become progressively longer, and the information they contain becomes increasingly detailed, but they also differ in their structure—specifically, in the number of independent and dependent clauses they contain. A dependent clause literally depends (hangs on, can't stand without) another clause.

The Simple Sentence

The *simple sentence* consists of a single independent clause. At its simplest, it contains a single subject and verb.

Consumers shop.

Other words and phrases can be added to this sentence, but it remains simple so long as "Consumers shop" is the only clause.

Most consumers shop unwisely.

Even if the sentence contains more than one grammatical subject or more than one verb, it remains simple in structure.

Most consumers *shop* unwisely and *spend* more than they can afford. *[two verbs]*

Both female consumers and their husbands shop unwisely. *[two subjects]*

The sentence structure in the example that uses two verbs (shop and spend) is known as a *compound predicate.* The sentence structure in the example that uses two subjects (consumers and husbands) is known as a *compound subject.* If, however, you were to add both another subject and another verb to the original simple sentence, you would have the next sentence type, a compound sentence.

The Compound Sentence

The *compound sentence* consists of at least two independent clauses and no subordinate clauses. The information conveyed in these clauses should be of roughly equal importance.

Producers manufacture, and consumers shop.

Producers manufacture, marketers sell, and consumers shop.

As with the simple sentence, you can also add qualifying phrases to the compound sentence, and it remains compound, as long as no dependent clauses are added.

Consumers shop in predictable ways, so producers manufacture with different target groups in mind.

Consumers shop recklessly during holidays; marketers are keenly aware of this fact.

Note that a compound sentence can connect its independent clauses with either a coordinate conjunction or a semicolon. (The primary use of the semicolon is as a substitute for a coordinate conjunction, separating two independent clauses.) If you were to substitute a subordinating conjunction for either of these connectors, however, you would have a sentence with one independent clause and one dependent clause. For example:

> *Because* consumers shop in predictable ways, producers manufacture with different target groups in mind.

This revision changes the compound sentence into the next sentence type, the complex sentence.

The Complex Sentence

The *complex sentence* consists of a single independent clause and one or more dependent clauses. The information conveyed in the dependent clause is subordinated to the more important independent clause (a matter we take up in more detail momentarily in the subordination section). In the following example, the subject and verb of the main clause are underlined, and the subordinating conjunctions are italicized:

> *Although* mail-order merchandising—*which* generally saves shoppers money—has increased, most <u>consumers</u> still <u>shop</u> unwisely, buying on impulse rather than deliberation.

This sentence contains one independent clause (consumers shop). Hanging upon it are two introductory dependent clauses (although merchandising has increased, and which saves) and a participial phrase (buying on impulse). If you converted either of these dependent clauses into an independent clause, you would have a sentence with two independent clauses (a compound sentence) and a dependent clause. In the following example, the subjects and verbs of the two main clauses are underlined, and the conjunctions are italicized:

> Mail-order <u>merchandising</u>—*which* generally saves shoppers money—<u>has increased</u>, *but* <u>consumers</u> still <u>shop</u> unwisely, buying on impulse rather than deliberation.

This revision changes the complex sentence into the next sentence type, the compound-complex sentence.

The Compound-Complex Sentence

The *compound-complex sentence* consists of two or more independent clauses and one or more dependent clauses.

> Consumers shop in ways that can be predicted by such determinants as income level, sex, and age; consequently, producers use market research that aims to identify different target groups for their products.

This sentence contains two independent clauses (consumers shop, and producers use) and two dependent clauses (that can be predicted, and that aims).

So Why Do the Four Sentence Types Matter?

The four types of sentences are about different ways of organizing and prioritizing information. Simple sentences give one clearly defined idea at a time. Compound sentences allow you to piggy-back several of these together, indicating that they go together and are equal in some way, whether you add them onto each other or contrast them. Complex sentences indicate relationship among ideas: "Before I did *X*, I did *Y*, although I didn't want to." Each of these sentence types has force; they just foreground and relate their ideas in different ways.

Try this 18.1: *Composing the Four Sentence Shapes*

As we have done with the consumers-shop example, compose a simple sentence and then a variety of expansions: a compound subject, a compound predicate, a compound sentence, a complex sentence, and a compound-complex sentence.

To prevent this exercise from becoming merely mechanical, keep in mind how different sentence shapes accomplish different ends. In other words, make sure your compound sentence balances two items of information, that your complex sentence emphasizes one thing (in the main clause) over another (in the subordinate clause), and that your compound-complex sentence is capable of handling and organizing complexity.

COORDINATION, SUBORDINATION, AND EMPHASIS

A *clause* is a group of words containing a subject and a predicate. The syntax of a sentence can give your readers cues about whether the idea in one clause is equal to (coordinate) or subordinate to the idea in another clause. In this context, grammar operates as a form of implicit logic, defining relationships among the clauses in a sentence according to the choices that you make about coordination, subordination, and the order of clauses. In revising your sentences, think of coordination and subordination as tools of logic and emphasis, helping to rank your meanings.

Coordination

Coordination uses grammatically equivalent constructions to link ideas. These ideas should carry roughly equal weight as well. Sentences that use coordination connect clauses with coordinating conjunctions (such as *and, but,* and *or*). Here are two examples.

Historians organize the past, *and* they can never do so with absolute neutrality.

Homegrown corn is incredibly sweet, *and* it is very difficult to grow.

If you ponder these sentences, you may begin to detect the danger of the word *and.* It does not specify a precise logical relationship between the things it connects but instead simply adds them.

Notice that the sentences get more precise if we substitute *but* for *and.*

> Historians organize the past, *but* they can never do so with absolute neutrality.

> Homegrown corn is incredibly sweet, *but* it is very difficult to grow.

These sentences are still coordinate in structure; they are still the sentence type known as compound. But they achieve more emphasis than the *and* versions. In both cases, the *but* clause carries more weight because *but* always introduces information that qualifies or contradicts what precedes it.

Reversing the Order of Coordinate Clauses for Emphasis

In both the *and* and *but* examples, the second clause tends to be stressed. The reason is simple: *the end is usually a position of emphasis.*

You can see the effect of clause order more starkly if we reverse the clauses in our examples.

> Historians are never absolutely neutral, but they organize the past.

> Homegrown corn is very difficult to grow, but it is incredibly sweet.

Note how the meanings have changed in these versions by emphasizing what now comes last. Rather than simply having their objectivity undermined (Historians are never absolutely neutral), historians are now credited with at least providing organization (they organize the past). Similarly, whereas the previous version of the sentence about corn was likely to dissuade a gardener from trying to grow it (it is very difficult to grow), the new sentence is more likely to lure him or her to nurture corn (it is incredibly sweet).

Nonetheless, all of these sentences are examples of coordination because the clauses are grammatically equal. As you revise, notice when you use coordinate syntax, and think about whether you really intend to give the ideas equal weight. Consider as well whether reversing the order of clauses would more accurately convey your desired emphasis to your readers.

So Why Does the Order of Coordinate Clauses Matter?

As you've seen, the clause placed last tends to get emphasis. This fact provides a useful drafting and revising strategy: manipulate the order of clauses to get the one you wish to emphasize at the end rather than the beginning of the sentence.

■ Try this 18.2: *Rearranging Coordinate Clauses for Emphasis*

Rearrange the parts of the following coordinate sentence, which is composed of four sections, separated by commas. Construct at least three versions, and jot down how the meaning changes in each version.

> I asked her to marry me, two years ago, in a shop on Tremont Street, late in the fall.

Then subject two sentences of your own to the same treatment. Make sure to describe how the meaning changes in each case because it will get you accustomed to seeing the effects of the rearrangements.

Subordination

In sentences that contain *subordination,* there are two "levels" of grammar—the main clause and the subordinate clause—that create two levels of meaning. When you put something in a main clause, you emphasize its significance. When you put something in a subordinate clause, you make it less important than what is in the main clause.

As noted in the discussion of complex sentences, a subordinate clause is linked to a main clause by words known as *subordinating conjunctions.* Here is a list of the most common ones: *after, although, as, as if, as long as, because, before, if, rather than, since, than, that, though, unless, until, when, where, whether,* and *while.* All of these words define something *in relation to* something else:

> *If* you study hard, you will continue to do well.
>
> You will continue to do well, *if* you study hard.

In both of these examples, *if* subordinates "you study hard" to "you will continue to do well," regardless of whether the *if* clause comes first or last in the sentence.

Reversing Main and Subordinate Clauses

Unlike the situation with coordinate clauses, the emphasis in sentences that use subordination virtually always rests on the main clause, regardless of the clause order. Nevertheless, the principle of end-position emphasis still applies, though to a lesser extent than among coordinate clauses. Let's compare two versions of the same sentence.

> Although the art of the people was crude, it was original.
>
> The art of the people was original, although it was crude.

Both sentences emphasize the idea in the main clause (original). Because the second version locates the although clause at the end, however, the subordinated idea (crude) has more emphasis than it does in the first version.

You can experiment with the meaning and style of virtually any sentence you write by reversing the clauses. Here, taken almost at random, is an earlier sentence from this chapter, followed by two such transformations.

> When you put something in a subordinate clause, you make it less important than what is in the main clause.
>
> Put information in a subordinate clause if you want to make it less important than what is in the main clause.
>
> If you want to make information less important than what is in the main clause, put it in a subordinate clause.

So Why Does It Matter What Goes in the Subordinate Clause?

This can be complicated, but as we've shown, subordination qualifies ideas in the independent clause. So emphasis tends to be placed on the information in the independent clause. But this tendency can be in conflict with the "rule" that you empower whatever you put at the end of the sentence. A complex sentence ending with a subordinate clause would still put somewhat greater emphasis on the content of the subordinate clause just because it is at the end.

◼ **Try this 18.3:**   *Experimenting with Coordination, Subordination, and the Order of Clauses*

Do two rewrites of the following sentence, changing the order of clauses and subordinating or coordinating as you wish. We recommend that you make one of them end with the word *friendly.*

> Faculty members came to speak at the forum, and they were friendly, but they were met with hostility, and this hostility was almost paranoid.

How does each of your revisions change the meaning and emphasis?

Parallel Structure

One of the most important and useful devices for shaping sentences is *parallel structure* or, as it is also known, *parallelism.* Parallelism is a form of symmetry: it involves placing sentence elements that correspond in some way into the same (that is, parallel) grammatical form. Consider the following examples, in which the parallel items are underlined or italicized:

> The three kinds of partners in a law firm who receive money from a case are popularly known as <u>finders</u>, <u>binders</u>, and <u>grinders</u>.

> The Beatles acknowledged their musical debts <u>to</u> American rhythm and blues, <u>to</u> English music hall ballads and ditties, and later <u>to</u> classical Indian ragas.

> There was <u>no way that</u> the president *could gain* the support of party regulars *without alienating* the Congress, and <u>no way that</u> he <u>could appeal</u> to the electorate at large *without alienating* both of these groups.

> In the entertainment industry, the money that <u>goes out</u> to hire *film stars* or *sports stars* <u>comes back</u> in increased ticket sales and video or television rights.

As all of these examples illustrate, at the core of parallelism lies repetition—of a word, a phrase, or a grammatical structure. Parallelism uses repetition to organize and emphasize certain elements in a sentence so that readers can perceive more clearly the shape of your thought. In the Beatles example, each of the prepositional phrases beginning with *to* contains a musical debt. In the president example, the repetition of the phrase *no way that* emphasizes his entrapment.

Parallelism has the added advantage of economy: each of the musical debts or presidential problems might have had its own sentence, but in that case the prose would have been wordier and the relationships among the parallel items more obscure. Along with this economy comes balance and emphasis. The trio of rhyming words (finders, binders, and grinders) that concludes the law firm example gives each item equal weight; in the entertainment industry example, "comes back" answers "goes out" in a way that accentuates their symmetry.

■ Try this 18.4: *Finding Examples of Parallelism*

List all of the examples of parallelism in the following famous passage from the beginning of the Declaration of Independence:

> We hold these truths to be self-evident: that all men are created equal; that they are endowed by their Creator with certain inalienable rights; that, among these, are life, liberty, and the pursuit of happiness.

Remember that parallelism can occur with clauses, phrases, and prepositional phrases. You might find it useful to review the entries for these terms in the glossary in Chapter 19. After you have completed your list, what do you notice about the way that the parallel structures accumulate? And what is the effect of the placement and phrasing of these parallelisms? In other words, try to describe how this famous passage develops stylistically.

One particularly useful form of balance that parallel structure accommodates is known as *antithesis* (from the Greek word for "opposition"), a conjoining of contrasting ideas. Here the pattern sets one thing against another thing, as in the following example:

> Where bravura failed to settle the negotiations, tact and patience succeeded.

"Failed" is balanced antithetically against "succeeded," as "bravura" against "tact and patience." Antithesis commonly takes the form of "if not *X*, at least *Y*" or "not *X*, but *Y*."

When you employ parallelism in revising for style, there is one grammatical rule you should obey. It is important to avoid what is known as *faulty parallelism*, which occurs when the items that are parallel in content are not placed in the same grammatical form.

> **Faulty:** *To study* hard for four years and then *getting* ignored once they enter the job market is a hard thing for many recent college graduates to accept.

> **Revised:** *To study* hard for four years and then *to get* ignored once they enter the job market is a hard thing for many recent college graduates to accept.

As you revise your draft for style, search for opportunities to place sentence elements in parallel structure. Try this consciously: include and underline three uses of it in a draft of your next writing assignment. Remember that parallelism can occur with *clauses, phrases,* and *prepositional phrases.* Often the parallels are hidden in the sentences of your draft, but they can be brought out with a minimum of labor. After you've acquired the habit of casting your thinking in parallel structures, they will rapidly become a staple of your stylistic repertoire, making your prose more graceful, clear, and logically connected.

So Why Does Parallel Structure Matter?

Ideas that are put in parallel form seem equal in importance, even though the last element in a series always gets more weight. Parallelism creates an effect of balance and in so doing can also foreground the content of two parallel but opposing elements—antithesis. *Chiasmus* is a rhetorical pattern that generates emphasis on the basis of parallelism, antithesis, and the emphatic power of the terminal position. The most famous chiasmus to most Americans: "Ask not," intoned JFK, "what your country can do for you; ask what you can do for your country."

Try this 18.5: *Correcting Errors in Parallelism*

Rewrite the following examples of faulty parallelism using correct parallel structure. In the last of these sentences you will need to contemplate the thinking behind it as well as its form.

1. The problems with fast food restaurants include the way workers are exploited, eating transfatty acids, and that the food can damage your liver.
2. Venus likes to play tennis and also watching baseball games.
3. In the 1960s the use of drugs and being a hippie was a way for some people to let society know their political views and that they were alienated from the mainstream.

PERIODIC AND CUMULATIVE SENTENCES: TWO EFFECTIVE SENTENCE SHAPES

The shape of a sentence governs the way it delivers information. The order of clauses, especially the placement of the main clause, affects what the sentence means.

There are two common sentence shapes defined by the location of their main clauses; these are known as *periodic* and *cumulative* sentences.

The Periodic Sentence: Delaying Closure for Emphasis

The main clause in a periodic sentence builds to a climax that is not completed until the end. Often, a piece of the main clause (such as the subject) is located early in the sentence, as in the following example.

> The *way* that beverage companies market health—"No Preservatives," "No Artificial Colors," "All Natural," "Real Brewed"—*is* often, because the product also contains a high percentage of sugar or fructose, *misleading.*

We have italicized the main clause to clarify how various modifiers interrupt it. The effect is suspenseful: not until the final word does the sentence consummate its fundamental idea. Pieces of the main clause are spread out across the sentence. (The term *periodic* originates in classical rhetoric to refer to the length of such units within a sentence.)

Another version of the periodic sentence locates the entire main clause at the end, after introductory modifiers.

> Using labels that market health—such as "No Preservatives," "No Artificial Colors," "All Natural," and "Real Brewed"—while producing drinks that contain a high percentage of sugar or fructose, *beverage companies are misleading consumers.*

As was previously discussed, the end of a sentence normally receives emphasis. When you use a periodic construction, the pressure on the end intensifies because the sentence needs the end to complete its grammatical sense. In both of the preceding examples, the sentences "snap shut." They string readers along, delaying *grammatical closure*—the point at which the sentences can stand alone independently—until they arrive at climactic ends. (Periodic sentences are also known as *climactic sentences.*)

You should be aware of one risk that accompanies periodic constructions. If the delay lasts too long because there are too many interrupters before the main clause is completed, your readers may forget the subject that is being predicated. To illustrate, let's add more subordinated material to one of the preceding examples.

> The way that beverage companies market health—"No Preservatives," "No Artificial Colors," "All Natural," "Real Brewed"—is often, because the product also contains a high percentage of sugar or fructose, not just what New Agers would probably term "immoral" and "misleading" but what a government agency such as the Food and Drug Administration should find illegal.

Arguably, the additions (the not just and but clauses after fructose) push the sentence into incoherence. The main clause has been stretched past the breaking point. If readers don't get lost in such a sentence, they are at least likely to get irritated and wish the writer would finally get to the point.

Nonetheless, with a little care, periodic sentences can be extraordinarily useful in giving emphasis. If you are revising and want to underscore some point, try letting the sentence snap shut upon it. Often the periodic potential is already present in the draft, and stylistic editing can bring it out more forcefully. Note how minor the revisions are in the following example:

> **Draft:** The novelist Virginia Woolf suffered from acute anxieties for most of her life. She had several breakdowns and finally committed suicide on the eve of World War II.

> **Revision:** Suffering from acute anxieties for most of her life, the novelist Virginia *Woolf* not only *had* several *breakdowns but,* finally, on the eve of World War II, *committed suicide.*

This revision has made two primary changes. It has combined two short sentences into a longer sentence, and it has made the sentence periodic by stringing out the main clause (italicized). What is the effect of this revision? Stylistically speaking, the revision radiates a greater sense of its writer's authority. The information has been arranged for us. After the opening dependent clause ("Suffering . . ."), the subject of the main clause ("Woolf") is introduced, and the predicate is protracted in a *not only/but* parallelism. The interrupters that follow "had several breakdowns" (finally, on the eve of World War II) increase the suspense before the sentence snaps shut with "committed suicide."

In general, when you construct a periodic sentence with care, you can give readers the sense that you are in control of your material. You do not seem to be writing off the top of your head, but rather from a position of greater detachment, rationally composing your meaning.

The Cumulative Sentence: Starting Fast

The cumulative sentence is in many respects the opposite of the periodic. Rather than delaying the main clause or its final piece, the cumulative sentence begins by presenting the independent clause as a foundation and then *accumulates* a number of modifications and qualifications. As the following examples illustrate, the independent clause provides quick grammatical closure, freeing the rest of the sentence to amplify and develop the main idea.

> *Robert F. Kennedy was assassinated* by Sirhan B. Sirhan, a twenty-four-year-old Palestinian immigrant, prone to occultism and unsophisticated left-wing politics and sociopathically devoted to leaving his mark in history, even if as a notorious figure.

> *There are two piano concerti* composed solely for the left hand, one by Serge Prokofiev and one by Maurice Ravel, and both commissioned by Paul Wittgenstein, a concert pianist (and the brother of the famous philosopher Ludwig Wittgenstein) who had lost his right hand in combat during World War I.

Anchored by the main clause, a cumulative sentence moves serially through one thing and another thing and the next thing, close to the associative manner in which people think. To an extent, then, cumulative sentences can convey more immediacy and a more conversational tone than can other sentence shapes. Look at the following example:

> The film version of *Lady Chatterley's Lover* changed D. H. Lawrence's famous novel a lot, omitting the heroine's adolescent experience in Germany, making her husband much older than she, leaving out her father and sister, including a lot more lovemaking, and virtually eliminating all of the philosophizing about sex and marriage.

Here we get the impression of a mind in the act of thinking. Using the generalization of changes in the film as a base, the sentence then appends a series of parallel participial phrases (omitting, making, leaving, including, eliminating) that moves forward associatively, gathering a range of information and laying out possibilities. Cumulative sentences perform this outlining and prospecting function very effectively. On the other hand, if we were to add four or five more changes to the sentence, readers would likely find it tedious, or worse, directionless. As with periodic sentences, overloading the shape can short-circuit its desired effect.

So Why Do Periodic and Cumulative Sentences Matter?

Each offers writers different opportunities and creates different effects on readers. The rhetoric of periodic sentences is all about suspense and delay. It puts maximum emphasis on the way the suspension ends. Cumulative sentences are all about up-front impact plus elaboration.

▬ Try this 18.6: *Writing Periodic and Cumulative Sentences*

If you consciously practice using periodic and cumulative constructions, you will be surprised how quickly you can learn to produce their respective effects in your own writing. You will also discover that both of these sentence shapes are already present in your prose in some undiscovered and thus unrefined way. It is often simply a case of bringing out what is already there. Try including at least one of each in the next paper you write.

Toward that end, compose a simple sentence on any subject, preferably one with a direct object. Then construct two variations expanding it, one periodic and one cumulative. Here, as a model, is an example using the core sentence "James Joyce was a gifted singer."

> **Periodic:** Although known primarily as one of the greatest novelists of the twentieth century, James Joyce, the son of a local political functionary who loved to tip a few too many at the pub, was also a gifted—and prizewinning—singer.

> **Cumulative:** James Joyce was a gifted singer, having listened at his father's knee to the ballads sung in pubs, having won an all-Ireland prize in his early teens, and having possessed a miraculous ear for the inflections of common speech that was to serve him throughout the career for which he is justly famous, that of a novelist.

Can't think of a core sentence? Okay, here are a few:

> Why do airlines show such mediocre films?

> The Abu Ghraib prison scandal rocked the nation.

> Manny Ramirez and friends lifted the curse of the Bambino.

> Every senator is a millionaire.

CUTTING THE FAT

If you can reduce verbiage, your prose will communicate more directly and effectively. In cutting the fat, you need to consider both the diction and the syntax. When it comes to diction, the way to eliminate superfluous words is deceptively simple: ask yourself if you need all of the words you've included to say what you want to say. Such revision requires an aggressive attitude. Expect to find unnecessary restatements or intensifiers such as "quite" and "very" that add words but not significance.

Sometimes, by the way, the problem is not just a matter of syntax but a matter of confidence. A lot of writing becomes obscure because the writer is trying to hide what he or she has to say with various "throat clearings" and other defensive verbiage. If you don't say anything clearly enough to be understood, you can't be accused of being wrong. If you find yourself bogged down in language, take a moment to write as directly as possible an answer to the question, "What I'm really trying to say here is . . . "

Expletive Constructions

The syntactic pattern for "*It* is true that more government services mean higher taxes" is known as an *expletive* construction. The term *expletive* comes from a Latin word that means "serving to fill out." The most common expletives are *it* and *there*. Consider how the expletives function in the following examples.

> *There* are several prototypes for the artificial heart.

> *It* is obvious that the American West exerted a profound influence on the photography of Ansel Adams.

Compare these with versions that simply eliminate the expletives.

> The artificial heart has several prototypes.

> The American West exerted a profound influence on the photography of Ansel Adams.

As the revisions demonstrate, most of the time you can streamline your prose by getting rid of expletive constructions. The "It is obvious" opening, for example, causes the grammar of the sentence to subordinate its real emphasis. In some cases, however, an expletive can provide a useful way of emphasizing, as in the following example: "There are three primary reasons that you should avoid litigation." Although this sentence subordinates its real content (avoiding litigation), the expletive provides a useful frame for what is to follow.

Static versus Active Verbs: "To Be" or "Not to Be"

Verbs energize a sentence. They do the work, connecting the parts of the sentence with each other. In a sentence of the subject–verb–direct object pattern, the verb—known as a *transitive verb*—functions as a kind of engine, driving the subject into the predicate, as in the following examples.

> John F. Kennedy effectively *manipulated* his image in the media.

> Thomas Jefferson *embraced* the idea of America as a country of yeoman farmers.

Verbs energize a sentence. A transitive verb functions as an engine, driving the subject into the predicate.

By contrast, *is* and other forms of the verb *to be* provide an equal sign between the subject and the predicate but otherwise tell us nothing about the relationship between them. *To be* is an *intransitive* verb; it cannot take a direct object. Compare the two preceding transitive examples with the following versions of the same sentences using forms of the verb *to be*.

> John F. Kennedy *was* effective at the manipulation of his image in the media.

> Thomas Jefferson's idea *was* for America to be a country of yeoman farmers.

Rather than making things happen through an active transitive verb, these sentences let everything just hang around in a state of being. In the first version, Kennedy did something—*manipulated* his image—but in the second he just *is* (or *was*), and the energy of the original verb has been siphoned into an abstract noun, manipulation. The revised Jefferson example suffers from a similar lack of momentum compared with the original version: the syntax doesn't help the sentence get anywhere.

Certain situations, however, dictate the use of forms of *to be*. For definitions in particular, the equal sign that an *is* provides works well. For instance, "Organic gardening *is* a method of growing crops without using synthetic fertilizers or pesticides." As with choosing between active and passive voices, the decision to use *to be* or not should be just that—a conscious decision on your part.

If you can train yourself to eliminate every unnecessary use of *to be* in a draft, you will make your prose more vital and direct. In most cases, you will find the verb that you need to substitute for *is* lurking somewhere in the sentence in some other grammatical form. In the preceding sentence about Kennedy, *manipulate* is implicit in *manipulation*. In Table 18.1, each of the examples in the left-hand column uses a form of *to be* for its verb (italicized) and contains a potentially strong active verb lurking in the sentence in some other form (underlined). These "lurkers" have been converted into active verbs (italicized) in the revisions in the right-hand column.

Clearly, the examples in the left-hand column have problems other than their reliance on forms of *to be*—notably wordiness. *To be* syntax tends to encourage this circumlocution and verbosity.

■ **Try this 18.7:** *Finding the Active Verb*

Take a paper you've written and circle the sentences that rely on forms of *to be*. Then, examine the other words in these sentences, looking for lurkers. Rewrite the sentences, converting the lurkers into vigorous verbs. You will probably discover many lurkers, and your revisions will acquire more energy and directness.

Action Hidden in Nouns and to Be Verbs	**Action Emphasized in Verbs**
The cost of the book *is* ten dollars.	The book *costs* ten dollars.
The acknowledgment of the fact *is* increasingly widespread that television *is* a replacement for reading in American culture.	People increasingly *acknowledge* that television *has replaced* reading in American culture.
A computer *is* ostensibly a labor-saving device—until the hard drive *is* the victim of a crash.	A computer ostensibly *saves* labor—until the hard drive *crashes*.
In the laying of a flagstone patio, the important preliminary steps to remember *are* the excavating and the leveling of the area and then the filling of it with a fine grade of gravel.	To *lay* a flagstone patio, first *excavate* and *level* the area and then *fill* it with a fine grade of gravel.

TABLE 18.1 Static and Active Verbs

Active and Passive Voices: Doing and Being Done To

In the *active voice,* the grammatical subject acts; in the *passive voice,* the subject is acted upon. Here are two examples.

Active: Adam Smith wrote *The Wealth of Nations* in 1776.

Passive: *The Wealth of Nations* was written by Adam Smith in 1776.

The two sentences convey identical information, but the emphasis differs—the first focuses on the author, the second on the book. As the examples illustrate, using the passive normally results in a longer sentence than using the active. If we consider how to convert the passive into the active, you can see why. In the passive, the verb requires a form of *to be* plus a past participle. (For more on participles, see the Glossary of Grammatical Terms in Chapter 19.) In this case, the active verb *wrote* becomes the passive verb *was written,* the grammatical subject (Smith) becomes the object of the preposition *by,* and the direct object (*The Wealth of Nations*) becomes the grammatical subject.

Now consider the activity being described in the two versions of this example: a man wrote a book. That's what happened in life. The grammar of the active version captures that action most clearly: the grammatical subject (Smith) performs the action, and the direct object (*The Wealth of Nations*) receives it, just as in life. By contrast, the passive version alters the close link between the syntax and the event: the object of the action in life (*The Wealth of Nations*) has become the grammatical subject, whereas the doer in life (Smith) has become the grammatical object of a prepositional phrase.

Note, too, that the passive would allow us to omit Smith altogether: "*The Wealth of Nations* was written in 1776." A reader who desired to know more and was not aware of the author would not appreciate this sentence. More troubling, the passive can also be used to conceal the doer of an action—not "I made a mistake" (active) but rather "A mistake has been made" (passive).

In summary, there are three reasons for avoiding the passive voice when you can: (1) it's longer, (2) its grammatical relationships often reverse what happened in life, and (3) it can omit the performer responsible for the action.

On the other hand, sometimes there are good reasons for using the passive. If you want to emphasize the object or recipient of the action rather than the performer, the passive does that for you: "*The Wealth of Nations* was written in 1776 by Adam Smith" places the stress on the book. The passive is also preferable when the doer remains unknown: "The president has been shot!" is probably a better sentence than "Some unknown assailant has shot the president!"

Especially in the natural sciences, the use of the passive voice is a standard practice. There are sound reasons for this disciplinary convention: science tends to focus on what happens to something in a given experiment, rather than on the actions of that something. Compare the following sentences.

Passive: Separation of the protein was achieved by using an electrophoretic gel.

Active: The researcher used an electrophoretic gel to separate the protein.

If you opted for the active version, the emphasis would rest, illogically, on the agent of the action (the researcher) rather than on what happened and how (electrophoretic separation of the protein).

More generally, the passive voice can provide a way to avoid using the pronoun *I,* whether for reasons of convention, as indicated earlier, or for other reasons. For example, the following passive sentence begins a business memo from a supervisor to the staff in the office.

> The Inventory and Reprint departments have recently been restructured and merged.

Like many passive sentences, this one names no actor; we do not know for sure who did the restructuring and merging, though we might imagine that the author of the memo is the responsible party. The supervisor might, then, have written the sentence in the active voice.

> I have recently restructured and merged the Inventory and Reprint departments.

But the active version is less satisfactory than the passive one for two reasons: one of practical emphasis and one of sensitivity to the audience (tone). First, the fact of the changes is more important for the memo's readers than is the announcement of who made the changes. The passive sentence appropriately emphasizes the changes; the active sentence inappropriately emphasizes the person who made the changes. Second, the emphasis of the active sentence on *I* (the supervisor) risks alienating the readers by taking an autocratic tone and by seeming to exclude all others from possible credit for the presumably worthwhile reorganization.

On balance, *consider* is the operative term when you choose between passive and active as you revise the syntax of your drafts. Recognize that you do have choices—in emphasis, in relative directness, and in economy. All things being equal and disciplinary conventions permitting, the active is usually the better choice.

■■ Try this 18.8: *Converting Passive to Active*

Identify all of the sentences that use the passive voice in one of your papers. Then, rewrite these sentences, converting passive into active wherever appropriate. Finally, count the total number of words, the total number of prepositions, and the average sentence length (words per sentence) in each version. What do you discover?

For more practice, here's another exercise. Compose a paragraph of at least half a page in which you use only the passive voice and verbs of being, followed by a paragraph in which you use only the active voice. Then, rewrite the first paragraph using only active voice, if possible, and rewrite the second paragraph using only passive voice and verbs of being as much as possible. How do the paragraphs differ in shape, length, and coherence?

About Prescriptive Style Manuals

Be wary of these. They almost always value one style and tone over another as self-evidently good and right. Despite Strunk & White's rule (in *The Elements of Style*), three words are not better than six in every rhetorical situation. And their edict against it notwithstanding, passive voice has its place, its own special advantages; active is not always better. Much depends on context. The key to growing as a stylist is learning to see the choices.

Experiment!

A key idea of this chapter is that there are not necessarily right and wrong choices when it comes to sentence style but instead better and best choices for particular situations. The from-the-hip plain style of a memo or a set of operating instructions for your lawn mower is very likely not the best style choice for a good-bye letter to a best friend, a diplomatic talk on a sensitive political situation, or an analysis of guitar styles in contemporary jazz.

Is style a function of character and personality? Is it, in short, personal, and thus something to be preserved in the face of would-be meddlers carrying style manuals and grammar guides? Well, as you might guess at this point in the book, the answer is yes and no. We all need to find ways of using words that do not succumb to the mind-numbing environment of verbal cliché in which we dwell. It helps, then, to become more self-conscious about style and not assume that it is inborn. Staying locked into one way of writing because that is "your style" is as limiting as remaining locked into only one way of thinking.

This chapter has presented some terms and techniques for experimenting with sentence styles. Equipped with these, you might profitably begin to read and listen for style more self-consciously. Find models. When a style appeals to you, figure out what makes it work. Copy sentences you like. Try imitating them. Know, by the way, that imitation does not erase your own style—it allows you to experiment with new moves, new shapes into which to cast your words.

ASSIGNMENTS: Stylistic Analysis

1. Analyze the style—the syntax, but also the diction—of two writers doing a similar kind of writing; for example, two sportswriters, two rock music reviewers, or two presidents. Study first the similarities. What style characteristics does this type of writing seem to invite? Then study the differences. How is one writer (Bush, Reagan, or Clinton, for example) recognizable through his or her style? The American Rhetoric website would be a wonderful place to go hunting.

2. Analyze your own style, past and present. Assemble some pieces you have written, preferably of a similar type, and study them for style. Do you have some favorite stylistic moves? What sentence shapes (simple, compound, complex, compound-complex, highly parallel, periodic, or cumulative) dominate in your writing? What verbs? Do you use forms of *to be* a lot, and so forth?

3. Whether we recognize it or not, most of us have a "go to" sentence—the sentence shape we repeatedly go to as we write and talk. If a person's "go to" sentence takes the form "Although _____, the fact is that _____," we might see that person as inclined to qualify his or her thoughts ("Although") and as someone who is

disinclined to immediately impose his or her ideas on others ("the fact that" comes in the second half of the sentence, where it gets a lot of emphasis but is also delayed and qualified by the sentence's opening observation).

First, select one sentence in something you've been reading that you think is typical of that writer's way of putting sentences together. Describe that sentence shape and speculate about what it accomplishes and how it reveals the writer's characteristic mode of thinking in some way.

Then find a "go to" sentence of your own in something that you've written. What does this structure reveal to you about how you think?

4. For many people, Lincoln's Gettysburg Address is one of the best examples of the careful matching of style to situation. Delivered after a long talk by a previous speaker at the dedication of a Civil War battlefield on a rainy day, the speech composed by Abraham Lincoln (some say on the back of an envelope) is a masterpiece of style. Analyze its sentence structure, such as its use of parallelism, antithesis, and other kinds of repetition. Which features of Lincoln's style seem to you to be most important in creating the overall effect of the piece? (Or do this with any popular journalist you read regularly and who you think has an especially effective style. Or look for another inspirational speech and see if such occasional writing has anything in common.)

5. Do a full-fledged stylistic revision of a paper. The best choice might well be an essay you already have revised, resubmitted, and had returned because in that case, you are less likely to get distracted by conceptual revision and so can concentrate on stylistic issues. As you revise, try to accomplish each of the following:

   a. Sharpen the diction.

   b. Blend concrete and abstract diction.

   c. Experiment with the order of and relation among subordinate and coordinate clauses.

   d. Choose more knowingly between active and passive voice.

   e. Cut the fat, especially by eliminating unnecessary *to be* constructions.

   f. Vary sentence length and shape.

   g. Use parallelism.

   h. Experiment with periodic and cumulative sentences.

   i. Fine-tune the tone.

CHAPTER 19

Common Grammatical Errors and How to Fix Them

THIS CHAPTER APPEARS AT THE END OF THE BOOK not because grammar is unimportant, but because the end of the book is a convenient place for you to consult when you have questions about correctness.

There is more to thinking about grammar than the quest for error-free writing, as Chapter 18 on sentence style demonstrates, with its emphasis on how to analyze writers' syntactical choices and how to think about the relationship between a writer's style and his or her characteristic ways of thinking. Studying the nine basic writing errors in this chapter will enable you to find your way around in a sentence more easily, and thus to build better sentences yourself.

The first part of this chapter, Why Correctness Matters, makes the case for learning to recognize a pattern of error in your drafts and learning to prioritize the most serious problems, creating a hierarchy of error, rather than treating (and worrying about) all errors equally and all at the same time. Achieving grammatical correctness is a matter of both knowledge—how to recognize and avoid errors—and timing: when to focus on possible errors.

Following the opening rationale on correctness, the chapter offers a quick-hit guide to punctuation followed by discussion of the nine most important grammatical errors to avoid:

- Sentence fragments
- Comma splices and fused (run-on) sentences
- Errors in subject–verb agreement
- Shifts in sentence structure (faulty predication)
- Errors in pronoun reference
- Misplaced modifiers and dangling participles
- Errors in using possessive apostrophes
- Comma errors
- Spelling and diction errors that interfere with meaning

For each of these, the chapter offers a definition with examples, and then talks you through how to fix it—with a Test Yourself section at the end.

At the end of the chapter, a brief Glossary of Grammatical Terms defines and illustrates many of the key terms used earlier in the chapter and throughout the book.

Following this chapter is an appendix that provides solutions to the various Test Yourself examples that illustrate the chapter's lessons.

WHY CORRECTNESS MATTERS

This chapter addresses the issue of grammatical correctness and offers ways of recognizing and fixing (or avoiding) the most important errors. The first guideline in editing for correctness is to *wait* to do it until you have arrived at a reasonably complete conceptual draft. We have delayed until the end of the book our consideration of technical revisions precisely because if you are too focused on producing polished copy up-front, you may never explore the subject enough to learn how to have ideas about it. In other words, it doesn't make sense for you to let your worries about proper form or persuasive phrasing prematurely distract you from the more important matter of having something substantial to polish in the first place. Writers need a stage in which they are allowed to make mistakes and use writing to help them discover what they want to say. But at the appropriate time—the later stages of the writing process—editing for correctness becomes very important.

When a paper obeys the rules of grammar, punctuation, and spelling, it has achieved *correctness*. Unlike editing for style, which involves you in making choices between more and less effective ways of phrasing, editing for correctness locates you in the domain of right or wrong. As you will see, there are usually a number of ways to correct an error, so you are still concerned with making choices, but leaving the error uncorrected is not a viable option.

Correctness matters deeply because your prose may be unreadable without it. If your prose is ungrammatical, not only do you risk incoherence (in which case your readers will not be able to follow what you are saying) but also you inadvertently invite readers to dismiss you. Is it fair of readers to reject your ideas because of the way you've phrased them? Perhaps not, but the fact is they often will. A great many readers regard technical errors as an inattention to detail that also signals sloppiness at more important levels of thinking. If you produce writing that contains such errors, you risk not only distracting readers from your message but also undermining your authority to deliver the message in the first place.

THE CONCEPT OF BASIC WRITING ERRORS (BWEs)

You get a paper back, and it's a sea of red ink. But if you look more closely, you'll often find that you haven't made a million mistakes—you've made only a few, but over and over in various forms. This phenomenon is what the rhetorician Mina Shaughnessy addressed in creating the category of "basic writing errors," or BWEs. Shaughnessy argues that to improve your writing for style and correctness, you need to do two things:

- Look for a *pattern of error,* which requires you to understand your own logic in the mistakes you typically make.
- Recognize that not all errors are created equal, which means that you need to *address errors in some order of importance*—beginning with those most likely to interfere with your readers' understanding.

The following BWE guide, Nine Basic Writing Errors and How to Fix Them, reflects Shaughnessy's view. First, it aims to teach you how to recognize and correct the basic kinds of errors that are potentially the most damaging to the clarity of your writing and to your credibility with readers. Second, the discussions in the guide seek to help you become aware of the patterns of error in your writing and discover the logic that has misled you into making them. If you can learn to see the pattern and then look for it in your editing and proofreading—expecting to find it—you will get in the habit of avoiding the error. In short, you will learn that your problem is not that you can't write correctly but simply that you have to remember, for example, to check for possessive apostrophes.

Our BWE guide does not, as we've mentioned, cover *all* of the rules of grammar, punctuation, diction, and usage, such as where to place the comma or period when you close a quotation or whether to write out numerals. For comprehensive coverage of the conventions of standard written English, you can consult one of the many handbooks available for this purpose. Our purpose is to provide a short guide to grammar—one that identifies the most common errors, provides remedies, and offers the logic that underlies them. This chapter's coverage of nine basic writing errors and how to fix them will help you eliminate most of the problems that routinely occur. We have arranged the error types in a hierarchy, moving in descending order of severity (from most to least problematic).

WHAT PUNCTUATION MARKS SAY: A QUICK-HIT GUIDE

These little signs really aren't that hard to use correctly, folks. A few of them are treated in more specific contexts in the upcoming discussion of BWEs, but here are the basic rules of punctuation for the five basic signs.

The *period* (.) marks the end of a sentence. Make sure that what precedes it is an independent clause; that is, a subject plus verb that can stand alone.

The period says to a reader, "This is the end of this particular statement. I'm a mark of closure."

Example: Lennon rules.

The *comma* (,) separates the main (independent) clause from dependent elements that modify the main clause. It also separates two main clauses joined by a conjunction—known as a compound sentence. Information that is not central to the main clause is set off in a comma sandwich. The comma does *not* merely signify a pause.

The comma says to the reader, "Here is where the main clause begins (or ends)," or "Here is a break in the main clause." In the case of compound sentences (containing two or more independent clauses), the comma says, "Here is where one main clause ends, and after the conjunction that follows me, another main clause begins."

Examples: Lennon rules, and McCartney is cute.

Lennon rules, although McCartney is arguably more tuneful.

The *semicolon* (;) separates two independent clauses that are not joined by a conjunction. Secondarily, the semicolon can separate two independent clauses that are joined by a conjunction if either of the clauses already contains commas. In either case, the semicolon both shows a close relationship between the two independent clauses that it connects and distinguishes where one ends and the other begins. It is also the easiest way to fix comma splices (see BWE 2 later in this chapter).

The semicolon says to the reader, "What precedes and what follows me are conceptually close but grammatically independent and thus equal statements."

Example: Lennon's lyrics show deep sympathy for the legions of "Nowhere Men" who inhabit the "Strawberry Fields" of their imaginations; McCartney's lyrics, on the other hand, are more upbeat, forever bidding "Good Day, Sunshine" to the world at large and "Michelle" in particular.

The *colon* (:) marks the end of a setup for something coming next. It provides a frame, pointing beyond itself, like a spotlight. The colon is quite dramatic, and unlike the semicolon, it links what precedes and follows it formally and tightly rather than loosely and associatively. It usually operates with dramatic force. It can frame a list to follow, separate cause and effect, or divide a brief claim from a more expanded version of the claim. The language on at least one side of the colon must be an independent clause, though both sides can be.

The colon says to the reader, "Concentrate on what follows me for a more detailed explanation of what preceded me" or "What follows me is logically bound with what preceded me."

Examples: *Rubber Soul* marked a change in The Beatles' song-writing: the sentimentality of earlier efforts gave way to a new complexity, both in the range of their subjects and the sophistication of their poetic devices. Nowhere is this change more evident than in a sequence of songs near the album's end: "I'm Looking Through You," "In My Life," "Wait," and "If I Needed Someone."

The *dash* (—) provides an informal alternative to the colon for adding information to a sentence. Its effect is sudden, of the moment—what springs up impulsively to disrupt and extend in some new way the ongoing train of thought. A *pair of dashes* provides an invaluable resource to writers for inserting information within a sentence. In this usage, the rule is that the sentence must read coherently if the inserted information is left out. (Note that to type a dash, type two hyphens with no space between, before, or after. This distinguishes the dash from a hyphen [-], which is the mark used for connecting two words into one.)

The dash says to the reader, "This too!" or, in the case of a pair of them, "Remember the thought in the beginning of this sentence because we're jumping to something else before we come back to finish that thought."

Examples: For all their loveliness, the songs on *Rubber Soul* are not without menace—"I'd rather see you dead little girl than to see you with another man."

In addition to the usual lead, rhythm, and bass guitar ensemble, *Rubber Soul* introduced new instruments—notably, the harpsichord interlude in "In My Life," the sitar spiraling though "Norwegian Wood"—that had not previously been heard in rock'n'roll.

NINE BASIC WRITING ERRORS AND HOW TO FIX THEM

If you're unsure about some of the terms you encounter in the discussions of BWEs, see the Glossary of Grammatical Terms at the end of this chapter. You'll also find brief Test Yourself questions interspersed throughout this section. Do them: it's easy to conclude that you understand a problem when you are shown the correction, but understanding is not the same thing as actively practicing. There's an appendix to this chapter that (as mentioned earlier) contains answers to these sections, along with explanations.

BWE 1: Sentence Fragments

The most basic of writing errors, a *sentence fragment,* is a group of words punctuated like a complete sentence but lacking the necessary structure: it is only part of a sentence. Typically, a sentence fragment occurs when the group of words in question (1) lacks a subject, (2) lacks a predicate, or (3) is a subordinate (or dependent) clause.

To fix a sentence fragment, either turn it into an independent clause by providing whatever is missing—a subject or a predicate—or attach it to an independent clause upon which it can depend.

Noun Clause (No Predicate) as a Fragment

A world where imagination takes over and sorrow is left behind.

This fragment is not a sentence but rather a noun clause—a sentence subject with no predicate. The fragment lacks a verb that would assert something about the subject. (The verbs *takes over* and *is left* are in a dependent clause created by the subordinating conjunction *where.*)

Corrections

A world *arose* where imagination takes over and sorrow is left behind. *[new verb matched to a world]*

She entered a world where imagination takes over and sorrow is left behind. *[new subject and verb added]*

The first correction adds a new verb (arose). The second introduces a new subject and verb, converting the fragment into the direct object of *she entered.*

Verbal as a Fragment

Falling into debt for the fourth consecutive year.

Falling in the preceding fragment is not a verb. Depending on the correction, *falling* is either a verbal or part of a verb phrase.

Corrections

The company was falling into debt for the fourth consecutive year. *[subject and helping verb added]*

Falling into debt for the fourth consecutive year *led the company to consider relocating. [new predicate added]*

Falling into debt for the fourth consecutive year, *the company considered relocating. [new subject and verb added]*

In the first correction, the addition of a subject and the helping verb *was* converts the fragment into a sentence. The second correction turns the fragment into a gerund phrase functioning as the subject of a new sentence. The third correction converts the fragment into a participial phrase attached to a new independent clause. (See the Glossary of Grammatical Terms and look under *verbal* for definitions of *gerund* and *participle.*)

Subordinate Clause as a Fragment

I had an appointment for 11:00 and was still waiting at 11:30. Although I did get to see the dean before lunch.

Although is a subordinating conjunction that calls for some kind of completion. Like *if, when, because, whereas,* and other subordinating conjunctions (see the Glossary of Grammatical Terms), "although" always makes the clause that it introduces dependent.

Corrections

I had an appointment for 11:00 and was still waiting at 11:30, *although* I did get to see the dean before lunch. *[fragment attached to preceding sentence]*

As the correction demonstrates, the remedy lies in attaching the fragment to an independent clause on which it can depend (or, alternatively, making the fragment into a sentence by dropping the conjunction).

Sometimes writers use sentence fragments deliberately, usually for rhythm and emphasis or to create a conversational tone. In less formal contexts, they are generally permissible, but you run the risk that the fragment will not be perceived as intentional. In formal writing assignments, it is safer to avoid intentional fragments.

■ **Test yourself:** *Fragments*

There are fragments in each of the following three examples, probably the result of their proximity to legitimate sentences. What's the problem in each case, and how would you fix it?

1. Like many other anthropologists, Margaret Mead studied non-Western cultures in such works as *Coming of Age in Samoa.* And influenced theories of childhood development in America.

2. The catastrophe resulted from an engineering flaw. Because the bridge lacked sufficient support.

3. In the 1840s the potato famine decimated Ireland. It being a country with poor soil and antiquated methods of agriculture.

A Further Note on Dashes and Colons

Beyond what the punctuation guide has offered, the particular virtues of the dash and colon as ways to correct sentence fragments deserve brief mention. One way to correct a fragment is to replace the period with a dash: "The campaign required commitment. Not just money." becomes "The campaign required commitment—not just money." The dash offers you one way of attaching a phrase or dependent clause to a sentence without having to construct another independent clause. In short, it's succinct. (Compare the correction that uses the dash with another possible correction: "The campaign required commitment. It also required money.") Moreover, with the air of sudden interruption that the dash conveys, it can capture the informality and immediacy that the intentional fragment offers a writer.

You should be wary of overusing the dash as the slightly more presentable cousin of the intentional fragment. The energy it carries can clash with the decorum of formal writing contexts; for some readers, its staccato effect quickly becomes too much of a good thing.

One alternative to this usage of the dash is the colon. It can substitute because it also can be followed by a phrase, a list, or a clause. As with the dash, it must be preceded by an independent clause. And it, too, carries dramatic force because it abruptly halts the flow of the sentence.

The colon, however, does not convey informality. In place of a slapdash effect, it trains a light on what is to follow it. Hence, as in this sentence you are reading, it is especially appropriate for setting up certain kinds of information: explanations, lists, or results. In the case of results, the cause or action precedes the colon; the effect or reaction follows it.

BWE 2: Comma Splices and Fused (or Run-On) Sentences

A comma splice consists of two independent clauses connected ("spliced") with a comma; a fused (or run-on) sentence combines two such clauses with no conjunction or punctuation. The solutions for both comma splices and fused sentences are the same.

1. Place a conjunction (such as *and* or *because*) between the clauses.
2. Place a semicolon between the clauses.
3. Make the clauses into separate sentences.

All of these solutions solve the same logical problem: they clarify the boundaries of the independent clauses for your readers.

Comma Splice

He disliked discipline, he avoided anything demanding.

Correction

Because he disliked discipline, he avoided anything demanding. *[subordinating conjunction added]*

Comma Splice

Today most TV programs are violent, almost every program is about cops and detectives.

Correction

Today most TV programs are *violent; almost* every program is about cops and detectives. *[semicolon replaces comma]*

Because the two independent clauses in the first example contain ideas that are closely connected logically, the most effective of the three comma splice solutions is to add a subordinating conjunction ("because") to the first of the two clauses, making it depend on the second. For the same reason—close conceptual connection—the best solution for the next comma splice is to substitute a semicolon for the comma. The semicolon signals that the two independent clauses are closely linked in meaning. In general, you can use a semicolon where you could also use a period.

The best cures for the perpetual comma splicer are to learn to recognize the difference between independent and dependent clauses and to get rid of the "pause theory" of punctuation. All of the clauses in our two examples are independent. As written, each of these should be punctuated not with a comma but rather with a period or a semicolon. Instead, the perpetual comma splicer, as usual, acts on the "pause theory": because the ideas in the independent clauses are closely connected, the writer hesitates to separate them with a period. And so the writer inserts what he or she takes to be a shorter pause—the comma.

But a comma is not a "breath" mark; it provides readers with specific grammatical information, in each of these cases mistakenly suggesting there is only one independent clause separated by the comma from modifying information. In the corrections, by contrast, the semicolon sends the appropriate signal to the reader: the message that it is joining two associated but independent statements. (Adding a coordinating conjunction such as *and* would also be grammatically correct, though possibly awkward.)

Fused Sentence

The Indo-European language family includes many groups most languages in Europe belong to it.

Correction

The Indo-European language family includes many groups. Most languages in Europe belong to it. *[period inserted after first independent clause]*

You could also fix this fused sentence with a comma plus the coordinating conjunction *and*. Alternatively, you might condense the whole into a single independent clause.

Most languages in Europe belong to the Indo-European language family.

Comma Splices with Conjunctive Adverbs

Quantitative methods of data collection show broad trends, however, they ignore specific cases.

Sociobiology poses a threat to traditional ethics, for example, it asserts that human behavior is genetically motivated by the "selfish gene" to perpetuate itself.

Corrections

Quantitative methods of data collection show broad *trends; however,* they ignore specific cases. *[semicolon replaces comma before* however]

Sociobiology poses a threat to traditional ethics; for example, it asserts that human behavior is genetically motivated by the "selfish gene" to perpetuate itself. *[semicolon replaces comma before* for example]

Both of these examples contain one of the most common forms of comma splices. Both of them are compound sentences—that is, they contain two independent clauses. (See the section entitled The Compound Sentence in Chapter 18.) Normally, connecting the clauses with a comma and a conjunction would be correct; for example, "Most hawks hunt alone, but osprey hunt in pairs." In the preceding two comma splices, however, the independent clauses are joined by transitional expressions known as conjunctive adverbs. (See the Glossary of Grammatical Terms.) When a conjunctive adverb is used to link two independent clauses, it *always* requires a semicolon. By contrast, when a coordinating conjunction links the two clauses of a compound sentence, it is *always* preceded by a comma.

In most cases, depending on the sense of the sentence, the semicolon precedes the conjunctive adverb and has the effect of clarifying the division between the two clauses. There are exceptions to this general rule, though, as in the following sentence:

The lazy boy did finally read a *book, however;* it was the least he could do.

Here *however* is a part of the first independent clause and qualifies its claim. The sentence thus suggests that the boy was not totally lazy because he did get around to reading a book. Note how the meaning changes when *however* becomes the introductory word for the second independent clause.

The lazy boy did finally read a *book; however,* it was the least he could do.

Here the restricting force of *however* suggests that reading the book was not much of an accomplishment.

▬ Test yourself: *Comma Splices*

What makes each of the following sentences a comma splice? Determine the best way to fix each one and why, and then make the correction.

1. "Virtual reality" is a new buzzword, so is "hyperspace."
2. Many popular cures for cancer have been discredited, nevertheless, many people continue to buy them.
3. Elvis Presley's home, Graceland, attracts many musicians as a kind of shrine, even Paul Simon has been there.
4. She didn't play well with others, she sat on the bench and watched.

BWE 3: Errors in Subject–Verb Agreement

The subject and the verb must agree in number, a singular subject taking a singular verb and a plural subject taking a plural verb. Errors in subject–verb agreement usually occur when a writer misidentifies the subject or verb of a clause.

Agreement Problem

Various kinds of vandalism has been rapidly increasing.

Correction

Various kinds of vandalism *have* been rapidly increasing. *[verb made plural to match kinds]*

When you isolate the grammatical subject (kinds) and the verb (has) of the original sentence, you can tell that they do not agree. Although vandalism might seem to be the subject because it is closest to the verb, it is actually the object of the preposition *of* The majority of agreement problems arise from mistaking the object of a preposition for the actual subject of a sentence. If you habitually make this mistake, you can begin to remedy it by familiarizing yourself with the most common prepositions. (See the Glossary of Grammatical Terms, which contains a list of these.)

Agreement Problem

Another aspect of territoriality that differentiates humans from animals are their possession of ideas and objects.

Correction

Another aspect of territoriality that differentiates humans from animals *is* their possession of ideas and objects. *[verb made singular to match subject* aspect*]*

The subject of the sentence is *aspect.* The two plural nouns (humans and animals) probably encourage the mistake of using a plural verb (are), but *humans* is part of the *that* clause modifying *aspect,* and *animals* is the object of the preposition *from.*

Agreement Problem

The Republican and the Democrat both believe in doing what's best for America, but each believe that the other doesn't understand what's best.

Correction

The Republican and the Democrat both believe in doing what's best for America, but each *believes* that the other doesn't understand what's best. *[verb made singular to agree with subject* each*]*

The word *each* is *always* singular, so the verb (believes) must be singular as well. The presence of a plural subject and verb in the sentence's first independent clause (the Republican and the Democrat both believe) has probably encouraged the error.

Test yourself: *Subject-Verb Agreement*

Diagnose and correct the error in the following example.

The controversies surrounding the placement of Arthur Ashe's statue in Richmond was difficult for the various factions to resolve.

A Note on Nonstandard English

The term *standard written English* refers to language that conforms to the rules and conventions adhered to by the majority of English-speaking writers. The fact is, however, that not all speakers of English grow up hearing, reading, and writing standard written English. Some linguistic cultures in America follow, for example, a different set of conventions for subject–verb agreement. Their speakers do not differentiate singular from plural verb forms with a terminal "–s," as in standard English.

She walks home after work.

They walk home after work.

Some speakers of English do not observe this distinction so that the first sentence becomes:

She walk home after work.

These two ways of handling subject–verb agreement are recognized by linguists not in terms of right versus wrong but rather in terms of dialect difference. A *dialect* is a variety of a language that is characteristic of a region or culture and is sometimes unintelligible to outsiders. The problem for speakers of a dialect that differs from the norm is that they can't always rely on the ear—on what sounds right—when they are editing according to the rules of standard written English. Such speakers need, in effect, to learn to speak more than one dialect so that they can edit according to the rules of standard written English in situations where this would be expected. This often requires adding a separate proofreading stage for particular errors, like subject–verb agreement, rather than relying on what sounds right.

BWE 4: Shifts in Sentence Structure (Faulty Predication)

This error involves an illogical mismatch between subject and predicate. If you continually run afoul of faulty predication, you might use the exercises in a handbook to drill you on isolating the grammatical subjects and verbs of sentences because that is the first move you need to make in fixing the problem.

Shift

In 1987, the release of more information became available.

Correction

In 1987, more *information* became available *for release. [new subject]*

It was the information, not the release, that became available. The correction relocates *information* from its position as object of the preposition *of* to the subject position in the sentence; it also moves *release* into a prepositional phrase.

Shift

The busing controversy was intended to rectify the inequality of educational opportunities.

Correction

Busing was intended to rectify the inequality of educational opportunities. *[new subject formulated to match verb]*

The controversy wasn't intended to rectify, but busing was.

Test yourself: *Faulty Predication*
Identify and correct the faulty predication in this example:
The subject of learning disabilities is difficult to identify accurately.

BWE 5: Errors in Pronoun Reference

There are at least three forms of this problem. All of them involve a lack of clarity about whom or what a pronoun (a word that substitutes for a noun) refers to. The surest way to avoid difficulties is to make certain that the pronoun relates back unambiguously to a specific word, known as the antecedent. In the sentence "Nowadays appliances don't last as long as they once did," the noun *appliances* is the antecedent of the pronoun *they*.

Pronoun–Antecedent Agreement A pronoun must agree in number (and gender) with the noun or noun phrase that it refers to.

Pronoun Error

It can be dangerous if a child, after watching TV, decides to practice what they saw.

Corrections

It can be dangerous if *children,* after watching TV, *decide* to practice what *they* saw. *[antecedent (and verb) made plural to agree with pronouns]*

It can be dangerous if a child, after watching TV, decides to practice what *he or she* saw. *[singular pronouns substituted to match singular antecedent* child]

The error occurs because *child* is singular, but its antecedent pronoun, *they,* is plural. The first correction makes both plural; the second makes both singular. You might also observe in the first word of the example—the impersonal "it"—an exception to the rule that pronouns must have antecedents.

Test yourself: *Pronoun-Antecedent Agreement*

What is wrong with the following sentence, and how would you fix it?

Every dog has its day, but all too often when that day happens, they can be found barking up the wrong tree.

Ambiguous Reference A pronoun should have only one possible antecedent. The possibility of two or more confuses relationships within the sentence.

Pronoun Error

Children like comedians because they have a sense of humor.

Corrections

Because children have a sense of humor, *they* like comedians. *[subordinate* because *clause placed first, and relationship between noun* children *and pronoun* they *tightened]*

Children like comedians because *comedians* have a sense of humor. *[pronoun eliminated and replaced by repetition of noun]*

Does *they* in the original example refer to *children* or *comedians?* The rule in such cases of ambiguity is that the pronoun refers to the nearest possible antecedent, so here *comedians* possess the sense of humor, regardless of what the writer may intend. As the corrections demonstrate, either reordering the sentence or repeating the noun can remove the ambiguity.

▬ **Test yourself:** *Ambiguous Reference*

As you proofread, it's a good idea to target your pronouns to make sure that they cannot conceivably refer to more than one noun. What's wrong with the following sentences?

1. Alexander the Great's father, Philip of Macedon, died when he was twenty-six.
2. The committee could not look into the problem because it was too involved.

Broad Reference Broad reference occurs when a pronoun refers loosely to a number of ideas expressed in preceding clauses or sentences. It causes confusion because the reader cannot be sure which of the ideas the pronoun refers to.

Pronoun Error

As a number of scholars have noted, Sigmund Freud and Karl Marx offered competing but also at times complementary critiques of the dehumanizing tendencies of Western capitalist society. We see this in Christopher Lasch's analysis of conspicuous consumption in *The Culture of Narcissism.*

Correction

As a number of scholars have noted, Sigmund Freud and Karl Marx offered competing but also at times complementary critiques of the dehumanizing tendencies of Western capitalist society. We see *this complementary view* in Christopher Lasch's analysis of conspicuous consumption in *The Culture of Narcissism. [broad* this *clarified by addition of noun phrase]*

The word *this* in the second sentence of the uncorrected example could refer to the fact that "a number of scholars have noted" the relationship between Freud and Marx, to the competition between Freud's and Marx's critiques of capitalism, or to the complementary nature of the two men's critiques.

Beware of *this* as a pronoun: it's the most common source of broad reference. The remedy is generally to avoid using the word as a pronoun. Instead, convert *this* into an adjective, and let it modify some noun that more clearly specifies the referent: "this complementary view," as in the correction or, alternatively, "this competition" or "this scholarly perspective."

▬ **Test yourself:** *Broad Reference*

Locate the errors in the following examples, and provide a remedy for each.

1. Regardless of whether the film is foreign or domestic, they can be found in your neighborhood video store.
2. Many experts now claim that dogs and other higher mammals dream; for those who don't own such pets, this is often difficult to believe.

A Note on Sexism and Pronoun Usage

Errors in pronoun reference sometimes occur because of a writer's praiseworthy desire to avoid sexism. In most circles, the following correction of the preceding example would be considered sexist.

It can be dangerous if a child, after watching TV, decides to practice what *he* saw.

Though the writer of such a sentence may intend *he* to function as a gender-neutral impersonal pronoun, it in fact excludes girls on the basis of gender. Implicitly, it also conveys sexual stereotypes (for example, that only boys are violent or perhaps stupid enough to confuse TV with reality).

The easiest way to avoid the problem of sexism in pronoun usage usually lies in putting things into the plural form because plural pronouns (we, you, they) have no gender. (See the use of *children* in the first correction of the pronoun–antecedent agreement example.) Alternatively, you can use the phrase *he or she.* Many readers, however, find this phrase and its variant, *s/he,* to be awkward constructions. Another remedy lies in rewriting the sentence to avoid pronouns altogether, as in the following revision.

It can be dangerous if a child, after watching TV, decides to practice *some violent activity portrayed on the screen.*

BWE 6: Misplaced Modifiers and Dangling Participles

Modifiers are words or groups of words used to qualify, limit, intensify, or explain some other element in a sentence. A misplaced modifier is a word or phrase that appears to modify the wrong word or words.

Misplaced Modifier

At the age of three he caught a fish with a broken arm.

Correction

At the age of three *the boy with a broken arm* caught a fish. *[noun replaces pronoun; prepositional phrase revised and relocated]*

The original sentence mistakenly implies that the fish had a broken arm. Modification errors often occur in sentences with one or more prepositional phrases, as in this case.

Misplaced Modifier

According to legend, General George Washington crossed the Delaware and celebrated Christmas in a small boat.

Correction

According to legend, General George Washington crossed the Delaware *in a small boat* and *then* celebrated Christmas *on shore. [prepositional phrase relocated; modifiers added to second verb]*

As a general rule, you can avoid misplacing a modifier by keeping it as close as possible to what it modifies. Thus, the second correction removes the implication that Washington celebrated Christmas in a small boat. When you cannot relocate the modifier, separate it from the rest of the sentence with a comma to prevent readers from connecting it to the nearest noun.

A dangling participle creates a particular kind of problem in modification: the noun or pronoun that the writer intends the participial phrase to modify is not actually present in the sentence. Thus, we have the name dangling participle: the participle has been left dangling because the word or phrase it is meant to modify is not there.

Dangling Participle

After debating the issue of tax credits for the elderly, the bill passed in a close vote.

Correction

After debating the issue of tax credits for the elderly, *the Senate passed the bill* in a close vote. *[appropriate noun added for participle to modify]*

The bill did not debate the issue, as the original example implies. As the correction demonstrates, fixing a dangling participle involves tightening the link between the activity implied by the participle (debating) and the entity performing that activity (the Senate).

Test yourself: *Modification Errors*

Find the modification errors in the following examples and correct them.

1. After eating their sandwiches, the steamboat left the dock.
2. The social workers saw an elderly woman on a bus with a cane standing up.
3. Crossing the street, a car hit the pedestrian.

BWE 7: Errors in Using Possessive Apostrophes

Adding "-'s" to most singular nouns makes them show possession, for example, the plant's roots, the accountant's ledger. You can add the apostrophe alone, without the "s," for example, to make plural nouns that already end with s show possession: the flowers' fragrances, the ships' berths (although you may also add an additional s).

Apostrophe Error

The loyal opposition scorned the committees decisions.

Corrections

The loyal opposition scorned the *committee's* decisions.
The loyal opposition scorned the *committees'* decisions. *[possessive apostrophe added]*

The first correction assumes there was one committee; the second assumes there were two or more.

Apostrophe Error

The advisory board swiftly transacted it's business.

Correction

The advisory board swiftly transacted *its* business. *[apostrophe dropped]*

Unlike possessive nouns, possessive pronouns (my, your, yours, her, hers, his, its, our, ours, their, theirs) *never* take an apostrophe.

Test yourself: *Possessive Apostrophes*

Find and correct any errors in the following sentence.

The womens movement has been misunderstood by many of its detractors.

BWE 8: Comma Errors

As with other rules of punctuation and grammar, the many that pertain to comma usage share an underlying aim: to clarify the relationships among the parts of a sentence. Commas separate the parts of a sentence grammatically. One of their primary uses, then, is to help your readers distinguish the main clause from dependent elements, such as subordinate clauses and long prepositional phrases. They do not signify a pause, as was discussed under BWE 2.

Comma Error

After eating the couple went home.

Correction

After *eating,* the couple went home. *[comma added before independent clause]*

The comma after *eating* is needed to keep the main clause visible, or separate; it marks the point at which the prepositional phrase ends and the independent clause begins. Without this separation, readers would be invited to contemplate cannibalism as they moved across the sentence.

Comma Error

In the absence of rhetoric study teachers and students lack a vocabulary for talking about their prose.

Correction

In the absence of rhetoric *study,* teachers and students lack a vocabulary for talking about their prose. *[comma added to separate prepositional phrase from main clause]*

Without the comma, readers would have to read the sentence twice to find out where the prepositional phrase ends—with *study*—to figure out where the main clause begins.

Comma Error

Dog owners, despite their many objections will have to obey the new law.

Correction

Dog owners, despite their many *objections,* will have to obey the new law. *[single comma converted to a pair of commas]*

A comma is needed after *objections* to isolate the phrase in the middle of the sentence (despite their many objections) from the main clause. The phrase needs to be set off with commas because it contains additional information that is not essential to the meaning of what it modifies. (Dog owners must obey the law whether they object or not.) Phrases and clauses that function in this way are called *nonrestrictive.*

The test of nonrestrictive phrases and clauses is to see if they can be omitted without substantially changing the message that a sentence conveys ("Dog owners will have to obey the new law," for example). Nonrestrictive elements always take two commas—a comma "sandwich"—to set them off. Using only one comma illogically separates the sentence's subject (dog owners) from its predicate (will have to obey). This problem is easier to see in a shorter sentence. You wouldn't, for example, write "I, fell down." As a rule, commas virtually never separate the subject from the verb of a sentence. (Here's an exception: "Ms. Smith, a high fashion model, watches her diet scrupulously.")

Comma Error

Most people regardless of age like to spend money.

Correction

Most *people,* regardless of *age,* like to spend money. *[comma sandwich added]*

Here commas enclose the nonrestrictive elements; you could omit this information without significantly affecting the sense. Such is not the case in the following two examples.

Comma Error

People, who live in glass houses, should not throw stones.

Correction

People *who live in glass houses* should not throw stones. *[commas omitted]*

Comma Error

Please return the library book, that I left on the table.

Correction

Please return the library *book that* I left on the table. *[comma omitted]*

It is incorrect to place commas around *who live in glass houses* or a comma before *that I left on the table.* Each of these is a *restrictive clause*—that is, it contains information that is an essential part of what it modifies. In the first sentence, for example, if *who live in glass houses* is left out, the fundamental meaning of the sentence is lost: People should not throw stones. The word *who* is defined by restricting it to *people* in the category of glass-house dwellers. Similarly, in the second example the *that* clause contributes an essential meaning to *book;* the sentence is referring to not just any book but to a particular one, the one on the table.

So remember the general rule: if the information in a phrase or clause can be omitted—if it is nonessential and therefore nonrestrictive—it needs to be separated by commas from the rest of the sentence. Moreover, note that nonrestrictive clauses are generally introduced by the word *which,* so a *which* clause interpolated into a sentence takes a comma sandwich. (The dinner, which I bought for $20, made me sick.) By contrast, a restrictive clause is introduced by the word *that* and takes no commas.

Test yourself: *Comma Errors*

Consider the following examples as a pair. Punctuate them as necessary, and then briefly articulate how the meanings of the two sentences differ.

1. The book which I had read a few years ago contained a lot of outdated data.
2. The book that I had read a few years ago contained a lot of outdated data.

BWE 9: Spelling/Diction Errors That Interfere with Meaning

Misspellings are always a problem in a final draft, insofar as they undermine your authority by inviting readers to perceive you as careless (at best). If you make a habit of using the spellchecker of a word processor, you will take care of most misspellings. But the problems that a spellchecker won't catch are the ones that can often hurt you most. These are actually diction errors—incorrect word choices in which you have confused one word with another that it closely resembles. In such cases, you have spelled the word correctly, but it's the wrong word. Because it means something other than what you've intended, you end up misleading your readers. (See Making Distinctions in Chapter 17.)

The best way to avoid this problem is to memorize the differences between pairs of words that are commonly confused with each other but that have distinct meanings. The following examples illustrate a few of the most common and serious of these errors. Most handbooks contain a glossary of usage that *cites* more of these *sites* of confusion.

Spelling/Diction Error: *It's* versus *Its*

Although you can't tell a book by it's cover, its fairly easy to get the general idea from the introduction.

Correction

Although you can't tell a book by *its* cover, *it's* fairly easy to get the general idea from the introduction. *[apostrophe dropped from possessive and added to contraction]*

It's is a contraction for *it is. Its* is a possessive pronoun meaning "belonging to it." If you confuse the two, *it's* likely that your sentence will mislead *its* readers.

Spelling/Diction Error: *Their* versus *There* versus *They're*

Their are ways of learning about the cuisine of northern India besides going their to watch the master chefs and learn there secrets—assuming their willing to share them.

Correction

There are ways of learning about the cuisine of northern India besides going *there* to watch the master chefs and learn *their* secrets—assuming *they're* willing to share them. *[expletive* there, *adverb* there, *possessive pronoun* their *and contraction* they're *inserted appropriately]*

There as an adverb normally refers to a place; *there* can also be used as an expletive to introduce a clause, as in the first usage of the correction. (See the discussion of expletives under Cutting the Fat in Chapter 18.) *Their* is a possessive pronoun meaning "belonging to them." *They're* is a contraction for *they are.*

Spelling/Diction Error: *Then* versus *Than*

If a person would rather break a law then obey it, than he or she must be willing to face the consequences.

Correction

If a person would rather break a law *than* obey it, *then* he or she must be willing to face the consequences. *[comparative* than *distinguished from temporal* then]

Than is a conjunction used with a comparison, for example, "rather *X* than *Y*." *Then* is an adverb used to indicate what comes next in relation to time, for example, "first *X*, then *Y*."

Spelling/Diction Error: *Effect* versus *Affect*

It is simply the case that BWEs adversely effect the way that readers judge what a writer has to say. It follows that writers who include lots of BWEs in their prose may not have calculated the disastrous affects of these mistakes.

Correction

It is simply the case that BWEs adversely *affect* the way that readers judge what a writer has to say. It follows that writers who include lots of BWEs in their prose may not have calculated the disastrous *effects* of these mistakes. *[verb* affect *and noun* effects *inserted appropriately]*

In their most common usages, *affect* is a verb meaning "to influence," and *effect* is a noun meaning "the result of an action or cause." The confusion of *affect* and *effect* is enlarged by the fact that both of these words have secondary meanings: the verb *effect* means "to cause or bring about"; the noun *affect* is used in psychology to mean "emotion or feeling." Thus, if you confuse these two words, you inadvertently make a meaning radically different from the one you intend.

▄ Test yourself: *Spelling/Diction Errors*

Make corrections as necessary in the following paragraph.

Its not sufficiently acknowledged that the behavior of public officials is not just an ethical issue but one that effects the sale of newspapers and commercial bytes in television news. When public officials don't do what their supposed to do, than their sure to face the affects of public opinion—if they get caught—because there are dollars to be made. Its that simple: money more then morality is calling the tune in the way that the press treats it's superstars.

GLOSSARY OF GRAMMATICAL TERMS

adjective An adjective is a part of speech that usually modifies a noun or pronoun—for example, *blue, boring, boisterous.*

adverb An adverb is a part of speech that modifies an adjective, adverb, or verb—for example, *heavily, habitually, very.* The adverbial form generally differs from the adjectival form via the addition of the ending "–ly"; for example, *happy* is an adjective, and *happily* is an adverb.

clause (independent and dependent) A clause is any group of words that contains both a **subject** and a **predicate**. An **independent clause** (also known as a **main clause**) can stand alone as a sentence. For example, "The most famous revolutionaries of this century have all, in one way or another, offered a vision of a classless society." The subject of this independent clause is *revolutionary,* the verb is *have offered,* and the direct object is *vision.*

By contrast, a **dependent** (or **subordinate**) **clause** is any group of words containing a subject and verb that cannot stand alone as a separate sentence because it depends on an independent clause to complete its meaning. The following sentence adds two dependent clauses to our previous example: "The most famous revolutionaries of this century have all, in one way or another, offered a vision of a classless society, *although* most historians would agree *that* this ideal has never been achieved."

The origin of the word *depend* is "to hang": a dependent clause literally hangs on the independent clause. In the preceding example, neither "although most historians would agree" nor "that this ideal has never been achieved" can stand independently. The *that* clause relies on the *although* clause, which in turn relies on the main clause. *That* and *although* function as **subordinating conjunctions;** by eliminating them, we could rewrite the sentence to contain three independent clauses: "The most famous revolutionaries of this century have all, in one way or another, offered a vision of a classless society. Most historians would agree on one judgment about this vision: it has never been achieved."

comma splice A comma splice consists of two independent clauses incorrectly connected (spliced) with a comma. See BWE 2.

conjunction (coordinating and subordinating) A conjunction is a part of speech that connects words, phrases, or clauses, for example, *and, but, although.* The conjunction in some way defines that connection: for example, *and* links; *but* separates. All conjunctions define connections in one of two basic ways. Coordinating conjunctions connect words or groups of words that have equal grammatical importance. The coordinating conjunctions are *and, but, or, nor, for, so,* and *yet.* Subordinating conjunctions introduce a dependent clause and connect it to a main clause. Here is a partial list of the most common subordinating conjunctions: *after, although, as, as if, as long as, because, before, if, rather than, since, than, that, though, unless, until, when, where, whether,* and *while.*

conjunctive adverb A conjunctive adverb is a word that links two independent clauses (as a conjunction) but that also modifies the clause it introduces (as an adverb). Some of the most common conjunctive adverbs are *consequently, furthermore, however, moreover, nevertheless, similarly, therefore,* and *thus.* Phrases can also serve this function, such as *for example* and *on the other hand.* When conjunctive adverbs are used to link two independent clauses, they always require a semicolon: "Many pharmaceutical chains now offer their own generic versions of common drugs; however, many consumers continue to spend more for name brands that contain the same active ingredients as the generics." When conjunctive adverbs occur within an independent clause, however, they are enclosed in a pair of commas, as is the case with the use of *however* earlier in this sentence.

coordination Coordination refers to grammatically equal words, phrases, or clauses. Coordinate constructions are used to give elements in a sentence equal weight or importance. In the sentence "The tall, thin lawyer badgered the witness, but the judge interceded," the clauses "The tall, thin lawyer badgered the witness" and "but the judge interceded" are coordinate clauses; *tall* and *thin* are coordinate adjectives.

dependent clause (*See* clause)

direct object The direct object is a noun or pronoun that receives the action carried by the verb and performed by the subject. In the sentence, "Certain mushrooms can kill you," *you* is the direct object.

gerund (*See* verbals)

fused (or run-on) sentence A fused sentence incorrectly combines two independent clauses with no conjunction or punctuation. See BWE 2.

independent clause (*See* clause)

infinitive (*See* verbals)

main clause (*See* clause)

noun A noun is a part of speech that names a person (woman), place (town), thing (book), idea (justice), quality (irony), or action (betrayal).

object of the preposition (*See* preposition)

participle and participial phrase (*See* verbals)

phrase A phrase is a group of words occurring in a meaningful sequence that lacks either a subject or a predicate. This absence distinguishes it from a clause, which contains both a subject and a predicate. Phrases function in sentences as adjectives, adverbs, nouns, or verbs. They are customarily classified according to the part of speech of their key word: "over the mountain" is a **prepositional phrase;** "running for office" is a **participial phrase;** "had been disciplined" is a **verb phrase;** "desktop graphics" is a **noun phrase;** and so forth.

predicate The predicate contains the verb of a sentence or clause, making some kind of statement about the subject. The predicate of the preceding sentence is "contains the verb, making some kind of statement about the subject." The simple predicate—the verb to which the other words in the sentence are attached—is *contains.*

preposition, prepositional phrase A preposition is a part of speech that links a noun or pronoun to some other word in the sentence. Prepositions usually express a relationship of time (after) or space (above) or direction (toward). The noun to which the preposition is attached is known as the object of the preposition. A preposition, its object, and any modifiers comprise a prepositional phrase. "*With love from me to you*" strings together three prepositional phrases. Here is a partial list of the most common prepositions: *about, above, across, after, among, at, before, behind, between, by, during, for, from, in, into, like, of, on, out, over, since, through, to, toward, under, until, up, upon, with, within,* and *without.*

pronoun A pronoun is a part of speech that substitutes for a noun, such as *I, you, he, she, it, we,* and *they.*

run-on (or fused) sentence A run-on sentence incorrectly combines two independent clauses with no conjunction or punctuation. See BWE 2.

sentence A sentence is a unit of expression that can stand independently. It contains two parts, a **subject** and a **predicate.** The shortest sentence in the Bible, for example, is "Jesus wept." "*Jesus* is the subject; *wept* is the predicate.

sentence fragment A sentence fragment is a group of words incorrectly punctuated like a complete sentence but lacking the necessary structure; it is only a part of a sentence. "Walking down the road" and "the origin of the problem" are both fragments because neither contains a **predicate.** See BWE 1.

subject The subject, in most cases a noun or pronoun, names the doer of the action in a sentence or identifies what the predicate is about. The subject of the previous sentence, for example, is "the subject, in most cases a noun or pronoun." The simple subject of that sentence—the noun to which the other words in the sentence are attached—is *subject.*

subordination, subordinating conjunctions *Subordination* refers to the placement of certain grammatical units, particularly phrases and clauses, at a lower, less important structural level than other elements. As with coordination, the grammatical ranking carries conceptual significance as well: whatever is grammatically subordinated appears less important than the information carried in the main clause. In the following example, Microsoft is subordinated both grammatically and conceptually to Apple: "Although Microsoft continues to upgrade the operating system and special features on its computers, the more stylish and virus-free Apple MacIntosh computers continue to outclass them." Here *although* is a **subordinating conjunction** that introduces a subordinate clause, also known as a **dependent clause.**

verb A verb is a part of speech that describes an action (goes), states how something was affected by an action (became angered), or expresses a state of being (is).

verbals (participles, gerunds, and infinitives) Verbals are words derived from verbs. They are verb forms that look like verbs but, as determined by the structure of the sentence they appear in, they function as nouns, adjectives, or adverbs. There are three forms of verbals.

An **infinitive**—composed of the root form of a verb plus *to (to be, to vote)*—becomes a verbal when it is used as a noun (*To eat* is essential), an adjective (These are the books *to read*), or an adverb (He was too sick *to walk*).

Similarly, a **participle**—usually composed of the root form of a verb plus "–ing" (present participle) or "–ed" (past participle)—becomes a verbal when used as an adjective. It can occur as a single word, modifying a noun, as in *faltering negotiations* or *finished business*. But it also can occur in a participial phrase, consisting of the participle, its object, and any modifiers. Here are two examples:

Having been tried and convicted, **the criminal was sentenced to life imprisonment.**

Following the path of most resistance, **the masochist took deep pleasure in his frustration.**

"Having been tried and convicted" is a participial phrase that modifies *criminal;* "Following the path of most resistance" is a participial phrase that modifies *masochist.* In each case, the participial phrase functions as an adjective.

The third form of verbal, the **gerund,** resembles the participle. Like the participle, it is formed by adding "–ing" to the root form of the verb, but unlike the participle, it is used as a noun. In the sentence "Swimming is extraordinarily aerobic," the gerund *swimming* functions as the subject. Again like participles, gerunds can occur in phrases. The gerund phrases are italicized in the following example: "*Watching a film adaptation* takes less effort than *reading the book* from which it was made."

When using a verbal, remember that although it resembles a verb, it cannot function alone as the verb in a sentence: "Being a military genius" is a fragment, not a sentence.

ASSIGNMENT: Grammar and Style Quiz

Here is an error-laden paragraph to rewrite and correct by making changes in grammar and punctuation as necessary. You may need to add, drop, or rearrange words, but do not add any periods. That way, you will be able to test yourself on your ability to use commas plus conjunctions, semicolons, colons, and dashes rather than avoid these options by separating each independent clause into a simple sentence. The quiz also contains a few stylistic problems addressed in Chapters 17 and 18. A discussion of the errors and how to fix them can be found in the appendix to this chapter.

[1] It is a fact that fraternities and sororities are a major part of student life at the

[2] university, students are preoccupied with pledging. This is not approved of by

[3] most members of the faculty, however, they feel helpless about attacking them.

[4] Perceiving that the greek societies are attractive to the students but at the same

[5] time encouraging anti-intellectualism, it is not an issue that can be addressed

[6] easily. The student, who wants to be popular and cool feels that he should not

[7] talk in class, because interest in academics or having ideas outside class is

[8] uncool. Its more important to pledge the right house then being smart. If the

[9] administration would create alternatives to Greek life such as a honors program

[10] students lives would be more enriched. Although for now raising the cumulative

[11] grade point necessary to pledge and remain active would be a good start.

[12] Contrary to the Universitys stance against gender discrimination Greek life

[13] perpetuates gender stereotypes; for example, the dances at each house for

[14] freshman women but not men. Some of the best students agree with this but

[15] mistakenly believes that most faculty endorse the system.

CHAPTER 19 APPENDIX

Answer Key (with Discussion)

TEST YOURSELF SECTIONS

Test Yourself: Fragments

Original example: Like many other anthropologists, Margaret Mead studied non-Western cultures in such works as *Coming of Age in Samoa*. And influenced theories of childhood development in America.

Problem: The second sentence is actually a fragment, a predicate in need of a subject.

Possible correction: Like many other anthropologists, Margaret Mead studied non-Western cultures (in such works as *Coming of Age in Samoa*) in ways that influenced theories of childhood development in America.

Comment: There are many ways to fix this example, but its original form leaves ambiguous whether the fragment refers only to *Mead,* or to *many other anthropologists* as well. The correction offered includes the other anthropologists in the referent and diminishes the emphasis on Mead's book by placing it within parentheses. Although the correction uses a subordinating *that* to incorporate the fragment into the first sentence, it keeps this information in an emphatic position at the end of the sentence.

Original example: The catastrophe resulted from an engineering flaw. Because the bridge lacked sufficient support.

Problem: The second sentence is actually a dependent clause; *because* always subordinates.

Possible correction: The catastrophe resulted from an engineering flaw: the bridge lacked sufficient support.

Comment: Because the colon has causal force, this is an ideal spot to use one, identifying the "flaw."

Original example: In the 1840s the potato famine decimated Ireland. It being a country with poor soil and antiquated methods of agriculture.

Problem: The second sentence is actually a fragment, a subject plus a long participial phrase.

Possible correction: In the 1840s the potato famine decimated Ireland, a country with poor and antiquated methods of agriculture.

Comment: The cause of this kind of fragment is usually that the writer mistakenly believes that *being* is a verb rather than a participle that introduces a long phrase (modifying "Ireland" in this case). It would also be correct simply to change the period to a comma in the original sentence.

Test Yourself: Comma Splices

Original example: "Virtual reality" is a new buzzword, so is "hyperspace."

Problem: This is a comma splice—both clauses are independent, yet they are joined with a comma.

Possible correction: "Virtual reality" is a new buzzword; so is "hyperspace."

Comment: Because the clauses are linked by association—both naming buzzwords—a semicolon would show that association. A writer could also condense the clauses into a simple sentence with a compound subject, for example, "Both 'virtual reality' and 'hyperspace' are new buzzwords."

Original example: Many popular cures for cancer have been discredited, nevertheless, many people continue to buy them.

Problem: A comma splice results from the incorrectly punctuated conjunctive adverb *nevertheless.*

Possible correction: Many popular cures for cancer have been discredited; nevertheless, many people continue to buy them.

Comment: Without the semicolon to separate the independent clauses, the conjunctive adverb could conceivably modify either the preceding or the following clause. This problem is usually worse with *however.*

Original example: Elvis Presley's home, Graceland, attracts many musicians as a kind of shrine, even Paul Simon has been there.

Problem: This is a comma splice—the two independent clauses are linked by a comma without a conjunction. The problem is exacerbated by the number of commas in the sentence; the reader cannot easily tell which one is used to separate the clauses.

Possible correction: Elvis Presley's home, Graceland, attracts many musicians as a kind of shrine—even Paul Simon has been there.

Comment: Although one could justly use a semicolon here, the dash conveys the impromptu effect of an afterthought.

Original example: She didn't play well with others, she sat on the bench and watched.

Problem: Because the second clause develops the first one, a writer might think that it is dependent on the first; conceptually, yes, but grammatically, no.

Possible correction: She didn't play well with others; she sat on the bench and watched.

Comment: If the writer wanted to link the two clauses more tightly, a colon would be appropriate instead of the semicolon.

Test Yourself: Subject–Verb Agreement

Original example: The controversies surrounding the placement of Arthur Ashe's statue in Richmond was difficult for the various factions to resolve.

Problem: The grammatical subject of the main clause (controversies) is plural; the verb (was) is singular.

Possible corrections: The controversies surrounding the placement of Arthur Ashe's statue in Richmond were difficult for the various factions to resolve (or, The controversy . . . was).

Comment: An error of this kind is encouraged by two factors: the distance of the verb from the subject and the presence of intervening prepositional phrases that use singular objects, either of which a writer might mistake for the grammatical subject of the main clause.

Test Yourself: Faulty Predication

Original example: The subject of learning disabilities is difficult to identify accurately.

Problem: The predicate matches the object of the preposition (learning disabilities) rather than the subject of the main clause (subject).

Possible correction: Learning disabilities are difficult to identify accurately.

Comment: Omitting the abstract opening (The subject of) enables the predicate (are) to fit the new grammatical subject (disabilities).

Test Yourself: Pronoun–Antecedent Agreement

Original example: Every dog has its day, but all too often when that day happens, they can be found barking up the wrong tree.

Problem: The plural pronoun *they* that is the grammatical subject of the second clause does not have a plural antecedent in the sentence.

Possible correction: Every dog has its day, but all too often when that day happens, the dog can be found barking up the wrong tree.

Comment: If a writer vigilantly checks all pronouns, he or she will identify the intended antecedent of the pronoun *they* to be the singular *dog*, and revise accordingly. The sentence would still be incorrect if the pronoun *it* were used instead of the repeated *dog* because *it* could refer to the nearest preceding noun, *day*.

Test Yourself: Ambiguous Reference

Original example: Alexander the Great's father, Philip of Macedon, died when he was twenty-six.

Problem: A reader can't be sure whether *he* refers to Alexander or to Philip.

Possible correction: Alexander the Great's father, Philip of Macedon, died at the age of twenty-six.

Comment: The correction rewords to remove the ambiguous pronoun. This solution is less awkward than repeating *Philip* in place of *he,* though that would also be correct.

Original example: The committee could not look into the problem because it was too involved.

Problem: A reader can't be sure whether *it* refers to *the committee* or to *the problem.*

Possible correction: The committee was too involved with other matters to look into the problem.

Comment: As with the previous example, rewording to eliminate the ambiguous pronoun is usually the best solution.

Test Yourself: Broad Reference

Original example: Regardless of whether the film is foreign or domestic, they can be found in your neighborhood video store.

Problem: The plural pronoun *they* does not have a plural antecedent in the sentence.

Possible correction: Regardless of whether the film is foreign or domestic, it can be found in your neighborhood video store.

Comment: Although the sentence offers two options for films, the word *film* is singular and so, as antecedent, requires a singular pronoun (it). It is probably worth noting here that *it* would still be correct even if the original sentence began, "Regardless of whether the film is a foreign film or a domestic film." The rule for compound subjects that use an either/or construction is as follows: the number (singular or plural) of the noun or pronoun that follows *or* determines the number of the verb. Compare the following two examples: "Either several of his aides *or* the *candidate is* going to speak" and "Either the candidate *or* several of his *aides are* going to speak."

Original example: Many experts now claim that dogs and other higher mammals dream; for those who don't own such pets, this is often difficult to believe.

Problem: The referent of the pronoun *this* is unclear. Precisely what is difficult to believe—that mammals dream or that experts would make such a claim?

Possible correction: Many experts now claim that dogs and other higher mammals dream; for those who don't own such pets, this claim is often difficult to believe.

Comment: Often the best way to fix a problem with broad reference produced by use of *this* as a pronoun is to convert *this* to an adjective—a strategy that will require a writer to provide a specifying noun for *this* to modify. As a rule, when you find an isolated *this* in your draft, ask and answer the question "This what?"

Test Yourself: Modification Errors

Original example: After eating their sandwiches, the steamboat left the dock.

Problem: This is a dangling participle—the grammar of the sentence conveys that the steamboat ate their sandwiches.

Corrections: After the girls ate their sandwiches, the steamboat left the dock. Or, After eating their sandwiches, the girls boarded the steamboat, and it left the dock.

Comment: The two corrections model the two ways of remedying most dangling participles. Both provide an antecedent (the girls) for the pronoun *their.* The first correction eliminates the participial phrase and substitutes a subordinate clause. The second correction adds to the existing main clause (steamboat left) another one (girls boarded) for the participial phrase to modify appropriately.

Original example: The social workers saw an elderly woman on a bus with a cane standing up.

Problem: Misplaced modifiers create the problems in this sentence, which implies that the bus possessed a cane that was standing up. The problem exemplified here is produced by the series of prepositional phrases—"*on* a bus *with* a cane"—followed by the participial phrase *standing up,* which is used as an adjective and intended to modify *woman.*

Possible correction: The social workers saw an elderly woman on a bus. She was standing up with the help of a cane.

Comment: Writers often try to cram too much into sentences, piling on the prepositions. The best remedy is sometimes to break up the sentence, a move that usually involves eliminating prepositions, which possess a sludgy kind of movement, and adding verbs, which possess more distinct movement.

Original example: Crossing the street, a car hit the pedestrian.

Problem: The dangling participle (Crossing the street) does not have a word to modify in the sentence. The sentence conveys that the car crossed the street.

Possible corrections: Crossing the street, the pedestrian was hit by a car. Or: As the pedestrian crossed the street, a car hit him.

Comment: The first solution brings the participial phrase closest to the noun it modifies (pedestrian). The second converts the participial into the verb (crossed) of a dependent *as* clause and moves *pedestrian* into the clause as the subject for that verb. As in the *steamboat* example, one correction provides an appropriate noun for the participial phrase to modify, and the other eliminates the participle.

Test Yourself: Possessive Apostrophes

Original example: The womens movement has been misunderstood by many of its detractors.

Problem: The possessive apostrophe for *womens* is missing. The trickiness here in inserting the apostrophe is that this word is already plural.

Possible correction: The women's movement has been misunderstood by many of its detractors.

Comment: Because the word is already plural, it takes a simple "–'s" to indicate a movement belonging to women—not "–s'" (womens').

Test Yourself: Comma Errors

Original paired examples:

> The book which I had read a few years ago contained a lot of outdated data.
>
> The book that I had read a few years ago contained a lot of outdated data.

Problem: In the first example, the modifying clause "which I had read a few years ago" is nonrestrictive: it could be omitted without changing the essential meaning of the sentence. Therefore, it needs to be enclosed in commas—as the *which* signals.

Possible correction: The book, which I had read a few years ago, contained a lot of outdated data.

Comment: The second example in the pair is correct as it stands. The restrictive clause, "that I had read a few years ago," does not take commas around it because the information it gives readers is an essential part of the meaning of *book*. That is, it refers to not just any book read a few years ago, as in the first example in the pair, but rather specifies the one containing outdated data. "The book that I had read a few years ago" thus functions as what is known as a *noun phrase.*

Test Yourself: Spelling/Diction Errors

Original example: Its not sufficiently acknowledged that the behavior of public officials is not just an ethical issue but one that effects the sale of newspapers and commercial bytes in television news. When public officials don't do what their supposed to do, than their sure to face the affects of public opinion—if they get caught—because there are dollars to be made. Its that simple: money more then morality is calling the tune in the way that the press treats it's superstars.

Problems: The paragraph confuses the paired terms discussed under BWE 9. It mistakes

> *its* for *it's* before *not sufficiently.*
>
> *effects* for *affects* before *the sale.*
>
> *their* for *they're* before *supposed.*
>
> *than* for *then* before *their sure.*
>
> *they're* for *their* before *sure.*
>
> *affects* for *effects* before *of public opinion.*
>
> *its* for *it's* before *that simple.*
>
> *then* for *than* before *morality.*
>
> *it's* for *its* before *superstars.*

Possible correction: It's not sufficiently acknowledged that the behavior of public officials is not just an ethical issue but one that affects the sale of newspapers and commercial bytes in television news. When public officials don't do what they're supposed to do, then they're sure to face the effects of public opinion—if they get caught—

because there are dollars to be made. It's that simple: money more than morality is calling the tune in the way that the press treats its superstars.

Comment: If you confuse similar words, the only solution is to memorize the differences and consciously check your drafts for any problems until habit takes hold.

GRAMMAR AND STYLE QUIZ

The answers offered here are not exclusive—the only ways to correct the problems. In some cases, we have offered various satisfactory remedies, and, as previously noted, a few of the suggested revisions—marked by a bullet—address editing for style (Chapters 17 and 18) rather than editing for correctness.

Line 1

- There are no grammatical errors per se, but "It is a fact that" is a wordy expletive that should be cut.

Line 2

- There is a comma splice between *university* and *students:* insert a semicolon as the preferred option.
- *This,* beginning the next sentence, is a broad reference and should be converted into an adjective, with a noun or noun phrase added, such as "This preoccupation" or "This dominance by Greek societies."
- In addition, a writer might recast the passive verb into the active: "Most faculty members do not approve of . . ."

Line 3

- There is a comma splice after *faculty:* insert a semicolon.
- The antecedent of the pronoun *them* is ambiguous: substitute a noun, such as *the Greeks.*

Line 4

- *Perceiving* is a dangling participle: either recast to include a subject in a dependent clause (such as "Because most faculty members perceive") or insert "most faculty members" as a referent for the participle before *it* in line 5.
- Capitalize *Greek.*

Line 5

- Fix faulty parallelism: introduce the second item (encouraging anti-intellectualism) with another *that* (but at the same time that they encourage).
- The *it is* (an expletive) creates problems with broad reference. If line 4 has been changed by eliminating the participle (using some version of the "Because most faculty members feel" option), recast the main clause. For example, following *anti-intellectualism,* the sentence might read, "this issue cannot be addressed

easily." If line 4 has retained the participial phrase, then the revision would need to read something like "most faculty members believe that this issue cannot be addressed easily."

Line 6

- The *who* clause is restrictive: the comma must be dropped.
- The *he* is sexist: use *he or she*, or change the number—to "Students who want . . . feel that they."

Line 7

- Fix faulty parallelism: change "interest in" to "be*ing* interested in" so as to match "hav*ing* ideas."

Line 8

- Possessive *Its* should be the contraction *It's*.
- Temporal *then* should be the comparative *than*.
- Fix faulty parallelism: change *being* to *to be* to match *to pledge*.

Line 9

- Change *a honors* to *an honors*.
- Insert commas around the nonrestrictive modifying phrase "such as an honors program": these will separate it from both the long introductory dependent *if* clause that precedes it and the main clause that follows.

Line 10

- Make *students* a plural possessive: *students' lives*.
- The "more enriched" is arguably wordy: "richer" is leaner.
- *Although* is a subordinating conjunction that creates a sentence fragment. The easiest solution is to cut it, though a writer could also attach the entire *although* clause to the previous sentence, using a comma or dash.

Line 11

- This is part of the fragment that began in line 10.

Line 12

- Fix the possessive: make it *University's*.
- Fix the case of the noun: make it *university's*.
- Place a comma after *discrimination* to separate the long introductory modifying phrases from the main clause.

Line 13

- The semicolon is incorrect because the sentence does not contain two independent clauses. A colon is better than a dash here, though both are technically correct.

Line 14

- Most rhetoricians consider *freshman* sexist: substitute *first-year*.
- The use of *this* is another egregious case of broad reference (ask, Agree with *this what?*). The best solution is probably to rewrite this part of the sentence to clarify the meaning. For example, make it "Some of the best students object to Greek life in these terms and oppose the administration's handling of the Greeks . . ."

Line 15

- Fix subject–verb agreement: make it "some . . . believe."

Here is how one corrected version of the quiz might look:

Fraternities and sororities are a major part of student life at the university: students are preoccupied with pledging. Most faculty members do not approve of this dominance by Greek societies; however, they feel helpless about attacking the Greeks. Because faculty members perceive that the Greek societies are attractive to the students but at the same time that they encourage anti-intellectualism, this issue cannot be addressed easily. The student who wants to be popular and cool feels that he or she should not talk in class, because being interested in academics or having ideas outside class is uncool. It's more important to pledge the right house than to be smart. If the administration would create alternatives to Greek life, such as an honors program, the students' lives would be richer. For now, raising the cumulative grade point necessary to pledge and remain active would be a good start to solving the problem of Greek domination. Contrary to the university's stance against gender discrimination, Greek life perpetuates gender stereotypes: for example, the dances at each house for first-year women but not men. Some of the best students object to Greek life in these terms and oppose the administration's handling of the Greeks. But many of these same students mistakenly believe that most faculty members endorse the system.

CREDITS

Chapter 3. Pages 31–32: Imperial Bedroom, Jonathan Franzen, in *How to Be Alone: Essays.* Picador. **Page 40:** Malcolm Gladwell, "Listening to Khakis: What America's Most Popular Pants Tell Us About the Way Guys Think." **Page 41:** "Brooklyn Heights, 4:00 A.M." by Dana Ferrelli. Reprinted by permission of the author.

Chapter 4. Pages 53–54: *Hua dan:* The Dance of Values in the Beijing Opera, reprinted by permission of the author. **Page 59:** Figure 4.2. ©The Dancers, by Sarah Kersh. Pen and ink drawing, 6" × 13.75". Used by permission of Sarah Kersh.

Chapter 5. Pages 79–82: "Playing by the Antioch Rules" by Eric Fassin, *New York Times,* December 26, 1993, p. 11. Copyright © 1993 by the New York Times Co. Reprinted by permission.

Chapter 6. Pages 95–96: Marketing the Girl Next Door: A Declaration of Independence? reprinted by permission of the author.

Chapter 8. Page 126: Excerpt from student paper on *The Tempest,* reprinted by permission of the author. **Pages 136–137:** Freewrite on a scene from the film *Good Bye Lenin!* by Sarah Kersh. Reprinted by permission of the author.

Chapter 10. Pages 175-176: September 11th: A National Tragedy? James Peck, from Aftermath: Thinking After September 11th: Occasional Papers of the Center for Ethics and Leadership.

PHOTO CREDITS

Chapter 1. Page 14: Figure 1.2. REUNION DES MUSEES NATIONAUX, ART RESOURCE, NY. James Abbott McNeil Whistler.

Chapter 4. Page 66: Figure 4.3. Artwork by Ian Falconer/The New Yorker © 2000 Conde Nast Publications Inc.

Chapter 8. Page 130: Figure 8.3. ©Jeff Widener/AP

Chapter 9. Page 146: Figure 9.3. SCALA/Art Resource, NY. Diego Rodgrigues Velázquez. Las Meninas. 1656.